De Sion exibit lex et verbum domini de Hierusalem

Essays on Medieval Law, Liturgy, and Literature in Honour of Amnon Linder

CULTURAL ENCOUNTERS
IN LATE ANTIQUITY AND THE MIDDLE AGES

VOLUME 1

De Sion exibit lex et verbum domini de Hierusalem

Essays on Medieval Law, Liturgy, and Literature in Honour of Amnon Linder

Edited by

Yitzhak Hen

BREPOLS

British Library Cataloguing in Publication Data

De Sion exibit lex et verbum domini de Hierusalem : essays on medieval law, liturgy, and literature in honour of Amnon Linder. – (Cultural encounters in late antiquity and the Middle Ages ; v. 1)

1. Liturgics – History – To 1500 2. Law, Medieval 3. Literature, Medieval

I. Hen, Yitzhak

264' .00902

ISBN 2503510914

D/2001/0095/13

ISBN 2-503-51091-4

Printed in the E.U. on acid-free paper.

Contents

Preface

Fodere quam vites melius est scribere libros:
Ille suo ventri serviet, iste animae.
Vel nova vel vetera poterit proferre magister
Plurima, quisque legit dicta sacrata patrum.
(Alcuin of York)

Amnon Linder reminds me in more than one respect of Alcuin of York. Like Alcuin, Linder is a man of prodigious learning, whose writings have ranged widely—from political and institutional issues to the study of liturgy and culture, covering more than a millennium of medieval history, from Constantine the Great to the *Opus Davidicum* of Johannes Angelus de Legonissa. Like Abbot Alcuin, the master of the Tours scriptorium, Linder insists on high standards of accuracy and clarity both in his own works, and in those of his students. Like Alcuin, the master of Charlemagne's court school, Amnon Linder retired in his prime (and at about the same age as Alcuin), not in order to relax and enjoy the *otium* of retirement, but in order to write and dedicate himself more fully to research. But, more than anything else, Linder, like Alcuin, was (and still is) a gifted and dedicated teacher. We all remember his lectures and seminars with great admiration, and those of us who became teachers ourselves try to follow his footsteps. He is a model to us all in this matter.

Linder has never confined himself to a single topic in his research and publications. He wrote his MA thesis on John of Salisbury's *Policraticus* and his PhD thesis was dedicated to the study of tyrannicide in the Middle Ages. Later on, as a professor of medieval history at the Hebrew University of Jerusalem, he showed much interest in the history of the Christian Holy Land and in Jewish-Christian relations in Late Antiquity and the Middle Ages. This particular interest gave birth to two seminal studies: *The Jews in Roman Imperial Legislation* (Jerusalem and Toronto, 1987; a Hebrew version was published in 1983) and *The Jews in the Legal Sources of the Early Middle Ages* (Jerusalem and Toronto, 1997). Shortly after their publication, these two monumental volumes became an indispensable tool for both students and scholars interested in Jewish history and in Jewish-Christian relations. In recent years Linder dedicated much time and scholarly effort to the study of medieval liturgy, and, in particular, the Crusader liturgy of the liberation and destruction of Jerusalem. The exciting results of this massive research will be published shortly by Brepols. There are others, far more qualified than I, to assess the significance of Linder's contribution to the corpus of scholarly writing on his chosen topics, but it does seem quite clear that his work has great significance in the broader context of medieval studies in our generation, and especially in the state of Israel.

The essays in this volume were gathered together as a *Festschrift* for Amnon Linder. They were written independently of one another by Linder's friends, colleagues, and students, and they deal with a wide variety of sources, both in date (from the fourth to the fifteenth century), geographical range (from the Holy Land to the British Isles), and methodology. Thus, the volume's internal organization is simply chronological, and there has been no attempt to harmonize the viewpoints or to present a coherent conclusion. The shared feature of all the papers collected here is the fact that they deal with topics close to Amnon Linder's heart—medieval law, liturgy, and literature. We offer him what we have written in gratitude and affection.

This volume could not have been published without the help and advice of many friends and colleagues. I would first like to extend my deep gratitude to the contributors for their cooperation and forbearance, and to Dina Linder for her discrete suggestions and assistance. Shelly Benvenisti and Ora Limor took a special interest in the progress of this enterprise, and provided much encouragement and support. I should also like to thank Tal Tovi for his help in preparing the manuscript for publication. Finally, warm thanks should go to the staff of Brepols for seeing the book through the press, and especially to Simon Forde, who championed our cause with Brepols.

Y. H.

Abbreviations

AASS	Acta Sanctorum (Antwerp and Brussels, 1643–)
BM	Bibliothèque Municipale
BNF	Bibliothèque Nationale de France
CCCM	Corpus Christianorum, Continuatio Mediaevalis (Turnhout, 1966–)
CCSL	Corpus Christianorum, Series Latina (Turnhout, 1952–)
CSEL	Corpus Scriptorum Ecclesiasticorum Latinorum (Vienna, 1866–)
DG	*Corpus juris canonici. Pars prior: Decretum magistri Gratiani*, ed. by E. Friedberg (Leipzig, 1879)
MGH	Monumenta Germaniae Historica
Epp.	Epistulae (Berlin, 1887–1939)
SRG	Scriptores Rerum Germanicarum in usum scholarum (Hannover, 1871–)
SRM	Scriptores Rerum Merovingicarum (Hannover, 1884–1951)
SS	Scriptores in folio (Berlin, 1826–)
PG	Patrologia Graeca, ed. by J.-P. Migne, 162 vols (Paris, 1857–66)
PL	Patrologia Latina, ed. by J.-P. Migne, 221 vols (Paris, 1841–64)
RHC	Recueil des historiens des croisades (Paris, 1841–1906)
Hocc.	Historiens occidentaux, 5 vols (Paris, 1844–95)
Hor.	Historiens orientaux, 5 vols (Paris, 1872–1906)
Settimane	Settimane di studio del Centro italiano di studi sull'alto medioevo (Spoleto, 1954–)

Reading Sacred Space: Egeria, Paula, and the Christian Holy Land

ORA LIMOR

Helena's visit to the Holy Land created a fashion among ladies of the Roman aristocracy. Many of them visited the Holy Places in Judea, Jordan, and Galilee, as well as the centres of monasticism in Egypt. Famous among them are Melania the Elder, her grand-daughter Melania the Younger, and Paula, but we also hear of Poemenia, Silvia, Fabiola, Flavia, and others.[1] Two of their journeys are known to us in detail: the journey made by Egeria in 381–384, and the one made by Paula in 385.[2] The accounts of Egeria's and Paula's journeys also mark the birth of a new literary

I remain indebted to my teacher Amnon Linder, who first set me on the path to the Christian Holy Land. I am also grateful to Bruria Bitton-Ashkelony, Elisheva Baumgarten, Israel Yuval, and to the participants of the seminar of the Center for Judaic Studies in Philadelphia, autumn 1999, for their instructive comments on the first draft of this paper.

[1] Helena's pilgrimage, as well as other fourth-century travels are described by E. D. Hunt, *Holy Land Pilgrimage in the Later Roman Empire (AD 312–460)* (Oxford 1982); K. G. Holum, 'Hadrian and St. Helena: Imperial Travel and the Origins of Christian Holy Land Pilgrimage', in *The Blessings of Pilgrimage*, ed. by R. Ousterhout (Urbana and Chicago 1990), pp. 66–83; F.X. Murphy, 'Melania the Elder: A Biographical Note', *Traditio,* 5 (1947), 59–77; N. Moine, 'Melaniana', *Recherches augustiniennes,* 15 (1980), 3–79; E. A. Clark, *The Life of Melania the Younger* (Lewiston, 1984); P. Devos, 'La servante de Dieux Poemenia', *Analecta Bollandiana,* 87 (1969), 189–208; P. Devos, 'Silvie, la sainte pélerine', *Analecta Bollandiana,* 91 (1973), 105–17; 92 (1974), 321–41.

[2] The standard editions of Egeria's travels are *Itinerarium Egeriae*, ed. by A. Franceschini

genre: the *itinerarium*, which appears simultaneously with the institutionalization of pilgrimage itself. Both accounts took the form of a letter. Egeria described her journey in a letter she wrote to a group of women whom she called 'loving sisters'—friends who were nuns or who belonged to some other kind of religious sisterhood, and who had remained behind in her homeland.[3] Paula's journey, on the other hand, is known to us from the obituary letter which Jerome wrote to Eustochium, Paula's daughter, in 404, after Paula's death.[4] The letter contains a biography of Paula and includes the account of her journey to the holy places. In what follows, I would like to examine the two letters, and especially their interpretive methods and means of deciphering sacred space, and to look at the means through which Christians appropriated the biblical-historical geography of the Holy Land, making it a Christian space.

The letters of Egeria and Jerome are very different from each other. Jerome wrote an elegant prose, following the rules of the Ciceronian literary tradition in which he had been brought up, while Egeria wrote a late vulgar Latin, very remote from the norms of classical Latin.[5] While Jerome and Paula represented the two cultures—the classical

---

and R. Weber, CCSL, 175 (Turnhout, 1965), pp. 27–103; P. Maraval, *Égérie. Journal de Voyage,* Sources chrétiennes, 296 (Paris, 1982). The latest English translations are E. Gingras, *Egeria: Diary of a Pilgrim,* Ancient Christian Writers, 38 (New York, 1970); J. Wilkinson, *Egeria's Travels* (London, 1971). The citations below are taken from Wilkinson's translation. The literature about Egeria's letter is vast. See M. Starowieyski, 'Bibliografia Egeriana', *Augustinianum,* 19 (1979), 297–318; S. Janeras, 'Contributo alla bibliografia Egeriana', in *Atti del Convegno internazionale sulla Peregrinatio Egeriae (1987)* (Arezzo, 1990), pp. 355–66; Paula's travels are described in two of Jerome's letters: Hieronymus, 'Epistula 46, Paula et Eustochium ad Marcellam', ed. by I. Hilberg, CSEL, 54 (Vienna and Leipzig, 1910), pp. 329–44; 'Epistula 108, Epitaphium sanctae Paulae', ed. by I. Hilberg, CSEL, 55 (Vienna and Leipzig, 1912), pp. 306–51; also in *Saint Jérôme Lettres*, ed. and trans. by J. Labourt (Paris 1955); for an English translation of Paula's travels, see J. Wilkinson, *Jerusalem Pilgrims before the Crusades* (Jerusalem, 1977), pp. 45–52. The citations below are also taken from Wilkinson's translation. See also J. N. D. Kelly, *Jerome. His Life, Writings, and Controversies* (London, 1975), p. 124.

[3] Egeria, 3:8; 5:8; 7:3; 19:19; 23:9; H. Sivan, 'Who Was Egeria? Piety and Pilgrimage in the Age of Gratian', *Harvard Theological Review,* 81 (1988), 59–72.

[4] Kelly, *Jerome,* pp. 118–19, 277–79; P. Nautin, 'Études de chronologie hieronymienne', *Revue augustiniennes,* 18 (1972), 209–18.

[5] Egeria's language and style have been the subject of many scholarly works. See E. H. Löfstedt, *Philologischer Kommentar zur Peregrinatio Aetheriae. Untersuchungen zur Geschichte der lateinischen Sprache* (Uppsala, 1911); W. Van Oorde, *Lexicon Aetherianum* (Amsterdam, 1929); R. A. Bastiaensen, *Observations sur le vocabulaire liturgique dans l'Itinéraire d'Égérie,* Latinitas christianorum primaeva, 17 (Utrecht, 1962); G. F. M. Vermeer, *Observations sur le vocabulaire du pélerinage chez Égérie et chez Antonine de Plaisance,* Latinitas christianorum primaeva, 19 (Utrecht, 1965); L. Spitzer, 'The Epic Style of the Pilgrim Aetheria', *Comparative*

and the biblical—Egeria knew only the biblical. Egeria wrote her letter for certain specific women readers and for no one else. She was not a writer, and did not know she was writing an itinerary, as very few Christian itineraries had yet been written.[6] Jerome, on the other hand, was a famous author. The letter he wrote, though apparently addressed to Eustochium, was in fact intended for the entire Christian world. His writing was very self-conscious and well crafted. It was also didactic in nature, unlike Egeria's. Egeria wrote her letter in the course of her journey, soon after seeing the things she described. Jerome, however, wrote his account of Paula's journey nearly twenty years after it happened, from far away. The location in time also determined the atmosphere of the two letters: the emotional immediacy of Egeria as against the scholarly distance of Jerome.[7]

We know many facts about Paula, all derived from Jerome's letters. She belonged to one of the most eminent families of the Roman aristocracy, received a classical and Christian education, and after being widowed joined a group of aristocratic Christian ladies who chose an ascetic way of life and devoted themselves to the study of the Scriptures under the guidance of Jerome.[8] Like Jerome, Paula studied Hebrew. Jerome related with admiration that she learnt the language easily and sang the psalms without a foreign accent.[9] In the autumn of 385, after dividing her considerable property among her heirs, she followed Jerome to the East. After visiting the Holy Places and the abodes of the famous monks in Egypt—a journey which took about a year—they settled in Bethlehem. Paula lived a severe ascetic life and died in Bethlehem at the age of fifty-six in the year 404.[10]

Nothing is known about Egeria except the facts contained in her letter, and even the few biographical details one may glean from it are hypothetical. Her letter has reached us only in part. It was discovered in 1884, without beginning or end, and without any details that might identify the writer.[11] Textual analysis revealed that it was written by a woman: an aristocratic woman of some financial means from southern France or Spain. Her extreme piety and her enthusiasm for the lifestyle of hermits indicate that she had chosen an ascetic way of life. After various attempts at identification, the writer was

---

Literature, 3 (1949), 225–58 (reprinted in idem, *Romanische Literaturstudien 1936–1956* (Tübingen, 1959), pp. 871–912).

[6] M. B. Campbell, *The Witness and the Other World. Exotic European Travel Writing 400–1600* (Ithaca and London 1988), pp. 7–8, 20–33.

[7] On the atmosphere of Egeria's letter, see especially Spitzer, 'The Epic Style'.

[8] E. A. Clark, 'Ascetic Renunciation and Feminine Advancement: A Paradox of Late Ancient Christianity', in *Ascetic Piety and Women's Faith. Essays on Late Ancient Christianity,* ed. by E. A. Clark (Lewiston, 1986), pp. 175–208.

[9] Ep. 108.

[10] Kelly, *Jerome*, p. 277.

[11] On the Codex Aretinus, VI, 3, see *S. Hilarii tractatus de mysteriis et hymni, et S. Silviae Aquitanae peregrinatio ad loca sancta,* ed. by G.-F. Gamurini (Rome, 1887).

finally identified as Egeria, the protagonist of a letter which the abbot Valerius of Vierzo in Galicia wrote to his monks in the seventh century.[12]

Thus, while Paula came from Rome and belonged to both the senatorial aristocracy and the centre of Christian intellectual life, Egeria came from the provinces, and although she was a woman of status and wealth, she was not comparable in this respect with Paula. Her education, as far as one can tell from her letter, also could not be compared with Paula's. She wrote a vulgar Latin, and if she knew classical literature, it is not visible in her letter. She knew little, if any, Greek,[13] and she had no knowledge of Hebrew. Biographically and culturally, Paula belonged to the Roman imperial and Christian centre, while Egeria belonged to the periphery. This also determined the fate of the two letters. Jerome's letter became famous throughout the Christian world, while Egeria's was almost forgotten.

The two works discussed here describe pilgrimages by women, a common phenomenon at this particular time, soon to disappear and to surface again only at the beginning of the Modern Era. Since most of the religious literature in late Antiquity and the Middle Ages was written by men, these particular works may broaden our view, directing attention to the religious experience of the silent half of the believers.[14] Yet, it is hard to decide how far we are allowed to draw our conclusions. Although many

---

[12] Z. Garcia, 'La lettre de Valérius aux moines du Vierzo sur la bienheureuse Aetheria', *Analecta Bollandiana,* 29 (1910), 377–99; Maraval, *Égérie*, pp. 336–49 (Latin text and French translation). For an English translation, see Wilkinson, *Egeria's Travels,* pp. 174–78. The identification of the author of the *peregrinatio* as the protagonist of Valerius's letter was made by Dom Ferotin in 1903: M. Ferotin, 'Le veritable auteur de la "Peregrinatio Silviae", la vierge espagnole Éthéria', *Revue des questions historiques,* 74 (1903), 367–97. For more details on Egeria, see Wilkinson, *Egeria's Travels*; Maraval, *Égérie*; and O. Limor, *Holy Land Travels. Christian Pilgrims in Late Antiquity* (Jerusalem, 1998), pp. 41–54 [in Hebrew].

[13] C. Milani, 'I grecismi nell'"Itinerarium Egeriae"', *Aevum,* 43 (1969), 220–34; C. Milani, 'Studi sul' "Itinerarium Egeriae". L'aspetto classico della lingua di Egeria', *Aevum*, 43 (1969), 381–452.

[14] On educated women in Late antiquity, see G. Clark, *Women in Late Antiquity* (Oxford, 1993), pp. 130–38; P. Dronke, *Women Writers of the Middle Ages* (Cambridge, 1984), pp. 1–26. Even today pilgrimage constitutes an expression of female devotion. According to the anthropologist Harvey Goldberg, who studies Jewish and Moslem pilgrimage to sacred tombs in North Africa, the initiative to set out on a pilgrimage comes usually from the mother of the family. This may derive from the fact that unlike the circumstances in institutionalized sacred spaces, like synagogues and churches, in which women can take no part in liturgy, near sacred tombs they are free to express their piety in the same ways as men. While in synagogues and churches there are rigid rules of religious behaviour, as well as a structured hierarchy in which women have no place, tombs create a more democratic space and allow an outlet for individual expressions of piety, both of men and of women (Harvey Goldberg, private conversation, October 1999).

women went on pilgrimage, and although the two journeys described here were undertaken by women, only Egeria wrote her journey in person. Egeria may well represent other women travellers of her time, but she may also be a unique voice. It is even harder to tell to what degree Paula represents other women pilgrims and women's piety in general. Paula's journey was related by Jerome, who travelled with her, and it is almost impossible to distinguish her viewpoint from that of Jerome. Because of the close friendship between Paula and Jerome, one may perhaps cautiously suppose that the religious point of view described by him was shared by Paula. Jerome wrote his account of Paula's journey as if he had seen the Holy Places with her eyes, while Paula saw the Holy Places with the eyes of her teacher, Jerome.[15]

The problem of the relationship between pilgrim (Paula), author (Jerome), and pilgrimage is even more complex. Although the pilgrimage described in letter 108 is the only long journey Jerome is known to have undertaken, and although he spent most of his time in his monastery, it is hard to believe that during the thirty-four years he was living in Palestine this was the only time he set out to tour the country, or at least to visit specific sites in it.[16] Jerome often went to Jerusalem, at least during the first years of his stay in Bethlehem. He also occasionally visited Caesarea, the imperial metropolis and the ecclesiastical centre of Palestine, and its famous library.[17] His scholarly meetings with Jews suggest travel, either to their places of residence or to other meeting points.[18] In his Latin translation of the *Onomasticon* of Eusebius, Jerome included many corrections and updatings, which indicate familiarity with sites.[19] His knowledge could have been derived from visitors to Bethlehem, but it is more plausible that he had 'contemplated Judaea with his own eyes', to use his own phrase from the introduction to the Book of Chronicles.[20] Yet, Jerome never described his other travels. Moreover, although Jerome deals with Holy Places and pilgrimage to them in several of his writings, his two classical works devoted entirely or at length to travel in the Holy Land are mediated through Paula. The first one is letter 108, mentioned above, a long part of which describes Paula's pilgrimage in detail. The fact that Jerome himself also took part in this tour is almost concealed in this rather lengthy description. The other work

---

[15] On the general problems of distinguishing the voices of medieval female saints from those of their male interpreters, see C. M. Mooney , 'Voice, Gender, and the Portrayal of Sanctity', in *Gendered Voices. Medieval Saints and their Interpreters,* ed. by C. M. Mooney (Philadelphia, 1999), pp. 1–15.

[16] J. Wilkinson, 'L'apport de Sainte Jérôme à la topographie', *Revue biblique,* 81 (1974), 245–57.

[17] Kelly, *Jerome*, p. 135.

[18] H. I. Newman, 'Jerome and the Jews' (unpublished doctoral thesis, The Hebrew University, 1997), pp. 103–22.

[19] Eusebius, *Das Onomasticon der biblischen Ortsnamen,* ed. by E. Klostermann, Griechischen christlichen Schriftsteller der ersten drei Jahrhunderte, 11 (Leipzig, 1904).

[20] See below.

dealing with Holy Land sites and with Christian devotion to the biblical sacred space is letter 46 addressed to the Roman lady Marcella, a friend who had stayed behind in Rome, written probably in 386, soon after Jerome and Paula had settled in Bethlehem.[21] Although the letter has been ascribed to Paula and Eustochium, most scholars agree that it was written by Jerome himself.[22] Letter 46 is considered 'the classical expression of Jerome's positive principal attitude concerning pilgrimage and visits to the holy sites of the Holy Land'.[23] Pilgrimage is described in this letter as both an emotional experience and a means for a deeper understanding of the Scriptures. The scholarly education of the Christian is not completed until he visited Jerusalem, 'Christian Athens'.[24]

Yet, if letter 46 expressed Jerome's convictions about pilgrimage to the holy places, why is it ascribed to Paula and Eustochium, as if the letter expressed their ideas, and not his?[25] And if Jerome took part in Paula's pilgrimage described in letter 108, why did he conceal this fact? Did he consider pilgrimage an act of devotion more suitable for women than for men? Were fourth-century pilgrims primarily women? We have two detailed descriptions of fourth-century pilgrimages undertaken by women—the itineraries of Egeria and of Paula—but not even one personal description of a pilgrimage undertaken by a male pilgrim. Even the gender of the Bordeaux Pilgrim, the author of the *Itinerarium burdigalense*, the first Holy Land description by a Christian that is known to us (dated 333), was recently questioned. The possibility that the author of this text may well have been a woman, a possibility that had not occurred to scholars before,

---

[21] Hieronymus, 'Epistula 46' (note 2 above).

[22] Dronke however believes the letter was written by Paula and Eustochium: Dronke, *Women Writers of the Middle Ages,* p. 17, but see P. Nautine, 'La lettre de Paule et Eustochium à Marcelle (Jérôme, Ep. 46)', *Augustinianum,* 24 (1984), 441–49; Newman, *Jerome and the Jews,* pp. 220–21; L. Perrone, 'The Mystery of Judaea (Jerome, Ep. 46). The Holy City of Jerusalem between History and Symbol in Early Christian Thought', in *Jerusalem: Its Sanctity and Centrality to Judaism, Christianity, and Islam,* ed. by L. I. Levine (New York, 1999), pp. 230–39.

[23] Newman, *Jerome and the Jews,* pp. 220–21; H. I. Newman, 'Between Jerusalem and Bethlehem: Jerome and the Holy Places of Palestine', in *Sanctity of Time and Space in Tradition and Modernity,* ed. by A. Houtman, M. J. H. M. Poorthuis, J. Schwartz (Leiden, Boston, and Köln, 1998), pp. 218–19; Perrone, 'The Mystery of Judaea'; P. Maraval, 'Saint Jérôme et le pélerinage aux lieux saints de Palestine', in *Jérôme entre l'occident et l'orient,* ed. by Y. M. Duval (Paris, 1988), pp. 345–53; Bruria Bitton-Ashkeloni, 'Pilgrimage: Perceptions and Reactions in the Patristic and Monastic Literature of the Fourth–Sixth Centuries' (unpublished doctoral thesis, The Hebrew University, 1995), pp. 85–98.

[24] Ep. 46, 9; see Hunt, *Holy Land Pilgrimage*, pp. 83–106.

[25] It is hard to determine with certainty that Jerome himself ascribed the letter to the two women. There is always a possibility that the title 'Paula et Eustochium ad Marcellam' is an addition of a later editor or scribe. Still, if the letter was written by Jerome, as most scholars believe, why should anyone ascribe this particular letter to another author?

was taken up by three historians in the last decade.[26] As things stand now, we have no conclusive proof that the author was either a man or a woman, but at least we are aware of the problem.

This being the case, Jerome's use of Paula's eyes while describing the holy places is even more telling. Jerome chose Paula as a means, a medium to deliver information and to express ideas about sacred space. The reason why he changed voices on this particular subject is still to be explained.

Egeria and Paula reached the Holy Land from the north. Egeria came from Constantinople, and Paula came from Antioch.[27] Both travelled with a group, riding on animals.[28] Egeria's pilgrimage to the Holy Land took three years, from Easter 381 to Easter 384.[29] In those three years, she visited the Holy Places of Palestine, Egypt, and Transjordan, and stayed for long periods in Jerusalem, where she took part in all the ritual ceremonies of the Jerusalem Church. Her letter has two parts: one (chapters 1–23) describes her visits to Sinai, Mount Nebo, Carneas, and Mesopotamia, and the other (chapters 24–49) describes the Jerusalem liturgy. According to Petrus Diaconus's account, written in the twelfth century and partially based on Egeria, she visited all the sites in the Holy Land.[30]

Paula's journey was much shorter. It lasted for about a year,[31] and only included the sites west of the Jordan and a visit to Egypt, the home of Christian monasticism. In contrast to Egeria, who came to the East with the aim of visiting all the Holy Places and not returning to her country until her curiosity was satisfied, Paula's journey was only a step towards becoming a nun in Bethlehem, her journey's final goal.[32] Still, one aspect

---

[26] The possibility that the writer of the *Itinerarium burdigalense* may well have been a woman, which had been first suggested by J. E. Taylor, *Christians and the Holy Places. The Myth of Jewish-Christian Origins* (Oxford, 1993), p. 313, was taken up by Laurie Douglass, who devoted an article to prove this assumption: L. Douglass, 'A New Look at the *Itinerarium burdigalense*', *Journal of Early Christian Studies,* 4 (1996), 313–33. In a recent article, Susan Weingarten discussed the evidence brought up by Douglass and gave it a different and very convincing interpretation, yet did not exclude the possibility: S. Weingarten, 'Was the Pilgrim from Bordeaux a Woman? A Reply to Laurie Douglass', *Journal of Early Christian Studies,* 7 (1999), 291–97.

[27] Egeria, 23; Ep. 108, 7.

[28] Egeria, 3:2; 11:4; Ep. 108, 7.

[29] Egeria, 17:1; P. Devos, 'La date de voyage d'Égérie', *Analecta Bollandiana,* 85 (1967), 165–94; P. Devos, 'Égérie à Édesse. S. Thomas l'Apôtre, le roi Abgar', *Analecta Bollandiana,* 85 (1967), 381–400; P. Devos, 'Égérie à Bethleem', *Analecta Bollandiana,* 86 (1968), 87–108.

[30] Petrus Diaconus, *De locis sanctis,* CCSL, 175 (Turnhout, 1965), pp. 37–47; 251–80 (at the foot of the *Itinerarium Egeriae* and of Beda Venerabilis, *De locis sanctis*).

[31] Kelly, *Jerome*, pp. 116, 124.

[32] Egeria, 23:10; Ep. 108, 14.

of her journey is worth mentioning: out of the 78 places she visited, 55 witnessed to Old Testament traditions and only 27 to New Testament traditions. This proportion is characteristic of this early period, but it also represents the special interest of Jerome, as an interpreter of the Old Testament.[33]

How did Egeria and Paula read sacred space? How did they make it their own? Egeria described her pilgrimage as a journey 'for the sake of prayer' (*gratia orationis*), a journey for liturgical purposes.[34] From this one may infer that Egeria believed that prayer in the Holy Places had a special quality: prayers offered there were more effective than elsewhere. The description of the liturgy of the Holy Places is the heart of Egeria's letter.[35] She says: 'It was always our practice when we managed to reach one of the places we wanted to see to have first a prayer, then a reading from the book, then to say an appropriate psalm and another prayer'.[36] Egeria describes here a well-organized 'practice' carried out by the monks in charge of the places. They would read to the travellers the passages in the Scriptures relating to the site, and recite prayers before and after the readings.

Before Egeria left the site, the monks gave her 'blessings' (*eulogiae*).[37] These were usually fruits which the monks had grown on their soil, and whose nurture on holy soil had somewhat sanctified them. Egeria does not inform us whether she regards these gifts as mere keepsakes, or whether she believes that they also have a special virtue, but perhaps her very silence in this matter reveals that such objects did not yet have the significance ascribed to them later. In the 560s, the anonymous pilgrim known as 'Antoninus' returned to his home town Piacenza with his bag filled with relics and souvenirs, all of which were said to have wondrous virtues, and especially the virtue of healing.[38]

In relating Paula's pilgrimage, Jerome did not use any special terminology, and he

---

[33] J. Wilkinson, 'Jewish Holy Places and the Origins of Christian Pilgrimage', in *The Blessings of Pilgrimage*, ed. by Ousterhout, pp. 41–53; J. Wilkinson, 'L'apport de Sainte Jérôme a la topographie'; Newman, *Jerome and the Jews,* pp. 220–78; Limor, *Holy Land Travels*, pp. 23–25.

[34] Egeria, 13:1; 17:1.

[35] Ibid., 24–49; Starowieyski, 'Bibliografia Egeriana', nos 164–214; A. Renoux, 'Hierosolymitana. Aperçu bibliographique des publications depuis 1960', *Archiv für Liturgiewissenschaft,* 23 (1981), 10–15; Wilkinson, *Egeria's Travels,* pp. 54–88.

[36] Egeria, 7:10.

[37] Ibid., 3:6; 11:1; 15:6; 21:3; B. Kötting, *Peregrinatio Religiosa: Wallfahrten in der Antike und das Pilgerwesen in der alten Kirche* (Münster, 1980), pp. 403–13.

[38] Antoninus calls these gifts 'benedictio'. *Itinerarium Antonini Placentini. Un viaggio in Terra Santa del 560–570 d.c.*, ed. by C. Milani (Milan, 1977); *Itinerarium Antonini Placentini*, ed. by P. Geyer, CCSL, 175 (Turnhout, 1975), pp. 127–74. See cc. 14, 18, 22, 23, 39, 40, 41, 42, 46.

even explicitly stated that he did not intend to write the description of a journey: 'I shall not describe her journey through Coele-Syria and Phoenicia, for I have not set out to write a travel-book about her, but am going to name only those places which are mentioned in Holy Scripture'.[39] When one compares the two texts, it is very noticeable that the liturgical aspect of the Holy Places, which is so important in Egeria's account, is entirely absent from that of Paula. For Egeria, a holy site is a 'ritual space', and is especially memorable on account of the ceremonies held there, which are 'according to the day and place' (*apte diei et loco*).[40] This special liturgical and theatrical experience —one that enacts sacred past events in the same time and in the same place in which they happened—is absent from the account of Paula's travels. For her, the visit is a purely textual experience, limited to seeing the place and reflecting on its significance. Similarly, Jerome does not mention any objects—benedictory gifts—which Paula takes with her from the Holy Places, and it seems that she keeps only memories and spiritual experiences.

These differences between the two texts may hint at deeper differences of attitude with regard to pilgrimage and the Holy Places. In contrast to Egeria, who is convinced both of the merits of pilgrimage and of the special qualities of the Holy Places, Jerome's ambivalent attitude is well known.[41] On the one hand, Jerome repeated the Pauline view that one place is no better than another where closeness to God is concerned. But, at the same time, Jerome, as a biblical scholar, knew the value of sites as an aid to understanding the text. His famous words at the beginning of his introduction to the Book of Chronicles are in no need of explication: 'In the same way that those who have seen Athens understand the Greek histories better, [. . .] so he who has contemplated Judaea with his own eyes and knows the sites of the ancient cities, and knows the names of the places whether the same or changed, will regard Scripture more lucidly'.[42] And so, even if he does not believe that the holy places have any 'intrinsic holiness',[43] he considers them of great importance as an aid to the comprehension of the Bible.[44] Historical sites are solid evidence for the events that took place there.

---

[39] Ep. 108, 8.

[40] The phrase *'apte diei et loco'* (according to day and place) is repeated fourteen times in Egeria's account. See especially Egeria 47:5; Limor, *Holy Land Travels,* pp. 48–50.

[41] J. Prawer, 'Jerusalem in the Jewish and Christian Perspective of the Early Middle Ages', Settimane, 26 (Spoleto, 1980), pp. 739–95 (revised version: 'Christian Attitudes towards Jerusalem in the Early Middle Ages', in *The History of Jerusalem. The Early Islamic Period 638–1099,* ed. by J. Prawer and H. Ben-Shammai (Jerusalem, 1996), pp. 311–47); P. Maraval, 'Saint Jérôme et le pélerinage aux lieux saints de Palestine'; Newman, *Jerome and the Jews*, pp. 220–40; Newman, 'Between Jerusalem and Bethlehem'; Bitton-Ashkeloni, 'Pilgrimage', pp. 81–135.

[42] PL, 29, col. 423.

[43] Taylor, *Christians and the Holy Places,* p. 312.

[44] The same idea is expressed in letter 46, 9; Newman, *Jerome and the Jews,* p. 232.

In view of Jerome's known opinions, one might indeed expect that his account would reflect the intellectual aspect of the journey, and that he would regard places as merely instrumental to the understanding of the text. And since Egeria represented a less learned pilgrimage, one might expect her to value places over texts, and emotions over scholarship. Yet, it is doubtful if one can say that these two texts represent two different kinds of pilgrimage, or two different ways of relating to the Holy Places.[45] Jerome constantly stresses the fervour, enthusiasm, reverence, courage, and faith shown by Paula on her journey.[46] Like Egeria, Jerome too speaks of the Holy Places in terms of longing and desire. Egeria called the places to which she made pilgrimage 'the places of my desire' or 'longed-for places' (*loca desiderata*).[47] She did not consider the difficult ascent to Mount Sinai to be work, for obedience to divine commandments was for her a fulfilment of desire.[48] The stories of the monks she met in Jerusalem made her long to undertake the 'labour' of visiting Job's grave,[49] and there are other examples. And Paula, for her part, decided not to remain in Egypt, among the praised monks of Nitria, because of her 'greater desire for the Holy Places' (*maius sanctorum locorum desiderium*).[50] The same word—*desiderium*—also recurs in other letters of Jerome in reference to the Holy Places.[51] Thus, despite a certain difference between Egeria's curiosity and almost childish enthusiasm[52] and Paula's gloomy seriousness,[53] they both have a similar motive for going eastwards—a longing for the holy places. The intellectual value Jerome ascribed to them cannot overshadow this primary emotional attraction, which probably was also one of the reasons why he and Paula settled in Bethlehem.

Similarly, despite the fact that Egeria stresses the liturgical aspect of the holy places, at the heart of this liturgy, there was always a textual experience—the reading of the texts in the places they spoke of. The fragmentary sentence which opens Egeria's

---

[45] For the difference between scholarly travels to holy places before Constantine, and later pilgrimage for the sake of places, see Taylor, *Christians and the Holy Places*. It seems that the distinction Taylor makes between these two types of travel is too sharp.

[46] Ep. 108, 6; 7; 9; 11; 12; 13; 14.

[47] Egeria, 10:7.

[48] Ibid., 3:2.

[49] Ibid., 13:1.

[50] Ep. 108, 14.

[51] Ibid., 8, 77; 22, 30. Jerome used the same words (*'desiderio sanctorum locorum'*) in describing the motives of Alexander, the bishop from Cappadocia, for his visit of the Holy Places in 220: *De viris inlustribus,* 62, ed. by E. C. Richardson, Texte und Untersuchungen zur Geschichte der altchristlichen Literatur, 14 (Leipzig, 1896), p. 36.

[52] Egeria says: 'tunc ego ut sum satis curiosa [. . .]' (16:3).

[53] For example the descriptions of Paula's visit to Gibea (8), Beth Zur (11), and to Lot's cave (11).

account is particularly revealing in this regard: 'sites were pointed out according to the Bible'.[54]

Egeria went around the Holy Land, and the Bible served her as a guidebook in her journey. Paula undoubtedly did the same. But Paula and Egeria adopted totally different interpretive strategies where the holy places were concerned. For Egeria, the appearance of a place was an illustration of the text. The height and steepness of a mountain, the size or width of a valley, or even the beauty of the places—all these had no value in themselves, but were visible characteristics which helped one to understand the events described in the text. The description of Mount Sinai is a good example:

> [The Mount of God] looks like a single mountain as you are going round it, but when you actually go into it there are really several peaks, all of them known as 'the Mount of God', and the principal one, the summit on which the Bible tells us that 'God's Glory came down', is in the middle of them. I never thought I had seen mountains as high as those which stood around it, but the one in the middle where God's glory came down was the highest of all, so much so that, when we were on top, all the other peaks we had seen and thought so high looked like little hillocks far below us. Another remarkable thing—it must have been planned by God—is that even though the central mountain, Sinai proper on which God's glory came down, is higher than all the others, you cannot see it until you arrive at the very foot of it to begin your ascent. After you have seen everything and come down, it can be seen facing you, but this cannot be done till you start your climb. I realized it was like this before we reached the Mount of God, since the brothers had already told me, and when we arrived there I saw very well what they meant.[55]

The sight of Mount Sinai and the experience of ascending it aroused Egeria's wonder, but that was hardly surprising, as it was the place of the giving of the Law. Geography reinforced the text and gave material reality to the great events described in it. Egeria is convinced that the way the 'Mount of God' towers above the surrounding high mountains, so that it cannot actually be seen before one climbs it but only afterwards, 'must have been planned by God'. It was here that the Lord descended to give the Israelites the Law, and the landscape itself reveals the uniqueness and sanctity of the place. The landscape is not just beautiful or sublime, but heavily charged with significance, demonstrating God's grace in his creation. Mount Sinai is the place where the Law—the 'Old Testament'—was given. Just as the formative historical event changed the face of human history and the march of time, it also left an impression on geography and the appearance of the site. For Egeria, as well as for other Christian

---

[54] Egeria 1:1; J. Ziegler, 'Die Peregrinatio Aetheriae und die heilige Schrift', *Biblica,* 12 (1931), 162–98.

[55] Egeria, 2:5–7.

observers, sacred space is a text, to be interpreted and deciphered, just like the Holy Scriptures and in parallel to them.[56]

Egeria does not give the difficult ascent of Mount Sinai the contemplative, ascetic, or penitential significance which can be ascribed to a religious act. Her pilgrimage is not a symbolical experience.[57] The abbot Valerius, who read her description in the seventh century gave significance of this kind to her journey.[58] In his time, it seems, pilgrimage and the dangers it involved were already regarded as having a value of themselves. For Egeria, however, the purpose of her visit was to understand the text. She was amazed to see how much the landscape reinforced an understanding of the text, and her compensation for the hard labour was merely seeing the place and not any benefits the act might bring her.

Egeria saw many holy sites, and in all of them the monks read her the appropriate passages from the Bible: 'Indeed, whenever we arrived, I always wanted the Bible passages to be read to us'.[59] After coming down from Mount Sinai, Egeria saw many other places, and she enumerated them until she became weary, and ended her description with the following advice: 'I know it has been rather a long business writing down all these places, and it is far too much to remember. But you, loving sisters, will better discern what happened in these places if you read the holy Books of Moses'.[60] Here, Egeria used the word *'pervidere'* which means 'to look over', 'to survey', 'to discern', and it could be inferred from this that the pilgrimage was in fact unnecessary, as Egeria's sisters at home were able to see and understand all that Egeria had seen simply by reading the Scriptures. In another place she wrote: 'I already knew the land of Goshen from my first visit to Egypt, but I wanted to see all the places where the children of Israel had been [. . .]'.[61] Here again she used the word *'pervidere',* the word she used in connection with the reading of the text, as if she was suggesting that reading and travelling were in fact the same. Reading reflected the travel and vice versa.

For Jerome the connecting link between the place and the text was not the place's appearance, but its name. In his account of Paula's pilgrimage there is hardly any description of places. On the other hand, place-names are regarded as providing a key to an understanding of the text. The Christians inherited the taste of the ancients for etymology, and their belief that there was a connection between the names and their

---

[56] O. Limor, 'The Formation of the Christian Sacred Map' (forthcoming). On the meaning of the ascent to Sinai, see J. Elsner, *Art and the Roman Viewer: The Transformation of Art from Pagan World to Christianity* (London, 1997), p. 108.

[57] On these aspects of Christian pilgrimage, see J. Sumption, *Pilgrimage. An Image of Medieval Religion* (London, 1975).

[58] See n. 12 above.

[59] Egeria, 4:3.

[60] Ibid., 5:8: '[. . .] sed cum leget affectio vestra libros sanctos Moyse, omnia diligentius pervidet, quae ibi facta sunt'.

[61] Ibid., 7:1: '[. . .] tamen ut perviderem omnia loca, quae filii Israel tetigerant [. . .]'.

bearers.[62] A name was a condensation of an experience, its significance and its history, not just a word reflecting a thing. Names were considered a sort of key to the understanding of the figures or the places to which they belonged. Jerome wrote an etymological dictionary of biblical names, *Liber interpretationis hebraicorum nominum*, in which he gave the etymology of biblical names, including the names of places.[63]

This is also the approach in his account of Paula's journey. Jerome gives the etymology of fifteen names: Zion means 'citadel' or 'watchtower'; Ariel means the 'Lion of God'; Bethlehem is the 'House of Bread'; Efrata is 'Karpophorus', a most fertile region; Tower Ader means 'of the flock'; Gaza means 'strength' or 'riches of God'; Esckol means 'cluster'; Kiriath-Sepher is the 'village of letters'; Caphar Barucha is the 'village of blessing'; Zoara means 'small'; the Samaritan is 'the Guardian'; Adummim means 'of blood'; Achor is 'tumult' and disturbance; Bethel is 'house of God'; Sior means 'muddy'. For many places he gives both the biblical and the present name, according to the didactic value he ascribed to the biblical geography: Acco–Ptolemais; Lydda–Diospolis; Emmaus–Nicopolis and so on. A name can have a positive significance. On arriving in Bethlehem, Paula exclaimed with joy mingled with tears: 'Blessed Bethlehem, "House of Bread", birthplace of the Bread that came down from heaven [. . .]'.[64] But 'she had no wish to go to Kiriath Sepher ("village of Letters"), for, despising the letter that killeth, she had found the spirit that giveth life'.[65] By this Jerome explicitly negated the literal reading of the text and exchanged it for a spiritual one.[66]

It would seem that the interpretation of these names—Bethlehem and Kiryath Sepher—contained the essence of Jerome's concept of the relationship between places and texts. Bethlehem was the goal of Paula and Jerome's journey. It was a spiritual goal, a lofty objective which involved also a deep religious meaning. The chapter describing Bethlehem is the most elaborated in the text, made up of a tissue of passages from various books of the Bible which are given together with a complex interlacing of meanings, and it shows us that it was no accident that the town was chosen as Paula and Jerome's place of residence.[67] As for Kiryath Sepher, the very meaning of the name was

---

[62] A. Kamesar, *Jerome, Greek Scholarship, and the Hebrew Bible. A Study of the Quaestiones Hebraicae in Genesim* (Oxford, 1993), pp. 103–04.

[63] Hieronymus, *Liber interpretationis hebraicorum nominum*, ed. by P. de Lagarde, CCSL, 72 (Turnhout, 1959); M. Thiel, *Grundlagen und Gestalt der Hebräischkenntnise des frühen Mittelalters,* Biblioteca degli 'Studi Medievali', 4 (Spoleto, 1973).

[64] Ep. 108, 10.

[65] Ibid., 108, 11.

[66] On the various Christian biblical interpretations, see H. De Lubac, *Exégèse médiévale. Les quatre sens de l'écriture*, 4 vols (Paris, 1959); on these specific words of Jerome, see P. Devos, 'Une fausse lecture dans la lettre 108 de S. Jérôme (Epitaph Sae Paula)', *Analecta Bollandiana,* 87 (1969), 213; Thiel, *Grundlagen,* p. 274.

[67] Concerning the reasons for Jerome's choice of Bethlehem, see Newman, 'Between

enough to make Paula decide not to go there. The essence of the Christian reading of the Scripture according to Jerome and the significance of Paula's pilgrimage was nothing else than a search for the 'spirit that giveth life'—the Christian allegorical interpretation of the Scriptures—and a negation of the 'letter that killeth'—the rival Jewish literal interpretation.

Egeria was not concerned with the interpretation of names. None of the names she mentioned was given an interpretation. It seems that etymologies did not form part of her cultural universe. She went from place to place and stopped in order to read the Scriptures, or, more exactly, to hear them read to her by the monks. Egeria spoke of reading and listening, Jerome of memory and reflection. Paula, in the holy places, 'meditated, remembered, recalled'.[68] Egeria saw a place and listened to a text; Paula came to a place and thought of its significance. For her, the places were important not only because of the events that took place there, but because of the meaning of these events for believers. Paula's visit to Gibeah is a good example: 'At the city of Gibeah, which was razed to the ground, she paused to remember her own sins, and those of the concubine who was cut into pieces and remembered also the six hundred Benjamites who were spared on account of the Apostle Paul'.[69] In the holy places, Paula meditated on the text.[70]

Was Egeria then ignorant of allegorical reading? It should be pointed out that the liturgical part of Egeria's letter shows that spiritual interpretation was by no means unfamiliar to her and could gain her admiration.[71] She had no knowledge of Jerome or his interpretations, but she listened on many occasions to the sermons of Cyril, Bishop of Jerusalem, which she praised highly.[72] Just as Paula accepted Jerome's authority as a teacher, so Egeria accepted that of Cyril, who advocated a spiritual understanding of prophecy.[73] This being the case, the straightforward historical approach of the geographical section of the work is even more striking. For Egeria, the exodus from Egypt, the journey across Sinai, the giving of the Law, the death of Moses—events that had received allegorical and typological interpretations in early Christianity—were represented as historical events with a geographical locations, and nothing else. Egeria was well versed in the Bible, and knew how to read a text. One may suppose that her preference for the historical meaning of the text and her avoidance of typological interpretation was deliberate and reflected her personal inclination.

Jerusalem and Bethlehem', pp. 224–27; Kelly, *Jerome,* pp. 127–28; Hunt, *Holy Land Pilgrimage,* pp. 173–74.

[68] 'recordata est' (8, 11, 12), 'contemplata est' (11), 'venerata est' (13), 'mirata est' (13).

[69] Ep. 108, 8. See Jude 19–20; Romans 11. 1.

[70] Dronke, *Women Writers*, p. 19.

[71] Egeria, 24–49.

[72] Cyrillus Hierosolymitanus, *Catecheses*, PG, 33, cols 331–1128; Although probably very old, Cyril was still bishop when Egeria visited Jerusalem.

[73] See especially Egeria, 46.

There is another difference between Jerome and Egeria. Jerome was a teacher and his letter had a didactic aim. He taught Christians how they should look at holy places, and how they should understand them. Egeria's reading was much more private. She wanted to share her experience and her knowledge with her sisters, but she did not try to give her experience a universal or doctrinal status. In the following centuries, Jerome would be accepted as the biblical scholar *par excellence* of the Christian world. His way of reading the Bible and his exegetic methods became authoritative, and moreover, the only possible ones. Indeed by translating and interpreting the Hebrew text, Jerome made an enormous contribution to the Christian world, but this contribution had its price. It closed off other possibilities of reading. Christians in the Middle Ages did not have to approach the Hebrew Bible by themselves. They had Jerome. They read the Holy Scriptures, and especially the Old Testament, through Jerome's eyes. Egeria, who did not know Jerome, tells us, in her humble and naive way, about other possible ways of reading the Bible that were in use in her time, and for that we are greatly indebted to her.[74]

Three elements are indispensable for the creation of sacred space: place, ritual, and text.[75] While Egeria puts great emphasis on liturgy, Jerome concentrates on the interpretation of the text and on its deeper meaning. The absence of the liturgical dimension and the benedictory gifts in Paula's journey and the absence of the typological dimension in Egeria's point to the variety of religious experience, and to the different ways of representing the encounter with the holy places right from the beginning of Christian pilgrimage. Paula and Jerome, generally speaking, continued a tradition of scholarly pilgrimage (represented by Melito of Sardis in the second century and Origen in the third century)[76] whose purpose was chiefly a better understanding of the text, while Egeria's experience was already closer to the type of Christian pilgrimage known in the Middle Ages—that is, pilgrimage as a religious act in its own right.[77] At the same time, Egeria's unmediated relationship to the biblical text, and her constant emphasis on the connection between place and text, make her pilgrimage a textual experience as well, and the fact that Paula and Jerome settled in Bethlehem 'where Mary and Joseph found nowhere to lodge'[78] endows the place with a special significance. Furthermore, even in the following centuries, when pilgrims came to the holy places for the sake of their benedictory, remedial, or penitential virtues, the places never lost their textual character. This after all was the essential difference between pilgrimage to other places and pilgrimage to the Holy Land, which remained always a 'textual pilgrimage', a pilgrimage to the Land of the Text.

---

[74] As a matter of fact, Egeria shows us how the Jewish historical reading of the Bible could have been accepted as a Christian reading.

[75] J. Smith, *To Take Place. Toward Theory in Ritual* (Chicago, 1987), p. 86.

[76] Hunt, *Holy Land Pilgrimage,* pp. 3–4, 100–101.

[77] On these later aspects, see Sumption, *Pilgrimage*.

[78] Ep. 108, 14.

Le judaïsme et les juifs dans l'hagiographie et la liturgie visigothique

BAT-SHEVA ALBERT

L'hagiographie remplit une fonction importante dans la liturgie: la *Passio,* la *Vita,* ou des extraits de ces ouvrages, serviront de *lectio* pendant la messe. Dans l'office cathédral, elles figurent dans les missels ou bréviaires ainsi que dans les lectionnaires. Ces ouvrages serviront surtout de lecture édifiante pour le public monastique. Il faudra attendre longtemps pour que des collections de Vies des Saints comme la célèbre Légende Dorée de Jacques de Voragine (1255–66) soient destinées à la lecture d'une audience laïque plus largement alphabétisée.

Toutefois, l'hagiographie du haut moyen âge n'excluait pas totalement le public laïc et analphabète. A l'époque carolingienne, les Passions et les Vies des Saints ou plutôt des remaniements ou des extraits choisis à cet effet, étaient lus ou même déclamés aux foules accourues dans les sanctuaires pour la fête du saint patron qui y était enseveli: c'était le cas notamment à l'abbaye de S. Gall et à la tombe de S. Rémi de Reims,[1] usage d'ailleurs plusieurs fois séculaire au neuvième siècle.[2] On déplore l'absence de témoignages analogues pour l'Espagne visigothique; or la participation des fidèles aux processions organisées au sixième siècle en l'honneur de S. Eulalie de Mérida laisse deviner que l'histoire de son martyre était connue, soit par l'intermédiaire des homélies, soit par celui de la liturgie, soit encore par des recits populaires déjà séculaires.

---

[1] Voir B. Albert, *Le pèlerinage à l'époque carolingienne* (Louvain-la-Neuve, Bruxelles et Leuven, 1999), pp. 217, 237–38.

[2] Ibid. Infra nn. 36–38, sermon de S. Augustin en l'honneur de S. Eulalie de Mérida.

Quelle est la place réservée à l'hagiographie dans la polémique anti-judaïque? Pour répondre à cette question, il importera de repérer les passages liturgiques qui citent des ouvrages hagiographiques où les juifs jouent un rôle de premier plan: l'usage qu'en fera (ou ignorera) la liturgie sera étudié à un niveau plus étendu. Si manifestement les offices n'étaient compris que par une audience restreinte et surtout monastique, quel retentissement ces passages eurent-ils sur la polémique anti-judaïque et sur les attitudes et relations judéo-chrétiennes? L'ignorance des laïcs n'échappait certes pas aux réformateurs ecclésiastiques et princiers: dès lors, quel rôle pastoral et éducatif assignaient-ils à la liturgie? Problème qui sera particulièremnt épineux pour l'Espagne visigothique dont la production liturgique, dite mozarabe, fut d'une splendeur, d'une originalité et d'une complexité inégalées.

Quant à l'*Adversus Judaeos*, il serait légitime de penser que la liturgie, plutôt que la littérature polémique sous ses divers aspects, pouvait effectivement toucher le plus grand nombre d'auditeurs. Si encore les disputations judéo-chrétiennes, phénomène tardif, se dérouleront devant une audience aristocratique et ecclésiastique assez nombreuse et capable d'en appréhender l'essentiel, les ouvrages de polémique, munis d'un bagage patristique et éxégétique bien fourni, réclamaient une éducation ecclésiastique poussée. Sachant que la liturgie visigothique, si riche et complexe, n'était pas aisément accessible aux fidèles, on admettra toutefois qu'elle pouvait leur offrir des éléments de polémique anti-judaïque et présenter l'image du juif telle qu'elle se profile à partir des Passions ou des Vies des Saints lues au cours des offices.

L'image du juif dans l'hagiographie du haut moyen âge a fait l'objet d'un article fort important de Gilbert Dahan.[3] Dahan estime qu'il n'y eu pas de systématisation du caractère négatif du juif dans l'hagiographie du haut moyen âge, bien qu'il admette que son reflet est plutôt négatif.[4] En outre, il ne mentionne qu'un seul ouvrage hagiographique originaire de l'Espagne visigothique, notamment la *Vita Mancii,* où les juifs agissent comme tortionnaires qui tuent le malheureux Mancius.

Or les juifs figurent également dans deux *Passiones* visigothiques célèbres décrivant respectivement le martyre de S. Eulalie de Mérida et celui de S. Vincent et de ses soeurs Sabine et Cristète. Notre objectif se proposera de replacer ces Passions dans le cadre historique des relations judéo-chrétiennes dans l'Espagne visigothique ainsi que de retrouver et de retracer leur emprunt par la liturgie.

Deux remarques s'imposent au départ: il ne sera question ici que de Passions ou de *Vitae* dont le caractère historique des protagonistes demeure improuvable; cela excluera d'office des évêques éminents comme Césaire d'Arles (470–543) ou Ferréol d'Uzès dont les relations et les démêlés avec les juifs de leurs diocèses reposent probablement sur un fond historique et qui ont déjà fait l'objet d'importants travaux.[5]

---

[3] G. Dahan, 'Saints, démons et juifs', dans *Santi e demoni nell'alto medioevo occidentale (secoli V–XI),* Settimane, 36 (Spoleto, 1989), pp. 609–42.

[4] Ibid., pp. 634–36.

[5] Pour Césaire d'Arles et les juifs, voir W. E. Klingshirn, *Caesarius of Arles. The Making*

Par contre, les évènements qui forment la trame des *Passiones* visigothiques que nous examinerons ne peuvent être corroborés par d'autres témoignages. Dès lors, ces ouvrages présentent le portrait—type du juif tel que le concevaient les auteurs ecclésiastiques de ces ouvrages, image qui pouvait servir des objectifs pastoraux, voire missionaires, de l'époque de leur rédaction. Notons toutefois qu'une présence juive dans les lieux où se déroulent ces Passions est établie pour la plus célèbre d'entr'elles, celle de S. Eulalie de Mérida. L'évidence épigraphique a conservé des stèles funéraires juives originaires de Mérida datant des sixième-septième ou du huitième siècle,[6] temps probable de la rédaction définitive de la Passion d'Eulalie. D'ailleurs l'histoire des évêques et de la communauté catholiques de Mérida sous la royauté visigothique arienne, relatée dans la *Vita Sanctorum Patrum Emeretensium* qui date du septième siècle, viendra confirmer leur présence au sixième siècle dans cette cité.

Or les juifs habitaient Mérida à l'époque romaine: on y a découvert une stèle funéraire qui daterait du deuxième siècle.[7] D'après la Passion, le martyre d'Eulalie daterait de la fin du troisième ou du début du quatrième siècle; il s'en suit que l'intervention du juif dans ce récit repose pour le moins sur l'histoire d'un habitat juif fort ancien à Mérida et sur celle de relations judéo-chrétiennes séculaires.

Remarquablement, un ouvrage juif espagnol du XIIe siècle, le *Sefer ha-Kabbala* d'Abraham ibn David, renvoie l'établissement de la communauté juive à Mérida à la destruction du Temple par Titus. Ce dernier aurait exilé des notables juifs à Mérida, et parmi eux, un artisan nommé Baruch et d'autres familles juives. Plus tard, un des juifs de Mérida, rabbi ben Albalia, aurait quitté la ville pour s'installer à Cordoue. Or ben Albalia était un ancêtre de l'auteur, Abraham ibn David: cette tradition familiale juive faisait elle aussi remonter l'origine de la communauté juive de Mérida à l'époque romaine.[8]

Quant à la présence des juifs à Avila, théâtre du martyre de Vincent et de ses soeurs Sabine et Cristète, les données seront plutôt d'ordre spéculatif car on ne dispose pas d'informations relatives à l'existence de communautés dans cette ville à l'époque

---

of a Christian Community in Late Antique Gaul (Cambridge, 1994), pp. 108–110; ég. Dahan, 'Saints', pp. 616, 622.

[6] A. F. Rabello, *The Jews in Visigothic Spain in Light of the Legislation* (Jerusalem, 1983), pp. 120–21; A. M. Jorge, 'Church and Culture in Lusitania in the V–VIII Centuries. A Late Roman Province on the Crossroads', dans *The Visigoths*, ed. A. Ferreiro (Leiden 1999), p. 115, signale l'existence de ghettos [*sic*] dans la vallée du Tage et dans l'aire de Braga sans fournir des précisions ou des références bibliographiques.

[7] Rabello, *The Jews*, p. 119.

[8] *Sefer ha-Quabbalah. The Book of Tradition by Abraham ibn David*, ed. G. D. Cohen (New York, 1967), p. 59, cité par J. Castaño, 'Mesianismo seudo-isidoriano en autores judíos de Castilla y Fez en torno a 1492', Seminario 'Judíos en tierras de Islam, II', Casa de Velásquez, Madrid, 16 Noviembre 1998, pp. 11–12. Je remercie mon collègue et ami, Claudio Dov Stuchinski d'avoir attiré mon attention sur cet article.

romaine. Pour l'époque visigothique catholique (587–711), cette *Passio* serait le seul indice de leur présence. Connaissant l'existence d'une communauté juive à Tolède au milieu du septième siècle,[9] on pourra concevoir une présence juive à Avila à l'époque visigothique, temps de la rédaction de la Passion de Vincent et de ses soeurs.

Autre observation digne d'attention: ces *Passiones* et les fêtes des martyrs qui en sont les héros feront l'objet de cultes locaux, 'nationaux', parfois même internationaux[10] dont l'écho solennel dans la liturgie hispanique aurait diffusé l'image du juif offerte par ces ouvrages. La question demeure: cette liturgie pouvait-elle exercer quelque influence sur l'appréhension du dogme chrétien par les mentalités populaires? On tentera d'évaluer l'impact de la liturgie visigothique, plus particulièrement celle du *Passionaire hispanique* sur la formation religieuse des fidèles.

L' Importance pastorale de la liturgie mozarabe et du 'Passionaire hispanique'

Création littéraire impressionante, la liturgie hispanique ou mozarabe ne prévoyait qu'une participation fort limitée des laïcs, et la séparation entre le clergé et les fidèles y sera très marquée. C'est ainsi que le canon XVIII du IVe concile de Tolède (a. 633) stipulait que l'évêque et les prêtres communieront devant l'autel, les clercs dans le choeur, tandis que le peuple communiera à l'extérieur du choeur.[11] En général, il s'agissait de répéter *Amen* aux pétitions contenues dans les litanies, le *Pater Noster* inclu, que l'officiant récitait phrase par phrase. Le Vendredi Saint, la participation des fidèles créait un effet impressionant grâce à la répétition criée ou chantée d'*Indulgentia.* A l'avis de Díaz y Díaz, la participation des fidèles, même passive, serait devenue progressivement plus ardue car les formules liturgiques, destinées à une audience cléricale, se firent graduellement plus élaborées. Notons toutefois que certaines sections des offices révêtent un caractère doctrinal accusé: on y relève de nombreuses formules qui paraissent anti-ariennes.[12] A l'évidence, ces textes liturgiques seront souvent des créations d'auteurs identifiables qui les rédigèrent dans un but didactique défini à l'intention de de la communauté entière.[13]

---

[9] Le *Placitum* de 654, ce serment prêté dans la cathédrale de Tolède par des juifs baptisés qui s'engageaient par serment à ne plus observer les observances et les coutumes juives et de demeurer dorénavant des chrétiens sincères, définit ces convertis comme des *'ex hebraeis'* de la ville de Tolède: Rabello, *The Jews,* pp. 143–45.

[10] Pour la diffusion de ces cultes, voir infra, pp. 22seq., 27seq.

[11] IVe concile de Tolède (633), c. 18, *Concilios Visigóticos e Hispano—Romanos,* ed. J. Vives, T. Marín Martínez, et G. Martínez Díez (Barcelona et Madrid, 1963), p. 198. Voir à ce propos J. N. Hillgarth, 'Popular Religion in Visigothic Spain', dans *Visigothic Spain: New Approaches,* ed. E. James (Oxford 1980), pp. 17, 21.

[12] Voir infra, nn. 79 et 85.

[13] M. C. Díaz y Díaz, 'Literary Aspects of the Visigothic Liturgy', dans idem, *Vie chrétienne*

C'étaient surtout les sections de la liturgie eucharistique qui convenaient à une élaboration littéraire. En effet, celles-ci étaient beaucoup plus longues que les sections correspondantes de la liturgie romaine et se prêtaient mieux que la liturgie gallicane à l'expression créatrice des auteurs. La *Inlatio*, l'équivalent hispanique de la Préface romaine (c'est-à-dire l'introduction à la partie centrale de l'office, débutant par le *Sursum corda* et finissant avec le *Sanctus*) illustrera cette caractéristique. Elle contiendra un élément doxologique, une section de prières et une introduction presque formulaire au *Sanctus*. La longueur des *Inlationes* hispaniques varie entre onze et quatre-vingt-huit lignes, face à une variation de douze à quinze lignes pour la Préface romaine. Dans le cycle sanctoral hispanique les variations seront encore plus remarquables: il s'agit d'une moyenne de quarante-six lignes pour la *Inlatio* du cycle sanctoral, comparée à une moyenne de trente-et-une lignes dans le cycle temporel. Il s'entend donc que c'était surtout le cycle sanctoral qui permettait aux auteurs liturgiques de donner libre cours à leur génie créateur.[14] On verra plus loin l'importance de ces données pour l'appréciation de la messe dédiée aux martyrs d'Avila, Vincent, Sabine et Cristète.[15]

Si le cycle sanctoral permettait l'éclosion du talent littéraire des auteurs, on se demandera néanmoins quand, pourquoi et comment on utilisa le Passionaire. C'est seulement au VIIIe siècle que l'Eglise romaine introduisit peu à peu la lecture des Passions dans la liturgie. Or en Espagne, ainsi qu'en Afrique, en Gaule et à Milan, la lecture des Actes des saints était déjà pratiquée au cinquième siècle. Cette lecture était certainement d'usage courant au septième siècle, témoin de la sévère législation anti-juive et de la rédaction des ouvrages de polémique anti-judaïques importants, notamment le *De Fide Catholica contra Judaeos* d'Isidore de Séville (*c*. 560–636) suivi plus tard par les ouvrages de l'archevêque Julien de Tolède (680–690).[16] Dans la lettre-prologue à sa *Vita Aemiliani*, l'évêque Braulion de Saragosse (*c*. 585–651) déclare l'avoir rédigée pour qu'on puisse en faire la lecture dans la messe du saint. Plus significativement, il ajoute que la *Vita* tiendra lieu de sermon, car il ne faut pas lasser les fidèles par de trop longues cérémonies; finalement, il faudra rédiger une messe en l'honneur du saint, et c'est son ami Eugène de Tolède qui s'en chargera.[17] De toute évidence, les *Vitae* des saints hispaniques remplissaient une fonction homélitique de premier plan, et la masse des fidèles les connaissaient.

---

et culture dans l'Espagne du VIIe au Xe siècles (Aldershot, 1992), pp. 64–74. Pour le contenu anti-arien ou peut-être anti-judaïque des Passions visigothiques, infra, pp. 34–38.

[14] Díaz y Díaz, 'Literary Aspects', pp. 62–63.

[15] Infra, pp. 39–41.

[16] Pour une mise au point récente, bien documentée et qui accepte la thèse de l'auteur sur les motifs religieux de la politique anti-juive visigothique, voir R. González-Salinero, 'Catholic Anti-Judaism in Visigothic Spain', dans *The Visigoths*, ed. Ferreiro, pp. 123–50.

[17] B. de Gaiffier, 'La Lecture des actes de martyrs dans la prière liturgique en Occident. A propos du Passionaire hispanique', *Analecta Bollandiana*, 72 (1954), 141–43, 153.

Indubitablement, ce fut le IVe concile de Tolède (633) qui établit l'uniformité du culte.[18] Suite à cette décision, des messes dédiées aux martyrs qui jusqu'à là étaient récitées dans les régions qui abritaient leurs tombes furent introduites dans des formulaires dorénavant utilisés par toutes les églises du royaume.

Qui plus est, les exigences de la liturgie désormais nationale dictaient la rédaction d'un récit circonstancié; on rédigea donc des passions sur des modèles déjà appréciés.[19] Voilà pourquoi De Gaiffier place la rédaction du *Passionaire hispanique*, collection des vies des martyrs, dans la seconde partie du septième siècle.

Nous verrons que le contenu anti-judaïque des Passions que nous examinerons ici permettra d'émettre des hypothèses plus précises sur la date de leur rédaction définive.[20] En effet, de nombreux offices contiennent des allusions et même des citations de textes plus anciens extraits des Passions ou des vies des saints[21] mais ce seront precisément les thèmes relatifs aux juifs et au judaïsme qui aideront à replacer les diverses strates du texte dans leur contexte historique.

On connaît déjà le caractère 'élitiste' de la liturgie hispanique, presque incompréhensible pour les fidèles qui se voyaient d'ailleurs interdits d'accéder de près à une partie du service religieux. Or l'utilisation du Passionaire revêtait une importance primordiale pour l'édification des fidèles: s'ils ne pouvaient que partiellement comprendre la liturgie, au moins connaissaient-ils la vie des martyrs. La fonction homélitique de ces textes est claire: ils confrontaient les fidèles avec les modèles d'un christianisme ultimatif qui ne reculent pas devant la mort, mais au contraire la recherchent souvent par une confrontation aggressive avec le pouvoir païen. Inutile d'ajouter que ces situations héroïques ne correspondaient nullement à celle des catholiques triomphants de l'Espagne du septième siècle. L'idéal chrétien du sacrifice personnel demeurait certes éternel, mais le Passionaire aidera également à véhiculer des messages doctrinaires plus récents et encore actuels dans l'Espagne du VIIe siècle; ils contiendront par conséquent des formules anti-ariennes, et en ce qui concerne notre propos, également anti-judaïques. Concluons donc: le *Passionaire hispanique*, rédigé au courant du septième siècle,[22] fut utilisé dans la liturgie, surtout dans le sanctoral, et permit au le clergé visigothique de transmettre son message doctrinaire aux laïcs ignares qui seront les fervents adeptes du culte des saints.

Ayant établi l'impact homélétique et doctrinal du Passionaire, notre démarche se proposera de faire le portrait du juif tracé par ses textes et de peser son influence sur les relations judéo-chrétiennes dans l'Espagne visigothique. L'image du juif et le bagage typologique qui l'entoure nous permettront de préciser la datation de ces Passions.

---

[18] IVe concile de Tolède (633), c. 2, *Concilios*, p. 188.

[19] De Gaiffier, 'La Lecture', p. 162.

[20] Pour la datation de la rédaction des Passions d'Eulalie de Mérida, de Vincent d'Avila et des ses soeurs d'après leurs thèmes anti-juifs, infra, pp. 24–26 et 37–38.

[21] Díaz y Díaz, 'Literary Aspects', p. 64.

[22] Voir infra, p. 24 pour la datation du Passionaire.

Finalement, l'on suivra la diffusion du culte, son reflet dans la liturgie et l'usage qu'elle fit du récit de ces martyrs pour diffuser ce portrait et ses formules anti-judaïques et parfois anti-juives.

Les Passions et les juifs

Disons d'emblée que la comparaison entre la *Passio S. Eulaliae* et la *Passio SS. Vincentii Sabinae et Christetae* et leur utilisation liturgique présentent des analogies aussi bien que de nettes différences: les juifs y apparaissent comme témoins de la vérité du christianisme et de l'indiscutable sainteté des martyrs: ils finissent par se convertir. Ceci dit, la propagation de leurs cultes respectifs variera largement: alors que celui d'Eulalie fut dès son origine un culte à résonnances internationales, celui de Vincent et de ses soeurs fut à ses débuts purement local mais s'assura plus tard un succès à l'échelle nationale.

LA *PASSIO S. EULALIAE*

Le récit se déroule à l'époque de Dioclétien (284–305). Eulalie, adolescente noble âgée de treize ans, apprend le martyre des chrétiens et exprime son désir de les rejoindre. Effrayés, ses parents, l'envoie hors de la ville de Mérida. Elle parvient à s'échapper, retourne à Mérida et affronte le *praetor* qui veut l'obliger à rester païenne. Elle refuse obstinément, est cruellement torturée, et finalement à l'instant de sa mort son âme monte aux cieux sous la forme d'une colombe blanche.

L'épisode de sa rencontre avec le juif se situe sur le chemin du retour à Mérida. Le juif la salue et lui conseille de brûler de l'encens aux dieux pour sauver sa vie. Lui rendant son salut, Eulalie répond qu'elle aspire à mourir pour Jésus. Quand le juif réalise qu'elle passe devant lui comme du feu, il comprend que les anges la protègent, et ce miracle divin s'est produit pour que 'leur insensée dureté de coeur puisse voir les grandes actions du Christ'.[23]

Trois remarques s'imposent à la lecture de ce texte. D'abord, la rencontre entre le juif et Eulalie paraît amicale: il la salue et elle lui rend son salut en lui souhaitant longue vie.[24] Pourtant cette amitié ne doit pas faire illusion: de fait, les salutations échangées prouvent uniquement l'innocence et la sainteté d'Eulalie. Le juif par contre, adoptant un ton soit-disant paternel, essaye de l'empêcher d'atteindre à la sainteté sublime du martyre en lui présentant l'option de la vie terrestre obtenue à un prix innaceptable, celui du sacrifice au culte païen.[25] D'ailleurs la conclusion de la Passion efface le doute sur le caractère véritable du juif: elle trace un parallélisme assez flou entre le juif et

---

[23] A. Fábrega Grau, *Pasionario hispánico, s. VII–XI,* t. II, 8, Eulaliae Emeriten, 6 (Madrid et Barcelona, 1955), p. 70.

[24] Ibid.

[25] Ibid.

'l'ennemi premier de la chair'.[26] Formule problématique, il s'entend, car si 'l'ennemi premier de la chair' ne désigne pas clairement le démon, on pourra suggérer que dans l'Espagne du VIIe siècle l'*adversarius fidei* ne saurait être nul autre que le juif; le paganisme, encore pratiqué, n'avait plus de représentants officiels pas plus d'ailleurs que l'arianisme latent,[27] tandis que les juifs demeuraient l'unique adversaire organisé et 'officiel' du catholicisme visigothique.

Arrêtons-nous également à l'apparition du feu et des anges protégeant la martyre, thème qui n'est pas sans évoquer la colonne de feu marchant devant les Enfants d'Israël pendant l'Exode,[28] l'Eternel lui-même guidant ainsi leur itinéraire pendant la nuit. Cette analogie était bien faite pour convaincre les juifs: le Christ, par l'entremise de ses anges, a rapporté sa protection sur la martyre chrétienne, nouvelle fille d'Israël, et la guide vers sa fin héroïque, indiquant aux juifs le chemin qui les délivrera de la servitude de l'Ancien Testament vers le salut chrétien du Nouveau. L'intention missionaire de l'épisode du juif est évidente, ce qui aidera à dater la rédaction la Passion telle qu'elle nous est parvenue dans le *Passionaire hispanique*.

LA DATATION

L'antiquité du culte d'Eulalie de Mérida est indubitable, puisque Augustin lui avait déjà consacré un sermon.[29] Malheureusement, le texte de la Passion du cinquième siècle ne nous est pas parvenu; par conséquent, on ignore s'il différait peu ou prou de celui du septième siècle. Fábrega Grau, l'éditeur du *Pasionario hispánico,* précise que la version finale daterait de la fin du septième ou du début du huitième siècle et fut rédigée sous l'influence de la législation du roi Erwig, datant de 681.[30] Rappelons toutefois qu'Erwig promulga une loi qui rendait le baptême obligatoire pour les juifs, leur famille et leurs esclaves dans le délai d'un an.[31] Or une lecture attentive de la Passion d'Eulalie révèle que notre épisode se déroule dans une climat entourant les relations judéo-chrétiennes qui s'accorde mal avec celui qui régnait au temps d'Erwig et de sa législation. Malgré sa ruse (oserait-on dire perfidie?), le juif de Mérida, symbole de son peuple, fait preuve d'une disposition à la conversion, le miracle parvenant à le convaincre de la vérité chrétienne. A partir de là, on entrevoit deux hypothèses de travail qui permettraient de

---

[26] Ibid. 20, pp. 77–78.

[27] Pour le culte des idoles et le paganisme à la fin du septième siècle, voir par example le XVIe concile de Tolède (693), c. 2, *Concilios,* p. 498. Pour l'arianisme latent, infra, pp. 35–36.

[28] L'Exode, 13. 21.

[29] Pour le sermon d'Augustin, infra, nn. 36–38.

[30] Fábrega Grau, *Pasionario hispánico,* p. 82.

[31] *Leges visigothorum,* 12.3.3., texte dans J. Juster, 'La condition légale des juifs sous les rois visigoths', *Études d'histoire juridique offertes à Paul Frédéric Girard* (Paris, 1912), p. 4, n. 3. Le résumé des lois d'Erwig fut approuvé par le XIIe concile de Tolède (681), *Concilios,* c. 8, pp. 395–97, cf. n. 33.

préciser la date de la rédaction. La première confirmerait l'antiquité certaine de la Passion, la situant soit dans la seconde partie du quatrième ou au début du cinquième siècle car Augustin, sacré évêque d'Hiponne en 396, écrivit un sermon en l'honneur de la sainte.[32] Doctrine officielle de l'église catholique, la conversion des juifs s'effectuera par la persuasion; le miracle sera une arme pacifique mais efficace pour l'obtenir. L'intervention miraculeuse regroupera la communauté chrétienne autour du culte des martyrs, souvenirs encore vivaces des persécutions; le témoignage du juif (autre adversaire de la foi) du miracle qui précéda le martyre viendra renforcer cette cohésion.

La seconde thèse de travail replacerait la date de la rédaction après l'échec de la conversion forcée des juifs par le roi Sisebut en 612. Isidore de Séville, le dirigeant incontesté de l'église visigothique, qui avait, tacitement du moins approuvé la coercition exercée par Sisebut, la récusa partiellement au IVe concile de Tolède réuni en 633 qu'il présida et dont il rédigea les décisions. Il recommanda d'user dorénavant de la persuasion pour amener les juifs à la conversion, mais les juifs convertis de force seront tenus de demeurer chrétiens.[33] Décision qui inaugure une période d'efforts persistants de convertir les juifs par la persuasion certes, mais une persuasion accompagnée d'une législation royale et conciliaire progressivement plus sévère et punitive pour les récalcitrants, et à laquelle nous ne pourrons nous arrêter ici.[34] Par contre, ce fut le roi Erwig (680–687) qui, avec l'approbation du XIIe concile de Tolède,[35] réintroduisit la conversion forcée, le roi et l'église admettant indirectement que les mesures moins brutales avaient échoué. Voilà un climat qui ne se prête plus guère à la conversion par la persuasion, même par l'entremise d'un miracle convaincant; c'est pourquoi une datation qui placerait la rédaction de la *Passio Eulaliae* entre 612 et 680 paraît plus plausible.

LE CULTE

Le culte d'Eulalie de Mérida était un des cultes les plus anciens et les répandus dans la péninsule ibérique; de plus, il jouissait d'une popularité internationale certaine à partir du cinquième siècle, succès qui ne se démentira pas jusqu'au neuvième siècle.

LE CULTE INTERNATIONAL

Une brève description de l'expansion du culte de S. Eulalie hors de la Péninsule sera d'intérêt, bien que la liturgie qui peut-être l'accompagnait nous échappe. On en retiendra toutefois les aspects relatifs à notre propos, tout en observant que pour le culte des saints hispaniques, la popularité internationale est toujours un reflet fidèle de l'extension du culte à l'échelle nationale.

---

[32] Sermon d'Augustin, infra, nn. 36–38.

[33] IVe concile de Tolède, c. 57, *Concilios,* pp. 210–11.

[34] Voir Juster, *La condition légale,* pp. 280–98; Rabello, *The Jews*, pp. 59–68.

[35] XIIe concile de Tolède (681), *Concilios,* pp. 395–96.

Le sermon d'Augustin en l'honneur de S. Eulalie[36] est remarquable à deux égards: d'abord, parce qu'il fut prononcé pour la fête de la martyre, ce qui laisse supposer l'existence d'une célébration liturgique appropriée, malheureusement disparue, dans l'Afrique du début du cinquième siècle. Ensuite, parce qu'il indique que l'histoire de l'intervention du juif dans le déroulement du martyre figurait déjà dans la version de la Passion telle que l'évêque d'Hiponne la connaissait. S'il ne relate pas l'épisode du juif, Augustin y fait très clairement allusion. En effet, il rappelle à ses auditeurs la haine des juifs (et des païens) envers les chrétiens.[37] Le rapprochement tracé entre les sentiments haineux des juifs et des païens envers la communauté chrétienne et l'histoire du martyre d'Eulalie ne saurait être fortuite: le *praetor* païen et le juif sont les ennemis déclarés et topologiques d'Eulalie et du christianisme. De toute évidence, l'audience d'Augustin connaissait elle aussi le récit du martyre d'Eulalie; voilà pourquoi il se contenta de condamner les ennemis jurés de la foi chrétienne et de faire les louanges de la martyre dans les termes du genre.[38]

D'après des témoignages du cinquième au septième siècle,[39] le culte d'Eulalie se répandit également en Aquitaine et en Francie. Ce sera le témoignage de Grégoire de Tours[40] qui retiendra l'attention.Cela, parce qu'il ignore manifestement l'intervention du juif. On imagine qu'il n'aurait pas manquer d'y référer car il rapporte le fameux récit du juif, père dénaturé, qui tua son fils qui s'était converti.[41] Par ailleurs, Grégoire rapporte (les aurait-il inventés?) de nombreux détails relatifs au culte d'Eulalie à Mérida. Notons que son témoignage est pratiquement contemporain du conflit qui confronta Masona, l'évêque catholique de la cité, au roi Léovigild (568–586) qui

---

[36] G. Morin, 'Une page inédite de Saint Augustin: Sermo de die sanctae Eulaliae', *Revue bénédictine,* 8 (1891), pp. 417–18.

[37] Ibid., p. 418: 'et ipsi [sc. Iudaei] oderunt nos'. On notera que'Eulalie figure également dans le calendrier de Carthage (VIe siècle) et dans le Psautier latin de S. Catherine du Mt Sinaï, qui représente probablement une église nord-africaine à la veille de la conquête arabe. Ces notices indiqueraient la persistance du culte en Afrique du Nord.

[38] Ibid.: 'Sancta Eulalia [. . .] sancta et fortis femina, quae per affectum vicit sexus, sicut sancta Crispina'. Pour le portrait d'Eulalie comme ascète féminine parfaite, *femina virilis,* voir J. Petruccione 'The Portrait of St Eulalia of Mérida in Prudentius' *Peristephanon* 3, 1', *Analecta Bollandiana,* 108 (1990), 81–104.

[39] Pour la basilique de Béziers dédiée à Eulalie en 455, ainsi que le monastère de Fécamp fondé en 688 par S. Waningus, venu d'Aquitaine, voir C. Garcia Rodriguez, *El culto de los santos en la España romana y visigoda* (Madrid, 1966), p. 27.

[40] Grégoire de Tours, *Liber in Gloria Martyrum,* ed. B. Krusch, MGH, SRM I:2 (Hannover, 1885), pp. 44–45.

[41] Ibid. c. 9, p. 44: le caractère dénaturé du père juif est mis en relief: 'Si cum his infantibus [sc. christianis] communicasti oblitus paterna pietate ad ulciscendam Moysaicae legis iniuriam parricida in te durus exsistam. Ed apprehensum puerum in os fornacis ardentis proiecit, adiectaque ligna. [. . .]'

supportait l'évêque arien Suna, lutte dont l'aboutissement renforça le statut et le culte d'Eulalie, patronne de la communauté catholique de Mérida;[42] or l'histoire de ce conflit ignore la description du culte par Grégoire qui raconte qu'en octobre, trois arbres donnent des fleurs en forme de colombe, identique à l'aspect revêtu par l'âme de la sainte lors de son ascension. L'abondance de ces fleurs sera signe d'abondance agricole, la carence, signe de péché et de pénitence pour la communauté. En cas de sincère repentir, les arbres fleuriront et les fleurs enbaumeront. Ce signe de pardon sera fêté par une procession, et ajoute Grégoire, que les fleurs ont un pouvoir thérapeuthique. La source du récit de l'arbre miraculeux est inconnue, et il ne figure pas dans la *Vita Sanctorum Patrum Emeretensium*, qui décrit le culte de la martyre sous l'épiscopat de Masona (deuxième partie au VIe siècle). Il semblerait s'agir d'une tradition 'populaire', peut-être répandue par des marchands qui fréquentaient Mérida à cette époque,[43] et serait une indication de l'importance du culte au sixième siècle.

Eulalie figure également dans des calendriers et des martyrologes non-hispaniques. L'usage liturgique des calendriers et davantage encore l'importance des martyrologes présente un problème épineux: leur valeur historique dépend souvent de leurs sources littéraires. La mention d'un saint dans ces documents ne saurait constituer une preuve suffisante ni de l'envergure de leur commémoration dans la liturgie ni de l'importance, voire de la présence même de leur culte dans l'espace où ils furent rédigés. Rappelons cependant que les calendriers réflètent la tradition vivante de la communauté, et la présence de la martyre dans des calendriers non-hispaniques démontre pour le moins qu'elle était célèbre à l'étranger. C'est ainsi qu'on la retrouvera sur le calendrier lapidaire de Naples (IXe siècle), un calendrier non-liturgique, qui est un appel à la dévotion envers les saints, quel que soit leur pays d'origine.[44] Eulalie fera également acte de présence dans les martyrologes, qui partagent une caractéristique commune qui exigera une explication: l'intervention du juif ne figure dans aucune de ces sources, qui contiennent pourtant des notices assez détaillées décrivant son martyre. Cette lacune proviendrait-elle d'un emprunt à une source commune, antérieure à la rédaction du *Passionaire hispanique* du septième siècle, qui ignorait cet épisode? Pourtant Augustin paraît avoir connu ce passage.[45] Autre éventualité: l'épisode du juif aurait été délibérément éliminé parce qu'il ne contribuait rien d'essentiel à la narration du martyre, le juif n'y remplissant qu'un rôle accessoire, et les notices des martyrologes étant par définition un résumé succint du récit martyriel. Quoi qu'il en soit, les notices figurant dans les martyrologes seront, comme les calendriers dont ils sont issus, des indications de l'importance des martyrs qui y figurent, sans pour autant prouver l'existence d'un culte. Le martyrologe de Bède confond probablement Eulalie de Mérida avec son homonyme de Barcelone. L'histoire du martyre d'Eulalie de Barcelone

---

[42] Pour le culte d'Eulalie à Mérida, infra, pp. 29–31.

[43] Pour l'importance de Mérida, ibid.

[44] H. Delehaye, 'Hagiographie Napolitaine', *Analecta Bollandiana,* 57 (1939), 58.

[45] Supra, n. 37.

est presque identique à celle d'Eulalie de Mérida et serait peut-être un plagiat.[46] Or Bède rapporte la date de la fête (dix décembre) de la sainte de Mérida, alors que celle de la martyre de Barcelone était célébrée le douze février: cette erreur mène à l'inévitable conclusion que la mention de la martyre, basée sur des sources douteuses, serait d'une valeur exclusivement littéraire. Au neuvième siècle, les martyrologes issus de Lyon renfermeront d'importantes notices sur la sainte, mais celles-ci ignorent également sa rencontre avec le juif.[47] Pourtant le martyrologe composé par le diacre Florus de Lyon (*c.* 852), lui-même visigoth, suggère la connaissance d'une oraison visigothique en l'honneur de la sainte[48] qui rapporte sa mort par crucifixion, alors que le *Passionaire hispanique* n'en dit mot. Il serait permis de penser que Florus aurait puisé son information dans une autre source où l'intervention du juif ne figurait pas. Cela,d'autant plus que le diacre Florus (*c.* 790–*c.* 860) et ses patrons d'origine visigothique, les archevêques de Lyon Agobard (815–840) et Amolon (841–851), témoignèrent tous trois un vif intérêt pour le judaïsme, curiosité qui d'ailleurs accompagnait une hostilité plus vive encore qui anima leurs campagnes contre le judaïsme dans l'empire carolingien.[49] On supposera, non sans raison, que Florus aurait rapporté quelque terme désobligeant sur le juif de Mérida s'il avait connu le *Passionaire hispanique*. Si on retrouve encore la mention d'Eulalie dans l'espace auxerrois dans la seconde moitié du neuvième siècle,[50] son culte, s'il était suivi dans l'empire carolingien, (ce que rien ne permet d'affirmer), restait très limité. Ce sera en Espagne que le culte et la liturgie dédiés à la martyre prendront leur grand essor.

---

[46] J. Vives, 'Eulalia, virgen martir de Barcelona', *Diccionario de Historia Eclesiastica de España*, ed. Q. Aldea Vaquero, T. Marin Martinez, et J. Vives Gatell (Madrid, 1972), II, 883.

[47] J. Dubois et G. Renaud, *Edition pratique des martyrologes de Bède, de l'Anonyme Lyonnais et de Florus* (Paris, 1976), p. 221.

[48] *Martyrologe de Florus,* ibid.: 'cujus beatum corpus per triduum jussu praesidis pependit in ligno'. A comparer avec l'oraison *alia* 174, *Oracional visigotico,* ed. J. Vives, Monumenta Hispaniae Sacra, Serie Liturgica, 1 (Barcelona, 1946), p. 58: 'Eulaliae corpusculum in crucem pendentem. [. . .]' On notera que le *Passionaire hispanique* ne mentionne pas la crucifixion d'Eulalie de Mérida. Le Martyrologe Anonyme de Lyon (*c.* 806) dénote également une forte influence hispanique, voir R. Guerrero, 'L'hagiographie hispanique en Gaule vers le Haut Moyen Age. Circulation et diffusion des *Passions hispaniques*', dans *L'Europe, héritière de l'Espagne wisigothique,* ed. J. Fontaine et C. Pellistrandi (Madrid, 1992), p. 147.

[49] B. Albert, '*Adversus Iudaeos* in the Carolingian Empire', dans *Contra Iudaeos. Ancient and Medieval Polemics between Christians and Jews,* ed. O. Limor and G. G. Stroumsa, (Tübingen, 1996), pp. 135–42.

[50] Eulalie figurait dans le santoral privé d'Heiric d'Auxerre (841–876/7), lui-même hagiographe important: D. Iognat-Prat, 'Influences spirituelles et culturelles du monde wisigothique dans la seconde moitié du IXe siècle', dans *L'Europe, héritière de l'Espagne wisigothique*, ed. Fontaine et Pellistrandi, pp. 247–48.

Le culte d'Eulalie en Espagne (VIe–VIIe siècles)

Au septième siècle, le culte d'Eulalie de Mérida joua un rôle prépondérant dans le développement de cette cité. L'essor économique de la ville aux sixième et septième siècles est indiqué par la quantité des monnaies qui y furent frappées; de 587 à 682, l'atelier de frappe de Mérida émit probablement la majeure quantité de monnaies du royaume, ce qui représente un siècle de suprématie monétaire.[51]

Difficile de savoir si c'était l'éclosion économique de la ville qui contribua à répandre le culte, ou si au contraire, la réputation du culte et l'attraction qu'il exerçait aidèrent l'épanouissement de son économie. Quoi qu'il en soit, ce fut sous le règne du grand roi Léovigild (568–586), le dernier souverain arien, que le culte d'Eulalie rallia les catholiques de la cité autour de leur évêque Masona. Le roi, qui tenta un dernier et vain effort pour unifier son royaume par l'arianisme, ordonna que la basilique S. Eulalie soit remise à l'évêque arien; pour affaiblir la communauté catholique, il voulut s'emparer de la tunique de la sainte pour la ramener à Tolède. La tentative échoua grâce aux prières de l'évêque, et les catholiques rendirent des actions de grâce à la sainte, et victorieux, se réjouirent par une procession.[52] On comprendra que l'auteur ecclésiastique anonyme de la *Vita Sanctorum Patrum Emeretensium* ait voulu exalter la sainte patronne de la cité et son évêque; on devine toutefois que le conflit qui, de 573 à 582–583, opposa le roi à Masona revêtait sans doute un aspect personnel[53] et certainement politique plus significatif si l'on considère la situation économique et stratégique de Mérida, située à proximité de la frontière du royaume suève que Léovigild devait conquérir en 586. On retiendra un aspect de ce conflit qui eut, semble-t-il des répercussions importantes sur le culte et la liturgie: Eulalie serait devenue la championne et le symbole incontesté du catholicisme vainqueur de l'hérésie arienne.[54] De plus, l'ordre de ramener la tunique de la martyre à Tolède traduirait certes son

---

[51] R. Collins, 'Mérida and Toledo: 550–585', dans *Visigothic Spain,* ed. James, pp. 206–07. Récemment, D. M. Metcalf, 'Visigothic Monetary History. The Facts, What Facts?', dans *The Visigoths,* ed. Ferreiro, p. 203, a publié les résultats des derniers travaux numismatiques, qui contribuent à confirmer la suprématie de Mérida: parmi les monnaies de cuivre trouvées à Séville, 63 furent frappées à Mérida, 10 à Tolède, 6 à Cordoue; les monnaies trouvées à Alcalá del Rio (5 km de Séville, en amont sur le Guadalquivir): 7 frappées à Séville, 4 à Mérida, 1 à Tolède; monnaies trouvées à Cullera: 4 frappées à Mérida, 3 à Tolède. Pour les pièces d'or, on compte quatre ateliers de frappe principaux qui frappèrent entre 37 et 60% des monnaies, le nombre plus exact étant sans doute situé entre ces deux chiffres: celui de Séville émit 15%, celui de Tolède 15%, Cordoue 8%, alors que l'atelier de Mérida frappa 22% des monnaies d'or.

[52] *Vita Sanctorum Patrum Emeretensium,* V, 5, 12, 6.7. ed. et trans. J. N. Garvin, Catholic University of America Studies in Medieval and Renaissance Latin Language and Literature, 19 (Washington DC, 1946), p. 208, cité dans Rodriguez, *El culto de los santos,* p. 434.

[53] C'est l'avis de E. A. Thompson, *The Goths in Spain* (Oxford 1969), p. 78.

[54] Pour les aspects anti-ariens de la liturgie en l'honneur d'Eulalie, infra, p. 35.

dessein de soumettre Mérida à l'autorité de la capitale, mais il serait également l'écho du succès du culte de la sainte vers la fin du sixième siècle. Sans doute l'hôpital-hospice que Masona fit construire auprès de la basilique S. Eulalie serait l'indice encore hésitant d'un pèlerinage. En fait, les fouilles de l'église S. Eulalie ont livré des données sur la *civitas christiana.* L'emplacement du sépulcre de la sainte a engendré un ensemble cimetériel important et la construction d'une église qui a subi de nombreuses reconstructions. La zone nord de la cité romaine fut remodelée, comme l'indique l'important bâtiment de l'église Santa Catalina, sise près de celle de S. Eulalie. C'est Santa Catalina qui a été identifiée comme le xénodoche d'inspiration byzantine, à la fois hôpital et abri pour les pèlerins, édifié par les soins de Masona. Cette institution charitable contribua certainement à attirer les pèlerins souffrants à Mérida.[55] Quoi qu'il en soit, vers le milieu du septième siècle, le célèbre moine Fructueux de Braga (d. *c.* 665) se rendit en pèlerinage à Mérida,[56] indication que les pèlerins se recrutaient déjà dans une aire assez éloignée. C'est à la même époque que l'on retrouve des reliques de la sainte dans des églises du sud de l'Espagne, preuve supplémentaire de sa renommée péninsulaire.[57]

LA LITURGIE

Dans la liturgie hispanique, le martyr se profile comme témoin du Christ. S'il agit toujours *pro Christo,* il sera à la fois un *alter Christus* qui se sacrifie pour le monde entier. Le martyr servira de modèle aux fidèles qui seront tenus de l'imiter comme lui-même a imité le Christ, et il interviendra en leur faveur comme l'avocat de la grâce salvatrice. Mais le martyre des vierges sera le martyre ultimatif et sublime car leur union mystique avec Jésus y sera consommée.[58]

---

[55] Supra, le témoignage de Grégoire de Tours, à peu près contemporain de Masona, sur les fleurs thérapeuthiques des arbres de Mérida. Pour les fouilles importantes à Mérida, voir G. Ripoll López, 'The Transformation and Process of Acculturation in Late Antique Hispania: Select Aspects from Urban and Rural Archaeological Documentation', dans *The Visigoths,* ed. Ferreiro, pp. 272–73.

[56] *Vita Fructuosi,* 11, cité par M. C. Díaz y Díaz, 'Notes for a Chronology of the Pasionario Hispánico, dans idem, *Vie chrétienne et culture,* no. V, p. 43.

[57] J. Vives, *Inscriptiones cristianas de la España visigoda et romana* (Barcelona, 1941–42), cité dans Rodriguez, *El culto de los santos,* pp. 450–51: inscriptions des églises de Salpensa, Cadix et Loja.

[58] J. Camarero Cuñado, *La figura del santo en la Liturgia Hispánica. Estudio teológico-litúrgico a la luz de los formularios eucarísticos de los Santos en las tradiciones del rito hispánico* (Salamanca et Madrid 1982), pp. 439, 442, 447.

LES CALENDRIERS

Bien que l'on sache déjà que les calendriers ne sauraient apporter la preuve décisive de l'existence d'un culte, l'omniprésence d'Eulalie dans les calendriers d'origine visigothique sera un indice formel de sa popularité en Espagne tout au long du moyen âge. Il faudra néanmoins séparer les calendriers liturgiques de ceux qui sont une simple liste de saints. En Espagne, on attendra le dixième ou le onzième siècle pour une série de calendriers qui correspondent à la liturgie hispanique.[59] Si Eulalie ne figure pas dans le calendrier épigraphique de Carmona,[60] (Ve–VIe siècles) qui n'est pas un calendrier liturgique, on n'en sera guère surpris: cette liste de saints est incomplète et n'enregistre les fêtes qu'à partir de Noël; or celle d'Eulalie est célébrée le dix décembre. La martyre figurera toutefois dans tous les calendriers liturgiques postérieurs. A titre d'exemple, pour le dixième siècle, elle sera présente dans le calendrier de Ripoll (Xe–XIe siècle, plus probablement Xe), dans le calendrier écrit en 976 par Vigila (d'où son nom de *Vigilano*) et Sarracius au monastère d'Albelda,dans celui du monastère de San Millán de la Cogolla, datant de 994,[61] ainsi que dans le dénommé 'Calendrier de Cordoue' présenté en 976 par l'évêque Recemundus au calife. Son succès ne se démentit pas après le remplacement du rite mozarabe par le rite romain (1085). On répère la fête de la martyre dans un calendrier joint au missel du rite romain de San Millán, écrit en minuscule visigothique (seconde moitié du XIe siècle) qui est postérieur au changement de rite au monastère (1090).[62] Popularité qui se maintient encore aux quatorzième et quinzième siècles, puisque sa fête figure respectivement dans un calendrier de Tarrazone (XIVe–début du XVe siècle) et dans un calendrier de Saragosse qui date du milieu du quinzième siècle.[63] Par définition, les notices dans les calendriers liturgiques

---

[59] On rappellera que Dom Férotin, qui publia la majorité de ces calendriers, ainsi que d'autres spécialistes comme García Villada sont d'avis que ces calendriers sont plus anciens, et les attribuent au cinquième ou sixième siècle, mais la tradition manuscrite ne remonte pas plus haut que les dixième à onzième siècles: J. Vives, 'Liturgia. Calendarios litúrgicos', *Diccionario de Historia Eclesiastica de España,* II, 1325; également J. Vives et A. Fábrega, 'Calendarios Hispánicos anteriores al siglo XII', *Hispania Sacra,* 2.3 (1949), 119–47.

[60] J. Vives, 'Santoral visigodo en calendarios e inscriptiones', *Analecta Sacra Tarraconensia,* 14 (1941), 54.

[61] Vives et Fábrega, 'Calendarios Hispánicos', p. 134: Eulalie figure dans le calendriee de Ripoll sous son homonyme de Barcelone, mais la date est celle de la fête de la martyre de Mérida: 'IIII Ids deb. Barch.Eulalie virg'; pp. 145–46, calendriers dit *Vigilano,* et *Emilianense*: '10 dec Scae eolaliae'.

[62] J. Janini, 'Dos calendarios Emilianenses del siglo XI', *Hispania Sacra,* 15. 29 (1972), 187; p. 194: '1° IIII KL DCBRs Passio sce eulalie urg. Mr'.

[63] V. Saxer, 'Manuscrits liturgiques. Calendriers et litanies des saints du XIIe au XVIe siècles conservés à la bibliothèque capitulaire de Tarazona', *Hispania Sacra,* 25.49 (1972), 138, 153.

comme d'ailleurs dans les martyrologes[64] se doivent d'être brèves. Ce sera dans la liturgie même qu'il faudra rechercher des formules anti-judaïques ou leurs traces.

LES MANUELS LITURGIQUES

Eulalie représente le cas le plus clair d'un saint fêté depuis l'antiquité par un office personnel et sollennel, la comparaison des formulaires, la critique textuelle est formelle à cet égard. Son office contient des textes qui échappent à toute comparaison, comme si son contour se perdait dans la nuit des temps; contrairement aux textes relatifs à la liturgie de Léocadie, martyre dont le culte prit un grand essor au septième siècle et dont les offices furent composés en plein essor liturgique du septième siècle, ceux consacrés à Eulalie manquent d'harmonie, preuve de leur indiscutable antiquité.[65]

L'*Oracional* de Vérone, attribué à l'église de Tarragone, contient les oraisons matinales qui sont récitées après les Psaumes et débutent par les antiphones ou versets extraits de l'Ecriture récités avant ou après les Psaumes.On ne saurait exagérer son importance: l' *Oracional* est un des manuscrits les plus anciens de l'Espagne visgothique puisqu'il date de 700–734. C'est Julien de Tolède (d.690) qui l'aurait rédigé en y intégrant des oraisons de sa plume et des éléments liturgiques d'une grande antiquité, les plus récentes datant au plus tard du début du septième siècle.[66] L'*Oracional* se distingue par la richesse extraordinaire de ses formules,de son contenu biblique, théologique, hagiographique et liturgique ainsi que par celui de sa forme littéraire. Aucune collection liturgique ne contient une quantité aussi impressionante (1121!)[67] et variée d'oraisons complètes différentes; nombre d'entre elles ne figurent dans aucun des manuscrits visigothiques ni dans aucune des éditions.[68]

La place d'honneur d'Eulalie y est mise en évidence, réflétant forcément la prépondérance de son culte. En effet, pour l' Advent, la seconde partie de ces oraisons est intitulée *'de sanctis'*; le schéma dominical y est minutieusement observé, tout en augmentant le nombre des oraisons *'Ad matitunum'* suivant la fête et son importance:

---

[64] Par exemple le texte conservé dans le MS Aem. 39 (Madrid, Academia de la Historia), datant de la conquête de Valence par Jacques I d'Aragon en 1238, qui serait un exemple très ancien d'un martyrologe espagnol. Voir J. Vives, 'El supuesto Pasionario de San Millán de la Cogolla', *Hispania Sacra,* 12 (1959), 449: decembre, 48: 'Eolalia virgo passa est in Emerita sub Calpurniano preside et imperatore era Cca Xla Va'.

[65] P. Rovalo, 'Temporal y Santoral en el adviento; su relacíon a través del oficio visigodo', *Hispania Sacra*, 19 (1966), 299.

[66] M. C. Díaz y Díaz, 'La fecha de implantacíon del Oracional festivo visigótico', *Boletín arqueológico,* 113–20 (1971–72), 242, qui cite Félix, le biographe de Julien de Tolède.

[67] Cela sans compter les antiphones et autres textes similaires plus courts (respons, alleluias) qui sont écrits dans les marges: Vives, *Oracional visigotico,* p. xv.

[68] Ibid., p. xiii.

le dimanche, l'office contient trois oraisons *'alia'.*[69] Or, après l'office dédié à Marie qui compte vingt-neuf oraisons *'alia',*[70] celui d'Eulalie a droit au nombre le plus élevé des *'alia',* soit vingt-six oraisons.[71] Dans un manuscrit plus tardif, le manuscrit de Silos (London, British Museum Add.30.852) datant du début du neuvième siècle mais réflétant une tradition visigothique certaine,[72] le nombre des oraisons en l'honneur d'Eulalie ne le cède qu'à celles dédiées à Léocadie de Tolède,[73] sainte vénérée dans la capitale à partir du septième siècle. Lorsque le siège de Tolède obtint la suprématie après le décès d'Isidore de Séville (636), réunissant ainsi la capitale religieuse à la capitale royale, Léocadie devint en quelque sorte une sainte 'nationale': quatre conciles de Tolède furent tenus dans la basilique qui lui était dédiée.[74] De même, dans l'Antiphonaire visigothique de la cathédrale de Tolède, manuscrit qui date du milieu du dixième siècle, l'office en l'honneur d'Eulalie est plus long que celui de Léocadie.[75] Parmi les oraisons consacrées à Eulalie par *l'Oracional,* trois oraisons contiennent semble-t-il des références obliques aux juifs, adversaires et ennemis de l'église.[76] La troisième de ces prières ajoute qu'avec l'assistance divine, les implorants pourront s'évader des 'pièges tendus par les impies', et celui qui vénère Eulalie ne craignera pas les persécuteurs; les hérétiques combattus par la martyre seront vaincus.[77] On se demandera si les ennemis, les impies, les persécuteurs et les hérétiques désignent d'une manière générale et topologique les adversaires et ennemis de l'église visigothique. Julien de Tolède, on s'en souvient, réunit dans l' *Oracional* des oraisons 'antiques' et des oraisons dont il était l'auteur.[78] Dans quelle de ces deux catégories faudrait-il classer nos oraisons? Il semblerait que les *persequentes* seraient un souvenir très précis des

---

[69] L'oraison *'alia'* est la seconde des sept oraisons du canon mozarabe de la messe; l'officiant y implore Dieu de purifier les fidèles de leurs fautes et d'accepter leur offrande et leur prière.

[70] *Oracional visigotico,* nos 153–83, pp. 51–60.

[71] Ibid., nos 472–93, pp. 158–66. Notons que le martyr hispanique le plus vénéré en Espagne et dans la chrétienté, Vincent de Saragosse (d. 304) n'a droit qu'à vingt-deux oraisons.

[72] Les formules de cet *Oracional,* dit de Londres, auraient été rédigées par Braulion, évêque de Saragosse (631–651), élève et ami d'Isidore de Séville: Díaz y Díaz, 'La Fecha', p. 240, n. 71.

[73] Ibid., p. 229, *Oracional* de Londres: Léocadie, oraisons 10–29, Eulalie, 30–32, 33–45. Notons également que dans le Sacramentaire de Vich, dont le manuscrit date de 1038, l'*ordo* d'onction des prêtres et des évêques mentionne six saintes: Marie, Félicité, Perpetua, Agnès, et Cécile. Eulalie est l'unique sainte hispanique: *El Sacramentario de Vich,* ed. Dom A. Olivar, Monumenta Hispaniae Sacra, Serie Litúrgica, 4 (Madrid et Barcelona, 1963), pp. 223–25.

[74] Rodriguez, *El Culto,* pp. 246–53.

[75] *Antifonario visigotico de la Catedral de Léon,* ed. L. Brou et J. Vives, Monumenta Hispaniae Sacra, Serie Litúrgica, 5, 1 (Madrid, 1959): Officium in diem sanctae Eulalie, no. 50–53, pp. 55–62; Officium in diem sanctae Leocadiae, pp. 50–55.

[76] *Oracional visigotico,* no. 169, p. 56.

[77] Ibid., no. 176, pp. 58–59.

[78] Supra, n. 66.

persécutions romaines ou des confrontations avec les pouvoirs ariens; les ennemis et les impies désigneraient les païens ou les juifs, tandis que de toute évidence les hérétiques seraient les ariens.[79] Dès lors, *l'Oracional* reproduirait ici une oraison antique qui rassemble dans un seul texte l'opposition anti-catholique telle qu'elle se présentait avant la conversion de 587. Cette hypothèse de travail soulève deux objections: sous la domination arienne, l'église catholique aurait-elle osé s'attaquer dans des termes si directs et aggressifs aux Ariens soutenus par la royauté? Il est permis d'en douter. D'autre part, l'hérésie arienne n'avait pas disparu avec la conversion, et Díaz y Díaz a déjà observé que la Passion d'Eulalie récèle des détails et des formules anti-ariennes.[80] L'arianisme continuait visiblement à inquiéter l'église catholique pourtant triomphante: l'archevêque Eugène de Tolède (d. 657) écrivit un petit traité, aujourd'hui perdu, sur la Trinité.[81] Au XVe concile de Tolède (688), Julien de Tolède contribua une 'affirmation manifeste de l'existence des trois substances dans le Christ', citant à l'appui une collection impressionante d'ouvrages patristiques.[82] En 694, soit plus de cent ans après la conversion au catholicisme, le XVIIe concile de Tolède ordonna de consacrer les trois premiers jours des conciles à des débats sur la Trinité, sur d'autres questions d'ordre spirituel ainsi qu'à la réforme des moeurs du clergé. D'ailleurs la répétition du nombre trois, symbole de la Trinité dans le texte du canon I de ce concile est particulièrement flagrante.[83] D'autres textes liturgiques traduisent la prépondérance du problème trinitaire:[84] l'insistance sur les formules trinitaires figure non seulement dans les collectes de psaumes, mais elle est placée en évidence dans la messe en l'honneur d'Eulalie qui figure dans le *Liber mozarabicum sacramentorum*, le missel visigothique.[85] Or au septième siècle l'arianisme représentait-il encore un réel danger pour

---

[79] Remarquons toutefois que les Ariens n'interviennent pas dans la Passion d'Eulalie puisqu'elle se déroule avant la conquête visigothique; les formules anti-ariennes qui y figurent dateraient de l'époque de la rédaction.

[80] M. C. Díaz y Díaz, 'Correctiones y conjéturas al Pasionario Hispánico', *Revista de archivos, bibliotecas y museos,* 63 (1957), 456, n. 10: par example *Passio Eulaliae*, *Pasionario,* 12, p. 73: 'Iesu Christe [. . .] qui unus trinum nomen es qui vitam aeternam tribuis'.

[81] Ildephonse de Tolède, *De viris illustribus,* dans *El 'De viris illustribus' de Ildefonso de Toledo, estudio y edicion critica,* ed. C. Codoñer Merino (Salamanca 1972), p. 133.

[82] XVe concile de Tolède, (688), *Concilios,* pp. 456–64.

[83] XVIIe concile de Tolède (694), c. 1, *Concilios,* p. 528.

[84] *Liber Orationum Psalmographus. Colectos de Salmos del Antiguo Rito Hispánico,* ed. Dom J. Pinell, Monumenta Hispaniae Sacra, Serie Litúrgica, 9 (Barcelona et Madrid, 1972), pp. 162–63: 'sed per ineffabilem potentiam *Trinitat*'; ac per potentiam *Trinitat*';

[85] *Le Liber mozarabicum sacramentorum et les manuscrits mozarabes,* ed. M. Férotin, Monumenta Ecclesiae Liturgica, 6 (Paris 1912), pp. xxviii–xxix: l'édition est basée sur le MS 35.3 (IXe siècle) de la Bibliothèque capitulaire Tolède; de plus, Férotin a utilisé sept manuscrits qui remontent à une date antérieure au onzième siècle. Ibid., p. 45: 'Missa in Diem Sancte Eulalie; c. 97, p. 48: 'unum uerum Deum in Trinitate professa'; c. 99, p. 49: 'Deum in Trinitate predicat

la foi catholique? La réponse ne saurait être définitive car la documentation présente un tableau complexe. Dans le discours qu'il adressa au VIIIe concile de Tolède (653), le roi Recceswinth déclara que les hérétiques ont été radicalement extirpés; les juifs seuls polluent encore son royaume, et les juifs apostats se rendent coupables d'une profanation plus détestable encore.[86] En 694, vers la fin du royaume visigothique, l'hostilité au judaïsme atteignit son apogée lorsque que le roi Egica et le XVIIe concile de Tolède condamnèrent tous les juifs à la servitude, les accusant de causer la ruine de l'église, de la patrie et du peuple entier.[87] King estime lui-aussi que l'hérésie, telle qu'elle se dessine à partir de la législation visigothique de la fin du septième siècle, n'était pas importante, tandis qu' à travers l'optique des souverains et de l'église, le judaïsme demeurait l'adversaire principal.[88] Si l'arianisme n'avait pas été totalement éliminé, il était incontestablement en voie de déclin car tous ses cadres avaient disparu. Dans ce cas, pourrait-on appréhender l'insistance si fréquente sur la Trinité formulée par les décisions conciliaires et dans la liturgie dans le cadre de l'opposition au judaïsme, qui, sans conteste, niait depuis toujours la divinité de Jésus et considérait la Trinité comme une des formes de l'idôlatrie? Ce serait une hypothèse à suivre: le XIIe concile de Tolède, réuni en 681 confirma, à la supplication du roi Erwig, sa sévère législation anti-juive, et y inclua une loi contre les 'blasphémateurs de la sainte Trinité'.[89] La formule n'est pas explicite, mais il s'agit de deux lois promulguées par Erwig. La première était une profession de foi qui contenait une abjuration du judaïsme, la récitation du symbole de Nicée-Constantinople I (381), la promesse de ne jamais retourner *'ad vomitum superstitionis judaice'*, de fuir la société des juifs et de demeurer dans celle des chrétiens pieux, d'accepter des mets chrétiens et d'aller régulièrement à l'église les dimanches et les jours fériés.[90] La seconde loi reproduisait le texte de ce serment de fidélité à la religion chrétienne qui était prêté par devant l'évêque et dont le formulaire prescrivait de jurer au nom de la sainte Trinité de répudier toutes les

---

adorandum'. Pour la signification des diverses parties de la messe dans la liturgie visigothique, supra, n. 69 et infra, p. 40, n. 112; p. 42, n. 118.

[86] VIIIe concile de Tolède (653), *Concilios,* p. 266.

[87] XVIIe concile de Tolède (694), c. 8, *De iudaeorum damnatione, Concilios,* pp. 534–36.

[88] P. D. King, *Law and Society in the Visigothic Kingdom* (Cambridge, 1972), p. 130, citant Recceswinth (*Leges. Visigothorum,* XII, 2,1 et XII, 2, 2, ed. K. Zeumer, MGH, Leges Nationum Germanicarum (Hannover, 1902), pp. 410–11) traitent de l'hérésie, sans spécifier autrement; les quinze lois restantes concernent uniquement les juifs et les juifs convertis: ('De omnium hereticorum adque Iudeorum cunctis erroribus amputatis').

[89] XIIe concile de Tolède (681), IX, *Concilios,* pp. 395–96: 'Item de blasphematoribus sanctae Trinitatis. Suivent toutes les lois anti-juives d'Erwig, pp. 396–97.

[90] *Leges. Visigothorum,* XII.3.14, *Professio Iudeorum, quomodo unusquisque eorum ad fidem veniens indiculum professionis sue conscribere debeat,* p. 442: 'me abinceps veraciter in sancta Trinitate profiteor credere'; ég. Juster, *La condition légale,* p. 288, n. 4; Rabello, *The Jews,* p. 164.

coutumes et observances juives et de plus, de professer la foi absolue en la Trinité.[91] On constate que les autorités visigothiques réalisaient que la profession du symbole trinitaire était difficilement acceptable pour les juifs baptisés; il s'avérait impératif non seulement de les forcer à s'y engager par serment, mais encore d'y revenir sans relâche dans les tomes des conciles, de la répéter incessament dans la liturgie. Cela, non seulement pour supprimer les reliquats ariens, dont on ne peut que supposer l'existence, mais pour inculquer le symbole trinitaire aux juifs récemment baptisés et toujours réfractaires. Il faudrait par conséquent considérer les formules et expressions trinitaires des oraisons consacrées à Eulalie dans l'*Oracional* ainsi que celles qui figurent dans sa messe dans le *Liber mozarabicum sacramentorum* dans un contexte pastoral à double objectif: poursuivre l'éradication de l'arianisme et éduquer les juifs convertis dans les principes de la Trinité.

Si la liturgie en l'honneur d'Eulalie révèle des éléments pastoraux qui devaient servir à l'instruction et l'édification des juifs baptisés ainsi que des allusions à l'hostilité des juifs à l'égard des chrétiens, on n'y relève pas d'expressions particulièrement hostiles comme celles qui caractérisent des ouvrages de polémique et surtout la législation royale et conciliaire de l'époque visigothique. Il en sera autrement pour la Passion de Vincent, Sabine et Christète.

La Passion de Vincent, Sabine et Cristète

Durant les persécutions du début du quatrième siècle, Vincent est arrêté dans une église et professe sa foi; le menaçant de torture, on lui ordonne de sacrifier à la statue de Jupiter, mais en chemin, il accomplit un miracle: un rocher se ramollit sous ses pieds et porte ses empreintes. Ses gardes le ramène chez lui et ses soeurs, Sabine et Cristète, le supplient de prendre la fuite. Tous trois sont arrêtés, subissent le martyre à Avila mais ne sont pas enterrés. Un juif, poussé par la curiosité, s'approche des dépouilles des martyrs: surgit un serpent qui l'encercle de la tête aux pieds. Terrorisé, le juif adresse ses prières à Jésus et promet d'ensevelir les trois martyrs et de leur édifier une basilique. Dûment délivré, il retourne à Avila, se fait baptiser, transfère les dépouilles des martyrs dans un sarcophage et fait bâtir une belle basilique où les implorants sincères obtiendront la guérison.[92] L'épisode du juif et du miracle qui provoque sa conversion est bien plus significatif que celui de la Passion d'Eulalie où le miracle du feu et des anges vient aider la sainte et en même temps parvient à convertir le juif. Par contre, dans

---

[91] *Leges. Visigothorum,* XII.3.15, *Conditiones sacramentorum ad quos iurare debeant hii qui ex Iudeis ad fidem venientes professiones suas dederint,* pp. 445–46: 'in sanctam Trinitatem crediturus sum', etc. Déjà dans le *placitum que* les juifs baptisés avaient signé après le VIIIe concile de Tolède (653), le serment par lequel ils s'engagèrent à renoncer aux pratiques juives fut prêté au nom de la Trinité: 'iuramus per eundem Patrem et Filium et Spiritum sanctum, qui est unus in trinitate Deus.

[92] *Pasionario Hispánico,* t. II, XL[VIII], 11–12, p. 363.

la Passion de Vincent et de ses soeurs, l'intervention du serpent s'adresse au juif seul,qui, remarquons-le, n'a pas rencontré les martyrs, et le force brutalement à se convertir. Le thème de la coercition physique qu'exerce le serpent, instrument divin, pourrait servir à préciser situer la datation.

LA DATATION

L'auteur de la Passion des trois martyrs s'est probablement basé sur la Passion de S. Léocadie, avec laquelle il partage une introduction commune; elle daterait donc au plus tôt du septième siècle.[93] Il est clair que la Passion des martyrs d'Avila était connue en Espagne à la fin du septième siècle. Elle fut utilisée par les auteurs du Bierzo, Valerius de Bierzo (*c.* 630–635) dans son *De genere monachorum*[94] ainsi que par l'auteur anonyme de la *Vita Fructuosi*.[95] A cette époque, sous les règnes d'Erwig et d'Egica, les autorités royales et ecclésiastiques intensifièrent progressivement la persécution des juifs, interdisant de pratiquer le judaïsme, forçant les juifs à accepter le baptême, confisquant tous leurs biens et finalement les réduisant en esclavage.[96] Mesures brutales, dont une partie du moins étaient sans précédent (la confiscation totale des biens et l'esclavage), l'adoption unanime de la force pour mener les juifs à la conversion, politique que la tradition patristique réprouvait,[97] révèlèrent ou intensifièrent un climat anti-juif aisément conforme à l'action coercitive du serpent dans la Passion de Vincent et de ses soeurs.

La brutalité du serpent serait un indice supplémentaire de l'origine visigothique assez tardive (milieu à la fin du VIIe siècle) de cette Passion. Or si ce contexte permet de corroborer la datation proposée par Díaz y Diáz, les chapitres 11 et 12 qui relatent l'épisode du serpent et du juif représentent peut-être une addition postérieure. Deux arguments viendraient appuyer cette hypothèse: le chapitre 10 qui se termine par une invocation au Christ serait une conclusion convaincante de l'ouvrage.[98] En outre, les manuscrits liturgiques les plus anciens, l'*Oracional* et le *Liber Commicus,*[99] ignorent la

---

[93] Au sujet du problème de la relation entre la Passion de Léocadie et celle de Vincent et de ses soeurs, voir Rodriguez, *El culto de los santos,* pp. 250–53.

[94] Sur cette oeuvre dont on ne connaît que des fragments, voir M. C. Díaz y Díaz, 'Sobre el tratado "De genere monachorum" de Valerio del Bierzo', *Anecdota Wisigothica,* 1, Acta Salamanticensia, Filosofia y Letras, XII, 2 (Salamanca, 1958), pp. 49–61.

[95] M. C. Díaz y Díaz, 'Notes for a Chronology of the Pasionario Hispánico', dans *Vie chrétienne et culture,* p. 42.

[96] Juster, *La condition légale,* pp. 288–96; XVIIe concile de Tolède, c. 8, *Concilios,* p. 535.

[97] On se souviendra que même Isidore de Séville préférait la persuasion à la coercition: IVe concile de Tolède, c. 57, *Concilios,* pp. 210–11.

[98] Rodriguez, *El culto de los santos,* p. 262.

[99] Le *Liber Commicus* était le lectionnaire-type, évangéliaire ou épistolaire qui contenait les textes de l'Ancien et du Nouveau Testament dont on faisait la lecture pendant la messe; il devait

fête des martyrs d'Avila. Quant au *Liber Commicus*, on notera que ce fut seulement après la conquête musulmane que de nombreuses églises en furent pourvues. Qui plus est, ce lectionnaire-type ne contenait pas les fêtes locales que chaque église pouvait commémorer selon ses propres traditions hagiographiques. On en conclura que l'exclusion de certains saints s'explique par les nombreuses lectures qui figurent dans les prières dédiées au commun des saints.[100] En admettant que la rédaction de la Passion de Vincent et de ses soeurs daterait du septième siècle et que leur culte était surtout local, on envisage que ni l'*Oracional* ni le *Liber Commicus* ne jugèrent nécessaire de leur accorder des oraisons ou des lectures particulières. En outre, si l'on admet que les chapitres 11 et 12 qui concluent la Passion furent ajoutées à la version originale, par son contenu et son message ostensiblement missionaire, cette addition ne saurait être postérieure à la fin du royaume visigothique: la conversion forcée des juifs au christianisme était absolument irréalisable sous la domination musulmane.

LE CULTE

Le culte ou même la mention des trois martyrs d'Avila en dehors de l'aire hispanique parait avoir été très réduit. Vraisemblablement, l'apparition tardive de leur Passion (à l'opposé de celle d'Eulalie) en serait la cause manifeste. Au début du neuvième siècle leur fête est mentionnée dans le martyrologe de Florus,[101] suggérant ainsi que les trois martyrs étaient peut-être commémorés dans l'espace lyonnais où la présence et l'influence culturelle visigothiques étaient notoires sous Charlemagne et Louis le Pieux.[102]

En Espagne, nos martyrs figurent dans les témoins datant du neuvième—dixième siècle: s' ils n'apparaissent pas dans le *Libellus Orationum* (London, British Museum MS 30.852) on les découvre dans le martyrologe de l'Escorial, qui est un mélange du martyrologe dit *Hieronymianum* (Xe siècle) avec un calendrier espagnol du début du neuvième siècle.[103] Parmi les sources datant du dixième, ils apparaissent respectivement dans le calendriers d'Albelda (dit *Vigilano*) et le calendrier de San Millán (*Emiliense*).[104]

---

servir pour l'Espagne entière; le titre est une allitération de *'Commatus'* comme l'affirme Julien de Tolède. Le manuscrit de Tolède, le plus ancien, date de 900 environ: *Liber Commicus,* ed. J. Perez de Urbel et A. Gonzalez y Ruíz-Zorrila, Monumenta Hispaniae Sacra, Serie Litúrgica, 2 (Madrid 1950), I, xl, xiv–xv.

[100] Ibid., p. lxxxvii. Les prières pour le commun des saints (ibid., II, 466–78) ne présentent pas d'intérêt pour notre propos.

[101] Dubois et Renaud, *Edition pratique des martyrologes*, p. 195.

[102] Supra, n. 51.

[103] J. Vives, 'Santoral visigodo en calendarios e inscriptiones', *Analecta Sacra Tarraconensia,* 14 (1941), 55.

[104] Ces deux calendriers contiennent une notice abrégée, ce qui pourrait indiquer leur ignorance du texte de la Passion: Cristète n'y figure pas: Vives et Fábrega, 'Calendarios His-

Les calendriers espagnols de rite romain, du onzième au quinzième siècles, contiennent une notice de la fête de Vincent et de ses soeurs, signe de leur intégration, comme tant de saints du rite mozarabe, dans le rite romain tel qu'il fut adopté en Espagne.[105] Toutefois, ce sera la liturgie qui indique que le culte des martyrs d'Avila atteindra un niveau national par son intégration dans le rite hispanique, sans pour autant rejoindre le succès de celui qui était voué à Eulalie de Mérida.

LA LITURGIE

On sait déjà que l'*Oracional* ne contient pas de service en l'honneur de Vincent et de ses soeurs; cette absence signifierait éventuellement qu'à l'époque de sa rédaction, à la fin du septième siècle, leur culte demeurait encore local. Par contre, d'autres livres liturgiques, l'Antiphonaire visigothique-mozarabe de la cathédrale de Léon ainsi que le *Liber mozarabicum sacramentorum* consacrent tous deux des offices aux martyrs d'Avila. Plus significativement pour notre propos, on retrouve l'épisode du serpent dans les deux ouvrages.

L'Antiphonaire est conservé par un manuscrit datant du dixième siècle des archives de la cathédrale de Léon. Il renferme tous les chants de la messe et de l'office cathédral, et serait l'oeuvre de plusieurs auteurs visigothiques éminents, Léandre de Séville, Jean de Saragosse, Isidore de Séville, Conantius de Palencia et finalement les trois archevêques de Tolède, Eugène, Ildephonse et Julien.[106] Trois oraisons de l'office de Vincent et de ses soeurs attribuent un rôle au serpent, mais cela dans un contexte qui ne fait aucune allusion aux juifs. Ces prières réassurent les implorants et leur promettent que les morsures du serpent ne pourront nuire aux saints; se fiant au contexte, il s'agirait des trois saints commémorés.[107] Rappelons que dans la Passion le serpent surgit auprès des dépouilles des martyrs sans les avoir rencontrés avant leur mort: il est clair qu'il il ne pouvait leur nuire, ni physiquement ni spirituellement. Alternativement, les saints seraient-ils ici les représentants de la communauté chrétienne, qui, contrairement au judaïsme, ne subit pas l'empreinte du Mal? Il se dégage la nette impression que l'auteur

---

panicos', p. 145: 'Sci uice(n)ti et sabine'.

[105] J. Janini, 'Dos calendarios Emilianenses del siglo XI', *Hispania Sacra,* 15. 29 (1972), 189: calendrier du XIe siècle, postérieur au changement du rite (1090) à l'abbaye de San Millán de la Cogolla; p. 192: 'VKL OCTOBR: [. . .] Uicenti sabine et Xρte mrum'; V. Saxer, 'Manuscrits liturgiques', p. 140: calendrier de Tarazona, début du XIVe siècle: 'Vincencii, Sabine et Xρistete'; p. 148: calendrier de Saragosse, milieu du XVe siècle: Vincent manque: 'Vigilia, Sabine et Xρistete'.

[106] 'Liturgia', *Diccionario de Historia Eclesiastica de España,* II, 1309.

[107] *Antifonario visigótico mozarabe de la Catedral de Léon,* ed. Dom L. Brou et J. Vives, Monumenta Hispaniae Sacra, Serie Litúrgica 5, 2 (Barcelona et Madrid, 1959), pp. 402–03: 'Ant(ifonarium): Santos tuos domine non nocerunt serpentium morsus'; 'Sancti tui domine morsibus serpentium non sunt exterminati'.

de ces prières se débattait avec le renversement du rôle biblique et traditionnel du serpent, *topos* de la tentation du Mal,[108] mais qui apparait ici comme l'envoyé de Dieu. Il est probable que l'auteur ignorait la Passion de S. Christine dont le culte en Espagne serait postérieur à l'époque visigothique.[109] D'après cette Passion, des serpents furent dispersés sur la tête et les épaules de Christine mais ces dangereux reptiles furent miraculeusement changés en petits enfants.[110] Ce texte, beaucoup plus complexe sur le plan théologique que notre Passion hispanique, explicite l'impact bienfaisant de la révélation chrétienne qui transforme les forces du Mal.[111] Dès lors, la 'métamorphose sprirituelle' du serpent, si elle ne laisse de surprendre, ne serait pas totalement étrangère à la tradition chrétienne.

Ce sera toutefois le *Liber mozarabicum sacramentorum* qui citera le texte de la Passion des trois martyrs et fera les louanges du serpent et de son intervention coercitive. La messe en l'honneur de Vincent et de ses soeurs débute par des prières qui mettent en relief l'importance et la victoire de la Trinité, symbolisée par la victoire des trois martyrs.[112] Notons que la répétition de la formule trinitaire conjuguée à la date de rédaction de la Passion pourrait indiquer l'intention pastorale de catéchiser des convertis. Ce sera toutefois dans la *Inlatio* que le thème du juif et du serpent sera le sujet d'un exposé doctrinal important. La *Inlatio*, une des formules du canon mozarabe, est une préface, la plus longue et sollennelle du sacramentaire: le prêtre élevait jusquà Dieu les supplications de la communauté. Finalement, le choeur terminait cette prière par le chant du *Sanctus* dont l'officiant répétait les derniers mots, *Hosanna in excelsis*. Cette préface contient également un élément doxologique.[113] Notre *Inlatio* comporte plusieurs sections. La première cite clairement le texte de la Passion,[114] et rapporte brièvement les circonstances de la conversion du juif. Suit une section doxologique, qui se propose de ranimer la mémoire chrétienne.[115] L'examen de cette doctrine révèle deux thèmes répétés avec diverses variantes. Le premier, directement inspiré par la Passion, vient

---

[108] On notera avec intérêt que le canon 57 du IVe concile de Tolède (633) qui interdit la conversion forcée des juifs, formule le contraste entre le serpent, agent de la mort que l'humanité a choisi de suivre et la conversion volontaire des juifs, appelés par la Grâce: *Concilios,* pp. 210–11.

[109] Rodriguez, *El culto de los santos,* p. 181: en Espagne le culte date du Xe siècle.

[110] Jacobus de Voragine, *The Golden Legend. Readings on the Saints,* trans. W. Granger Ryan (Princeton 1993), II, 387.

[111] T. J. Heffernan, *Sacred Biography* (New York et Oxford 1988), pp. 284–85.

[112] *Liber mozarabicum sacramentorum,* CXXII, 1096, pp. 502–03: 'Missa. Omnis fidelium turba et christiana religiositas universa, uterque sexus, uterque affectus, perfecta fide sinceraque deuotione in trino martyre uicisse Trinitate exsultet'. Alia 'non enim puniuit crudelitas quos cupit, quos in se Trinitas uictores effecit'.

[113] Díaz y Díaz, 'Literary Aspects of Visigothic Liturgy', p. 62.

[114] *Liber mozarabicum sacramentorum,* pp. 504–05.

[115] Ibid., p. 505.

souligner l'inversion du rôle biblique traditionnel du serpent maléfique ici métamorphosé en agent divin. Le serpent, qui chassa le premier homme du paradis, qui le persuada de manger la pomme, qui par une promesse le conduisit à la ruine, qui expulsa le juste du paradis, réussit à restituer le juif impie à la Mère l'Eglise et à lui extorquer la promesse de bâtir une église en l'honneur des martyrs.[116] Le contraste entre la fonction pernicieuse du serpent de la Genèse et la mission évangélatrice qu'il accomplit dans la narration de la Passion des trois martyrs d'Avila est formulé par l'emploi répété de *'illic'*, désignant le paradis, par opposition à *'hic'* pour décrire l'intervention du serpent de la Passion. Indiscutablement, ce style répétitif, si heureusement adapté au genre homélitique, exprime les intentions pastorales de l'auteur. Or le deuxième thème, moins placé en évidence, permet de déceler ce message. En effet, le texte revient plusieurs fois sur la coercition physique exercée par le serpent: la violence de la douleur, la terreur, la force, la peine de mort, les tourments,[117] tels sont les grands moyens qui ont contribué à convertir le juif d'Avila. Faudrait-il appréhender ces expressions comme une justification du recours à la violence ou alternativement, comme un appel à la force pour convertir les juifs tels qu'ils figurent dans la législation visigothique de la seconde moitié du septième siècle? Toujours est-il que dans la conjoncture de l'Espagne du septième siècle, les textes du *Passionaire hispanique* qui font intervenir et convertir des juifs ainsi que les textes liturgiques qui commémorent ces martyrs contribuèrent à exacerber l'ambiance anti-juive qui y régnait[118] et viennent compléter le triste tableau des relations judéo-chrétiennes déjà observé dans la législation royale et conciliaire.

---

[116] Ibid., p. 505: 'serpens quippe olim de paradyso protho-plastum expulit hominem: nunc ipse Iudeum hic reuocavit ad fidem; et que illum suasione uetitum inlexit edere pomum, hec istum *ui doloris fecit credere crucifixum.* Hec in illo totum quod fuit intellectuale subuertit, *que in isto totum adstringens quod erat corporis, os tantum ad confessionem seruauit.* Illic [per] promissionem hominum compulit ad ruinam, *hic terrore reuocauit ad gratiam.* Illic uanitate decepit, *quem hic uiolentia reparauit.* Illic pena mortis, hic efficitur causa salutis. Illic iustum de paradyso eicit, hic impium Ecclesie Matri restituit-Illic prostrauit electum, hic reparauit infirmum. Illic fictione sui liberum in homine uulnauit arbitrium: *hic tormentis acto fidelem extorsit promissum,* quo tibi, Deus, sacrum edificaret in honore Martyrum templum'.

[117] Voir n. 116, les expressions accentuées.

[118] On remarquera que le *Liber mozarabicum sacramentorum* contient d'autres textes antijuifs: Missa in Diem Sancti Stephani, 1233, p. 566; 1235, p. 567 et Missa de Adsumtione Santa Marie, Inlatio, p. 595.

Educating the Clergy: Canon Law and Liturgy in a Carolingian Handbook from the Time of Charles the Bald

YITZHAK HEN

From the seventh century onwards the Frankish Church grew immensely, both in terms of wealth and expansion.[1] Accordingly, there was a rapid increase in the number of rural churches, and it seems that by the turn of the ninth century most large rural settlements had a church and a priest.[2] This huge network of rural parishes, spread throughout the Frankish kingdoms and supervised by bishops and archbishops, was administered by tens of thousands of priests, deacons, and lesser clergy, who were

---

[1] See N. Gauthier, *L'évangélisation des pays de la Moselle. La province romaine de première Belgique entre Antiquité et Moyen-Age (IIIe–VIIIe siècles)* (Paris, 1980), esp. pp. 431–45; J. Semmler, 'Mission und Pfarrorganisation in den rheinischen, mosel- und maasländische Bistümern 5.–10. Jahrhundert', *Cristianizzazione ed organizzazione ecclesiastica delle campagne nell'alto medioevo: espansione e resistenze*, Settimane, 28 (Spoleto, 1982), pp. 313–88; idem, 'Zehntgebot und Pfarrtermination in karolingischer Zeit', in *Aus Kirche und Reich. Festschrift F. Kemp*, ed. by H. Mordek (Sigmaringen, 1983), pp. 33–44; M. Aubrun, *La paroisse en France des origines au XVe siècle* (Paris, 1986), esp. pp. 33–42; J. L. Nelson, 'Making Ends Meet: Wealth and Poverty in the Carolingian Church', *Studies in Church History,* 24 (1987), 25–36.

[2] Joseph Lynch estimates that there were approximately 250 dioceses in the Carolingian kingdom at around 800. This implies a growth of 150% in two centuries, if one accepts Edward James's estimation regarding Merovingian Gaul at around 600. See J. Lynch, *The Medieval Church. A Brief History* (London and New York, 1992), p. 72; E. James, *The Franks* (Oxford, 1988), pp. 149–50.

perceived by the Carolingian reformers as the key to the success of their reforms.[3] Hence there was unprecedented concern in Carolingian legislation with the education of priests and the quality of the pastoral care they provide. Bishops were straightforwardly requested to inquire whether their priests knew the essential Christian beliefs and whether they could perform their liturgical duties in a proper way. For example, the *Admonitio generalis*, Charlemagne's most comprehensive reformatory statement, announces:

> [. . .] that bishops are diligently to examine the priests throughout their dioceses as to their doctrinal beliefs, baptisms and celebration of the mass, to see that they hold the right beliefs and observe catholic baptism and properly understand the prayers of the mass, and that the psalms are sung in proper accordance with the division of the verses and they both understand the Lord's prayer themselves and preach it so that it may be understood by all, to the end that everybody may know what he asks from God, and that the 'Glory of the Fathers' is sung by everyone with full honour and the *sacerdos* himself sings, in common voice with the holy angels and the people of God, the 'Holy, Holy, Holy'. [. . .][4]

Subsequent royal legislation and conciliar decrees followed suit, and preserved the aims and preoccupation of Charlemagne's enactments for the reform of the Frankish clergy.[5]

Responding to the demands of the Carolingian legislators, several bishops throughout the Frankish kingdom issued their own statutes in an attempt to direct and supervise the education and the performance of their clergy.[6] These episcopal statutes,

---

[3] On the Carolingian ecclesiastical reforms, see R. McKitterick, *The Frankish Church and the Carolingian Reforms, 789–895* (London, 1977); eadem, 'Unity and Diversity in the Carolingian Church', *Studies in Church History,* 32 (1995), 59–82; J. M. Wallace-Hadrill, *The Frankish Church* (Oxford, 1983), pp. 258–303; G. Brown, 'Introduction', in *Carolingian Culture: Emulation and Innovation*, ed. by R. McKitterick (Cambridge, 1994), pp. 1–51, at pp. 11–28; R. Reynolds, 'The Organisation, Law and Liturgy of the Western Church, 700–900', in *The New Cambridge Medieval History, II: c. 700–c. 900*, ed. by R. McKitterick (Cambridge, 1995), pp. 587–621.

[4] *Admonitio generalis,* ed. by A. Boretius, MGH, Capitularia Regum Francorum, 1 (Hannover, 1883), no. 22, c. 70, p. 59. I cite the English translation of P. D. King, *Charlemagne. Translated Sources* (Kendal, 1987), p. 216.

[5] See, for example, *Concilium Aquisgranense (836)*, c. 23, ed. by A. Werminghoff, MGH, Concilia, 2:2 (Hannover, 1908), p. 710; *Concilium Meldense-Parisiense (845/6)*, c. 35, ed. by W. Hartmann, MGH, Concilia, 3 (Hannover, 1984), p. 101.

[6] On the *capitula episcoporum,* see McKitterick, *The Frankish Church*, pp. 45–79; P. Brommer, '*Capitula episcoporum*: Bemerkungen zu den bischöflichen Kapitularien', *Zeitschrift für Kirchengeschichte,* 91 (1980), 207–36; idem, *'Capitula episcoporum': die bischöflichen Kapitularien des 9. und 10. Jahrhunderts*, Typologie des sources du Moyen Age occidental, 43

or *capitula episcoporum*, were addressed by their authors to the priests of their dioceses, and they were designed to guide them in various canonical, liturgical, and administrative matters. These *capitula* also urged the priests to become acquainted with various doctrinal issues they might need to explain to their congregations.

The abundant Carolingian legislation as well as the *capitula episcoporum*, which bring us closer to the rural orbit, presupposed that the Frankish priests, from whom so much is expected, possessed decent copies of canonical texts and the ability to read and understand them. Consequently, the Carolingian period witnessed the production of a variety of handbooks which were designed to guide the priests in various doctrinal and liturgical matters. These handbooks were part of the overall attempt to form a suitable clergy at the diocesan level, and an illustrious example of such a handbook is Hrabanus Maurus's *De institutione clericorum*.[7] Hrabanus's treatise was composed in Fulda at the request of his students and fellow brothers, who were preparing for the priesthood. In the first part of *De institutione clericorum* Hrabanus introduces the reader to the Church, the ecclesiastical grades, the sacraments, and the mass. The second part is dedicated to the celebration of the divine office and the liturgical year, and the third part is a short *curriculum* of the liberal arts, which, according to Hrabanus, any priest should know.[8] Although Hrabanus's treatise was practical in purpose, it was still overloaded with information and too cumbersome for the use of a simple priest, whose education was rather basic. Simpler, shorter, and straightforward handbooks were needed for the education of the clergy,[9] and an example of such a handbook is a liturgico-canonical manuscript from the outstanding library of Saint-Benoît-sur-Loire (Fleury). This manuscript, which forms the second part of MS 240 in Dom Chazal's catalogue of the library,[10] is now divided between Orléans, BM 116 (94), fols 63–105 and Florence,

---

(Turnhout, 1985); J. Imbert, *Histoire du droit et des institutions de l'église en occident* (Paris, 1994), V.1, pp. 102–10.

[7] See Hrabanus Maurus, *De institutione clericorum libri tres*, ed. by A. Knoepfler, Veröffentlichungen aus dem kirchenhistorischen Seminar München, 5 (Munich, 1900). The composition of this treatise is dated to 819; see D. J. Sheerin, 'The Church Dedication "Ordo" Used at Fulda, 1 Nov. 819', *Revue bénédictine,* 92 (1982), 304–16.

[8] On this and similar treatises, see J. J. Contreni, 'The Pursuit of Knowledge in Carolingian Europe', in *The Gentle Voices of Teachers. Aspects of Learning in the Carolingian Age*, ed. by R. E. Sullivan (Columbus, 1995), pp. 106–41.

[9] On the production of such handbooks, see Y. Hen, 'The Knowledge of Canon Law among Rural Priests: The Evidence of Two Carolingian Manuscripts from around 800', *Journal of Theological Studies,* 50 (1999), 117–34; idem, 'A Liturgical Handbook for the Use of a Rural Priest (Brussels, BR 10127–10144)', in *Organizing the Written Word: Scripts, Manuscripts and Texts*, ed. by M. Mostert (Turnhout, in press). See also R. Meens, 'Priests and Books in the Carolingian Period' (forthcoming).

[10] This catalogue, compiled in 1720 by Dom Chazal, was stolen by Guglielmo Libri from the municipal library of Orléans and is now lost; see n. 24 below. See also M. Mostert, *The*

Biblioteca Medicea-Laurenziana, Ashburnham 82 (32), fols 1–72,[11] and it is on this handbook that I wish to concentrate in this paper.

Let us first consider the format of this particular manuscript. Fleury, MS 240, fols 63–176 was a modest volume, consisting of 114 folios (42 folios in Orléans and 72 folios in Florence) that measure 190 x138 mm., with a written area of 156–66 x 97–107 mm.[12] The folios of the Orléans section, still bound with the first section of MS 240,[13] are numbered from 63 to 105,[14] whereas the Florence portion is numbered from 1 to 72. Traces of an older pagination, which continues consecutively the pagination of the Orléans section, can still be seen on the top right corner of some folios in the Florence manuscript.[15]

The original volume, as we can reconstruct it today, was divided into fourteen quires, all but one are regular gatherings of eight folios (four bifolia).[16] All the quires were signed with a Roman numeral at the lower margin of the last verso,[17] so that the Orléans section contains five quires (I–V) and the Florence section contains nine quires (VI–XIV). Although there is no uniformity in the arrangement of the parchment, it seems that the bifolia of most quires were arranged with the hair side uppermost, so that flesh faces flesh and hair faces hair within the quire.

Library of Fleury. A Provisional List of Manuscripts (Hilversum, 1989), p. 32 and no. 371, p. 105. Two incomplete copies of Chazal's catalogue survive; see ibid., no. 404, p. 110 and no. 911, p. 187. On Libri and his deeds, see the fascinating book by P. A. Maccioni-Ruju and M. Mostert, *The Life and Times of Guglielmo Libri (1802–1869)* (Hilversum, 1995).

[11] Cited hereafter as **O** and **F** respectively.

[12] L. Delisle, 'Notice sur plusiers manuscrits de la Bibliothèque d'Orléans', *Notices et extraits des manuscrits,* 31.1 (1883), pp. 367–69; idem, 'Notice sur plusiers manuscrits du fonds Libri conservés à la Laurentienne à Florence', *Notices et extraits des manuscrits,* 32.1 (1886), 39–40; C. Paoli, *I codici Ashburnhamiani della R. Biblioteca Mediceo-Laurenziana di Firenze* (Rome, 1887), I, pt. 1, pp. 42–44; C. Cuissard, *Catalogue général des manuscrits des bibliothèques publiques de France. Orléans* (Paris, 1889), pp. 45–48; W. von Hörmann, 'Bußbücherstudien', *Zeitschrift der Savigny-Stiftung für Rechtsgeschichte—kanonistische Abteilung,* 3 (1913), 413–97, at pp. 422–40; F. M. Carey, *De Scriptoria Floriacensi* (unpublished doctoral thesis, Harvard University, Cambridge, MA, 1923), pp. 39 and 81; Mostert, *The Library of Fleury*, no. 262 and 529, pp. 87 and 129 respectively.

[13] The first part of the Fleury manuscript (now Orléans, BM 116 (94), fols 1–62) is part of a different manuscript.

[14] The numbers 90 and 91 were assigned by mistake to the same folio.

[15] See **F**, fols 18r, 21r, 34r, 40r, 47r, 55r, 63r, 65r, and 67r.

[16] The only exception is quire I, which is a gathering of 10 folios (5 bifolia). A single folio (**F**, fol. 29) was added to quire IX as a fly-leaf at a later stage.

[17] The quire mark of quire XI is extremely faint, and the quire mark of quire XIII is practically invisible.

The folios were ruled four bifolia at a time before folding, guided by pricking at the outer margins. While in some quires the direct impression is found on the outside bifolium, in others it can be observed in the inside one. A single bounding line on each side of the folio was also ruled with a hard point, guided by pricking on the upper and lower margins of each folio. Some economy may be observed in the production of the manuscript, for rather inferior quality vellum was used, sometimes with very defective leaves.[18]

The text, for which at least three hands were responsible, is usually written in eighteen long lines to a page.[19] The script is a crude Caroline minuscule of the west Frankish type,[20] with some rather peculiar elements, such as the use of both uncial and straight-backed *d*, as well as uncial and minuscule *a*. Tall *s* is favoured, although round *s* occurs as well. There are very few ligatures, apart from the 'standard' ones, and not many abbreviations. The orthography displays confusion of *e* and *i*, *o* and *u*, *ch* and *c*, *ae* and *e*, *b* and *p*, *dd* and *d*, *v* and *b*, as well as *x* and *s*. The manuscript is thoroughly punctuated. Usually a medial point denotes both a main pause and a short one, with the occasional use of a question mark in the appropriate places. Each section of the text is headed with a title in either uncial (sometimes mixed with minuscule) or rustic capitals. There are no decorations throughout the entire manuscript.

On account of the palaeographical and codicological evidence, our manuscript can be dated to the third quarter of the ninth century,[21] and it seems that it was produced in the west Frankish kingdom, probably in the region of Fleury, to where its provenance leads.[22] Unfortunately, we know nothing of our handbook's history before it entered

---

[18] See, for example, **O**, fols 66 and 94; **F**, fols 27, 38, 51, 56, and 62.

[19] The exceptions are quire I, which is written in twenty lines (apart from the outer bifolium, fols 1 and 10, which are written in eighteen lines); quire VII, which is written in seventeen lines; and quires XII and XIII which are written in twenty-two lines.

[20] On the development of the Caroline minuscule, see B. Bischoff, *Latin Palaeography: Antiquity and the Middle Ages*, trans. by D. Ó Cróinín and D. Ganz (Cambridge, 1990), pp. 112–18; idem, 'Die karolingische Minuskel', in *Karl der Große: Werk und Werkung* (Aachen, 1965), 207–10; D. Ganz, 'The Preconditions for Caroline Minuscule', *Viator*, 18 (1987), 23–44.

[21] See H. Mordek, *Kirchenrecht und Reform im Frankenreich. Die Collectio Vetus Gallica, die älteste systematische Kanonessammlung des fränkischen Gallien*, Beiträge zur Geschichte und Quellenkunde des Mittelalters, 1 (Berlin and New York, 1975), p. 200, n. 525. An earlier date was suggested by von Hörmann, 'Bußbücherstudien', p. 457, yet, most scholars accept Mordek's dating. See, for example, R. Kottje, 'Bußpraxis und Bußritus', in *Segni e riti nella chiesa alto-medioevale occidentale*, Settimane, 33 (Spoleto, 1987), pp. 369–403, at p. 378, n. 41; *Capitula episcoporum*, ed. by P. Brommer, MGH, Capitula episcoporum, 1 (Hannover, 1984), p. 7.

[22] See, for example, Mordek, *Kirchenrecht und Reform*, p. 200, n. 525; Kottje, 'Bußpraxis und Bußritus', p. 378, n. 41; Brommer, *Capitula episcoporum*, p. 7; R. Haggenmüller, *Die Überlieferung der Beda und Egbert zugeschriebenen Bußbücher* (Frankfurt, Bern, and New York, 1991), p. 61.

Dom Chazal's catalogue in 1720, whence it was given the shelfmark MS 240.[23] Yet, this manuscript did not remain on the shelves of Fleury for long. In 1790, at the time of the French Revolution, Dom Chazal's MS 240 was transferred with many other Fleury manuscripts, first to Gien and then to Orléans. There it was examined in 1842 by the bibliomaniac Guglielmo Libri, who paradoxically held at the time the official title of 'Inspecteur des bibliothèques publiques'.[24] Taking advantage of the library's chaotic state and inaccurate cataloguing, Libri divided MS 240 into two separate booklets, leaving in Orléans the first part of the manuscript, containing the first five quires of our handbook, and taking with him the rest. In order to conceal the Fleury provenance of the nine quires he stole, Libri renumbered the folios and forged a new *ex libris* at the bottom of the last folio of the last quire, which reads *Sancte Justine de Padua*.[25] Libri, however, did not keep this particular manuscript for long, and five years after stealing it from Orléans he sold it with many other manuscripts from his collection to the fourth Earl of Ashburnham.[26] In 1878, after the death of the fourth Earl of Ashburnham and after some negotiations with the French, the fifth Earl of Ashburnham sold his father's Libri collection of manuscripts to the Italian government. The manuscripts were then deposited in the Florentine Biblioteca Medicea-Laurenziana, and among them were the nine quires Libri stole from Orléans.

The two separate sections of the Fleury handbook with which we are concerned have received much attention from scholars throughout the last century. André Wilmart used it as an early witness to the widespread anonymous *expositio missae* commonly known as *Dominus vobiscum*.[27] Roger Reynolds was interested in its version of the Ordinal of Christ,[28] while Susan Keefe examined the baptismal *formulae* that it contains.[29] Peter Brommer was drawn to it because of the first *capitula episcoporum* of

---

[23] At that stage it was, most probably, already bound with what is now Orléans, BM 116 (94), fols 1–62.

[24] J. Loiseleur, 'Les larcins de M. Libri à la bibliothèque de Orléans', *Bulletin de la Société archéologique et historique de l'Orlénais*, 8 (1883–86), 117–26.

[25] On Libri's habit to change, forge, and alter the *ex libris* of manuscripts he stole, see Maccioni-Ruju and Mostert, *The Life and Times of Guglielmo Libri,* pp. 209–13.

[26] On this sale, see Maccioni-Ruju and Mostert, *The Life and Times of Guglielmo Libri*, pp. 223–26. See also A. N. L. Munby, 'The Earl and the Thief: Lord Ashburnham and Count Libri', *Harvard Library Bulletin*, 17 (1969), 5–21; idem, 'The Triumph of Delisle. A Sequence to "The Earl and the Thief"', *Harvard Library Bulletin,* 17 (1969), 279–90.

[27] A. Wilmart, 'Expositio missae', in *Dictionaire d'archéologie chrétienne et de liturgie*, V, 1, ed. by F. Cabrol and H. Leclercq (Paris, 1922), cols 1014–27.

[28] R. Reynolds, *The Ordinals of Christ from their Origins to the Twelfth Century*, Beiträge zur Geschichte und Quellenkunde des Mittelalters, 7 (Berlin and New York, 1978), pp. 82–83.

[29] S. A. Keefe, 'Carolingian Baptismal Expositions: A Handlist of Tracts and Manuscripts', in *Carolingian Essays. Andrew W. Mellon Lectures in Early Christian Studies*, ed. by U.-R. Blumenthal (Washington, DC, 1983), pp. 169–237, at pp. 188, 199–200, 214.

Bishop Gerbald of Liège which it transmits,[30] and many scholars referred to the abundant penitential material found in it.[31] Yet, for all the interest in and importance of the various individual texts that this handbook contains, it should be examined as a functioning whole. The Fleury handbook is emphatically not a random gathering of unrelated texts bound together. Only by approaching it as a coherent collection of carefully chosen texts could one get a clearer and more accurate picture of its aims and function. It is, then, necessary to dwell a little longer on the content of the entire Fleury handbook in question.

The copying of our manuscript, as already mentioned, was executed by three different scribes, who worked, so it seems, simultaneously. The first scribe copied the first seven quires of the volume (**O**, fols 63–105 and **F**, fols 1–16), leaving the bottom half of the last verso of quire VII blank.[32] The second scribe copied the following six quires (VIII–XIII), finishing at **F**, fol. 63r,[33] and leaving the bottom of **F**, fol. 63r and fols 63v–64v blank. Later on, the second scribe (or someone with a very similar script) filled **F**, fols 63v–64v with the introduction to the text that appears in the last quire (XIV), and which was copied by a third scribe.

The division of labour between the first scribe and the other two reflects the content of the manuscript as well. Thus, the first half of our handbook, copied by the first scribe, is a *florilegium* of various texts, whose main purpose is to introduce the clergy to its duties and to inform them on basic issues concerning the Christian faith and dogma. It opens with a series of anonymous texts in a question-and-answer format on the Trinity,[34]

---

[30] Brommer, *Capitula episcoporum*, p. 7.

[31] See, for example, von Hörmann, 'Bußbücherstudien', pp. 422–40; Mordek, *Kirchenrecht und Reform*, p. 200, n. 525; F. L. Asbach, *Das Poenitentiale Remense und der sogen. Excarpsus Cummeani* (Regensburg, 1979), p. 21; Kottje, 'Bußpraxis und Bußritus', p. 378; Haggenmüller, *Die Überlieferung der Beda und Egbert*, pp. 61–62; L. Körntgen, *Studien zu den Quellen der frühmittelalterlichen Bußbücher*, Quellen und Forschungen zum Recht im Mittelalter, 7 (Sigmaringen, 1993), pp. 96,113; R. Meens, *Het tripartite boeteboek. Overlevering en betekenis van vroegmiddeleeuwse biechtvoorschriften* (Hilversum, 1994), pp. 237–38; *Paenitentialia minora Franciae et Italiae saeculi VIII–IX*, ed. by R. Kottje, L. Körntgen, and U. Spengler-Reffgen, CCSL, 156 (Turnhout, 1994), pp. xxxix–xl.

[32] At a later stage, probably at the beginning of the eleventh century, someone scribbled on the empty lines of **O**, fol. 16v and on the lower margin of **O**, fol. 17r a text on divination and prodigies.

[33] At a later stage, probably at the beginning of the eleventh century, someone scribbled on the empty lines of **O**, fol. 63r a short text on signs and divination.

[34] **O**, fol. 63r: 'De Trinitate. INTEROGATIO: Inter persona patris et filii et spiritus sancti quid interest? R.: Inter persona patris et filii et spiritus sancti, ita secernitur quod pater nec natus nec factus [. . .] spiritus vero sanctus ex patre filioque procedit'.

Christ's baptism,[35] the reasons for his incarnation,[36] and the meaning of *fides*, *spes,* and *caritas*.[37]

A series of questions and answers on the liturgical duties of the clergy and on the mass follows next,[38] part of which is taken from the so-called *Collectio Sangermanensis*.[39] A short tract in the question-and-answer format was then copied, under the heading *In nomine trino atque uno excursus de nominibus incognitis*.[40] This treatise, loosely modelled on selective passages from Isidore of Seville's *Etymologiae,*[41] surveys the various kinds of sacred books and their significance, and it is followed by another question-and-answer treatise on the genealogy of Christ.[42]

Two short expositions on baptism follow next. The first treatise, which maintains the question-and-answer format, is a brief instruction on the *ordo* of baptism,[43] modelled on the two letters written by Alcuin at around 798, one to a certain priest Oduinus and the other to some monks in Septimania.[44] The second of the baptismal tracts transmitted

---

[35] **O**, fols 63r–v: 'ITEM: Pro quid Christus filius dei in Iordane a Iohanne baptizatus est? Prima causa fuit ut qui homonatus erat [. . .] dum ipse dominus a Iohanne in Iordanem baptizatus est'.

[36] **O**, fol. 63v: 'INT.: Pro quales causas venit homo ad regnum dei? R.: Per fidem et spem et caritatem'.

[37] **O**, fols 63v–72r: 'INT.: Quid est fides? R.: Fides est divinitas confessio [. . .] quod latine bona gratia interpretatur'.

[38] **O**, fols 72r–74v: 'INT.: Quid sit munera? R.: Munera autem vocantur qui a manibus vel accipiuntur vel dantur [. . .] super terra propter ea fuit diluvium'.

[39] **O**, fols 72r–v. See A. J. Nürnberger, 'Über eine ungedruckte Kanonensammlung aus dem 8. Jahrhundert', in *25. Bericht der wissenschaftlichen Gesellschaft Philomathie in Neisse vom Oktober 1888 bis zum Oktober 1890* (Neisse, 1890), pp. 125–97, at p. 174; R. E. Reynolds, 'Unity and Diversity in Carolingian Canon Law Collection: The Case of the *Collectio Hibernensis* and its Derivatives', in *Carolingian Essays*, ed. by Blumenthal, pp. 99–135, at p. 122. On the *Collectio Sangermanensis*, whose longest form (Paris, BNF lat. 12444) was copied, most probably, at Fleury in the late eighth or early ninth century, see Reynolds, 'Unity and Diversity', pp. 106–07, 119–24.

[40] **O**, fols 74v–76r: 'In nomine trino atquae uno excarsum de nominibus incognitis. Liber cuius nomen est? R.: Quid interpretatur [. . .] hic liber evangelium nominatur'.

[41] See Isidore of Seville, *Etymologiarum sive originum libri XX*, ed. by W. M. Lindsay (Oxford, 1911), VI.

[42] **O**, fols 76r–77v: 'INT.: Liber generationis Iesus Christi filii David [. . .] ego sum alfa et o[mega] inicium et finis dicit dominus'.

[43] **O**, fols 77v–80r: 'INT.: Quur paganus caticuminus fit vel quid sit caticuminus? R.: Caticuminus Graecae [. . .] qui fuit in baptismo per gratiam vitae aeternae donatus'. On this treatise, see S. A. Keefe, 'Carolingian Baptismal Expositions', p. 214 (Text 54).

[44] See Keefe, 'Carolingian Baptismal Expositions', pp. 184–86 (Text 9). Alcuin's text, as pointed out by Keefe, 'was by far the most popular model for the Carolingian composers of

by our handbook is entitled *De baptismo*[45] and is, in fact, a short excerpt from Isidore of Seville's *Etymologiae*.[46]

After baptism, the cardinal points of the Nicaean creed are being dealt with in a series of simple questions and answers,[47] following which is a brief question-and-answer exposition on the meaning of the terms *canon*, *synodus*, and *ecclesia*,[48] selectively copied from Isidore of Seville's *Etymologiae*.[49] A brief survey of the first six ecumenical councils comes next.[50] This section, modelled again on Isidore of Seville's *Etymologiae*,[51] is also taken from the so-called *Collectio Sangermanensis*.[52]

The first *capitula episcoporum* of Bishop Gerbald of Liège (d. 809) was copied after the above mentioned *florilegium* of excerpts from Isidore and other canonical sources.[53] This document, composed around 805, is one of three statutes addressed by Gerbald to the priests of his diocese, in an attempt to instruct them on matters of clerical conduct, liturgical performance, the administration of baptism, penance, and various

---

baptismal instructions' (p. 185, n. 1). For a printed edition of these two letters, see Alcuin, *Epistolae* 134 and 137, ed. by E. Dümmler, MGH, Epp., 4 (Berlin, 1895), pp. 202–03 and 210–16 respectively. On Alcuin's views on baptism, see D. A. Bullough, 'Alcuin and the Kingdom of Heaven', in idem, *Carolingian Renewal: Sources and Heritage* (Manchester, 1991), pp. 161–240, esp. pp. 188–93.

[45] **O**, fols 80v–81r: 'Baptismum Graecae, Latine tinctio interpretatur [. . .] ita per unctionem sanctificatio Spiritus adhibetur'. On this treatise, see Keefe, 'Carolingian Baptismal Expositions', p. 188 (Text 13). The title appears at the bottom of **O**, fol. 80r.

[46] See Isidore of Seville, *Etymologiae*, VI:19:43–51.

[47] **O**, fols 81r–83v: 'Deum in quem credis? R.: Ego credo in deum patrem omnipotentem creatorem caeli et terra. D. Quare dicitur omnipotens [. . .] firmiter teneamus et operibus impleamus'. It is worth noting that throughout this section the questions are indicated with 'D' (*Discipulus*?), a feature common to many Carolingian didactic tracts; see Reynolds, 'Unity and Diversity', p. 122.

[48] **O**, fols 83v–84v: 'INT.: Quid sit canon vel quid continetur in canone? R.: Canon autem Greacae, Latine regula [. . .] in unitatem colligitur'.

[49] See Isidore of Seville, *Etymologiae*, VI:16:1–2, VI:16:12–13, and VIII:1:1–2 respectively.

[50] **O**, fols 84v–85r: 'Prima enim universalis synodus in Nicaea [. . .] et operationem adstruebant in Christo falsas se patrum catholicorum dicta'.

[51] See Isidore of Seville, *Etymologiae*, VI:16.

[52] See Nürnberger, 'Über eine ungedruckte Kanonensammlung', p. 161; Reynolds, 'Unity and Diversity', p. 122.

[53] **O**, fols 85r–88r: 'Haec sunt capitula ex divinarum scripturarum scripta quae electi sacerdotes custodienda atque adimplenda censuerunt. I. Ut unusquisque sacerdos [. . .] cum orationibus diligenter unguatur'. For a printed edition of Gerbald's first *capitula episcoporum*, see Gerbald of Liège, *Capitula I*, ed. by P. Brommer, MGH, Capitula episcoporum, 1, pp. 16–21.

rites for the sick and the dying.[54] Although Gerbald's *capitula episcoporum* were composed in response to the reform impetus originated in the court of Charlemagne, they became quite popular during the ninth and the tenth centuries, and were copied into many liturgico-canonical volumes.[55]

Following Gerbald's *capitula episcoporum* is the *expositio missae* known by its incipit *Dominus vobiscum*.[56] This anonymous treatise is an expository tract which explains in a straightforward manner the *canon* of the mass.[57] It was often attributed by scholars to Amalarius of Metz,[58] although the three manuscripts that bear any indication regarding its author, attribute it to Alcuin, Jerome, or Isidore of Seville.[59] Whatever attribution one may choose, there is little place to doubt that the mass exposition *Dominus vobiscum* was composed in the Carolingian period, most probably at the turn of the ninth century, and its origins should be sought in circles close to the Carolingian court. Shortly after its composition, this particular treatise became extremely widespread throughout the Frankish kingdom, and it was often incorporated into liturgico-canonical

---

[54] On Gerbald and his *capitula*, see W. A. Eckhardt, *Die Kapitulariensammlung Bischof Ghaerbalds von Lüttich* (Göttingen, 1955), pp. 54–59; McKitterick, *The Frankish Church and the Carolingian Reforms*, pp. 50–52; Brommer, '*Capitula episcoporum*: Bemerkungen zu den bischöflichen Kapitularien', esp. pp. 213–14; T. M. Buck, *Admonitio und praedicatio. Zur religiös-pastoralen Dimension von Kapitularien und kapitulariennahen Texten (507–814)*, Freiburger Beiträge zur Mittelalterlichen Geschichte, 9 (Frankfurt and Bern, 1997), pp. 343–44.

[55] On the reception and transmission of Gerbald's first statute, see Brommer's edition, pp. 5–6, and see there pp. 6–16 for a survey of the various manuscripts.

[56] **O**, fols 88r–105v and **F**, fols 1r–5v: *Expositio in missam. Dominus vobiscum. Salutat sacerdos populum* [. . .] *et omnes respondeant deo gratias.*

[57] On the *expositiones missae*, see Wilmart, 'Expositio missae', pp. 1014–27; H. Wegman, *Christian Worship in East and West. A Study Guide to Liturgical History*, trans. by G. W. Lathrop (Collegeville, 1985), pp. 194–96; M. M. Schaefer, 'Latin Mass Commentaries from the Ninth through Twelfth Centuries: Chronology and Theology', in *Fountain of Life. In Memory of Niels K. Rasmussen*, ed. by G. Austin (Washington, DC, 1991), pp. 35–49; Reynolds, 'Unity and Diversity', pp. 125–26. See also Y. Hen, *The Royal Patronage of Liturgy in Frankish Gaul to the Death of Charles the Bald*, Henry Bradshaw Society, subsidia 3 (London, 2001).

[58] See Amalarius of Metz, *Opera liturgica omnia*, ed. by J. M. Hanssens, Studi et Testi, 138 (1948), I, 284–338.

[59] These manuscripts are Budapest, Orszagos Szechenyi Konyvtar 316, fol. 29v (Alcuin); Rome, Biblioteca Casanatense 2010, fol. 190v (Isidore and Alcuin); and London, British Library 16413, fol. 19r (Jerome). See also R. Reynolds, 'Pseudonymous Liturgica in Early Medieval Canon Law Collections', in *Fälschungen im Mittelalter. Internationaler Kongress der Monumenta Germaniae Historica, 16–19 September 1986*, Schriften der MGH, 33 (Hannover, 1988), II, 67–77, esp. p. 71.

collections, such as Vatican City, Biblioteca Apostolica Vaticana, Pal. lat. 485,[60] or Sélestat, BM 132.[61]

A survey of the liturgical innovations instituted by the various popes follows next, under the title *De ordine missae et orationibus qui in ea continentur.*[62] This survey, undoubtedly based on the *Liber pontificalis,*[63] is shot with excerpts from the first book of Isidore of Seville's *De ecclesiastis officiis.*[64] This historical survey of the liturgy is followed by an extremely brief section which explain various parts of the mass,[65] and two anonymous tracts, one entitled *De duodecim sacrificiis,*[66] and the other *De decim precaepta* [*sic*] *legis.*[67] The various forms of liturgical chanting are the subject of the next piece,[68] after which a unique version of the Ordinal of Christ is added under the title *De septem gradus.*[69] This short composition, which illustrates the ecclesiastical

---

[60] The mass exposition *Dominus vobiscum* appears on fols 27v–36v. On this manuscript, see F. Paxon, '*Bonus liber*: A Late Carolingian Clerical Manual from Lorsch (Bibliotheca Vaticana MS Pal. lat. 485)', in *The Two Laws. Studies in Medieval Legal History Dedicated to Stephan Kuttner*, ed. by L. Mayeli and A. J. Tibbetts, Studies in Medieval and Early Modern Canon Law, 1 (Washington, DC, 1990), pp. 1–30, esp. pp. 13–14 on the *Dominus vobiscum.*

[61] The mass exposition *Dominus vobiscum* appears on fols 1r–16v. On this manuscript, see J.-P. Bouhot, 'Les pénitentiels attribués a Bède le Vénérable et a Egbert d'York', *Revue d'histoire des textes*, 16 (1986), 141–69, at pp. 146–51; H. Mordek, 'Karolingische Bischofskapitel in der Humanistenbibliothek zu Schlettstadt', *Zeitschrift für die Geschichte des Oberrheins,* 134 (1986), 414–21.

[62] **F**, fols 5v–11v: 'De ordine missae et orationibus que in ea continentur. In libro officiorum Isidori capitula XV, ordo autem missae [. . .] prima se omnium ecclesiarum scribebat'.

[63] See *Le liber pontificalis. Texte, introduction, et commentaire*, ed. by L. Duchesne, 2 vols, 2nd edn (Paris, 1886–92); with a third volume by C. Vogel (Paris, 1955–57). For an excellent assessment of the *Liber pontificalis*, see T. F. X. Noble, 'A New Look at the *Liber pontificalis*', *Archivum historiae pontificae,* 23 (1985), 347–59.

[64] **F**, fols 5v–6r (I:15); 6r–v (I:8); 6v–7r (I:17); and see Isidore of Seville, *De ecclesiasticis officiis*, ed. by C. M. Lawson, CCSL, 113 (Turnhout, 1989), pp. 16–17, 8, 19 respectively. Two more chapters of Isidore's *De ecclesiasticis officiis* are also mentioned on fol. 6v (I:13 and I:14) but without any citation.

[65] **F**, fols 11v–12r: 'Incipit expositio de introitum ad missa [. . .] Expositio collecta ad missam [. . .] De epistula [. . .] De responso [. . .] De alleluia [. . .] De evangelio [. . .]'.

[66] **F**, fols 12r–v: 'De duodecim sacrificiis. Duodecim sacrificiis veteris testamenti [. . .] per oleum fomenta carnis intelliguntur'.

[67] **F**, fols 12v–13r: 'De decim precaepta [*sic*] legis. De decim praecaepta [*sic*] legis in prima tabula [. . .] decimum non concupiscis rem proximi tui mundi cupiditatem'.

[68] **F**, fols 13r–16r: 'Pro quibus virtutibus cantatur omnis cursus. Pro qualibus virtutes cantatur omnis cursus in ecclesia dei [. . .] hora nona portae inferni fracte sunt et liberatus est Adam'.

[69] **F**, fols 16r–v: 'De septem gradus. Hic sunt septem gradus in quibus Christus adfuit [. . .]

hierarchy and, as demonstrated by Roger Reynolds, is a derivative of the so-called *Collectio Hibernensis*, completes the first part of our manuscript.[70]

The second part of the Fleury handbook, copied by the second and the third scribes, is dedicated to the practice of penance. This part of the handbook begins with a copy of the *Poenitentiale Martenianum*, one of the most extensive and incoherent penitentials from the ninth century, which is named after its first editor, Dom Edmond Martène.[71] It continues with the preface to the *Poenitentiale Remense*,[72] the prologue from the so-called *Poenitentiale Pseudo-Egberti*,[73] and another prologue from the *Poenitentiale Pseudo-Bedae*.[74] Finally, the penitential part is concluded with the so-called *Poenitentiale Floriacense*.[75]

---

et ferebatur in caelum'. For a printed edition of this text, see Reynolds, *The Ordinals of Christ*, p. 82; idem, 'Unity and Diversity', p. 130.

[70] See Reynolds, *The Ordinals of Christ*, pp. 82–83; idem, 'Unity and Diversity', p. 130.

[71] **F**, fols 17r–54v: 'De penitentibus in libro canonum instituta ecclese [*sic*] antiqua. [1] Ut sacerdos penitentiam [. . .] post partum id est XL diebus'. For a printed edition of the *Poenitentiale Martenianum*, see W. von Hörmann, 'Bußbücherstudien', *Zeitschrift der Savigny-Stiftung für Rechtsgeschichte—kanonistische Abteilung*, 4 (1914), 358–483, at pp. 360–480. On this penitential, see Reynolds, 'Unity and Diversity', pp. 112–14; C. Vogel, *Les libri paenitentiales*, Typologie des sources du Moyen Age occidental, 27 (Turnhout, 1978), p. 78; Meens, *Het tripartite boeteboek*, pp. 54–55.

[72] **F**, fols 54v–60r: 'Incipit de diversis malis. Diversarum culparum [. . .] in corpore quiescere videtur'. For a printed edition of the preface to the *Poenitentiale Remense*, see Asbach, *Das Poenitentiale Remense*, Anhang, pp. 7–14. On the *Poenitentiale Remense*, see Vogel, *Les libri paenitentiales*, p. 76; Kottje, 'Bußpraxis und Bußritus', pp. 378–79; Meens, *Het tripartite boeteboek*, esp. pp. 236–40.

[73] **F**, fols 60r–62v: 'Incipit excarsum de canones catholicorum patrum [. . .] ut alii timorem habeant'. For a printed edition, see H. J. Schmitz, *Die Bußbücher und das kanonische Bußverfahren* (Düsseldorf, 1898), pp. 661–63. On the *Poenitentiale Pseudo-Egberti*, see Vogel, *Les libri paenitentiales*, p. 71; A. J. Frantzen, *The Literature of Penance in Anglo-Saxon England* (New Brunswick, NJ, 1983), pp. 69–77; Haggenmüller, *Die Überlieferung der Beda und Egbert*; idem, 'Zur Rezeption der Beda und Egbert zugeschriebene Bußbücher', in *Aus Archiven und Bibliotheken. Festschrift für Raymund Kottje zum 65. Geburtstag*, ed. by H. Mordek, Freiburger Beiträge zur Mittelalterlichen Geschichte, 3 (Farnkfurt and Bern, 1992), pp. 149–59; Meens, *Het tripartite boeteboek*, pp. 56–57.

[74] **F**, fols 62v–63r: 'De modis paenitentiae. De remediis peccatorum [. . .] debent pendere iudicis'. For a printed edition, see Schmitz, *Die Bußbücher und das kanonische Bußverfahren*, p. 654. On the *Poenitentiale Pseudo-Bedae*, see Vogel, *Les libri paenitentiales*, pp. 70–71; A. Frantzen, 'The Penitentials Attributed to Bede', *Speculum*, 58 (1983), 573–97; idem, *The Literature of Penance*, pp. 69–77; Haggenmüller, *Die Überlieferung der Beda und Egbert*; idem, 'Zur Rezeption der Beda und Egbert', pp. 149–59; Meens, *Het tripartite boeteboek*, esp. pp. 55–56.

[75] **F**, fols 64r–72v: 'In Christi nomine incipiunt ordo ad dandam paenitentiam secundum

The content of our handbook suggests that it is not an arbitrary collection of unrelated texts, but a composite work clearly directed at the education of the clergy. As such it contains a large choice of texts carefully selected and arranged for brevity and clarity. It was well designed to equip the clergy with basic knowledge on most aspects of their pastoral duty, and it includes texts that should be known to every Christian priest. Furthermore, the question-and-answer format, which is well suited for instruction, and the straightforward manner in which these texts address the clergy, leave little place to doubt that didactic and pedagogical aims guided the compiler while selecting and arranging the material. Thus, it seems that our Fleury handbook is indeed a guidebook for the provision of basic information to a clerical audience preparing for the priesthood.

The production of such a handbooks, therefore, should be understood against the wider background of the ecclesiastical reforms pursued by the Carolingian kings and their advisers. The education of the Frankish clergy, as we have already noted, was a subject close to the heart of Charlemagne, and upon which his views were decided and obstinate. Charles the Bald followed his grandfather's example. He patronized scholarship with lavish donations to churches and monasteries, and he continued to support the instruction of the clergy.[76] Handbooks like the one from Fleury illustrate more than anything else the Carolingian reforms in action, for they reflect the remarkable effort made by the Carolingian reformers to create a new generation of educated clergy, who would be able to perform the Christian rites and to instruct the people on various doctrinal matters. These handbooks, it seems, translated the goals of the Carolingian legislation and the *capitula episcoporum* into reality, and they became an indispensable tool and an integral part of the equipment of the reformed Carolingian clergy. Hence, the Fleury handbook, which is certainly not a unique example, is a significant product of the Carolingian educational reform program, and it demonstrates how even as late as the third quarter of the ninth century such reformatory ideals were still preserved and promoted by ecclesiastical circles in the kingdom of Charles the Bald.

---

seniorum patrum traditionem [. . .] disperdit aut filius negavit homi[cidum]'. For a printed edition, see *Paenitentialia minora Franciae et Italiae,* ed. by Kottje et al., pp. 97–103, with comparative tables at pp. 1–60. On the *Poenitentiale Floriacense*, see Vogel, *Les libri paenitentiales*, p. 75; Meens, *Het tripartite boeteboek*, esp. p. 39; Körntgen, *Studien zu den Quellen der frühmittelalterlichen Bußbücher*, 113–18.

[76] On Charles the Bald and his role in promoting the Carolingian reforms, see J. L. Nelson, *Charles the Bald* (London and New York, 1992); Wallace-Hadrill, *The Frankish Church*, esp. pp. 268–78; R. McKitterick, 'Charles the Bald and his Library: The Patronage of Culture', *English Historical Review,* 95 (1980), 28–47; eadem, 'The Palace School of Charles the Bald', in *Charles the Bald: Court and Kingdom*, ed. by M. T. Gibson and J. L. Nelson (Aldershot, 1990), pp. 326–39; P. Riché, *Écoles et enseignement dans le Haut Moyen Age*, 2nd edn (Paris, 1989), pp. 76–79 and 103–10.

The Carolingian preoccupation with the education of the Frankish clergy was undoubtedly the broader context for the production of the Fleury manuscript with which we are concerned. Nonetheless, very little is known about the immediate and local circumstances which led to the compilation of such a handbook. Unfortunately, we do not know exactly when and where this manuscript was copied. The earliest indication for its Fleury provenance is Dom Chazal's catalogue of 1720, at which point it was already bound with another Fleury liturgico-caninical manuscript.[77] Yet, was it also copied at Fleury? To this question no clear and straightforward answer can be given. Judging from the palaeography and codicology of the manuscript, it seems probable that our handbook was indeed produced at the region of Orléans, where Fleury is situated. However, bearing in mind that it was produced at the third quarter of the ninth century, the Fleury attribution is somewhat problematic. During the third quarter of the ninth century the monastery of Fleury was plundered and destroyed by Viking raids,[78] and twice the monks were forced to flee. Shortly after the raid of 854 the monks were able to return to their monastery,[79] but in 865 they had to take a longer refuge in the city of Orléans,[80] which was also raided repeatedly by Viking parties coming up the Loire.[81] It is, therefore, hard to imagine the scriptorium of Fleury operating under such circumstances, and it is probable that our manuscript was produced in a place that suffered less damage and interruption, like, for example, the abbey of Micy.

Although not far removed from Fleury and Orléans, the abbey of Micy hardly suffered any damage at the hands of the Vikings who raided Neustria. Shortly after its refoundation at the instigation of Bishop Theodulf of Orléans, Micy became a centre of intellectual activity.[82] Even during the reign of Charles the Bald, when the region of

---

[77] This manuscript is Orléans, BM 116 (94), fols 1–62. See Mostert, *The Library of Fleury*, no. 528, p. 129, and see there for further bibliography.

[78] On the effects of the Viking raids on the Frankish kingdom, see J. M. Wallace-Hadrill, 'The Vikings in Francia', in *Early Medieval History* (Oxford, 1975), pp. 217–36; S. Coupland, 'The Vikings in Francia and Anglo-Saxon England', in *The New Cambridge Medieval History II*, ed. by McKitterick, pp. 190–201; idem, 'From Poachers to Gamekeepers: Scandinavian Warlords and Carolingian Kings', *Early Medieval Europe,* 7 (1998), 85–114; idem, 'The Frankish Tribute Payments to the Vikings and their Consequences', *Francia,* 26 (1999), 57–75; J. L. Nelson, 'The Frankish Empire', in *The Oxford Illustrated History of the Vikings*, ed. by P. Sawyer (Oxford, 1997), pp. 19–47.

[79] See Adrevald of Fleury, *Miracula sancti Benedicti*, I:34, ed. by E. de Certain, *Les miracles de saint Benoît* (Paris, 1858), pp. 75–76. For the date, see R.-H. Bautier, 'Le monastère et les églises de Fleury-sur-Loire sous les abbatiats d'Abbon, de Gauzlin et d'Arnaud (988–1032)', *Mémoires de la Société Nationale des Antiquaires de France* 4 (1969), pp. 71–156, at p. 79.

[80] See *Annales Bertiniani*, s.a. 865, ed. by F. Grant, J. Viellard, and S. Clémencet (Paris, 1964), p. 117; Adrevald of Fleury, *Miracula sancti Benedicti*, I:34, p. 76.

[81] See *Annales Bertiniani*, s.a. 854, 856, 865, 868, pp. 69, 72, 117, 143 respectively.

[82] On Micy and its history, see T. Head, *Hagiography and the Cult of Saints. The Diocese*

Orléans was harassed by the Vikings, the intellectual activity at Micy did not die out. Hagiography was still composed there, and manuscripts were regularly copied and collected.[83] Furthermore, the monks of Micy took an active role in the reform movement of the ninth century. At the request of Louis the Pious, a number of monks from Micy, led by Abbot Heric, reformed the abbey of Curbion near Blois.[84] Could it be that this reformatory zeal continued well into the third quarter of the ninth century, and together with the uninterrupted intellectual activity at Micy formed the impetus for the production of the Fleury handbook? It is impossible to answer this question with any certainty before some more suggestive evidence is unearthed. But still, it is a tempting speculation.[85]

---

of Orléans, 800–1200 (Cambridge, 1990), pp. 202–34. On Micy as an intellectual centre, see M. Gorman, 'Theodulf of Orléans and the Exegetical Miscellany in Paris lat. 15679', *Revue bénédictine,* 109 (1999), 278–323, esp. pp. 291–95.

[83] See Head, *Hagiography and the Cult of Saints*, esp. pp. 207–11; A. Poncelet, 'La bibliothèque de l'abbaye de Micy au IXe et au Xe siècle', *Analecta Bollandiana,* 23 (1904), 76–84; idem, 'Les saints de Micy', *Analecta Bollandiana,* 24 (1905), 5–97; L. Traube, *Hieronymi Chronicorum codicis Floriacensis fragmenta Leidensia Parisiana Vaticana phototypice edita* (Lyons, 1902), pp. xii–xx.

[84] See *Receuil des actes de Charles II le Chauve, roi de France*, ed. by G. Tessier (Paris, 1943–56), I, no. 27, pp. 67–71.

[85] I should like to thank Rob Meens for his comments on an earlier draft of this paper, and to Tom Head for his advice on Micy.

APPENDIX

Collation and contents of Orléans, BM 116 (94), fols 63–105 and Florence, Biblioteca Medicea-Laurenziana, Ashburnham 82 (32).

MS	QUIRE[86]	FOLIOS	CONTENT
O	I^{10}	63–72	
	II^{8}	73–80	Various canonical texts and expositions
	III^{8}	81–85r	
		85r–88r	The first statute of Bishop Gernald of Liège
		88r–v	
	IV^{8}	89–97	*Expositio missae, Dominus vobiscum*
	V^{8}	98–105	
F	VI^{8}	1–5v	
		5v–8	Various canonical texts and expositions
	VII^{8}	9–16	
	VIII^{8}	17–24	
	IX^{9}	25–32	
	X^{8}	33–40	
	XI^{8}	41–48	Various penitentials
	XII^{8}	49–56	
	XIII^{8}	57–64	
	XIV^{8}	65–72	

[86] The numbers in superscript indicate the number of folios in the quire.

Convergences of Oriental Christian, Muslim, and Frankish Worshippers: The Case of Saydnaya

BENJAMIN Z. KEDAR

The occasional convergence of worshippers belonging to different creeds is an aspect of religious life in the medieval Levant that has been largely neglected in historical research. One may distinguish between three sub-types of this phenomenon. The first is a convergence that is, in essence, merely spatial. In this case, adherents of different religions come to, or make a pilgrimage to, a site all consider holy. They may encounter one another at the holy site, and they may perform the same act, but no common service takes place. Such convergence occurred at al-Matariyya near Old Cairo. Here was a fountain at which the Holy Family was said to have rested during the flight to Egypt. Christians considered the fountain's water thaumaturgic, and its fame spread far and wide. A Coptic priest of the twelfth century, Abu al-Makarim, writes that when the envoys of the Greeks, the Franks, the Ethiopians, and the Nubians came to the caliph's court, they would customarily go to al-Matariyya, immerse in the spring's waters and pray.[1] The spring also attracted Muslim worshippers. Burchard of

---

An earlier version of this paper was presented at the workshop 'Expanding the Frontiers of Medieval Latin Christianity—The Crusades and the Military Orders', held at the Central European University, Budapest, 26–28 February 1999. My thanks to Dr A. Luttrell, Dr B. Major, Mr J. Reston Jr, Prof. L. Valensi, and Prof. J. Folda for their remarks and assistance.

[1] For a comprehensive discussion of the sources, see U. Zanetti, 'Matarieh, la Sainte Famille et les Baumiers', *Analecta Bollandiana*, 111 (1993), 21–68; Abu al-Makarim's remark on the envoys appears on p. 36. On him see idem, 'Abu l-Makarim et Abu Salih', *Bulletin de la société d'archéologie copte*, 34 (1995), 85–138. My thanks to Dr Daniel Baraz for having put at my

Strasbourg, the envoy whom Emperor Frederick I sent to Saladin in 1175, speaks of a fountain at which the Virgin and the Child hid for some time, and in which the Virgin washed the Child's clothes; the context leaves no doubt that he refers to Matariyya. Burchard relates that the fountain 'is venerated by the Saracens down to the present day, and they bring there candles and incense when they wash themselves there. At Epiphany a vast number of people flock there from all confines, and wash themselves in its water'. Burchard, who knows of Islam's positive perception of Mary and Jesus, mentions other places linked to the Virgin's stay in Egypt that attract both Christian and Muslim worshippers: for instance, a tall and ancient palm tree that bent toward the Virgin and the Child to allow her to pick some dates; the Saracens, who had initially tried to cut down the tree, now revere it, illuminating it with candles every night.[2] Here we have examples in which adherents of different creeds converge on the same site, venerate the same object for the same reason, and may even perform the same act—washing themselves in the waters of the holy fountain—but there is no trace of a common service.

The second sub-type is marked by convergence at the same service, with the service officiated by members of one religion, and members of another religion being allowed access—in other words, an inegalitarian convergence at a religious ceremony. This sub-type may be exemplified by the attendance of Muslims at the Miracle of the Easter Fire, which took place—and still takes place—in the Church of the Holy Sepulchre in Jerusalem on Holy Saturday. As is well known, in churches throughout Christendom the New Fire blessed on Holy Saturday is produced by the striking of flint, but in the Church of the Holy Sepulchre the fire was believed to descend from heaven upon the Tomb of Christ in its midst. While some Muslim authors of pre-crusade times branded the miracle a trick, others regarded it as genuine. Abu al-'Abbas Ahmad (d. 947) and al-Biruni (d. 1048) relate that Muslim officials take an active part in the ceremony, kindle the lamps of the mosque with the fire that appears in the Tomb, and report to their superiors the exact time of the fire's descent, which is believed to presage the future. Abu al-'Abbas Ahmad—like a contemporary tenth-century Greek polemicist—recounts that Jerusalem's Muslim governor shuts the Tomb's door before the fire's appearance and, when the fire's white light becomes visible within the Tomb, he unlocks its door, enters the Tomb, and kindles a candle from the fire. Al-Biruni has Christians and Muslims praying for the fire's coming.[3] Thus the descent of the Holy Fire

---

disposal his dossier on Matariyya, as well as some other material.

[2] Burchard's account appears in Arnold of Lübeck, *Chronica slavorum*, ed. by J. M. Lappenberg, MGH, SS, 21 (Hanover, 1869), p. 238; also in P. Lehmann and O. Glauning, 'Mittelalterliche Handschriftenbruchstücke der Universitätsbibliothek und des Georgianum zu München', *Zentralblatt für Bibliothekswesen*, Beiheft, 72 (Munich, 1940), pp. 65–66. For later western accounts see Zanetti, 'Matarieh', pp. 53–59.

[3] M. Canard, 'La Destruction de l'Église de la Résurrection par le calife Hakim et l'histoire de la descente du feu sacré', *Byzantion,* 25 (1965), 35–38.

assumes the features of a ceremony shared by Christians and Muslims; it is a Christian service that takes place in Christendom's holiest site, yet Muslims participate in it, albeit in a subordinate role. There is no evidence for such a Muslim role in the years after the caliph al-Hakim in 1009 ordered that the Church of the Holy Sepulchre be destroyed precisely on account of the Holy Fire, which he regarded as a fraud. When Abbot Richard of Saint-Vannes and Bishop Ulric of Orléans witnessed the fire's descent in the 1020s, the Muslims were menacing or mocking.[4]

Muslim partaking in Christian celebrations is attested in the Syrian town of Hama at a much later date. Al-Dimashqi (d.1327) relates that on Easter the Muslim women of Hama paint eggs and bake cakes even more than the Christian ones; on Christmas night the town's population, 'great and little, rich and poor, the [Muslim] soldiers and the [Muslim] prince, kindle torches on the roofs'; the same happens on the Feast of Christ's Circumcision.[5] Such Muslim participation in, or imitation of, Christian festivals was roundly condemned by fourteenth-century fundamentalists like Ibn Taymiyya (d. 1328).[6]

The third—apparently only rarely occurring—sub-type is that of an egalitarian convergence at a shared religious ceremony. An example appears in the chronicle of Ibn Duqmaq, an Egyptian writer of the second half of the fourteenth century. Ibn Duqmaq relates that in the year 717—that is, in 1317 AD—the wells of Jerusalem went dry and the only remaining source of water was that of the spring of Silwan (the biblical Shiloah, or Siloam). At that grave juncture all of Jerusalem's inhabitants, Muslims, Christians, and Jews, went out to an open space and implored God for rain. Their prayers were answered on the third day.[7] Here we find adherents of the three monotheistic religions praying side by side. But it is significant that this shared, proto-ecumenical prayer, elicited by a common, pressing need, did not take place on premises belonging to a specific religion, but in a neutral, open space, under the sky from which the rain was fervently expected to come down.[8]

---

[4] Hugh of Flavigny, *Chronicon* 2.21, ed. by G. H. Pertz, MGH, SS, 8 (Hannover, 1848), p. 395; Rodulfus Glaber, *Historiarum libri quinque,* ed. and trans. by J. France (Oxford, 1989), pp. 202–03.

[5] For a French translation, see R. Dussaud, *Topographie historique de la Syrie antique et médiévale* (Paris, 1927), p. 244.

[6] See, for instance, B. Shoshan, *Popular Culture in Medieval Cairo* (Cambridge, 1993), p. 68.

[7] Gotha, Landesbibliothek, MS Pertsch 1371, part 1, fol. 53v; ed. and trans. in J. Drory, 'Jerusalem in the Mamluk Period', in *Jerusalem in the Middle Ages. Selected Papers,* ed. by B. Z. Kedar (Jerusalem, 1979), p. 177 [in Hebrew].

[8] G. von Grunebaum mentions, without giving references, another kind of convergence: Christians visiting an ancient place of worship that was only incompletely integrated into Islam. See G. von Grunebaum, *Muhammadan Festivals,* 2nd edn (London, 1976), p. 79.

The Christians who figure alongside Muslims in the above examples are Oriental Christians. Now, were Franks—that is, Western Christians who settled in the Latin Kingdom of Jerusalem—involved in acts of religious convergence? The answer is, yes—but to a decidedly more limited extent.

There is some evidence for spatial convergence with Muslims. The canons of the Frankish cathedral of Sebaste allowed Muslims to visit the tomb of John the Baptist in the cathedral's crypt; according to Saladin's secretary, 'Imad al-Din, the canons amassed great wealth by exacting costly gifts from these Muslims.[9] Ibn Jubayr, the Muslim pilgrim from Spain, saw at Acre, in 1184, Franks and Muslims assembled at 'Ayn al-Baqar, the Spring of the Cattle, 'from which God brought forth the cattle for Adam'; the Muslims prayed facing south, near the *mihrab* of the mosque that had stood there in pre-crusade times, and the Franks prayed facing east, at an apse they had added to the original building.[10] Likewise, Jews and Muslims were allowed to pray near the Tombs of the Patriarchs, located within what was then the Frankish cathedral of Hebron. In all these instances, spatial convergence lacked a shared ritual element, with Franks and Muslims offering their different, distinctive prayers. In other words, in none of these cases did the convergence resemble that of al-Matariyya, where Christian and Muslim worshippers washed in the same waters.

In the above instances, Franks and Muslims converged for the same reason—at Sebaste to pray at the tomb of the Baptist, in Hebron to pray at the Tombs of the Patriarchs. But the Frankish appropriation of Muslim shrines brought about a spatial convergence of a different kind—one that entailed worship at the same site but for different reasons. Thus the Muslim Dome of the Rock, enclosing the spot from which Muhammad began his nocturnal ascent to heaven, became for the Franks the Lord's Temple. Muslims were allowed to perform their prayers just south of the shrine[11]—which, for them, continued to be the Dome of the Rock. In Acre, the principal mosque apparently became the Church of the Holy Cross, the town's cathedral—but a fraction of the original building, which contained the tomb of the prophet Salih, continued to serve as a small mosque in which Muslims could offer their obligatory prayers, with the tomb of the prophet near its *mihrab.*[12]

There is no evidence for the convergence of Franks and Muslims at a shared ceremony, though it is attested for Franks and Oriental Christians. Thus, on 20 April 1101, the second Holy Saturday observed in Frankish Jerusalem, Franks and Greeks prayed together in the Church of the Holy Sepulchre for the descent of the Holy Fire, with Frankish and Greek canons singing the readings alternately in Latin and Greek.

---

[9] 'Imad al-Din in Abu Shama, RHC, Hor., 4 (Paris, 1848), p. 302.

[10] *The Travels of Ibn Jubayr,* trans. by R. J. C. Broadhurst (London, 1952), pp. 318–19.

[11] John of Würzburg, ll. 315–21, in *Peregrinationes tres: Saewulf, Iohannes Wirziburgensis, Theodericus*, ed. by R. B. C. Huygens, CCCM, 139 (Turnhout, 1994), pp. 91–92.

[12] Broadhurst, *Travels of Ibn Jubayr*, p. 318; B. Z. Kedar, 'The Outer Walls of Frankish Acre', *'Atiqot,* 31 (1997), 169, 171.

There is reason to believe that this was the case in later years as well.[13] There is also evidence for processions held in common. In 1099, with the crusaders advancing to the decisive battle near Ascalon, Peter the Hermit called on Greeks and Franks in Jerusalem to hold processions and distribute alms. Again, during the crucial Frankish-Egyptian battle in 1123, Franks, Greeks, and Syrians held processions in Jerusalem.[14]

Against this background, it is worthwhile to dwell on an instance of spatial convergence of Oriental Christians, Muslims, and Franks, where—as at al-Matariyya—all worshippers shared a common cultic practice. This convergence (which has been largely neglected by crusade historians)[15] occurred in a locality that had never come under Frankish rule: the Greek convent of Our Lady of Saydnaya about twenty-five kilometres northeast of Damascus, that is, deep in Muslim territory. The objective of the worshippers was a miracle-working icon of the Virgin, Saydnaya's most treasured possession. The icon was said to date from Byzantine times, or from the ninth century; possibly Saydnaya had already been a holy site in pre-Christian times.[16]

From the late twelfth century on, the story of the icon of Saydnaya appears in Latin and Arabic texts; in the thirteenth century it was told also in Old French, and in the fifteenth in Ethiopian. Historians were perplexed by the fact that the earliest sources on this icon, kept in a Greek convent, were Western—but Daniel Baraz has recently demonstrated that the earliest Oriental account appears in an Arabic manuscript of the Sinai Monastery that dates from 1183 and thus presents an Arabic version roughly contemporaneous with the earliest Latin ones.[17] There are two main variants of the icon story. According to the first, the icon originated in Constantinople and was taken by some patriarch to Jerusalem, where an abbess of Saydnaya obtained it. According to the second variant, a female recluse at Saydnaya asked a monk (or a merchant) to bring her an icon of the Virgin from Jerusalem; the icon began to work miracles while the monk (or merchant) was returning from Jerusalem, and although the monk (or merchant) attempted to keep the icon for himself, he finally deposited it at Saydnaya. In any case, at Saydnaya the icon began to grow flesh from breasts to navel, emitting from the breasts an oil-like liquid that would heal the sick.[18]

---

[13] See especially the accounts by the so-called author of the L-text and by Bartolf of Nangis printed in Fulcher of Chartres, *Historia Hierosolymitana (1095–1127)*, ed. by H. Hagenmeyer (Heidelberg, 1913), pp. 831–36.

[14] Peter Tudebode, *Historia de hierosolymitano itinere*, ed. by J. H. Hill and L. L. Hill (Paris, 1977), pp. 144–45; Fulcher of Chartres, *Historia,* 3.18.2, p. 665.

[15] An amply annotated entry on 'Saidnaiya' appears in D. Pringle, *The Churches of the Crusader Kingdom of Jerusalem: A Corpus* (Cambridge, 1998), II, 219–21; but the author does not emphasize the convergence.

[16] For the last point see G. Raynaud, 'Le miracle de Sardenay', *Romania,* 11 (1882), 527, n. 3.

[17] D. Baraz, 'The Incarnated Icon of Saidnaya Goes West: A Re-examination of the Motif in the Light of New Manuscript Evidence', *Le Muséon,* 108 (1995), 181–91.

[18] For a brief recent survey of the legend's versions, see L. Minervini, 'Leggende dei cristiani

Burchard of Strasbourg's report of 1175 contains the earliest dated account of the icon's story. It reads as follows:

> Four miles from Damascus is a certain place located in the mountains that is called Saydaneia and is inhabited by Christians; there is a church, located in the rock [and] dedicated in honour of the Blessed Virgin, in which twelve virgin nuns and eight monks serve God and the Blessed Virgin. In that church I saw a wooden panel one ell long and half an ell broad, placed in the wall behind the altar, visible without obstruction through a window, and secured by a barred iron ceiling. On this panel there glittered once the painted image of the Blessed Mary, but now—which is wondrous to relate—the picture on the wood is made flesh, and oil more fragrant than the odour of balsam spreads from it unceasingly. By this oil many Christians and other people, who suffer from diverse illnesses, are restored to health and the oil never diminishes no matter how much one takes of it. Nobody dares to touch the said panel, but all are permitted to see it. The oil, guarded by a Christian monk, augments; and if one takes it for whatever sickness with devotion and sincere faith, he will undoubtedly obtain his request for the honour of the Blessed Virgin, at the celebration of Mass. All Saracens of that country flock to that place on the Assumption and the Nativity of the Glorious Virgin, together with the Christians, in order to pray there. The Saracens offer there their ceremonies with utmost devotion.[19]

It is noteworthy that Burchard is the only writer to dwell on the convergence of Christians and Muslims both at al-Matariyya and at Saydnaya; evidently the phenomenon of a Marian shrine attracting Christian and Muslim worshippers struck him as remarkable. As we have seen, he also mentions other Marian sites in Egypt honoured by Muslims.

The earliest evidence for the despatch of Saydnaya's miraculous liquid to the Catholic West dates from 1186. It appears in a thirteenth-century manuscript, now in the Royal Library of Belgium; Paul Devos published it in 1947. According to this account, one Guy Chat went to Jerusalem with Aymeric Brun, known from other sources as the lord of Montbrun who in 1178–79 had founded the monastery of Altavaux (Haute-Vienne, arr. Rochechouart). While the two men were in Jerusalem, a Templar knight, Gautier de Marangiers, returned from Saracen captivity—presumably in Damascus—and on his way back passed through Saydnaya; there he obtained some of the holy liquid, which he brought to Jerusalem. Aymeric Brun acquired some of it and in 1186 despatched it with Guy Chat to the church of Saint Mary of Altavaux,

orientali nelle letterature romanze del medioevo', *Romance Philology,* 49 (1995/96), 6–10. The author was still unaware of Baraz's find.

[19] I use the text edited by Lehmann and Glauning, 'Mittelalterliche Handschriftenbruchstücke', pp. 67–68, which is superior to that published by Lappenberg in MGH, SS, 21, pp. 239–40. I follow however Lappenberg's text with regard to the site's name. Translation is mine.

which he had founded. The account presents at some length the story of the icon of Saydnaya as told by Guy Chat: an ascetic Syrian woman of Sardena—the appellation Saydnaya is given here—asked a merchant to bring her an icon of the Virgin from Jerusalem. On the way, the icon spoke to the merchant twice, once telling him to leave the ship that was carrying him home, once reassuring him that Saracen robbers would not be able to harm him. On arrival in Sardena the merchant attempted to keep the icon for himself, but the icon spoke up and shamed him into surrendering it to the Syrian woman who, fearing the Saracens, hid it in a subterranean abode and worshipped it there. Then the miracle came to pass that the icon grew flesh from the navel upward, and from its breasts there emanated an oil-like liquid that later turned into flesh. On account of this miracle the Syrians of that place erected a church, which the Saracens allowed Christians from all over to visit.[20]

Devos discovered an independent corroboration of the despatch of the oil of Saydnaya in the year 1186. According to an entry in an inventory of relics of the priory of Altavaux, 'Aymeric Brun despatched with Guy Chat from Jerusalem to Altavaux some of the oil that emanates from the breasts of the image of God's Holy Mother, and some of the oil of the tomb of Saint Catherine, virgin and martyr'.[21] The oil of Saydnaya also reached other places. Gautier de Coincy (1177–1236), who devotes a section of his *Miracles Nostre Dame* to the story of Saydnaya, relates that a burgher who had seen the icon gave him at Soissons some of the oil that emanated from it.[22] The German Orientalist Johann Vansleb (Wansleben) writes that in 1670 he saw in Cluny's treasury a phial containing the 'precious balsam' from Saydnaya; he copied an inscription that identified it as having originated from 'the image of the Blessed Virgin Mary, transformed into flesh by God's will'.[23] Vansleb also reports that on 13 January 1672 he went to Saydnaya to see the image that changed miraculously into flesh and blood and gave rise to one of the Virgin's main feasts.[24]

Burchard's account of 1175 highlights the convergence of Christians and Saracens at Saydnaya; the account of the despatch of the miraculous liquid to Altavaux in 1186

[20] P[aul] D[evos], 'Les Premières versions occidentales de la légende de Saïdnaia', *Analecta Bollandiana,* 65 (1947), 272–73; the author doubts the authenticity of Burchard's account: ibid., pp. 259–72.

[21] Devos, 'Les premières versions', p. 276.

[22] Gautier de Coincy, 'Le Miracle Nostre Dame de Sardenay', vv. 610–17, in his *Les miracles de la Sainte Vierge*, ed. by [A.-E.] Poquet (Paris, 1857), col. 663.

[23] J. Vansleb, *L'Histoire de l'église d'Alexandrie* (Paris, 1677), p. 159; see also E. Cerulli, *Il libro etiopico dei Miracoli di Maria* (Rome, 1943), p. 273, n. 3. On Vansleb's career, see M. Martin, 'Vansleb (Wansleben), Johann Michael', in *The Coptic Encyclopaedia,* ed. by A. S. Atiya (New York, 1991), VII, 2299.

[24] Vansleb, *Histoire*, p. 158. For a list of pilgrims and other authors who mention Saydnaya, see J. Nasrallah, 'La Vierge Hodigitria (La Vierge Conductrice ou al-Hadia)', *Proche-Orient chrétien,* 38 (1988), 244–45, 247, 249–50. See also Postscript.

mentions a Templar knight who brought the liquid from Saydnaya to Jerusalem. The Christian-Muslim convergence and the Templar link with Saydnaya appear also in other accounts.

A brief, undated Latin account of the icon of Saydnaya (here called Sardenai) was published in 1882 by Gaston Raynaud; a part of it appears also in the chronicle of Alberic of Trois-Fontaines. According to this account, an emir of Damascus who had lost an eye recovered it at Saydnaya, in gratitude for which he and his successors gave the church of Saydnaya sixty measures of oil every year; this went on until the times of Saladin. The account adds that the Saracens are said to assemble at Saydnaya on the Feast of the Assumption and in September, and pray there to the Virgin according to their religion.[25] Similarly, the Copt Abu al-Makarim, who between 1171 and 1210 collected the materials for his Arabic-written *History of Churches and Monasteries*, reports that the priest in charge at Saydnaya told him that on the Feast of the Virgin, 'Christians, Muslims, Nestorians, Melkites, Syrians, and others, approximately four or five thousand people', gather at the place and take away with them bottles containing the miraculous oil; yet this does not affect the level of the pool in which the oil flowing from the icon is collected.[26] These Latin and Arabic accounts find a counterpart in an Old French continuation of the chronicle of William of Tyre, which claims that 'on the Feast of the Virgin in mid-August and in September, all the Saracens of that country' come to the church of *Nostre Dame Sainte Marie à la Roche,* also known as *Nostre Dame de Sardenay*.[27] One Latin account—apparently an interpolation into the account of the German pilgrim Thietmar, who visited the Holy Land in 1217[28]—imputes an unspiritual motive to the Saracen worshippers: Saydnaya abounds in wine, he says, and the Saracens are eager to come there in order to drink it clandestinely.[29] It is possible that the author of this account, perplexed by the presence of Muslim worshippers at a Christian sanctuary and aware of the vineyards in its vicinity, concocted this story.[30] Still, the same writer also mentions a Saracen matron who wailed and lamented throughout the church of Saydnaya because she had no vessel for the holy oil. On account of her great belief in its efficacy, the Virgin miraculously placed in her hand a

---

[25] Raynaud, 'Miracle', pp. 522–53; Alberic, *Chronica,* ed. by P. Scheffer-Boichorst, MGH, SS, 23 (Berlin, 1874), p. 936.

[26] Passage quoted and translated by Baraz, 'Incarnated Icon', p. 189.

[27] *Itinéraires à Jerusalem et descriptions de la Terre Sainte rédigés en français aux XIe, XIIe et XIIIe siècles*, ed. by H. Michelant and G. Raynaud (Geneva, 1882), p. 173; M. de Vogüé, *Les Églises de la Terre Sainte* (Paris, 1860), p. 451.

[28] The case for an interpolation is cogently presented by Devos, 'Premières versions', pp. 247–59.

[29] *Magistri Thietmari peregrinatio*, ed. by J. C. M. Laurent (Hamburg, 1857), pp. 18–19.

[30] On Saydnaya's vineyards, see P. P[eeters], S.J., in his review of H. Zayat's Arabic-written *History of Saidanaya*, in *Analecta Bollandiana,* 51 (1933), 435. Peeters accepts the story about the Saracens and the wine at face value; see ibid., pp. 435, 437.

flask filled with oil.[31] Thus it transpires that this author, too, must have believed that at least some Saracens were genuinely attracted to the oil issuing from the icon.

The Templar link with Saydnaya assumes various forms. An account of the miraculous icon that claims to amount to a translation of an account existing in the archives of Saydnaya asserts inter alia that the Saracens bring their sick from afar to Saydnaya to be healed with the holy liquid. It concludes by stating that the account's veracity is attested by 'the priors of the Templars, and by other, very many *religiosi,* both Latin and German, both clerics and laymen, who saw this with their eyes and touched [this] with their hands'.[32] The anonymous author of a kindred account extant in a thirteenth-century manuscript asserts that he learned about the icon being covered with flesh from the breasts downward from the testimony of brothers of the Temple who had seen the icon, from Brother Thomas who had touched it lightly with his finger, and from others who had seen it. He adds that the brothers of the Temple bring to their houses the liquid that emanates from the icon's flesh, and that they go to pray at Saydnaya at times of truce with the pagans.[33] Matthew Paris, too, relates that in times of truce with the pagans the Templars obtain the liquid, and that they do so in order to distribute it to pilgrims, who then go on to extol the Virgin in diverse parts of the world.[34] The Templar connection with Saydnaya figures also in Old French texts. A poem on the 'miracle de Sardenai', extant in a thirteenth-century manuscript, adduces the testimony of 'Master Thomas, who was chaplain of the Temple' and touched the icon with his hands—this Master Thomas being evidently Brother Thomas of the Latin account. Likewise, the poem mentions that at times of truce between Christians and pagans the brothers of the Temple, and other people, go to pray at Saydnaya and convey from there phials filled with the holy liquid.[35] And Gautier de Coincy asserts that many Templars who returned to France told him at length about the icon they had seen.[36]

Thus the Templars are depicted as playing a central role both in the diffusion of the story of Saydnaya's holy icon and in the distribution of its holy, thaumaturgic liquid.[37] It is a role that appears to have escaped the notice of most modern historians of the Order of the Temple. It may have been the dearth of healing shrines in the Kingdom of Jerusalem that drew the Templars to Saydnaya: the *Miracles de Notre-Dame de*

---

[31] *Magistri Thietmari peregrinatio,* p. 18.

[32] Cerulli, *Libro etiopico*, pp. 270–72. Cerulli dated the account to the twelfth century (pp. 269–70), but Devos convincingly argued for a later date: Devos, 'Premières Versions', pp. 249–51.

[33] Devos, 'Premières Versions', pp. 255–56.

[34] Matthew Paris, *Chronica majora*, ed. by H. R. Luard, Rolls Series, 57 (London, 1874), II, 487.

[35] Raynaud, 'Miracle', p. 536.

[36] Gautier de Coincy, 'Le Miracle Nostre Dame de Sardenay', vv. 618–24, col. 663.

[37] See Cerulli, *Libro etiopico,* p. 275; H. Nicholson, *Templars, Hospitallers and Teutonic Knights: Images of the Military Orders, 1128–1291* (Leicester, 1993), p. 117.

Rocamadour asserts that the main Marian shrines of the Holy Land did not serve as healing shrines,[38] and this was probably true also of the Church of the Holy Sepulchre and the country's other major foci of worship. The Templars may have been also attracted to Saydnaya on account of its far away, perilous location—deep in Muslim territory and accessible only at times of truce. Probably they derived some income from the holy oil. In any case, the Templars may be credited with making Catholic Christendom familiar with a cult that arose among Oriental Christians, beyond the boundaries of the Kingdom of Jerusalem—and that also attracted Muslim worshippers.

Among Latins, the fame of the cult of Saydnaya was not limited to Templars and simple pilgrims. Oliver, head of the cathedral school of Cologne, who participated in the Fifth Crusade, in September 1221 wrote a letter to the Egyptian sultan al-Kamil inviting him to convert to Christianity. In this letter he presented the oil-giving icon of the Virgin at 'Sardenai' as one example of images that arouse the devotion of Christian believers without turning them into idolaters. Oliver points out that the sultan's people cannot deny that oil drips abundantly from the icon; he comments also that Saracens do not dare to dwell there alongside the Christians.[39] And in 1240, when the Franks were allied with the sultan Isma'il of Damascus, Benoît of Alignan, the Franciscan bishop of Marseilles, 'went to Saint Mary of Sardenai on pilgrimage, with an appropriate safe-conduct from the said sultan'.[40] On his return to Acre the bishop strongly urged the Templar master, Armand of Périgord, to rebuild the castle of Saphet.[41] As other sources indicate that the Templars propagated the cult of Saydnaya, and as the lengthy account of Bishop Benoît's attempts to persuade the Templars to rebuild Safed suggests that he had been on friendly terms with them, it is plausible to assume that he went on pilgrimage to Saydnaya on a Templar recommendation.

Is it conceivable that the Templar espousal of Saydnaya contributed to sullying the Order's reputation and helped pave the way to its ultimate defamation and suppression? As is well known, during the trial of the Templars some of the accused brothers mentioned that Guillaume de Beaujeu, master of the Temple in the years 1273–91, cultivated excessive friendship with the Mamluk sultan and the Saracens, and kept some Saracens in his pay—assertions that were not entirely unfounded.[42] Possibly the

---

[38] *Les miracles de Notre-Dame de Roc-Amadour au XIIe siècle,* ed. and trans. by E. Albe (Paris, 1907), pp. 288–92.

[39] Oliver of Cologne, *Epistola salutaris regi Babilonis*, in *Die Schriften des Kölner Domscholasters Oliverus,* ed. by H. Hoogeweg (Tübingen, 1894), pp. 297–98. For the last point see also *Magistri Thietmari peregrinatio,* p. 18.

[40] R. B. C. Huygens, *De constructione castri Saphet. Construction et fonctions d'un château fort franc en Terre Sainte* (Amsterdam and New York, 1981), p. 35.

[41] Huygens, *De constructione castri Saphet,* pp. 36–37.

[42] See *Les Gestes des Chiprois*, ed. by G. Raynaud (Geneva, 1887), p. 242; M.-L. Bulst-Thiele, *Sacrae domus militiae templi hierosolymitani magistri. Untersuchungen zur Geschichte*

Templar connection with, and propagation of, a holy site honoured also by Saracens, aroused some further suspicion, but this is mere conjecture. In any case, in 1403 the Hospitallers attempted to negotiate a treaty with the Mamluk sultan that would allow them to repair, inter alia, the shrine of Saint Mary of 'Sardenaya', but the treaty was never put in force.[43] Still, western pilgrims continued to visit Saydnaya, as attested by numerous itineraries and travel descriptions.[44] Even Baedeker's handbook for travellers in Palestine and Syria, published in 1894, intimates that the iconosterium of the large Greek nunnery of Sednaya [*sic*] 'contains old pictures, one of which is said to be a miracle-working Madonna'.[45] And, down to the present, the shrine attracts Muslim worshippers, especially on Fridays.[46]

---

des Templerordens 1118/19–1314 (Göttingen, 1974), p. 283 with n. 99; M. C. Barber, *The Trial of the Templars* (Cambridge, 1978), p. 13.

[43] Text edited in A. Luttrell, 'Rhodes and Jerusalem: 1291–1411', *Byzantinische Forschungen,* 12 (1987), 204–05; see also pp. 196, 198. The treaty was noted by G. Raynaud, 'Le miracle de Sardenai (article complémentaire)', *Romania,* 14 (1885), 87.

[44] For a list see Nasrallah, 'La Vierge Hodigitria', p. 245; and Pringle, *Churches*, p. 221; Minervini, 'Leggende', p. 8, n. 20.

[45] K. Baedeker, *Palestine and Syria. Handbook for Travellers* (Leipzig, 1894), p. 376. The brochures now distributed at the monastery, *A Brief History of Convent* [*sic*] *of Our Lady of Saydanaya (near Damascus – Syria)* and R. Keriaky, *Saydnaya (History and Ruins)* (n.p., 1999), do not describe the icon as miracle-working at present.

[46] R. Burns, *Monuments of Syria: An Historical Guide* (London, 1992), p. 214; W. Dalrymple, *From the Holy Mountain. A Journey among the Christians of the Middle East* (New York, 1997), pp. 186–91.

Postscript: In the early fourteenth century, Nikolaus Omichsel of Passau made a pilgrimage to the Holy Land and brought back, inter alia, oil of the miraculous image of the Virgin of 'Sardinal'; he died in 1333 in Santiago de Campostela. See R. Plötz, 'Il cammino e i luoghi', in *Il mondo dei pellegrinaggi: Roma, Santiago, Gerusalemme,* ed. by P. Caucci von Saucken (Milan, 1999), p. 82.

Servise de Marriage and Law Enforcement in the Latin Kingdom of Jerusalem

SYLVIA SCHEIN

Though most of the legal sources of the Kingdom of Jerusalem are thirteenth-century jurists, scholars use their legal treatises for the twelfth century. This seems to be legitimate for a number of reasons. One of the main aims of the thirteenth-century jurists was to reconstruct the lost twelfth-century *Lettres du Sepulcre* (following Saladin's conquest of Jerusalem in 10 October 1187); namely, the collection of the *assises* of the kingdom, kept in the Church of the Holy Sepulchre. Secondly, though the jurists themselves express doubts as to whether they were describing actual laws or merely custom, and this finds expression in their treatises in the recurring phrase *assise ou usage*, they preserve the memories of jurists like Ralph of Tiberias, for example, who lived before 1187 and remembered the *assises* and customs (*usages*). Thirdly, the thirteenth-century jurists often used twelfth-century chronicles and diplomatic material. Moreover, some of the legislation regarding women, as described in thirteenth-century jurists' writings, appears in twelfth-century's sources.[1]

It is one of the *assises* described in detail by the thirteenth-century jurists that this study deals with. Namely, the *assise* known as *servise de marriage* granting lords the right to control the marriages of all women between the ages of twelve and sixty, who held fiefs or the baillage of fiefs owing *servise de cors*. The study of the application of the *assise* in the kingdom shows that in practice it was very seldom enforced. The

---

[1] J. Riley-Smith, *The Feudal Nobility and the Kingdom of Jerusalem, 1174–1277* (London, 1973), pp. 133–34; but see J. L. La Monte, 'Three Questions Concerning the Assises of Jerusalem', *Byzantina-Metabyzantina* (New York, 1949), I, 201–12.

comparison with the West (especially France and England) demonstrates that the feudal lords in the Latin Kingdom seem often to be unable to enforce the law upon their female vassals and, moreover, that the law was seldom used in practice.[2]

In twelfth-century England, monarchs and other feudal lords collected a fee for permission to marry, a custom unknown in the Kingdom of Jerusalem. Moreover, until 1215 lords could force a husband of their choice upon a widow. This is demonstrated by paragraph eight of the *Magna Carta* which stated that 'a widow should not be compelled to remarry so long as she prefers to remain without a husband'.[3] However, the baronial revolt and the reform of 1258 clearly show that the English monarchs continued to enforce marriages as well as disparagement.[4] Additionally, widows who refused to accept an unwanted husband lost their dower, which was taken, as a fine, by their lords. It was only later, in the late thirteenth and especially fourteenth century that feudal lords accepted monetary compensation for the loss of their right to consent over marriages of their vassals of both sexes.[5] In France too the king was known to control

---

[2] There are a number of studies dealing with various aspects of the subject of women in the Kingdom of Jerusalem. None however deals with the subject of law enforcement. See J. Richard, 'Le Statut de la femme dans l'Orient Latin', in *La Femme II,* Recueils de la Société Jean Bodin pour l'Histoire Comparative des Institutions, 12 (Brussels, 1962), pp. 377–87; J. A. Brundage, 'Marriage Law in the Latin Kingdom of Jerusalem', in *Outremer. Studies in the History of the Crusading Kingdom of Jerusalem*, ed. by B. Z. Kedar et al. (Jerusalem, 1982), pp. 258–71; H. E. Mayer, 'Studies in the History of Queen Melisande of Jerusalem', *Durbarton Oaks Papers,* 26 (1976), 93–189; B. Hamilton, 'Women in the Crusader States: The Queens of Jerusalem (1100–1190)', in *Medieval Women*, ed. by Derek Baker (Oxford, 1978), pp. 143–73; S. Lambert, 'Queen or Consort: Rulership and Politics in the Latin East, 1118–1228', in *Queens and Queenship in Medieval Europe. Proceedings of a Conference Held at King's College, London, April 1995*, ed. by A. J. Duggan (Woodbridge, 1997), pp. 153–69.

[3] J. C. Holt, *Magna Carta* (Cambridge, 1965), p. 318 and see also pp. 45–48, 113–16. E. Searle, 'Seigniorial Control of Women's Marriage: The Antecedents and Function of *Merchet* in England', *Past and Present,* 82 (1979), 3–14.

[4] S. L. Waugh, 'Marriage, Class and Royal Lordship in England under Henry III', *Viator,* 16 (1985), 181–207; J. Senderowitz Loengard, '*Rationabilis Dos*: Magna Carta and the Widow's "Fair share" in the Earlier Thirteenth Century', in *Wife and Widow in Medieval England*, ed. by Sue Sheridan Walker (Ann Arbor, 1993), pp. 59–80.

[5] According to the *Tractatus de legibus et consuetudinibus regni Anglie qui Glanvilla vocatur,* VII, 11–12, written between 26 November 1187 and 6 July 1189, if a widow marries without the consent of her lord she ought thereby to lose her dower; an heiress who marries without such consent is to be disinherited. See, *The Treatise on the Laws and Customs of the Realm of England Commonly Called Glanvill,* ed. by G. D. G. Hall (London, 1965), pp. 85–86. Henry of Bracton, who wrote *c.* 1259, argued that an heiress may not marry without the consent of her lord but if she marries 'she would not, as in former times, lose her inheritance beyond hope of recovery' but would have to pay a fine; similarly, a widow would not, as previously, lose her

in theory marriages of their vassals. The legal code of King Louis IX stipulated as law that a vassal was not permitted to marry off his daughter without the consent of their seigneur. The *Établissements de Saint Louis* (middle of the thirteenth century) stipulated that at least three candidates should be offered by both the family and the lord to an heiress (either a girl of marriageable age or a widow) and she should choose the best and the most suitable among them. At the same time, however, according to *coutumies* from the twelfth and thirteenth century, the consent of both parents or other members of the family and of the feudal lords, was necessary.[6]

This gradual disappearance of the coercive aspects of feudal right over marriages in England is to be explained as the result of the struggle of the nobility against the king. Moreover in England as well as in France it was also the result of the growing influence of the canon law concept of marriage over that of the nobility; namely, its insistence that marriages had to be based on the free consent of both the bride and the groom. The Church backed up its assertions about freedom of choice in marriage by annulling forced marriages arranged by either the families or feudal lords.[7]

The date of the *assise* of *servise de marriage* is unknown. Some historians ascribe it to the reign of Amalric I (1163–74). Its history is related by the jurist Philip of Navarre (who wrote his *Livre de forme de plait* in about 1250, and revised it in the 1260s) in an attempt to reconstruct the lost *assises* of the twelfth century. According to him, in the early years of the kingdom noble women could marry freely without the consent of their feudal lords. Then the lords and especially the kings of Jerusalem began to establish their right to control marriages, thus weakening the right of families over the marriages of their daughters. This led to the opposition of the nobility and a new rule was introduced: the king or another feudal lord was to propose three barons to a female heiress (either one who reached the marriage age or a widow) from among whom she was obliged to choose her husband. Although obliged to choose her husband

---

dower but would also have to pay a fine. Henry of Bracton, *De Legibus et consuetudinibus angliae*, ed. by Samuel Thorne, 4 vols (Cambridge, MA, 1968–77), III, 253–57. See also S. Sheridan Walker, 'Free Consent and Marriage of Feudal Wards in Medieval England', *Journal of Medieval History,* 8 (1982), 123–34; eadem, 'The Feudal Family and the Common Law Courts: The Pleas Protecting Rights of Wardship and Marriage *c.* 1225–1375', *Journal of Medieval History,* 14 (1988), 13–31.

[6] *Établissements de Saint Louis*, ed. by Paul Violet (Paris, 1881), c. 67, II, pp. 99–103. J. M. Turlan, 'Recherches sur le marriage dans la pratique coutumière (XIIe–XVIe s.)', *Revue historique de droit français et étranger,* 35 (1957), 477–528; H. Vidal, 'Les mariages dans la famille des Guillems seigneurs de Montpellier,' *Revue historique de droit français et étranger,* 62 (1984), 231–44; Hélène Débax, 'Stratégies Matrimoniales des Comtes de Toulouse (850–1270)', *Annales du Midi,* 100 (1988), 131–51.

[7] Christopher Brooke, *The Medieval Idea of Marriage,* new edn (1989; Oxford, 1994), pp. 128–33, 137–40 and *passim*; J. T. Noonan, 'Marriage in the Middle Ages: Power to Choose', *Viator,* 4 (1973), 419–34; Walker, 'Free Consent and Marriage', pp. 123–34.

from the three candidates proposed by her lord, under pain of losing her fief by *commise*, the heiress could refuse all of them on the grounds of disparagement or misalliance. According to John of Ibelin, should the heiress fail to choose one of the three candidates, she might be summoned by her lord to explain her reasons. If she failed to appear, she might be deprived forthwith of her fief. If she appeared, but failed to satisfy her lord that she had adequate reasons for refusal to marry one of his nominees, he might take control of her fief for a year and a day. At the end of that time he could require her once again to choose a husband from among three candidates. Failure to make a choice the second time presumably resulted in permanent loss of the fief. However, if the parent or friends of an heiress wanted her to marry someone other than the man proposed by the lord, they could offer the lord a sum of money to accept their candidate. Thus the king as well as other feudal lords found themselves forced to propose to a heiress candidates of her own social rank and of similar wealth or else she, with the advice of her family, might refuse the marriage. All this refers to heiresses who held fiefs which owed *servise de corps*; lords did not have any authority over marriages of heiresses who held fields which did not owe *servise de corps*.[8] This gave the family of an heiress more choice and undoubtedly presupposed its advice and consent, and thus considerably limited the control of overlords. Not only were they now obliged to propose three candidates instead of one, but the heiress could refuse them all on the grounds of disparagement or misalliance. Referring to the law, Philip of Navarre complains that in the third phase of its development it favoured the strengthening of the royal power and, consequently, the weakening of that *lignages*.[9] Actually as already pointed out by Peter Edbury, it was clearly a concession to the nobility.[10]

---

[8] *Livre de Philippe de Navarre*, *Assises de Jerusalem,* ed. by A. A. Beugnot, RHC, Lois, 1 (Paris, 1841), c. 86, pp. 558–59. *Livre de Jean d'Ibelin*, c. 227, in *Assises de Jerusalem,* ed. by A. A. Beugnot, RHC, Lois, 1 (Paris, 1841), c. 227, pp. 359–61; Richard, 'Le Statut', p. 379. P. W. Edbury, 'Feudal Obligations in the Latin East', *Byzantion*, 47 (1977), 345–47. J. Prawer, *Crusader Institutions* (Oxford, 1980), pp. 30–31. Brundage, 'Marriage Law', pp. 259–60, 268. For Philip de Navarre, see Riley-Smith, *The Feudal Nobility*, pp. 126–27; but see also M. Grandclaude, 'Liste d'Assises remontant au premier royaume de Jerusalem', *Mélanges Paul Fournier* (Paris, 1929), p. 340, who points out that it did not exist in 1177. See also n. 20 below. The *Livre au roi* (*c.* 1197–1205), in which the concept of monarchical power is more exalted than in the treatises of jurists like Philip of Navarre and John of Ibelin, presents a different version. Namely that the king may force a vassal's widow to marry one of his three nominees; this is an intermediate stage between that in which he had the right to impose a single nominee and that in which the widow could, under certain circumstances, refuse all three. *Livre au roi. Introduction, Notes et édition critique,* ed. by M. Greilsammer (Paris, 1995), c. 30, p. 219 (twelfth century) and nn. 127–29; eadem, 'Structure and Aims of the *Livre au roi*', in *Outremer. Studies in the History of the Crusading Kingdom of Jerusalem*, ed. by Kedar et al., pp. 218–26, esp. p. 222.

[9] See above n. 8.

[10] Edbury, 'Feudal Obligations', pp. 354–55.

However, several examples clearly demonstrate that the kings of Jerusalem had never enjoyed complete power of coercion over the marriages of their female vassals, not before the promulgation of the *assise* and not following it. One such example is that of Constance, widow of Raymond of Poitiers, Prince of Antioch. Constance married Raymond in 1137 while under ten years of age. When she became a widow in 1148, she was about twenty years old and a mother of four children, the eldest of whom, the future Bohemond III of Antioch, heir to the principality, was five years old. Two years later, in 1150, King Baldwin III of Jerusalem offered Constance three candidates: Yves of Nesle, Count of Soissons; Walter of Falconberg, whose family, the Saint-Omer, held the principality of Galilee in the past; and Ralph of Merle, a baron from the county of Tripoli. According to William of Tyre, 'any of these seemed with justice quite capable of protecting the region'. But Constance refused them all because, according to William, '[she] dreaded the yoke of marriage and preferred a free and an independent life. She paid little heed to the needs of her people and was more interested in enjoying the pleasure of life'.[11] William, however, was wrong. She did not dread the yoke of remarriage (what he considered to be her duty to both her principality and her overlord) but refused to marry the candidates offered to her by the king, her overlord, because she did not want to marry any of them. This became evident when in 1153 she married, in secret, a French nobleman, Renaud of Châtillon, whose family were the lords of Donzy, having asked the consent of King Baldwin III, only after she had chosen a husband for herself. William of Tyre remarked somewhat unkindly (and inaccurately) that 'many there were, however, who, marvelled that a woman so eminent, so distinguished and powerful, who had been the wife of a very illustrious man, should stoop to marry an ordinary knight'.[12]

Another example reads like an episode from a *chanson de geste*. In 1158 the beautiful Theodora, the niece of the Byzantine Emperor Manuel Comnenus, married King Baldwin III; when the king died in 1163, his widow, then only seventeen years old and childless, retired to Acre, which she received from her husband as her dower (*dos*) to be held for life if she were widowed. King Amalric, brother of Baldwin III, did not wish for his widowed sister-in-law to remarry, as he did not wish Acre, the largest and the richest city in the kingdom and traditionally a part of the royal domain, to pass into other hands; if Theodora remained a widow, Acre would revert to the crown at her death. In the winter of 1166/7, Theodora, then a widow for about three years living in retirement in Acre, eloped with her cousin Andronicus Comnenus, the Byzantine governor of Cilicia, then a married man in his forties. The couple eloped to Nur-al-Din's court in Damascus and lived there happily with their two children. Theodora died before 1182 when Andronicus became the Emperor of Byzantium. As Theodora's children

---

[11] William of Tyre, *Chronicon,* ed. by R. B. C. Huygens, CCCM, 63–63A (Turnhout, 1986), c. 17, 18, pp. 785–86.

[12] Ibid., c. 17, 26, pp. 795–96. Jonathan Phillips, *Defenders of the Holy Land. Relations between the Latin East and the West, 1119–1187* (Oxford, 1996), pp. 125–26.

were born out of wedlock, the dower lands of Acre returned to the crown.[13] Still, the story shows how little control the kings had over their female vassals.

Two additional cases, from the thirteenth century, demonstrate the impotence of the kings as overlords of female vassals. Between 1198 and 1205, Beatrice, the elder daughter of Joscelin of Courtenay and part heiress to his vast lands, married, against the will of King Aimery and therefore in breach of her *servise de marriage*, a German count, Otto of Henneberg. The king did not take any measures against the couple though they did not dispose freely of their fiefs until after the death of King Aimery in 1205.[14]

Isabella of Ibelin the elder daughter of John II of Beirut inherited upon his death in 1264 the lordship. She had been married as a child to the child-king of Cyprus Hugh II who died at the age of fourteen before the marriage was consummated (1267). His successor Hugh III of Cyprus, who in 1269 also became the King of Jerusalem, hoped to use Isabella to attract illustrious scions of the European knighthood to the East. She, however, refused to marry and instead had a liaison with Julian of Sidon. In 1272 she gave herself and her lordship to an Englishman, Hamo L'Estrange, who seems to have been one of the companions of Prince Edward of England (who came to the kingdom in 1271). In 1273 they put their lordship under the protection of Baibars. Therefore when King Hugh III tried to carry off Isabella to Cyprus, to marry her to a candidate of his choice, the Sultan at once cited the pact that Hamo had made with him and demanded her return. As the High Court gave the king no support he was obliged to send Isabella back to Beirut without being able to enforce *servise de marriage* from her (1275).[15]

In most of the cases mentioned above the heiresses not only broke the law refusing to accept the control of their lords over their marriages but also the law proclaiming that widows (except for those over sixty)[16] should as a matter of course remarry (after a year and one day from the day of the death of their husband); they could be forced to do so, and if need be on pain for forfeiture of their fiefs.[17]

---

[13] Ibid. c. 18, 22, pp. 842–44; c. 22, 11 (10), pp. 1020–21. William of Tyre's argument that 'the queen was treacherously abducted' by Andronicus is hardly convincing. See also Hamilton, 'Women', pp. 157–62.

[14] *Regesta regni Hierosolimitani*, ed. by R. Röhricht (Innsbruck, 1893), nos 828, 933, 978; Riley-Smith, *The Feudal Nobility,* p. 147; Edbury, 'Feudal Obligations', p. 347; Greilsammer, *Livre au roi*, p. 222 , no. 129.

[15] See S. Runciman, *A History of the Crusades* (Cambridge, 1954), III, 329–30, 342–43, 393; Riley-Smith, *The Feudal Nobility*, p. 224.

[16] *Livre de Jean d'Ibelin*, c. 228, pp. 362–64; Brundage, 'Marriage Law', pp. 270–71.

[17] *Livre au roi,* c. 30, pp. 220–22. The law regulating the period of mourning of a year and one day is recorded already by William of Tyre who, writing in the 1170s, argued that 'it was our custom, approved by a long usage, not to consider a remarriage of a widow, especially of one who was pregnant, within one year after the death of her husband, for that would not be honourable mourning'. William of Tyre, *Chronicon*, c. 21, 14(15), p. 981.

The cases clearly demonstrate that on these occasions the kings of Jerusalem failed to exercise their right to *servise de marriage*. This suggests perhaps that the law was only sporadically enforced till the 1180s; it was seldom enforced in the last two decades of the twelfth century and in the thirteenth century when the royal power considerably diminished and that of the class of high nobility increased. The futile attempt of King Hugh III to enforce his right upon Isabella of Beirut seems to suggest that in face of the opposition of the High Court at least in the 1270s the kings of Jerusalem were unable to enforce this law upon their female vassals. This, as well as the absence of cases which demonstrate the opposite,[18] all point out that perhaps the jurists record the reality of the twelfth rather than the thirteenth century. In the thirteenth century, when most of the kingdom's rulers, either *baillis* or consorts, were chosen by the High Court,[19] its members certainly insisted upon controlling the marriages in their own families.

Moreover, the examination of narrative sources and thus the practice of marrying off heiresses in the Latin Kingdom shows clearly that often before the promulgation of the *assise* of *servise de marriage* and after it, the kings offered the heiresses one candidate only. Maurice Grandclaude bases his dating of the *assise* as 'after 1177' on William of Tyre, who argues that in 1177 Sibylla of Montferrat, the daughter of King Amalric and widow of William Longsword of Montferrat, was offered by her brother King Baldwin IV only one candidate, namely, Duke Hugh III of Burgundy.[20] Sibylla actually refused to marry this candidate and married in 1180 another candidate offered to her by the king, Guy of Lusignan.[21] Both in 1177 and 1180 Sibylla was offered only one candidate and not three as allegedly the *assise* prescribed. There are few additional examples that suggest what was the common practice. Thus, in 1174, for example, King Amalric married off Stephanie of Millie, the lady and guardian of the lordship of Outrejourdain to his protégé Miles of Plancy. Following the murder of Miles (in October 1174), Baldwin IV arranged for her (in 1177) to marry Renaud of Châtillon,

---

[18] In 1177 for example Balian of Ibelin married the widow of King Amalric, Maria Comnena, 'domino rege id permittente'. William of Tyre, *Chronicon*, c. 21, 17(18), p. 986. This state of affairs in the Kingdom Jerusalem is in contrast not only to the West but also to principality of Antioch and county of Tripoli where the rulers took strong steps against lords who married an heiress without their permission. C. Cahen, *La Syrie du nord à l'époque des croisades et la principauté franque d'Antioche* (Paris, 1940), pp. 608–09; Riley-Smith, *The Feudal Nobility*, p. 148. J. Richard, 'The Political and Ecclesiastical Organization of the Crusader States', *A History of the Crusades*, ed. by K. M. Setton (Madison, 1985), V, 216–17.

[19] Riley-Smith, *The Feudal Nobility*, pp. 184–228. Lambert, 'Queen or Consort', pp. 153–69.

[20] William of Tyre, *Chronicon*, c. 20, 25(26), pp. 996–97; Grandclaude, 'Liste', pp. 340–41; Lambert, 'Queen or Consort,' pp. 159–60. Edbury in his 'Feudal Obligations', p. 355 n. 133, argues that Grandclaude's example 'would scarcely have been typical of feudal practice at that time'. In my opinion it is actually typical.

[21] William of Tyre, *Chronicon*, c. 22, 1, p. 1007. Hamilton, 'Women', pp. 163–67.

former Prince of Antioch.[22] There is no evidence that any other candidates were then offered to that lady. It follows thus that this *assise* can be added to the list which were described by the thirteenth-century jurists but which were never applied or enforced.[23] Moreover it is yet another example which shows that the jurists described theory rather than practice. In the Kingdom of Jerusalem, when law was concerned, these two, theory, and practice often did not coincide.

And the women? How did the actual state of affairs in the kingdom, namely, the failure to enforce the *assise* of *servise de marriage* stipulating the three candidates, the inability of the kings in some cases to enforce their candidates upon heiresses, and finally the practice of offering, or even forcing upon them, only one candidate, affect the position of women of the Latin Kingdom? As demonstrated above some of them like Constance of Antioch, Theodora, and Isabella of Ibelin, Lady of Beirut, succeeded in acting independently, evading both the constraints of the law, and of custom, to select their own husbands. These however are isolated cases and similar isolated cases are known to have taken place in both France and England.[24] Most of the heiresses in the kingdom were, however, in the same position as their counterparts in Europe whose marriage was arranged either by their family or their lords. As argued by Eileen Power,

> in feudal law a woman could be endowed by land and we know of endowable women holding land by every title recognized by law, including the most exalted ones. But, in practice, feudal marriage carried with it a certain denigration of woman as a person. While the Church subordinated woman to her husband, feudalism subordinated her to her fief. All feudal marriages of convenience were dictated by interests of land. In some ways an heiress—indeed an heir too—was much a chattel tied to the soil as was the manorial villein.[25]

This characterization expresses only too well the status of the heiresses in the Latin Kingdom. Except for the few who succeeded in acting freely, usurping from both their families and their lords the right to marry them, one may say it was most frequently that

---

[22] William of Tyre, *Chronicon*,, c. 21, 4, p. 964; c. 22, 5, p. 1012. B. Hamilton, 'The Titular Nobility of the Latin East: The Case of Agnes of Courtenay', *Crusade and Settlement. Papers Read at the First Conference for the Study of the Crusades and the Latin East, Presented to R. C. Smail*, ed. by Peter W. Edbury (Cardiff, 1985), pp. 200–01; E. Rey, 'Les Seigneurs de Mont-Réal et la Terre d'Outre Le Jourdain', *Revue de l'Orient Latin,* 4 (1896), 18–19 esp. pp. 16–17; Bernard Hamilton, 'Miles of Plancy and the Fief of Beirut', *The Horns of Hattin*, ed. by B. Z. Kedar (Jerusalem, 1992), p. 143 and n. 143.

[23] For examples of such *assises,* see Prawer, *Crusader Institutions,* pp. 27–45; Riley-Smith, *The Feudal Nobility*, pp. 34–37, 134–44, 229–30, and *passim*.

[24] Debax, 'Strategies', pp. 145–48; S. Shahar, *The Fourth Estate. A History of Women in the Middle Ages* (London and New York, 1983), pp. 131–36.

[25] E. Power, *Medieval Women*, ed. by M. M. Postan (Cambridge, 1975), p. 19.

their fate was dictated by either their family or their lords while the interest that dictated the choice of a husband for a heiress was that of the fief, the lordship, or the kingdom.[26] In the kingdom, marriages, it seems, were mainly dictated by the family wish to enlarge and to add to their fiefs or lordships, or when dictated by the king, to ensure military service owed to him from a lordship held by a heiress. Therefore, in the Latin Kingdom, in contrast to the West, marriages were to a large extent dictated by considerations evolving from the military needs of the state. Heiresses were often married to knights, newcomers in the land, in order to enable them to settle in the kingdom.[27] At the same time, one may say that similarly as in Europe, the more exalted was the status of the heiress in the feudal hierarchy the less freedom did she enjoy over her marriage.[28]

---

[26] I am at present working on the subject of the 'marriage policy' of the nobility in the Kingdom of Jerusalem.

[27] For example, Echiva of Bures, the heiress of the principality of Galilee married Walter of St Omer (*c.* 1159). See Edbury, 'Feudal Obligations', p. 338 and n. 65. Helvis the heiress of Ramleh married in 1150 Manasses of Hierges, a newcomer and a nephew of King Baldwin II. See H. E. Mayer, 'Manasses of Hierges in East and West', *Revue belge de philologie et d'histoire,* 66 (1988), 757–66 (reprinted H. E. Mayer, *Kings and Lords in the Latin Kingdom of Jerusalem* (Alderhot, 1994), no. XVI). In *c.* 1200–1204, Helvis, the daughter of Balian of Ibelin and Maria Comnena and widow of Reynald of Sidon, married Guy of Montfort, the brother of Simon of Montfort and a newcomer in the kingdom. P. W. Edbury, *John of Ibelin and the Kingdom of Jerusalem* (Bury St Edmunds, 1997), p. 25. Burgundia, the daughter of King Aimery of Lusignan (d. 1205), was married by him to Walter of Montbéliard who came to the kingdom with the forces of the Fourth Crusade (1204). Ibid., p. 27. Sibylla, the daughter of King Amalric, was married to newcomers twice; in 1176 to William of Montferrat and in 1180 to Guy of Lusignan: her sister Isabella was also married off twice to newcomers; in 1190 to Conrad of Montferrat and in 1192 to Henry of Champagne. Riley-Smith, *The Feudal Nobility,* pp. 111–20 and *passim*; Hamilton, 'Women', pp. 168–72.

[28] See Lambert, 'Queen or Consort', pp. 153–69. One may add also that the more important an heiress was, the earlier she was married. Feudal law followed the conventional Romano-canonical rule that the minimum age for marriage of females was twelve, proclaiming that an heiress under the age of twelve could not be induced to marry. *Livre de Philippe de Navarre,* c. 86, p. 559; *Livre de Jean d'Ibelin,* c. 171, p. 263. Brundage, 'Marriage Law', pp. 261–62. In practice, however, the heiress were often married at an earlier age. For example, Isabella, the daughter of King Amalric, married Humphrey IV of Toron in 1180 when she was only eight. Hamilton, 'Women', p. 167.

Did Laws of War Exist in the Crusader Kingdom of Jerusalem?

YVONNE FRIEDMAN

It is a moot point as to whether or not the crusaders, engaged in their war to conquer and rule the Holy Land (1095–1291), had established laws of war. As our first direct evidence for the existence of codified rules of war dates only from the thirteenth century,[1] this inescapably raises the question of how and when these codes developed. I argue that although we can assume that the crusader knights had codes based on custom, which bound them to a certain way of conducting warfare, there is, however, no solid evidence for the existence of codified, written rules of law in their former homelands for the period prior to the thirteenth century.

Let me state at the outset that I am well aware of the weaknesses of arguing *ex silentio*; however, it seems to me that while the laws of war were not yet defined in the countries the crusaders came from, they nevertheless brought with them some embryonic ideas and customs that would later develop into laws in Europe and probably also in the East. If I am correct, I feel it safe to assume these defined laws did not emerge *ex nihilo,* but were grounded in a prior distillation of custom. My approach is

[1] *Las siete partidas del Rey Don Alfonso el Sabio* (Madrid, 1807), partida II, tit. 21, 24, 26, 29. M. Keen, *The Law of War in the Late Middle Ages* (London, 1965). The first elaborate lay book of laws of war was Honoré Bonet's, *L'Arbre de batailles,* ed. by E. Nys (Brussels, 1883), trans. by G. W. Coopland, *The Tree of Battles of Honoré Bonet* (Liverpool, 1949). It was clearly indebted to the work of the canon lawyer John of Legnano, *Tractatus de bello, de represaliis, et de duello*, ed. by T. E. Holland, trans. by J. L. Brierly (Oxford, 1917); both were written in the fourteenth century.

developmental: if in the fourteenth century in France and England we find written codes, they were certainly based upon prior custom and social conventions defining the honourable way a warrior was expected to behave. My investigation of this question leads me to conclude that the participants in the First Crusade had some notion of what was right and wrong in war, even if they did not always act accordingly. Significantly, this existing custom was, in my opinion, altered by the encounter with a new reality on the campaigns to the Holy Land, which may in turn have changed customs in the East and even influenced, by way of returning crusaders, customs in the West. In essence, this paper is an initial, tentative attempt to explore what preceded the emergence of the written laws of war in the fourteenth century and to examine the interaction between European conventions and Holy Land reality. For the sake of discussion I have broadly divided the laws of war into two main categories—practical behaviour in war, which is easier to catalogue, and the more amorphous quantity of moral behaviour.

Unbridled Cruelty or Behavioural Norms?

I take as my starting point one of the bloodiest acts, with perhaps the exception of the taking of Jerusalem, as it appears in the context of the crusaders' conquest of Ma'arat a-Numan (11 December 1098). Upon first reading it seems to show a total lack of regard for law and order:

> Our men all entered the city, and each seized as his own whatever goods he found in houses or cellars, and when it was dawn they killed everyone, man or woman, whom they met in any place whatsoever. No corner of the city was clear of Saracen corpses, and one could scarcely go about the city streets except by treading on the dead bodies of Saracens. [. . .] While we were there [a month later] some of our men could not satisfy their needs, either because of the long stay or because they were so hungry, for there was no plunder to be had outside the walls. So they ripped up the bodies of the dead, because they used to find hidden bezants in their entrails, and others cut the dead flesh into slices and cooked it to eat.[2]

This contemporary description of the military victory at Ma'arat was one of the first in a series of descriptions of massacres by the crusaders which culminated in the conquest of Jerusalem in 1099. It has contributed to a popular image of the crusades not as a holy war, but as a lawless, violent adventure restrained neither by law nor by any ethical custom.[3] As depicted, the crusaders killed indiscriminately, looted and

---

[2] *Gesta Francorum et aliorum Hierosolimitanorum*, ed. by Rosalind Hill (London, 1962), pp. 80–81.

[3] T. Jones and A. Ereira, *Crusades* (London, 1994), pp. 9–12, based on a television series by the BBC (Christmas, 1994) used the motif of crusaders as cannibals as a motto.

plundered, and even descended to cannibalism.[4] Collaborated by other chroniclers,[5] the influence of the shocking nature of the story of Ma'arat is reflected in the detailed description of the *Tafurs*, the lawless and fearless cannibals, by the romantic *Chanson d'Antioch*.[6] The conquest of Ma'arat raises the acute question of whether this was an exceptional event caused by difficult circumstances or were the crusaders really devoid of any laws of war?[7] If the cruelty displayed during conquest can be seen as exceptional, were there any laws of war after the establishment of the Latin Kingdom, a kingdom that had to fight for its existence for long periods?

To understand the conduct of war as carried out by the crusaders it is crucial to examine their prior legacy. Did they deviate from the norms of warfare in their homelands; alternately, is it possible that no such norms existed and therefore they could not be expected to have had any? Again, we must distinguish here between formal modes of conduct and moral behaviour, noting however that it is not always possible to draw a precise distinction between these two categories. Every 'formal' code of behaviour has its underlying moral element.

After the disintegration of the Carolingian empire and its well-defined laws formulated in the *capitularia,* Western Europe seemingly became a lawless society. Many historians of the tenth- and eleventh-century 'Peace of God' movement attribute its emergence to the absence of such laws of war, leaving a social and governmental vacuum into which the Church moved in an attempt to restrict violence and lawless behaviour. Regulations promulgated by well-orchestrated Church councils were geared at arousing the *populus* against the violence of the warrior classes.[8]

The underlying interest of the Church was first and foremost proprietary, to defend its property and clergy against unrestricted violence. The 'Peace of God' was, however,

---

[4] For the motif of cannibalism in crusader propaganda both in the first and third crusades, see A. S. Ambrisco, 'Cannibalism and Cultural Encounters', *Medieval and Early Modern Studies*, 29.3 (1999), 499–528.

[5] Albert of Aachen, *Historia Ierosolymitana,* ed. and trans. by Susan B. Edgington, Oxford Medieval Texts (forthcoming) (hereafter cited as AA, by number of book and chapter). I am grateful to Sue Edgington for letting me use the text in advance of its publication. (Old version: RHC, Hocc., 4). Albert's set of priorities sounds strange to modern ears: 'It is wicked to tell, let alone to do—the Christians did not shrink from eating not only killed Turks or Saracens, but even dogs whom they snatched and cooked with fire'. See Fulcher of Chartres, *A History of the Expedition to Jerusalem, 1095–1127*, I, 25, trans. by Frances Rita Ryan, ed. by H. S. Fink (Knoxville, 1969), p. 112.

[6] Suzanne Duparc-Quioc, *La Chanson d'Antioche* (Paris, 1977), I, ll. 4039–118.

[7] Ademar de Chabannes relates how the Norman Roger de Toeni terrorized the Muslims by feigned cannibalism in Spain in 1020; see Ademar of Chabannes, *Chronicon*, ed. by P. Bourgain, CCCM, 129 (Tournhout, 1999), III, 55, 36, p. 174.

[8] F. S. Paxton, 'History, Historians and the Peace of God', in *The Peace of God,* ed. by T. Head and R. Landes (Ithaca and London, 1992), pp. 21–40.

formulated as a set of moral precepts: whoever violated the peace by killing a Christian was hurting Christ himself. The protection of the unarmed, particularly the clergy was supposed to restrain violent behaviour in battle. Did it?

Two generations after the main 'Peace of God' councils it was clear that although the movement strove to solve the problems of disorder it had not succeeded. Dolorosa Kenelly concluded that the movement of peace although 'an eminent practical approach to problems of disorder in its day, was unequal to the task of enforcing peace in feudal Europe'.[9]

Marcus Bull came to a parallel conclusion when he dismissed the existence of a significant link between the movement for peace and the First Crusade. In his opinion the ethical demands of the 'Peace of God' were pitched over the heads of the lesser *milites* and the greater *principes* who set out on the First Crusade. Moreover the movement failed: the thrust of the councils had passed its peak by the 1040s while violence continued. 'Peace ideals were at the most peripheral', he stated.[10]

Even if the Church councils failed to inaugurate a messianic period of peace in Europe, they could still have influenced the moral sensitivity of the warriors toward more humane behaviour in battle. Could the Church's efforts, coupled with lay chivalric ideas, have been decisive? To try to ascribe different standards of warriors' behaviour to secular tradition or to religious teaching may be impossible at this early stage.[11] Even if we could prove success in implementing moral inhibitions on the individual level, the behaviour of the crusaders as a group, as found in the conquest description from the First Crusade, seems far from influenced by any such ideals.

It should, moreover, be noted that the moral inhibitions the movement of peace strove to implement applied solely to Christians. War against the infidel was a different matter altogether. As the brutal attacks on the Jewish communities in the path of the crusade show, the First Crusaders did not shy from violence against unbelievers, nor did they think they were expected to show them any mercy. The chroniclers Guibert of Nogent[12] and Ralph of Caen[13] claimed that the crusaders combined two mutually exclusive elements—Christian piety and violence—so that those previously inhibited by

---

[9] Dolorosa Kenelly, 'The Peace of God: Fact or Fiction?' (unpublished doctoral dissertation, University of California, Berkeley, 1962), p. 238.

[10] M. Bull, *Knightly Piety and the Lay Response to the First Crusade*: *The Limousin and Gascony c. 970–1130* (Oxford, 1993), p. 68; and review by R. Landes, *Speculum,* 71 (1996), 135–38.

[11] C. J. Holdsworth, 'Ideas and Reality: Some Attempts to Control and Defuse War in the Twelfth Century', in *The Church and War,* ed. by W. J. Sheils (Oxford, 1983), pp. 59–78.

[12] Guibert de Nogent, *Dei Gesta per Francos*, ed. by R. B. C. Huygens, CCCM, 127A (Turnhout,1996), I, trans. by R. Levine as *The Deeds of God through the Franks* (Woodbridge, 1997), p. 28.

[13] Radulphus Cadomensis, *Gesta Tancredi Siciliae regis in expeditione Hierosolymitana*, RHC, Hocc., 3, pp. 605–06.

such a contradiction were now galvanized by sanctified warfare.[14] Should we then expect the crusaders in the East to change their code of behaviour when battling Muslims?

Laws of War

The term 'laws of war' encompasses four different sets of laws: (1) the laws of conquest; for example, division of spoils; (2) laws of conduct of war—negotiation and capitulation at sieges, but also technical laws such as how to charge, battlefield discipline, etc; (3) humane ethical laws restricting violence and cruelty in war; for example, giving quarter to a vanquished enemy; and (4) responsibility for one's own warriors—not to leave wounded soldiers in the field, ransoming of captives, defining who pays for whom. Broadly speaking I view the first two sets as a group—as belonging to the more easily defined practical sphere, and the latter two sets as a group—as belonging to the more elusive moral sphere.

The crusader chronicles, if they mention laws of war at all, usually refer to the first two sets of laws. They were more easily defined and more urgently needed, whereas the more problematic slippery moral sphere seems to have been formulated at a later date. In his *Etymologiae,* when Isidore of Seville (d. 636) wanted to define military laws (*jus militare*), he stayed within the sphere of the technical laws,[15] and his approach was adopted by later writers. The word used by the chroniclers of the crusades is in most cases *mos* 'custom', and not *lex* or *ius,* so that even when we look for the more rudimentary, technical laws of war we are in the sphere of custom and not in a period of codified, written laws.[16] And since unwritten law can only be extrapolated from examination of behaviour, I rely not only on the legal treatises of the period, but also on the chroniclers' actual description of crusader conduct and sometimes of crusader ideals. I will now proceed to examine each of these four sets of laws with an eye to

---

[14] Bull, *Knightly Piety*, p. 4.

[15] Isidore, *Etymologiae,* V, c. 7: 'jus militare est belli inferendi solemnitas, foederis faciendi nexus, signo dato egressio in hostem vel pugnae commissio; item, signo dato receptio; item, flagitii militaris disciplina, si locus deseratur; item, stipendiorum modus, dignitatum gradus, praemiorum honor [. . .] item, praedae decisio, et pro personarum qualitatibus divisio, ac principis portio'.

[16] According to Cheyette, any law in the West prior to the thirteenth century was synonymous with custom: 'We can use law, first of all to denote the ways the members of a society or group in society habitually perform certain acts, whether or not they consciously put those ways into words. This definition makes it impossible to distinguish law from custom and from morals and proper conduct, but for analysing the situation in eleventh to twelfth-century France it is adequate as neither distinction was evident in day to day practice'. F. L. Cheyette, 'Giving Each his Due', in *Debating the Middle Ages. Issues and Readings,* ed. by Lester K. Little and Barbara H. Rosenwein (Oxford, 1998), pp. 170–79.

clarifying how they elucidate the relationship between the knights' European legacy and their conduct in the Holy Land.

Practical Codes

THE LAWS OF CONQUEST

These old, long-established laws, deeply grounded in custom, governed the division of spoils: territory as well as moveable goods. According to the Frankish chronicler Gregory of Tours there existed, already in the Merovingian army, a clear set of rules governing division of spoils. The famous story about the vase of Soisson is instructive in this respect. At a meeting held at Soisson for a formal division of the booty a soldier breaks a vase looted from a church to prevent King Clovis from getting a disproportionate share of the spoils. The king's natural desire for reprisal is hampered by the fact that the rebellious soldier's act apparently has the backing of strong custom. The only recourse at the king's disposal was to draw on a correspondingly strong custom from the Merovingian 'laws of war': one that required the soldier to present himself on the battlefield in his full equipage. In the event his military outfit was found lacking he was liable to punishment. During the next military season, the king used this 'law' to his advantage. By asserting that the soldier's equipment was not up to standard requirements, the king argued he could therefore lawfully mete out a severe punishment—that is, decapitate the soldier, as he had decapitated the vase when he broke it.[17]

These kinds of laws were necessary both to muster and keep a medieval army in field. As there was no central government to pay salaries or to provide the necessary equipment for the warriors, they had to know in advance how the spoils of war would be divided, what material gains they could expect from their bellicose occupation. The costly expenditures associated with acquiring horse, armour, and training necessitated a system that made the soldier responsible for providing his own equipment; this system also clarified, both socially and economically, his allegiance to his military leader. Within this system the individual soldier knew his place in the rank of command and his rights to income from the profits of war. This custom continued to govern the division of spoils well into the Carolingian period.[18] Although a leader could arbitrarily

---

[17] Gregory of Tours, *Libri Historiarum X*, ed. by B. Krusch and W. Levison, MGH, SRM, 1.1 (Hannover, 1951), pp. 72–73. For a critical discussion of the historical background, see Ian N. Wood, 'Gregory of Tours and Clovis', in *Debating the Middle Ages*, ed. by Little and Rosenwein, pp. 73–91. Isidore counted the princely portion of spoils between the military laws, see n. 15, above.

[18] T. Reuter, 'Plunder and Tribute in the Carolingian Empire', *Transactions of the Royal Historical Society*, 35 (1985), 79–91.

disregard custom, any general who disregarded his soldiers' expectations of booty ran the risk of creating serious dissatisfaction in the ranks.[19]

One example from the East shows the Franks adhering to these conventions. As described by Walter the Chancellor the distribution of booty won by the Franks fighting at Tall-Danith by the Prince of Antioch in 1115 took place according to a well-defined practice: 'He directed the wealth, which was brought to him to be kept for him, as befitted so great a prince; the rest was to be shared out, as his sovereignty and the custom of the same court demanded'.[20] In addition, in the early customs of Ramle, preserved in the charter of Bethgibbelin (1168), the right of plunder was one of the privileges of the new settlers on the frontier, and part of their expected income.[21]

It may therefore come as a surprise that William of Tyre, a student of law himself,[22] claims that a different custom had become law in the Latin Kingdom. Writing about the charge of the Templars into Ascalon (1153), he observed:

> It was charged that he [the commander of the Templars] kept the rest back in order that his own people, being the first to enter, might obtain the greater and richer portion of the spoils and plunder. For when a city is taken by assault, *custom among the Christians has made it a law*, even to this day, that whatever anyone on entering seizes for himself, that he may hold in perpetual right for himself and his heirs. [. . .][23]

William Zajac has shown that although a clear custom governing division of spoils existed in the West, one which called for setting apart a princely portion for the leader of the combat and dividing the rest according to rank, the situation in the East prescribed a different conduct. The 'custom made law' that William of Tyre mentions, gave the soldiers proprietorial rights on any spoils they were first to lay hands on. This

---

[19] William G. Zajac, 'Captured Property on the First Crusade', in *The First Crusade, Origins and Impact,* ed. by J. Philips (Manchester, 1997), pp. 153–80.

[20] Walter the Chancellor, *The Antiochene Wars: A Translation and Commentary*, ed. by T. Ashbridge and S. Edgington (Aldershot, 1999), p. 106 and n. 180.

[21] '[. . .] et de omnibus lucris quae fecerint super paganos reddent nobis juxta consuetudinem Lithde quam alio nomine vocamus Ramas'. J. Delaville le Roulx, *Cartulaire générale de l'ordre des Hospitaliers de Saint-Jean de Jérusalem, 1100–1310*, 4 vols (Paris, 1894–1906), no. 399, p. 273. For an analysis of this charter, see J. Prawer, 'Colonization Activities in the Latin Kingdom', *Crusader Institutions* (Oxford, 1980), pp. 119–26; and R. Ellenblum, *Frankish Rural Settlement in the Latin Kingdom of Jerusalem* (Cambridge, 1998), pp. 76–77, 142–43.

[22] R. B. C. Huygens, 'Guillaume de Tyr, étudiant. Un chapitre (XIX,12) de son "Histoire" retrouvé', *Latomus*, 21 (1962), 811–29.

[23] William of Tyre, *Chronicon*, ed. by R. B. C. Huygens, CCCM, 63–63A (Turnhout, 1986) (hereafter cited as WT), 17, 2, 47: 'Nam in violenter effractis urbibus id hactenus apud nos *pro lege obtinuit consuetudo*, ut quod quisque ingrediens sibi rapit, id sibi et heredibus suis perpetuo *iure* possideat'.

custom can be shown to have been the working principle in most of the early military campaigns, as in Ma'arat and in Jerusalem, and quite a number of the later ones.[24] Thus, in the case of the divisions of spoils there did exist a law of arms known to the crusaders and presumably brought with them from Europe; nonetheless they chose, for tactical reasons, to disregard it when they came to the East and behave according to a different principle. This free for all system did, however, endanger the army during battle, as it induced the individual warrior to leave the disciplined charge in order to get first shot at the spoils.[25] It seems that the difference between the First Crusade's convention of free seizure of spoils and the later, well-disciplined distribution of booty by the military leader[26] may not be a question of early versus late conventions, but of different circumstances. We can perhaps distinguish between conquest of a city and battle. In conquering a city the aim was to dispossess the former inhabitants and therefore free looting was condoned, whereas on the battlefield order and timing were imperative and therefore the division of booty had to be better regulated.[27] William Zajac has dealt with this problem extensively[28] and as his eagerly awaited book on the laws of war in the Latin kingdom is forthcoming we need not go into further detail here.

[24] Fulcher of Chartres, in *Historia Hierosolymitana,* ed. by H. Hagenmeyer, I, 29, 1(Heidelberg, 1913), p. 304; see WT, 21, 23, 32. See Richard I giving 'each man the booty he gets', in *Chronicon Richardi Divinensis de tempore regis Ricardi primi*, ed. and trans. by J. Appleby (London, 1963), p. 22.

[25] This again led to special *ad hoc* edicts, forbidding the army to take spoils: 'Cautum est etiam *edicto publico et lege promulgatum*, ne quis hostium spoliis inhiare presumat; WT, 6, 18, 7; WT, 10, 17.

[26] After the battle of Montgisard-Gezer in 1177, Baldwin IV distributed the spoils and treasures according to the rules of war—*lege bellis distributis,* 1177; WT, 21, 23, 32. According to the *Chronicle of the Third Crusade. A Translation of the 'Peregrinorum et Gesta Ricardi',* trans. by Helen J. Nicholson, Crusade Texts in Translation, 3 (Aldershot, 1997), VI, c. 7, p. 344, Richard I divided the booty acquired at Betnoble equally between the warriors and those who stayed behind to guard the army, a sign of a well-organized and disciplined army.

[27] WT, 10,16, 62–64. But see Jean Sire de Joinville, *Histoire de Saint Louis, credo et lettre a Louis IX*, ed. by N. de Wailly (Paris 1874), c. XXXVI, 168, p. 92: 'Sire, fist li preudome, vous me faites grant honour, la vostre merci! mais ceste honour et ceste offre' (to divide 6000 livres among the soldiers while the king keeps all the wheat and barley to himself) 'que vous me faites, ne penrai-je pas, se Dieu plait; car je desferoie les bonnes coustumes de la Sainte-Terre, qui sont teix: car quant l'on prent les cités des ennemis, des biens que l'on treuve dedans, li roys en doit avoir le tiers, et li pelerin en doivent avoir les dous parts'. Thus the 'bonnes coustumes de la Sainte-Terre' seem to have changed by the middle of the thirteenth century, and anyway Louis did not act according to them.

[28] Zajac, 'Captured Property'.

As opposed to the unwritten conventions discussed in the preceding paragraphs, it is not surprising that the military service connected with land grants by the king[29] was the first aspect of military conventions distilled into written law in the Latin Kingdom,[30] as the entire social structure was based on the principle of lands or money-fiefs in exchange for military service. Whether the rules of military service were written in the lost *Letres dou Sepulchre* and reconstructed in the thirteenth century, or invented then,[31] in any event it is clear throughout the crusader period the right of the military leader to summon his men to war was not contested.[32] It was, however, restricted in time and place, as in the famous Assise of Bilbeis which limited the service of a knight to a region defined by where his horse could carry him.[33] The obligations of military service were defined by age, gender, and size of fiefs. Even if these laws were written only in the thirteenth century, the summons of the army to assemble for battle was seen quite early as a *legal edict*.[34]

To sum up, in the sphere of the laws of spoils and summons to war the crusaders in the East were apparently familiar with customs brought from Europe. While not disregarding this legacy entirely, they were not always guided by these customs. The new realities in the East called for modifications of the pre-existing laws and sometimes led to the growth of unique custom stemming from local circumstances.

LAWS OF CONDUCT OF WAR

Having examined the regulation of obligations and profits incurred in war, I return to the rules governing behaviour on the battlefield. An important facet of chivalrous education, aimed at moulding a youth into an efficient warrior, dealt with discipline and methods of warfare. It would be rash to assume that the great enterprise of the First

---

[29] S. Tibble, *Monarchy and Lordship in the Latin Kingdom of Jerusalem* (Oxford, 1989).

[30] The law was already clearly formulated in the Carolingian period. See Charlemagne's General Capitulary for the Missi, Spring, 802, in *The Reign of Charlemagne*, ed. by H. R. Loyn and J. Percival (London, 1975), no. 7.

[31] J. Edbury, 'Law and Custom in the Latin East: *Les Letres dou Sepulcre*', *Mediterranean Historical Review*, 10 (1995), 71–79.

[32] For the dating of these *assises* see M. Grandclaude, 'Liste d'assises remontant au premier royaume de Jérusalem (1099–1187)', *Mélanges Paul Fournier, Société d'histoire du droit* (Paris, 1929), pp. 329–45; and P. W. Edbury, *John of Ibelin and the Kingdom of Jerusalem* (Woodbridge, 1997).

[33] G. Paris and L. de Mas Latrie, *Les Gestes des Chiprois*, RHC, Documents Arméniens, 2 (Paris 1906), no. 202, p. 721: 'Le roy Amaury et ses hommes firent une assise que ja mais chevalier ne deüst ni feïst service a afaire de ville, ne de chasteau, ni en leuc que cheval ne peüst porter, se il ne fust assegié, ou sur son cours defendant'.

[34] WT, 11, 3, 18: 'lege edictali precipiens ut omnes illuc de singulis urbibus sine mora conveniant'.

Crusade was fought without any rules of command and discipline, although the rules were often broken due to circumstances. At crucial battles such as Dorylaeum (1097) and the Battle of Ascalon (1099) the army behaved as if it knew the laws of warfare and fought accordingly.[35] These rules included military discipline, and technical rules on how to charge in battle or conduct a siege.

Many historians of warfare assume that any theoretical knowledge of warfare in the crusader period was based on the classical work of Vegetius.[36] While Vegetius was indeed considered an authority,[37] medieval warriors were aware of the difference between the warfare of the Roman legion, mainly based on salaried infantry, and the needs of the medieval mounted knight. Thus the *Rule of the Templar Order*, a very elaborate handbook of their warfare formulated in the East,, was notoriously free of Vegetius' influence.[38] The rules of conduct in war as found in the thirteenth-century *Templar Rule* are mostly technical. Intended to regulate the everyday life of a monastic order, the *Rule* naturally included many paragraphs on ritual, conventional behaviour, etc., but precious little about the ethics of war. Being a military manual, it strongly emphasizes discipline, fortified by examples of the punishments for deviation from the rules.[39] The *Rule* contains numerous paragraphs dealing with punishment of cowardly behaviour in battle,[40] such as losing the banner or even just lowering it without permission,[41] leaving the battlefield without explicit orders from the commander, and

---

[35] J. France, *Victory in the East. A Military History of the First Crusade* (Cambridge, 1994), e.g. Fulcher of Chartres, I, 31, 7.

[36] Vegetius, *Epitome of Military Science,* trans. by N. P. Milner (Liverpool, 1993), esp. pp. 108–11 entitled 'General Rules of War', which was the part most frequently read in the Middle Ages. It does not contain the slightest hint of ethics or moral problems related to fighting.

[37] M. Prestwich, *Armies and Warfare in the Middle Ages: The English Experience* (New Haven, 1996), p. 184, cites Cambridge, Fitz-William Museum, MS Marlay. Add.1 fol. 2v, where the future Edward I is shown receiving the wisdom of Vegetius, *De re militari*. However, Prestwich himself concludes on p. 187: 'practical experience must have counted for much more than the dictates of Vegetius'. See John of Salisbury, *Policraticus. Of the Frivolities of Courtiers and the Footprints of Philosophers,* ed. and trans. by C. J. Nederman (Cambridge, 1990), VI, c. 19, p. 124. John wrote in c. 1159.

[38] See 'Introduction' to *The Rule of the Templars: The French Text of the Rule of the Order of the Knights Templars*, trans. by J. M. Upton-Ward (Woodbridge, 1992), Introduction.

[39] Ibid., no. 610, p. 157: 'It happened that Brother Jaques de Ravane was commander of the palace at Acre, and he took turcopoles and his sergeants, and made a raid on Casal Robert; and the Saracens of the land responded to the alarm and defeated them and seized some of the men; and he pleaded mercy for this and the habit was taken from him and he was put in irons, because he had made a raid without permission'.

[40] Ibid., no. 419; a brother who flees from the battle for fear of the Saracens while the piebald banner is aloft is expelled forever.

[41] Ibid., no. 611, p. 157.

breaking formation when charging into battle.[42] Although written in the Holy Land in the thirteenth century, this manual seems based on military usage and customs brought from Europe.[43]

In this case, as in the case of division of spoils, the military situation in the East reshaped existing custom to meet the special needs through more flexible conduct. The following stories show contrasting treatment of the same behaviour recklessly breaking the ranks. In 1147, William of Tyre tells us a warrior breaking the law was excused because he was successful:

> These troops kept making persistent and very spirited attacks upon the flanks of our army. Yet our soldiers under the commands (*proposita lege*) given them did not dare to break out of line against them. For, if contrary to the discipline of war (*rei militaris disciplinam*), they should break the ranks, they would be exposed to a harsh sentence as deserters from their places. In the retinue of that Turk who was with us, however, there was a certain knight who could not endure this situation and longed to relieve us of the annoyance. Regardless of the rules imposed (*legis inmemor*) and reckless of his life, he spurred his horse forward with great courage. He threw the spear which he was carrying against one of the four brothers, then ran him through with his sword in the midst of his ranks, and hurled the lifeless body to the ground. [. . .] It was discovered that he was an alien who might readily be pardoned for transgressing the rules (*legem propositam licebat ignorare*), especially as he did not know the language and had not understood the public edict. Accordingly, although he had undoubtedly acted contrary to the rules of military discipline (*rei militaris disciplinam*), yet, since he had been unaware of the command he was mercifully pardoned, and his deed was regarded as praiseworthy, rather because of its result than because it was right.[44]

In this passage William of Tyre uses the word *lex* three times, by which he clearly means military discipline. Although the breaking of the military code was condoned in this case, the emphasis on its legality shows that it was considered as binding and that disregarding it was contrary to accepted modes of warfare.

In the Third Crusade we find the same rules whose breach was condoned in 1147 now being strictly enforced:

> There was a certain knight whose valor would have won him renown if he had not infringed the rules of his order. Yet he seemed to have presumed that his action would be excused on the grounds of his bold prowess. This man was a Hospitaller named Robert of Bruges. He passed the royal standard and came up to the king. Then out of

[42] Ibid., no. 613, on charging without permission.

[43] *Leges Henrici Primi,* ed. by L. J. Downer (Oxford, 1972) cc. 13.12 and 10.1. M. Strickland, *War and Chivalry* (Cambridge 1996), pp. 115–24.

[44] WT, 16, 12, 21–40, trans. by Emily A. Babcock, II, 155–56.

> eagerness to engage the enemy and contrary to the discipline, he strongly spurred the excellent horse, on which he sat, abandoned the ranks of his comrades and before the others could advance in military order he charged alone into the enemy.[45]

Although the unruly knight courageously killed 'a very finely armed Turk', the master of his Order, Garnier of Nablus, ordered him to descend from his horse and had him disciplined severely—he had to return on foot to the tents and wait for his peers to beg mercy for him.

Thus, in the late twelfth century this law of war banning a reckless charge was apparently well known and regularly used. Nevertheless, at Mansurah in 1249, no less a person than Robert of Artois, the brother of King Louis IX, broke the law in the same way, charging headlong without waiting for permission, and with disastrous results.[46] It may be that the difference in discipline inheres in the difference between a member of the well-disciplined Military Orders and an individual knight striving to prove his valour by an exceptional feat even if that meant breaking the rules.

However, the most common discipline problem in battle was not to restrain overly courageous knights, but rather to keep the fainthearted from running away. Therefore, many of the sanctions against misdemeanours in the *Templar Rule* deal with this category of breach of discipline. In especially critical situations a commander might promulgate *ad hoc* rules of war, as Richard I did at Messina (1190): any common soldier running away was to lose a foot whereas a knight was to lose his belt, that is the symbol of his rank and military function.[47] For the common soldier the sanction was corporeal punishment, but the means for maintaining discipline in the ranks of the knights were more subtle, namely to use the notions of honour and shame as a deterrent. For knights, the fear of dishonour was the most effective sanction of the law of arms.[48] Other instances, described by chroniclers as 'laws of war',[49] are regulations for making camp, as when to pitch camp and how to keep watch. Not surprisingly these regulations were well known and usually adhered to by the crusaders in the East as by the armed forces in the West.

The rules of discipline probably existed before the crusades, inculcated as part of the military training. The main problem the commanders in the crusades faced was to

---

[45] *Chronicle of the Third Crusade,* V, c. 51, p. 330. Ambroise, *L'Estoire de la Guerre Sainte par Ambroise,* ed. by G. Paris (Paris, 1871), trans. by M. J. Hubert and J. L. La Monte, *The Crusade of Richard Lion-Heart by Ambroise* (New York, 1941), ll. 9908–46.

[46] Joinville, *Histoire de Saint Louis*, c. XLV, pp. 216–19.

[47] *Chronicon Richardi Divinensis de tempore regis Ricardi primi,* ed. and trans. by J. Appleby (London, 1963), p. 22: 'Sit lex servat sine remedio. Pedes pleno pede fugiens pedem perdat. Miles privitur cingulo'.

[48] M. Keen, *The Laws of War in the Late Middle Ages* (London, 1965), p. 20.

[49] For example, WT, 18, 13, 28; 16, 25, 13.

make the familiar rules valid and binding in the more fluid society of the crusader army on its way to fight in the Latin East.

More problematic, but still classed as belonging to the technical realm, were the laws of war governing the relationship between the belligerent sides. William of Tyre claimed that war was waged differently and less vigorously between men who hold the same law and faith than between those of diverse opinion and conflicting traditions.[50] If this indeed was the case, which comparison of the wars as conducted in the East and West by no means make certain, the technical laws of war were observed in the East as well. It was by no means a foregone conclusion that these rules were applicable in the East, in the engagement of a Muslim adversary. We do find agreements, however, made with the enemy and kept in line with the *lex pactorum*. In addition, the chivalrous idea of *diffidatio*—giving a formal defiance before attacking—was part of the normative behaviour towards the enemy.[51] In 1147 King Baldwin III was careful not to break a treaty with Anar of Damascus without prior notice. This example illustrates both phenomena: treaty keeping and defiance.

> There was an alliance and a temporary peace between Anar and King Baldwin which had existed also in the time of the king's father. Accordingly it was necessary that the governor be formally notified, in order that he might have a legitimate time, following the *custom of the land*, to assemble an army and make preparations for resistance. Otherwise the king would appear to have entered his territory suddenly and without official notice, which is contrary to the *law of treaties*.[52]

The same regard for customs of warfare emerges from what the chronicler wrote about Friedrich Barbarossa that 'his imperial majesty attacks no one without formal defiance. He always declares war on his enemies before attacking them. So the emperor sent a messenger with his sealed letter to Saladin'.[53] This was done not because of any notion of international law, which was still nonexistent,[54] but as part of the German

---

[50] WT, 13, 16, 53–55: 'Solet enim in hujusmodi conflictibus odiorum incentivum et inimicitiarum formitem dare maiorem sacrilegii et legis contempte dolor. Aliter enim et remissius solet inter consortes eiusdem legis et fidei pugna committi, aliter inter discolos et contradictorias habentes traditiones'.

[51] J. Gillingham, '1066 and the Introduction of Chivalry into England', in *Law and Government in Medieval England and Normandy,* ed. by G. Garnett and J. Hudson (Cambridge,1994), pp. 31–55, claims that *diffidatio* was a new custom in England in 1141 (p. 49).

[52] WT, 16, 8, 28–35.

[53] *Itinerarium peregrinorum,* trans. by Helen Nicholson, I, c. 18, p. 49. For the military aspects of defiance see M. Strickland, 'Provoking or Avoiding Battle? Challenge, Judicial Duel and Single Combat in Eleventh and Twelfth Century Warfare', in *Armies, Chivalry and Warfare in Medieval Britain and France,* ed. by M. Strickland (Stamford, 1998), pp. 317–43.

[54] W. Ullman, 'St Bernard and the Nascent International Law', in idem, *The Church and the*

emperor's chivalrous conduct. This notion of proper behaviour in war was, in this case, based both on the 'customs of the land' in the East and chivalrous traditions from the West. Can we identify any moral or ethical substance in this notion of chivalry or was it mainly a technical conception governing mounted fighting?

Ethical Codes

HUMANE ETHICAL LAWS RESTRICTING VIOLENCE AND CRUELTY IN WAR

I now move to the more elusive realm of moral behaviour. Were there rules similar to the examples furnished above defining ethical behaviour in war in the pre-crusade period? Can we extrapolate the existence of restraints on cruelty and violence from the actual conduct of war?

John France, who has written extensively about warfare both in the East[55] and in the West in the age of the crusades, maintains that combat was not without restraints: 'War had its ethics, and these were grafted on to the warrior ethos which infused the upper ranks of society and exalted the military virtues of bravery and loyalty to form what we call chivalry, the "Code of Conduct" of the European upper class'.[56] If operative ethics of war were part of the lay knights' social self-definition and cultural identity, when did they come into existence? Can one talk about chivalric *mores* in the West at the turn of the eleventh and twelfth centuries when the first crusades set out? It seems to me that when the crusaders left for the Holy Land these operative ethics were still in their embryonic stage. We search in vain for theoretical definitions of properly conducted warfare. Twelfth-century theoreticians of the law in the West found it more crucial to define a just war (*ius ad bellum*) than to ponder lawful behaviour in war (*ius in bello*). If the cause and aims were just, the actions taken in accordance with them were perceived as justifiable.[57] Seeing the crusade as the typical just war, and the main arena where a knight might win renown, the war against the infidel did not in principle have to be restrained.[58]

Law in the Earlier Middle Ages (London, 1975), ch. XVII, pp. 277–87.

[55] France, *Victory in the East*.

[56] J. France, *Western Warfare in the Age of the Crusades, 1000–1300* (London, 1999), p. 11.

[57] James Turner Johnson, 'Sources of the Western Just War Tradition', in *Just War and Jihad: Historical and Theoretical Perspectives on War and Peace in Western and Islamic Traditions,* ed. by J. Kelsay and J. T. Johnson (New York, 1991), pp. 3–30.

[58] See Otto of Freising, *The Deeds of Frederick Barbarossa,* trans. by C. C. Mierow (New York, 1966), p. 260: 'Let no one suppose we wage war at our whim. Since the war is just [. . .] let us act now to secure the highest praise of knighthood'.

It was the knightly code of chivalry, more than any other element in medieval culture that shaped the growing tradition of *ius in bello*.[59] The broader development of the idea of noncombatant immunity to include all persons not capable of bearing arms or not actually involved in bearing arms evolved from the code of chivalry and the self-restraint of the knightly class. This was not a law, but rather a dimly perceptible code of noble conduct on the battlefield.[60] At some point a denunciation of unseemly deeds that fly in the face of chivalrous behaviour seems to emerge. Can this be dated back to pre-crusade Europe? Was restraint in battle already an integral part of chivalry or did this moral sense simply not exist before the twelfth century?

Strickland assumed that William the Conqueror acted according to an existing social convention, which viewed this behaviour as appropriate when he offered compensation to the defenders of Dover in 1066 and protected the citizens of Exeter in 1068 once they had submitted.[61] But in trying to define the customs and *mores* on which William's conduct was based, Strickland doubts that there existed a 'law of war'—an *ius belli* that could guide the Conqueror at the end of the eleventh century.[62] Looking for precedents to prove the existence of such a code, Strickland returns to the Battle of Hastings (1066) as described by William of Malmesbury two generations later.[63] Although a bitterly fought war of conquest where no quarter was given, William the Conqueror punished a Norman knight, who gashed at the dead King Harold's thigh on the battlefield, by depriving this knight of his belt of knighthood. This punishment was apparently imposed for the knight's having behaved shamefully and for his having broken the code of knightly behaviour.[64] Assuming that this incident really happened as William of Malmesbury described it, it is still very problematic to try to date the growth of a general moral sense regarding what is honourable behaviour to a certain

---

[59] Johnson, 'Sources', p. 15.

[60] R. C. Stacey, 'The Age of Chivalry', in *The Laws of War,* ed. by M. Howard, G. Andreopoulos, and M. R. Shulman (New Haven, 1994), pp. 27–39.

[61] M. Strickland, *War and Chivalry. The Conduct and Perception of War in England and Normandy, 1066–1217* (Cambridge, 1996), p. 1.

[62] Ibid., p. 31.

[63] Ibid., pp. 4–5; William of Malmesbury, *De gestis regis Anglorum*, ed. by W. Stubbs, 2 vols, Rolls Series, 90 (London, 1887), II, 303. Incidentally, Karl Leyser uses the same example to trace the beginning of knighthood; see his, 'Early Medieval Canon Law and the Beginning of Knighthood, in *Institutionen, Kultur und Gesellschaft im Mittelalter, Festschrift für Josef Fleckenstein zu seinem 65. Geburtstag,* ed. by L. Fenske, W. Rosener, and T. Zotz (Sigmaringen, 1984), pp. 549–66. As if to prove that this conduct was still not commonplace, Bates also uses the same example to show the Conqueror as chivalrous; see *William the Conqueror* (London, 1989), p. 94.

[64] William of Malmesbury, *De gestis regis Anglorum,* II, 303: 'Jacentis femur unus militum gladio proscidit; unde a Willelmo ignominiae notatus, quod rem ignavam et pudendam fecisset, militia pulsus est'.

date.[65] It may well be that William the Conqueror's early chivalrous qualms stemmed from his abhorrence at dishonouring a king. Although he desired the rival king's death in order to inherit him, at the same time he did not want a king's body mutilated or treated with contempt. The time that passed between the event and its description is also critical. In trying to place the growth of chivalrous codes many historians name the twelfth century as the crucial period,[66] and William of Malmesbury may well make the conqueror behave according to the later *mores* of his own days.[67]

The same may be said about descriptions of chivalric behaviour in the East. For an example we again refer to William of Tyre, writing in the 1180s about Baldwin I's chivalrous behaviour in 1101. On a raid to Arabia, Baldwin found among his captives the wife of an Arab chieftain who was in labour. Not only did he refrain from hurting her, he provided her with a bed and other things needed for the birth, including two camels for milk and his own mantle for cover.[68] Baldwin's chivalrous behaviour was later repaid when her grateful husband saved the king's life at Ramle.[69] Curiously, Fulcher of Chartres, the king's chaplain and contemporary, knows nothing about this story which seems to fit the chivalrous ideas of the late twelfth century—saving a damsel in distress—better than the early years of the Latin Kingdom.[70] Even if this legendary feat did happen, contemporary chroniclers did not consider this a worthy subject for their histories. It may be that the king indeed felt compassion for the chieftain's wife, but this kind of humane behaviour toward a fragile enemy woman was not yet part of the social convention in the first years of the kingdom, as opposed to three generations later. The same Baldwin had no moral qualms about smoking out the women and children at the caves of Azopart (Bet Govrin?) and having some of the children beheaded with their mothers.[71] Presumably, Fulcher of Chartres accurately

---

[65] See William's treatment of his enemy's body after the battle and the story that he refused it a decent burial even after he was offered its weight in gold. For the different versions of Harold's burial see Strickland, *War and Chivalry*, p. 5, n. 18.

[66] See, for example, G. Duby, 'Au XIIe siècle: les "jeunes" dans la société aristocratique dans la France du nord-ouest', *Annales. Economies, Sociétés, Civilisations,* 19 (1964), 835–46; idem, *Les Trois ordres ou l'imaginaire du féudalisme* (Paris, 1978), pp. 347–52; M. Vale, *War and Chivalry: Warfare and Aristocratic Culture in England, France and Burgundy at the End of the Middle Ages* (Athens, GA, 1981); M. Keen, *Chivalry* (New Haven and London, 1984), p. 25 (dating the growth of tournaments); J. Flori, 'La notion de chevalerie dans les chansons de geste du XIIe siècle. Étude historique du vocabulaire', *Le Moyen Age,* 81 (1975), 211–44, 407–45.

[67] But see Gillingham, '1066 and the Introduction of Chivalry'.

[68] WT, 10, 10, 15–26.

[69] Ibid., 10, 20, 7–28; Fulcher of Chartres, II, 19, 1; 20, 1–2.

[70] Fulcher of Chartres was probably together with the king at the time, see II, 5.

[71] AA, VII, 40: 'When these two hundred and twenty had been beheaded, and their wickedness repaid on their heads by the genius of the most Christian Prince to avenge the pilgrims, only their women and children remained in the holes, with the pilgrim's spoils. When

reflects the prevailing state of affairs in his description of his feelings as a participant in battle in the early years of the Latin Kingdom: 'One struck, his enemy fell. The one knew no pity, the other asked none'.[72] And, as we have seen, the first decades of the Latin Kingdom of Jerusalem were characterized by fierce battles with no quarter given.

By the end of the twelfth century, however, there seem to be established conventions governing the ethical side of war. These conventions develop into written codes by the fourteenth century,[73] a state of affairs paralleling what we noted earlier with regard to the technical rules.

As an example of the later development in the East we may take the evidence of a Muslim chronicler. During the siege of Acre, Beha ad-Din tells us, the young boys were bored and wanted to take part in the fighting. A combat was arranged, a kind of tournament, between boys from both sides. When one of them won he was told by the elder spectators how to behave toward his opponent, namely, to take him as captive for ransom. By then, giving quarter and holding for ransom had become the accepted norm, a rule that one could teach to children and which was in principle binding on both sides.[74] Although killing of prisoners of war still occurred on both sides, by the end of the twelfth century it was no longer considered the right thing to do.

If the Battle of Hastings is not a reliable source for early chivalrous codes of restraint in battle, we can turn to Orderic Vitalis's *Ecclesiastical History,* which is often used to prove the existence of early chivalrous behaviour in the West.[75] The main example is the 'battle of the two kings' at Brémule 1119.[76] Orderic tells us admiringly that although nine hundred men fought only three were killed:

---

these knew of the murder of their men, because not one of them ever returned to them, they scarcely dared to go out. Because of this Baldwin was violently angry with them and he ordered wood, tow and straw to be brought in front of the mouth of every cave and set alight, until they were forced to emerge by the smoke and heat. At length, overwhelmed by the fierceness of the smoke and heat, the mothers and children, who lacked the strength of men, came out, albeit reluctantly and at once were given to the soldiers as booty and separated. Some of them were ransomed with their mothers, others indeed were beheaded with their mothers'.

[72] Fulcher of Chartres, II, 12, 1.

[73] *The Tree of Battles of Honoré Bonet*, trans. by G. W. Coopland (Liverpool, 1949), IV, 46: 'And written law allows that, so soon as a man has surrendered, and is a prisoner, mercy should be shown him, unless there were a risk of his escaping, with the result of prolonged war, damage or mischief'.

[74] Beha-ad-Din, *The Life of Saladin*, trans. by C. L. Conder, Palestine Pilgrims' Text Society, 12 (London, 1897), pp. 161–62.

[75] Marjorie Chibnall, *The Ecclesiastical History of Orderic Vitalis* (Oxford, 1978). Holdsworth, 'Ideas and Reality', uses Orderic as the main source for restraint in battle.

[76] Marjorie Chibnall, 'Anglo-French Relations in the Work of Orderic Vitalis', in *Documenting the Past: Essays in Medieval History Presented to George Peddy Cuttino,* ed. by J. S. Hamilton and Patricia J. Bradley (Woodbridge, 1989), pp. 5–19.

> They were all clad in mail and spared each other on both sides, out of fear of God and fellowship in arms; they were more concerned to capture than to kill the fugitives. As Christian soldiers they did not thirst for the blood of their brothers, but rejoiced in a just victory given by God.[77]

Whereas Holdsworth sees this description of chivalrous feelings as wishful thinking on the part of Orderic, he does not contest his description of facts.[78] The technical advancement in production of mail, making the knights better protected, as well as the proprietorial interests of the fighters may have counted for more than chivalrous inhibitions as an explanation to the low number of casualties. Nevertheless, another incident told by Orderic about the same battle seems to indicate that the battle of Brémule more resembled a huge tournament than a war: William Crispin tried to kill the English king who was saved by the collar of his hauberk. He was then taken captive by Roger fitz Robert who defended him from being lynched by flinging himself over his body.[79] This concern for the welfare of a prisoner of war seems to prove a beginning of a more chivalrous warfare in the West, although the fact that William Crispin was a noble captive, a rich prize, may have played a part. But this happened twenty-five years after the First Crusade set out, at a period when one can already find in the East the same reluctance to lose a valuable captive by killing him and giving quarter have become a common occurrence.

There is one striking point in the descriptions of chivalrous behaviour in battle both in the West and in the East: Chivalrous laws were for knights. They were implemented according to rank and social class. The distinction between combatants and noncombatants correlated with the social distinction between knights and infantry. This idea was not based on reality, as the infantry were certainly combatants. However, in the eyes of the knights warfare was their business and theoretically only they were supposed to take part in the game of war. Therefore foot soldiers could not expect any mercy after the battle and were often mercilessly killed on the spot. Mercy to a captured opponent was profitable if he could ransom himself, and ransom payments were among the most important profits of war, as the crusader learned from their Muslim enemies with their long tradition of taking captives for ransom. This did not include the infantry who were too poor to be worth the bother and accordingly suffered a harsh treatment. Therefore, armed townsmen and peasants could be and often were massacred at will in the early years of crusader conquest.

In the West the chivalric values were closely tied to the self-definition of the knights as a distinct social class.[80] When the Count of Anjou decided to free four

---

[77] Chibnall, *The Ecclesiastical History of Orderic Vitalis,* XII, 18, p. 241.

[78] Holdsworth, *Ideas and Reality*, p. 72.

[79] Chibnall, *The Ecclesiastical History of Orderic Vitalis,* XII, 18, p. 239.

[80] Margaret Switten, '*Chevalier* in French and Occitan Literature', in *The Study of Chivalry,*

captives who had composed a song in his honour the reason given was predominantly the solidarity towards members of the same social status: 'He has an inhuman heart who has no compassion for those of his own profession. Are we not knights? We therefore owe a special compassion to knights in need'.[81]

Thus in the middle of the twelfth century the profession of knighthood included the principle of benevolence towards fellow knights. This professional sensitivity towards people of one's own rank did not stop at the religious barrier. The same compassion, or mercenary feelings of greed, that spared the lives of prisoners of war in the West was sometimes shown towards highborn Muslim opponents in the East. The ethical customs of war were made up by the upper echelons of society to defend themselves.

To sum up, the chivalrous concept of showing mercy to a vanquished enemy was probably not yet part of the common legacy the crusaders brought with them from the West, although this idea was beginning to gain momentum.[82] It figures predominantly in chivalrous literature from the latter half of the twelfth century and seems to have become a social convention quite late. It could be that there was a parallel development in the East and West or it may even be possible that the crusaders were the first to absorb these *mores* in the East and that western chivalry learned it from returning crusaders. In the case of ethical laws, the crusaders do not seem to have come with a clear set of conventions and customs. Restraint practised in war, if it was learned at all, grew out of the everyday situation in the East and the growth of a social *ordo* of chivalry.

Resources and Approaches, ed. by H. Chickering and T. H. Seiler (Kalamazoo, 1988), pp. 403–48.

[81] *Chroniques des Comtes d'Anjou et des seigneurs d'Amboise,* ed. by L. Halphen and R. Poupardin (Paris, 1913), p. 196: 'Inhumani, inquit, cordis est qui sue non compatitur professioni. Si nos milites sumus, militibus debemus compassionem, presertim subactis'.

[82] Gillingham, '1066 and the Introduction of Chivalry', p. 52, cites William of Tyre's western contemporary, Giraldus Cambrensis, *Opera*, ed. by J. F. Dimock et al., 8 vols, Rolls Series (London, 1861–91), V, 246: 'In France, knights are held in captivity; here they are decapitated. There they are ransomed; here killed'. After an eloquent oration in favour of sparing the captives' lives (ibid. pp. 250–52) they are, however, killed. In the same way Gillingham proves early chivalric ethics in the west by citing William of Poitiers's panegyric exalting the Conqueror for treating rebels more mercifully than he might have done: 'He did not kill the rebel William of Arques, because the duke did not behave like other princes in killing prisoners of war or exacting the death penalty even when he was entitled to do so by custom or established law' (*iuxta ritum sive legum instituta*); Guillaume de Poitiers, *Histoire de Guillaume le Conquérant,* ed. and trans. by R. Foreville (Paris, 1952), I, pp. 8–20, 58, 62–65. But of course this also means that the established usage was to kill rebels.

RESPONSIBILITY FOR ONE'S OWN WARRIORS: RANSOM OF CAPTIVES

What kind of support could a vanquished warrior expect from his fellow fighters? If he were wounded, would anybody come to his aid? If he were taken captive, would anybody help him to regain his freedom?

To the best of my knowledge there was no law either in the West or the Christian East that regulated tending to wounded soldiers. But from the fact that almost every chronicler describing a battle mentions the wounded, it seems we can infer that they were indeed cared for in the best possible way, which may not have amounted to much.[83] Albert of Aachen mentions medical care given to Godfrey of Bouillon after a bear wounded him on the First Crusade (1097).[84] From the quick response to this crisis it seems we can extrapolate that from an early period some medical assistance was available on or near the battlefield. In the twelfth century, the transmission of medical knowledge in the West includes military surgery[85] and, in the East, the Hospitallers cared not only for sick pilgrims, but probably performed surgery on the battlefield.[86] Apparently a wounded knight could expect his comrades to come to his aid, to attempt to save his life. The success rate was of course another matter altogether.[87]

What could a captive expect from his comrades? There seems to be a gap between the enthusiasm to risk life and limb to save captives and the willingness to ransom them. In the East the call to liberate captives was used as a battle-cry both in the ill-fated crusade of 1101 and at the Battle of Tall-Danith 1115 when the bugles were sounded and the prince exhorted the army 'to deliver their captive comrades and slaughter the enemy'.[88] Although such a goal could not be enforced by law, it apparently could sway the warrior to fight more valiantly. Feelings of responsibility towards one's brothers-in-arms seem to slacken considerably when ransoming captives is the issue. Many captives were freed via paying of ransom, but evidently the problem of raising the money and

---

[83] Robert the Monk, *Historia Hierosolymitana*, RHC, Hocc., 3, p. 764, on medical care after the battle of Nicea. S. Edgington, 'Medical Knowledge in the Crusading Armies: The Evidence of Albert of Aachen and Others', in *The Military Orders. Fighting for the Faith and Caring for the Sick,* ed. by M. Barber (Aldershot, 1994), pp. 320–26.

[84] AA, III, 4, and Edgington, 'Medical Knowledge', p. 321.

[85] Linda M. Paterson, 'Military Surgery: Knights, Sergeants, and Raimon of Avignon's Version of the *Chirurgia* of Roger of Salerno', in *The Ideals and Practice of Medieval Knighthood,* ed. by C. Harper-Bill and Ruth Harvey (Woodbridge,1988), pp. 117–46.

[86] B. Z. Kedar, 'A Twelfth-Century Description of the Jerusalem Hospital', in *The Military Orders: Welfare and Warfare,* ed. by H. Nicholson (Aldershot, 1998), pp. 3–26, esp. pp. 7–8.

[87] See Usamah ibn Munquid's derogatory views on Frankish medicine in *An Arab-Syrian Gentleman and Warrior in the Period of the Crusades,* trans. by P. K. Hitti (New York, 1929), pp. 162–63.

[88] Walter the Chancellor, *The Antiochene Wars*, p. 102.

negotiating redemption was often seen as the captive knight's private hassle and not as the commanders' responsibility.[89]

In the West, the Church had a long tradition of seeing ransom of captives as an important act of charity.[90] As charity was not enforced by law, by viewing ransom as one of many charities this placed it in competition with more prestigious goals, among them endowments to ecclesiastical institutions.

Ransom of captives found its place in canon law and was promulgated by the Church as saintly behaviour. Gregory the Great (597),[91] whose letter was later incorporated in the canon law in Gratian's *Decretum,* decreed that church vessels could be alienated for only one reason—ransom of captives.[92] And this was apparently done. Prominent leaders of the early medieval church like Caesarius of Arles[93] and Adalbert of Prague[94] worked strenuously to ransom captives and to buy freedom from slavery. When the Vikings captured Emma, the wife of the Viscount of Limoges, church vessels were sold to ransom her (1010).[95] The monks of Cluny stripped the altar of their church to free their abbot Mayol.[96] However, none of the above examples of early ransom in the West were connected with knights taken captive in battle. Ransoming of non-combatants did not necessarily reflect on the conducts of the knights or the lords. It may also be that the Church's positive view of ransom of captives shifted the burden of responsibility off the shoulders of the lay forces, and therefore ransom was still the private plight of the captive.

Strickland thinks, however, that ransom of captives was already the norm in the West in the early eleventh century. Thus the treaty between Hugh of Lusignan and Count William V of Aquitaine, drawn up in the first quarter of the eleventh century, assumes the ransoming of captured knights as a norm of conduct. This norm might, however, be violated: the treaty reveals that Hugh's opponent Geoffrey de Thouars had

---

[89] Y. Friedman, 'The Ransom of Captives in the Latin Kingdom of Jerusalem', in *Autour de la Première Croisade,* ed. by M. Balard (Paris, 1996), pp. 177–89.

[90] C. Osiek, 'The Ransom of Captives: Evolution of a Tradition', *Harvard Theological Review*, 74 (1981), 356–86.

[91] Gregory the Great, *Registrum epistolarum*, ed. by D. Norberg, VII, Ep. 35, CCCM, 140–140A (Turnhout, 1982), pp. 498–99.

[92] DG, I:2, C. XII, q. II, c. 13–16, pp. 690–91, 'Vasa sacra, nisi pro redemptione captivorum non sunt alienanda'.

[93] W. Klingshirn, 'Charity and Power: Caesarius of Arles and the Ransoming of Captives in sub-Roman Gaul', *Journal of Roman Studies,* 75 (1985), pp. 183–203.

[94] Johannis Canaparius, *Vita S. Adalberti episcopi*, c. 12, MGH, SS, 4, ed. by G. H. Pertz et al. (Berlin, 1841) p. 586; M. Toch, 'The European Jews of the Early Middle Ages: Slave-traders?', *Zion,* 64 (1999), 39–64, and esp. p. 52, nn. 60–64 [in Hebrew]. I want to thank Michael Toch for enlightening me on this subject.

[95] Ademar of Chabannes, *Chronicon* III, 44, p. 164.

[96] Rodulfus Glaber, *Historiarum libri quinque*, I, iv, 9, p. 19.

mutilated some of Hugh's knights, and in reprisal Hugh refused to ransom some of Geoffrey's men he had captured.[97] While the treaty seems to prove a convention of ransom, and even a price for a knight, it does not prove that taking responsibility for one's knight was a regular practice. In the West a knight who was lucky enough to be held for ransom knew that he had to fend for himself.[98]

This lack of tradition of ransom stands in contrast to the situation in Spain. In Spain, another arena of conflict with the Muslims, the town *militia* saw themselves as responsible for ransoming the soldier they had sent to battle from quite an early period.[99] This custom became part of the written law in the thirteenth-century *Las siete partidas*.[100] A special official called *alfaqueque* was commissioned to negotiate ransom and his commercial benefits were strictly defined.[101] Giving money for ransom was regarded as a prestigious kind of charity suitable for lay nobles in Spain much earlier than elsewhere in the West and in the East. Thus around 1100 the Countess of Valence left in her will money for ransoming captives and for the upkeep of bridges, another usual form for charity supposed to be suitable for lay nobles.[102] In the frontier war of the Spanish Reconquista, ransom of captives was clearly the norm.

The crusaders arriving in the East do not seem to have been ready to ransom their comrades. The lord's responsibility to ransom his men did not become part of the law of the Latin Kingdom. The thirteenth-century assizes stipulated that vassals had to contribute to the ransom of their king, and even sell their fief if they were without heirs.[103] Judging from the long time King Baldwin II was in captivity (sixteen months,

---

[97] J. Martindale, 'Conventum inter Guillelmum Aquitanorum comes et Hugonem Chiliarchum', *English Historical Review*, 84 (1969), 528–48, at p. 543: 'Et ut vidit Ugo quod non haberet terram cepit de caballarios Toarcinse XLIII ex meliores. Potuissetque habere pacem et suas terras firmas et iusticiam de malifacto; et si accipere voluisset redemptionem, potuisset capere solidos l milia'. Strickland, *War and Chivalry*, p. 134.

[98] See Guibert of Nogent's story about his father who was taken captive by William the Conqueror (1054) and not likely to be freed, as 'it was the custom of this count never to hold prisoners for ransom, but to condemn them to captivity for life'. But apparently he gained his freedom somehow anyway, as he was present at Guibert's birth. *Self and Society in Medieval France, the Memoirs of Guibert of Nogent*, ed. by J. F. Benton (New York, 1970), c. 13, p. 69.

[99] J. W. Brodman, 'Municipal Ransoming Law on the Medieval Spanish Frontier', *Speculum*, 60 (1985), 318–30; J. F. Powers, *A Society Organized for War* (Berkeley, 1988).

[100] *Las siete partidas del muy noble rey Don Alfonso el Sabio*, ed. by G. López, 4 vols (Madrid, 1843–44).

[101] *Las siete partidas*, partida II, tit. 30, 2–3

[102] *Liber Feudorum Maior, Cartulario real que se conserva en el Archivo de la Corona de Aragon*, ed. by F. M. Rosell (Barcelona, 1944), n. 142, *Testamentum Valentiae comitissae Paliarensis*, 19.2.1101, p. 138: 'et alia parte sit per captivos et per pontes'.

[103] *Livre de Jean d'Ibelin*, in *Assises de Jerusalem*, ed. by A. A. Beugnot, RHC, Lois, 1 (Paris, 1841), c. 249, p. 397.

from April 1123 to August 1124) this law was not in force in the first half of the twelfth century. Other notable captives of that period, such as Bohemond, Joscelin of Courtney, and later Reynauld de Chatillon (almost sixteen years in captivity) and Baldwin of Ibelin had to ransom themselves or look for help from the Byzantine Emperor or Armenian princes who were more used to seeing ransom as their task. The early crusaders did not expect to be ransomed by their peers, and only reluctantly contributed towards the ransom of their lord. The law stipulated that a son had to ransom his father, but not vice versa, and some of the early crusaders left resources at home in case they needed to be ransomed and no help was forthcoming in the East.

In the thirteenth century, after captivity became a more widespread and common phenomenon and many found themselves in that quandary, we see a slow change in customs and conventions. But this change did not have sufficient time to become an important part of the written law. The law governing ransom of captives in the Latin kingdom lagged much behind the clearly formulated law in Spain. In the fourteenth century these laws were incorporated in western customs and were recorded in such works as *The Tree of Battle* as part of the laws of war. But by that time the Latin Kingdom was no longer in existence.

Conclusion

The embryonic laws of war in the Latin Kingdom grew out of the interaction between the customs brought from the West, where the enemy was usually a Christian neighbour, and the new situation faced when fighting a Muslim adversary. Paradoxically, war with infidels, in Spain and the Holy Land, promoted the development of a more regulated warfare than the internecine struggles. Although changes in conduct of warfare proceeded at differing rates for different customs and places, all were influenced by the encounter with the enemy. The more flexible technical laws of warfare changed according to the special needs that arose while fighting a Muslim enemy. Changes in the sphere of moral behaviour in battle are more difficult to chart. They did not develop as a result of a growing moral sensitivity. Once again, contact with the infidel and their practices seems to have influenced crusader *mores*. The need to free captives from infidel hands made the crusaders aware of the more advanced customs in the East, where ransom of captives was practised for centuries before the crusades. The life on the frontier with a Muslim enemy taught the crusaders in Spain to take responsibility for their brothers-in arms. The same process seems to have started in the Latin East. But due to the Latin Kingdom's brief existence, these trends did not develop as fully as in Spain, nor did the laws of war in the Latin Kingdom of Jerusalem reach the same level. Nonetheless, the laws that did emerge in the Latin East and were brought to Europe by the returning crusaders, may have contributed to the development of laws of war in the West as articulated in the fourteenth-century codified laws of war.

Pilgrimage in Crusader Acre: The *Pardouns dAcre*

DAVID JACOBY

Western pilgrimage to the Holy Land entered a new era after the crusader conquest of Jerusalem in 1099. It became a mass movement, which continued until the collapse of Frankish rule in the Levant in 1291. It has been suggested, however, that the volume of pilgrimage shrank after 1187 as a result of several factors: the loss of Jerusalem to Saladin in that year, Muslim rule over the city until 1291, except from 1229 to 1244, and periods of tense political relations and military confrontations between Latins and Muslims.[1] To be sure, these factors undoubtedly had an impact on pilgrimage and occasionally impaired or even prevented access to Jerusalem or to other holy sites. Yet quantitative and circumstantial evidence provided by public and notarial documents, more reliable that narrative sources,[2] points to an increase in the number of pilgrims reaching the Holy Land in the course of the thirteenth century.[3] Acre fulfilled an exclusive role in the pilgrim traffic during the

---

[1] See M.-L. Favreau-Lilie, 'Durchreisende und Zuwanderer. Zur Rolle der Italiener in den Kreutzfahrerstaaten', in *Die Kreuzfahrerstaaten als Multikulturelle Gesellschaft. Einwanderer und Minderheiten im 12. und 13. Jahrhundert*, ed. by H. E. Mayer, Schriften des Historischen Kollegs, Kolloquien, 37 (München, 1997), pp. 206, 209–11, 217.

[2] Sources examined by B. Z. Kedar, 'The Passenger List of a Crusader Ship, 1250', *Studi Medievali,* 13 (1972), 267–79 (reprinted in idem, *The Franks in the Levant, 11th to 14th Centuries* (Aldershot, 1993), no. XVI); D. Jacoby, 'Il ruolo di Acri nel pellegrinaggio a Gerusalemme', in *Il cammino di Gerusalemme*, ed. by M. S. Calò Mariani (Bari, in press), nn. 39–42.

[3] Favreau-Lilie, 'Durchreisende und Zuwanderer', pp. 210–11, contends that the number of

Frankish period. Shortly after its conquest by the Latins in 1104 it became the only Levantine port through which pilgrims transited on their way to and from the holy sites.[4]

The agreement reached by Frederick II with Sultan al Kamil in 1229, which secured the return of Christian rule over Jerusalem and a safe corridor to the city,[5] obviously stimulated pilgrimage. A few years later, in 1234, Aubrey of Trois-Fontaines noted that many Latins and other Christians were visiting the Holy Sepulchre.[6] In Jerusalem the patriarchs appear to have enjoyed substantial revenues from pilgrimage from 1229 to 1244.[7] An agreement reached in Acre by the Templars and the Hospitallers with Marseillais merchants, ratified the following year, granted the two Orders permission to take each year out of Marseilles up to 1,500 pilgrims on board two of their respective ships.[8] If these indeed sailed with such numbers of passengers, the total of pilgrims leaving Marseilles on these vessels alone must have reached the 6,000 mark each year.

One would assume that the renewed loss of Jerusalem to the Muslims in 1244 severely reduced western pilgrimage, yet the evidence points to its continuation on a large scale after that event. In 1248 it was expected that the Genoese vessel *Oliva* would take 1,100 passengers to Acre.[9] A Marseillais statute of 1253 reveals that ships

---

pilgrims passing through crusader ports was reduced by the opening of an alternative pilgrimage route via Egypt. This construct rests on a misunderstanding of the charter granted in 1208 by Sultan al 'Adil to Venice: *Urkunden zur älteren Handels- und Staatsgeschichte der Republik Venedig,* ed. by G. L. F. Tafel and G. M. Thomas (Vienna, 1856–57), II, 187–88, with correct dating by W. Heyd, *Histoire du commerce du Levant au moyen âge* (Leipzig, 1885–86), I, 401–04. The charter ensured the safety of Venetian ships sailing to Alexandria and those transporting pilgrims, yet does *not* imply that these arrived in the Egyptian port. Acre was the only destination of Venetian ships carrying pilgrims, as illustrated by various sources, including the Venetian maritime legislation of 1233 and 1255: *Gli statuti marittimi veneziani fino al 1255,* ed. by R. Predelli and A. Sacerdoti (Venice, 1903), pp. 74–75, par. 5, and p. 165, par. 115. See also Jacoby, 'Il ruolo di Acri'.

[4] See Jacoby, 'Il ruolo di Acri'.

[5] See S. Runciman, *A History of the Crusades*, 3 vols (Cambridge, 1953–54), III, 186–88.

[6] Albericus Trium Fontium, *Chronica*, ed. by P. Scheffer-Boichorst, MGH, SS, 23 (Hannover, 1874), p. 935.

[7] See B. Hamilton, *The Latin Church in the Crusader States. The Secular Church* (London, 1980), pp. 288–89.

[8] *Cartulaire général de l'Ordre des Hospitaliers de Saint-Jean de Jérusalem (1100–1310),* ed. by J. Delaville le Roulx (Paris, 1894–1906), II, 462–64, 469, nos 2067 and 2079. By then the two Orders had been engaging in the transportation of pilgrims from Marseilles for fifteen years at least: see H. E. Mayer, *Marseilles Levantehandel und ein akkonensisches Fälscheratelier des 13. Jahrhunderts*, Bibliothek des Deutschen historischen Instituts in Rom, 38 (Tübingen, 1972), pp. 80–81.

[9] *Genoese Shipping in the Twelfth and Thirteenth Century,* ed. by E. H. Byrne (Cambridge, MA, 1930), p. 81, doc. XV; see also J. H. Pryor, 'The Naval Architecture of Crusader Transport

transporting 1,000 pilgrims were not exceptional.[10] It follows that, except in times of warfare in the Mediterranean or in Acre itself, numerous pilgrims reached that city either in the spring or in the autumn, each time presumably well beyond ten thousand. It is noteworthy that pilgrims travelled from Acre to Jerusalem even in 1260, despite Mongol razzias and the threat of a Mongol invasion, which created rather unstable conditions in the region.[11] In 1271 the Venetian brothers Niccolò and Matteo Polo, together with the former's son, the later famous Marco Polo, took advantage of their stay at Acre to visit Jerusalem, which implies that pilgrimage was routinely continuing.[12] The Dominican Riccoldo da Monte Croce reports that on the day of Epiphany in 1289 there were more than 10,000 pilgrims of all nations on the banks of the River Jordan, at the place where according to tradition Christ had been baptized.[13] Even if we do not take this figure at face value, we may safely assume that a large number of pilgrims had reached the Jordan in early January, although most pilgrims preferred to visit the Holy Land in the spring in order to attend the Easter festivities in Jerusalem.

Most pilgrims sailed home on the same ships that had brought them to Acre. These ships remained in Levantine waters for a short period only, a whole month at most. As a result the pilgrims' stay was limited in time and their departure could not be postponed, unless they opted to remain in the Holy Land for a longer period, as throughout the winter months when transmediterranean shipping was at a standstill. At various occasions political or military circumstances prevented pilgrims and crusaders from visiting Jerusalem or other holy sites or from reaching Acre in time for their return voyage, and they were thus unable to fulfill their pilgrimage vow. It is in this context that the *pardouns dAcre* should be considered.

Though well known, this short French text has never been closely examined. It appears in a single fourteenth-century manuscript of the British Library after an itinerary of pilgrimage to various sites in the Holy Land.[14] It lists forty locations and

---

Ships: A Reconstruction of Some Archetypes for Round-Hulled Sailing Ships', *The Mariner's Mirror,* 70 (1984), 374–75 (reprinted in idem, *Commerce, Shipping and Naval Warfare in the Medieval Mediterranean* (London, 1987), no. VII).

[10] *Les statuts municipaux de Marseille,* ed. by R. Pernoud (Monaco and Paris, 1949), I, c. 35, pp. 49–50.

[11] On conditions in Syria-Palestine at that time, see P. Jackson, 'The Crisis in the Holy Land in 1260', *English Historical Review,* 95 (1980), 481–513; R. Amitai-Preiss, *Mongols and Mamluks. The Mamluk-Ilkhanid War, 1260–1281* (Cambridge, 1995), pp. 26–45.

[12] Marco Polo, *Il Milione. Prima edizione integrale*, ed. by F. Benedetto (Florence, 1928), cc. X–XI, pp. 7–8.

[13] The figure is recorded in an unpublished manuscript of his *Liber peregrinationis*, cited by E. Panella, 'Ricerche su Riccoldo da Monte Croce', *Archivum fratrum praedicatorum,* 58 (1988), 8–9.

[14] *Itinéraires à Jérusalem et descriptions de la Terre Sainte rédigés en français aux XIe, XIIe et XIIIe siècles,* ed. by H. Michelant and G. Raynaud (Genève, 1882), pp. 235–36 and 229–35

specifies the period for which remission of divine temporal punishment was granted at each of them. However, the *pardouns dAcre* do not deal only with individual sites. Once they are projected on thirteenth-century maps of Acre, they turn out to provide a pilgrimage itinerary, in line with the Holy Land itinerary preceding them in the manuscript. Two sets of maps reflect the topography of Acre in the late thirteenth century, one coming from the workshop of the Genoese cartographer Pietro Vesconte and the other appearing in the manuscripts of Paolino Veneto's *Universal Chronicle*. While similar in various ways, the two sets of maps display some wide discrepancies between them with respect to the configuration of quarters and streets, the location of buildings, and the inscriptions identifying urban districts or structures. To some extent, though, they are complementary, which proves to be extremely useful for our purposes, especially if they are combined with evidence culled from written sources.[15]

The first site mentioned in the *pardouns dAcre* is *la bourde la vile*, the meaning of which remains unclear.[16] In any event, this site was located outside the city walls like the following one, the church of St Nicholas located in the cemetery bearing the same name, which extended along the northern section of the Old City's eastern flank.[17] In order to reach the next site, the church of the Teutonic Order, one entered the Old City through the Gate of St Nicholas opening in the outer wall and the *Porta peregrinorum* in the inner one. Both gates are identified by inscriptions on the Vesconte and Paolino maps.[18] Originally the appellation St Nicholas was applied to a gate in the single wall protecting Acre before 1187. After the building of the outer wall between 1198 and

---

respectively. The mistakes appearing in the extant version of the *pardouns dAcre* may be safely ascribed to the copyist, who worked after the fall of Acre and was unfamiliar with the city's topography.

[15] On the maps, see D. Jacoby, 'Crusader Acre in the Thirteenth Century: Urban Layout and Topography', *Studi medievali,* 3rd ser., 20 (1979), 2–7 (reprinted in idem, *Studies on the Crusader States and on Venetian Expansion* (Northampton, 1989), no. V). Both maps appear in that study, in addition to my own reconstruction of Acre's topography.

[16] B. Dichter, *The Orders and Churches of Crusader Acre* (Acre, 1979), is the first attempt to list Acre's ecclesiastical institutions in the Frankish period and to deal with their history, yet his work is incomplete, riddled with errors, and unreliable. The forthcoming third volume of D. Pringle, *The Churches of the Crusader Kingdom of Jerusalem. A Corpus*, will offer solid evidence in this respect. I have not attempted here to locate all the forty sites mentioned in the *pardouns dAcre.*

[17] Location of the church mentioned in a charter of 1254: Delaville le Roulx, *Cartulaire*, II, 779–80, no. 2732. Evidence for this church from the same period is in *Tabulae ordinis theutonici,* ed. by E. Strehlke (Berlin, 1869), pp. 68–69, no. 86. I use 'Old City' here for the urban area enclosed by a single wall existing before the addition of the suburb Montmusard, on which see below, n. 19.

[18] The inscription on Vesconte's map reads *turris peregrinorum*, whereas that on Paolino's map is simply *peregrinorum*.

1212, the name of St Nicholas was transferred to a gate in that wall similarly facing the cemetery.[19] This would explain the renaming of the gate formerly called St Nicholas. There is reason to believe that its new appellation, *Porta peregrinorum*, was connected with the itinerary described by the *pardouns dAcre*. It signalled the beginning of urban pilgrimage in Acre proper.

From the Pilgrims' Gate one proceeded southwards to the nearby church of the Teutonic Order, close to the *turris Alamanorum* depicted on Vesconte's map and situated in the area identified by the inscription *Alamani* on Paolino's map. From the *pardouns dAcre* we may gather that St Leonard was positioned to the north of the German church on the way to St Romanus 'of the gardens', *de zardinis* or *a zardini* on the maps, located close to the north-eastern corner of the Old City. From there the itinerary led westward, to St Samuel of the Premonstratensian canons, the property of which included a tower *in muro Accon*, most likely along the Old City's northern wall. The possession of this tower had been confirmed by King Baldwin V in 1185.[20] It should be observed that several Latin ecclesiastical institutions in Acre pursued a systematic acquisition policy aimed at creating clusters of property around their main building.[21]

The next sites mentioned in the *pardouns dAcre* appear on the maps of Acre, Vesconte's topography being more reliable. After the nunnery of St Lazarus of Bethany came St Mary 'of the knights', signalled on the maps as *dei cavalieri* or *militum*, and the cathedral of the Holy Cross somewhat further south. From there one continued southward to the church of S. Marco in the Venetian quarter and westward to S. Lorenzo in the Genoese compound,[22] within which the abbey of St Mary of the Valley

---

[19] On the inner and outer walls, see D. Jacoby, 'Montmusard, Suburb of Crusader Acre: The First Stage of its Development', in *Outremer. Studies in the History of the Kingdom of Jerusalem, presented to Joshua Prawer,* ed. by B. Z. Kedar, H. E. Mayer, and R. C. Smail (Jerusalem, 1972), pp. 211–17 (reprinted in Jacoby, *Studies on the Crusader States*, no. VI) . D. Pringle, 'Town Defences in the Crusader Kingdom of Jerusalem', in *Medieval City under Siege,* ed. by A. Corfis and M. Wolfe (Woodbridge, 1995), pp. 81–84, proposes a different chronology for the fortification of Montmusard, with which I disagree. I shall return elsewhere to that issue.

[20] The charter is edited by H. E. Mayer, 'St. Samuel auf dem Freudenberg und sein Besitz nach einem unbekannten Diplom Balduins V.', *Quellen und Forschungen aus italienischen Archiven und Bibliotheken,* 44 (1964), 67–71, esp. 69–70 (reprinted in idem, *Kreuzzüge und lateinischer Osten* (London, 1983), no. VIII).

[21] See D. Jacoby, 'Les communes italiennes et les Ordres militaires à Acre: Aspects juridiques, territoriaux et militaires (1104–1187, 1191–1291)', in *État et colonisation au Moyen Age,* ed. by M. Balard (Lyon, 1989), pp. 198–208 (reprinted in D. Jacoby, *Trade, Commodities and Shipping in the Medieval Mediterranean* (Aldershot, 1997), no. VI).

[22] On these two quarters, see Jacoby, 'Crusader Acre', pp. 26–36. S. Lorenzo is depicted in a conventional way on the Vesconte map.

of Josaphat was positioned.[23] Then followed S. Pietro in the Pisan quarter,[24] St Anna at the western edge of the latter,[25] the hospital of the Holy Spirit, built on Pisan land and administered by the Crociferi Order of Bologna,[26] the church of St Andrew on the southern shore of the Old City, as marked on Paolino's map, and that of the Templars in the latter's south-west corner. From there the itinerary proceeded northward along the western shore of the city, reaching the Dominican church and later St Michael, which was situated close to St Michael's Gate, marked on Paolino's map as the most western opening along the northern flank of the Old City. Further east lay the church and the *domus infirmorum* of the Hospitallers, called *paleis des malades* in the *pardouns dAcre*. Both structures appear on Paolino's map. These were the last pilgrimage stations in the Old City.

From there the itinerary crossed into the suburb of Montmusard, leading to St Gilles and to the Cistercian abbey of St Mary Magdalen,[27] then to the hospital of St Catherine, located close to the shore, and to the monastery of the Holy Trinity in its vicinity.[28] It proceeded northward along the shore to St Bridget of Kildare, named after a saint popular in Ireland and England,[29] to the hospital named after St Martin, built by the Bretons, which does not appear on the maps,[30] then to the north-east towards the hospital of the Order of St Lazarus 'of the knights'.[31] All these three institutions were located within the *vicus Anglorum* or English quarter, situated at the northern tip of Montmusard. St Lazarus was close to the *bovaria Templi*, located to its east, and to the St Lazarus Gate, apparently the second one from the shore opening in the inner wall of

---

[23] As we may gather from a house in the Genoese quarter bordering on the courtyard of the abbey (9 December 1261): *Chartes de Terre Sainte provenant de l'abbaye de N.-D. de Josaphat,* ed. by H.-F. Delaborde (Paris, 1880), pp. 109–10, no. 53.

[24] On which see Jacoby, 'Crusader Acre', pp. 19–26.

[25] *Documenti sulle relazioni delle città toscane coll'Oriente cristiano e coi Turchi fino all'anno MDXXXI,* ed. by G. Müller (Florence, 1879), p. 14, no. 11. See also Jacoby, 'Crusader Acre', p. 20.

[26] Müller, *Documenti*, pp. 94–95, no. 63. See also M.-L. Favreau-Lilie, 'Die italienischen Kirchen im Heiligen Land (1098–1291)', *Studi veneziani,* new ser., 13 (1987), 41–44.

[27] The proximity of the two institutions is attested in 1225: Delaville le Roulx, *Cartulaire,* II, 344–45, no. 1828.

[28] Paolino marks the former and Vesconte the latter approximately in the same urban area. Their proximity is attested in 1253: Strehlke, *Tabulae*, pp. 82–84, no. 104. On the suburb, see Jacoby, 'Montmusard', pp. 205–17.

[29] See D. Jacoby, 'Some Unpublished Seals from the Latin East', *Israel Numismatic Journal,* 5 (1981), 86–88.

[30] Ibid., pp. 86–87.

[31] Ibid., p. 86 and n. 23. I mistakenly followed there the Vesconte map, which mentions *Sanctus Laurentius de cavaleriis*, yet no such institution existed in Acre. Paolino's map has the right inscription for the hospital, *Sanctus Lazarus militum.*

Montmusard.[32] The English hospital named after St Thomas of Canterbury stood to the north of St Lazarus.[33] St Bartholomew was on the way from there to the hospital of St Anthony, located next to St Anthony's Gate at the southeastern corner of Montmusard.[34] The Franciscan monastery, which was the next station, must have been in the vicinity. Its siting on Vesconte's map as *Fratres minores* differs from that on Paolino's map, where it is marked as *locus minorum*. St Denys appears on both maps just north of the wall separating Montmusard from the Old City. St Georges, the last site mentioned in our itinerary, must have been nearby in the suburb.

The *pardouns dAcre* do not offer any evidence regarding the date of their composition, yet contain various clues that enable us to arrive at some conclusions in this respect. Our itinerary mentions a number of institutions situated in the suburb of Montmusard, which began to develop after 1191.[35] St Thomas of Canterbury was transferred from the Old City to the suburb in 1228–29,[36] and St Martin of the Bretons was established there in 1254 or 1255.[37] St Bridget offers the latest possible date, since it is mentioned for the first time in 1264 as an existing institution.[38] It follows that the *pardouns dAcre* were compiled between 1254 and 1264, yet a more accurate dating is possible. A brief look at its text reveals wide discrepancies in the remission of temporal punishment gained at the various sites. These discrepancies are particularly flagrant when we compare the indulgences obtained at the churches located within the quarters of the three major maritime powers. Whereas the rate of both S. Marco of the Venetians and S. Pietro of the Pisans was five years, the indulgence acquired at S. Lorenzo of the Genoese was limited to forty days. The only plausible explanation for this wide gap is that the latter reflects conditions existing after the war of St Sabas, which ended in 1258 with the decisive victory of Venice and Pisa over Genoa, the destruction of the Genoese quarter and the exodus of the Genoese settlers from Acre. However, the Genoese church of S. Lorenzo was preserved, as revealed by a small legacy from which it benefited in 1264. Genoese merchants occasionally visited Acre after 1258, yet the absence of an official Genoese representative residing in the city clearly weakened the standing of S.

---

[32] Location attested in 1240: Comte de Marsy, 'Fragment d'un cartulaire de l'ordre de Saint Lazare en Terre Sainte', *Archives de l'Orient latin,* 2.2 (1884), 155–57, doc. 39. Vesconte's map depicts the *bovaria Templi* next to St Lazarus and, therefore, is more accurate in this respect. Yet this implies that the St Lazarus Gate was not the most western one, as on that map. Its siting is correctly reflected on Paolino's map.

[33] See the document cited in the previous note.

[34] For its location, see Jacoby, 'Montmusard', pp. 209 (map of Pietro Vesconte) and 216.

[35] See above, n. 19.

[36] See A. Forey, 'The Military Order of St Thomas of Acre', *English Historical Review,* 92 (1977), 486–88 (reprinted in idem, *Military Orders and Crusades* (Aldershot, 1994), no. XII).

[37] J. Delaville le Roulx, 'Titres de l'hôpital des Bretons d'Acre', *Archives de l'Orient latin,* 1 (1881), 425–26.

[38] See Jacoby, 'Some Unpublished Seals', pp. 86–88

Lorenzo.[39] We may thus conclude that the *pardouns dAcre* were composed between 1258 and 1264.

This approximate dating does not yet reveal when Acre's urban pilgrimage was established. In accordance with Jewish tradition, Acre was not considered by Christians part of the Holy Land, it had no claim to sanctity, nor could it boast of any holy sites.[40] It could therefore not compete with Jerusalem nor with any major shrines before 1187, and this was again the case from 1229 to 1244, when Jerusalem was once more under Frankish rule. Until 1187 Acre functioned exclusively as a transit station for pilgrims. Conditions changed during the two periods in which Jerusalem was in Muslim hands, from 1187 to 1229 and again since 1244. During the first of these periods the Christians still entertained some hope that they would recover the Holy City. The second loss of Jerusalem in 1244 and, especially, the failure of King Louis IX of France to achieve what Frederick II had succeeded in doing, buried all prospects in this respect. Therefore, the most likely date for the emergence of the institutionalized Acre pilgrimage is after the departure of Louis IX from Acre in 1254.[41]

The visit to forty sites included in the long and winding itinerary through the Old City of Acre and its suburb of Montmusard, which entailed spiritual benefits, was primarily intended for pilgrims and crusaders who had endured the hardship and expenses of the voyage from the West to the Holy Land, yet were prevented from reaching Jerusalem or other major shrines because of unfavourable conditions. It would seem, however, that the substitute pilgrimage in Acre rapidly acquired respectability and was also adopted by pilgrims who had access to these sites. This is suggested by the fourteenth-century manuscript, which reproduces the *pardouns dAcre* after the pilgrimage itinerary through the Holy Land. In all likelihood this manuscript follows a model executed before the fall of Acre in 1291.

The establishment of institutionalized pilgrimage in Acre raises a series of tantalizing questions, not all of which can be answered. Which driving force or multiple

---

[39] On the impact of the war on that quarter, see D. Jacoby, 'L'Expansion occidentale dans le Levant: Les Vénitiens à Acre dans la seconde moitié du treizième siècle', *Journal of Medieval History,* 3 (1977), 228 (reprinted in idem, *Recherches sur la Méditerranée orientale du XIIe au XVe siècle. Peuples, sociétés, économies* (London, 1979), no. VII); also idem, 'Crusader Acre', pp. 27–29. An additional illustration of Genoa's weak position in Acre in 1267 is provided by the complaint of a Genoese cleric before his city's bishop. He was prevented from enjoying the prebend he was entitled to as canon of Acre's cathedral, although he had been appointed to that dignity by the pope: L. Balletto, 'Fonti notarili genovesi del secondo Duecento per la storia del Regno latino di Gerusalemme', in *I Comuni italiani nel Regno crociato di Gerusalemme*, ed. by G. Airaldi and B. Z. Kedar, Collana storica di fonti e studi, 48 (Genova, 1986), pp. 273–74, doc. 21.

[40] See A. Graboïs, 'Les Pèlerins occidentaux en Terre Sainte et Acre: d'Accon des croisés à Saint-Jean d'Acre', *Studi medievali,* 24 (1983), 251–52, 260–61.

[41] On which see Runciman, *A History of the Crusades,* III, 280.

forces were behind that move? Why were only forty sites included in the itinerary, about two thirds of those who seem to have been eligible? Why and how were they chosen and the others excluded? Which factors determined the range of spiritual benefits at each station? And how did the various institutions manage to cooperate, despite their widely different ranking in this respect? It is clear that the itinerary was not only devised out of altruistic motives for the benefit of pilgrims. It was also a self-serving device, since the institutions included in it expected the devotion of settlers, pilgrims, and crusaders to translate into growing revenues and patronage. Their cooperation and accord were indispensable for the establishment and institutionalization of the urban pilgrimage.

A brief look at the gradation of indulgences, even without being exhaustive, may provide some partial answers to the questions posed above. St Thomas of Canterbury and St Magdalen, both charitable institutions of unassuming standing, appear well above all the other sites, granting respectively more than fifteen and full eleven years of indulgence. A second group in the range of eight years or more comprises the Templars, the Hospitallers with their infirmary, St Lazarus of Bethany, and St Bridget. A third group with seven years includes prominent resettled institutions, namely the Holy Sepulchre, the Bishopric of Bethlehem, and St Georges of Lydda, in addition to the Holy Spirit of the Bolognese Crociferi. In the five-year range we find the Venetian S. Marco, the Pisan S. Pietro, St Mary 'of the knights', and St Andrew. The following group with four years or more includes the first site of the itinerary, *la bourde la vile*, St Nicholas, the church of the Teutonic knights and the recently established St Martin of the Bretons. The cathedral church of the Holy Cross and the Dominicans are in the three-year group, while the Franciscan church offers only three hundred days. As noted earlier, S. Lorenzo provides no more than forty days and stands at the lower end of the hierarchy.

The review of these data does not yield a clear picture, yet warrants some suggestions. The relatively low rank of the cathedral church of the Holy Cross seems to imply that the bishops of Acre were not the initiators of the urban pilgrimage, nor those who determined the grading in terms of indulgences. This assumption is strengthened by the fact that many ecclesiastical institutions in Acre, especially relocated bishoprics, were not subordinated to the city's bishop, while others attempted to free themselves from episcopal authority or else fought to retain or enlarge their ecclesiastical rights and the revenues deriving from them.[42] One may wonder, therefore, whether the patriarch of Jerusalem James Pantaleon, in the East from 1255 to 1259 and pope under the name Urban IV since 1261, or else the papal legate Thomas Agni of Lentino, who arrived at Acre in 1259, were in any way involved in the establishment

---

[42] See Hamilton, *The Latin Church*, pp. 301–05; J. Riley-Smith, *The Knights of St John in Jerusalem and Cyprus, c. 1050–1310* (London, 1967), pp. 405–10; Favreau-Lilie, 'Die italienischen Kirchen', pp. 19–22, 28–41, 75–85.

of Acre's pilgrimage.[43] In any event, there is no evidence of direct papal intervention in this respect between 1254 and 1264, the period in which the pilgrimage itinerary was ultimately institutionalized.[44] The high ranking of St Thomas is rather surprising, since the house of this English military Order at Acre did not enjoy direct patronage from King Henry III.[45] Turning to the major military Orders, one perceives that the Templars and the Hospitallers are rated well above the Teutonic Order, a fact that appears to reflect their respective ecclesiastical standing and political leverage. Indeed, at various occasions thirteenth-century popes called upon the first two Orders to support their action in the Holy Land. Political factors were also at play with respect to the churches of the Venetian and Pisan communes on the one hand and the Genoese S. Lorenzo on the other, as mentioned earlier. It is also noteworthy that the Dominicans preceded by far the Franciscans, and that wide gaps existed between various charitable institutions.

It is likely that to some extent the grading of institutions was related to the possession of relics. These constituted an important asset in that context, although most of them were not as precious as the relics preserved in the major shrines of the Holy Land. Several religious houses resettling in Acre after 1191 brought with them some of the treasures they had salvaged from their original locations. Other relics were acquired elsewhere, as in Constantinople after the Latin conquest of 1204, and brought to Acre. A cross that had belonged to the monastery of St Lazarus at Bethany was carried via Jerusalem and Tyre to Acre, yet did not remain there since Conrad of Montferrat sent it in 1192 to Genoa, as a reward for the latter's support of his cause.[46] The Templars had a large collection of relics, the most precious of which was a cross supposed to have curative properties. It attracted many sick people and was carried through the streets of Acre in penitential procession.[47] Another relic owned by the Templars was supposedly the diadem with precious stones which Melchior, King of Arabia and Nubia, had offered to Christ. According to a fourteenth-century source, German noblemen had brought it to Acre around 1200, yet the Templars took hold of it later.[48] In 1283 the Hospitallers

---

[43] On the activity of these two prelates in the East, see Hamilton, *The Latin Church*, pp. 267–72. Many documents issued by them in the Levant were obviously lost.

[44] On the other hand, in 1288 Pope Nicholas IV awarded an indulgence of one year and forty days to those visiting the Hospitaller chapel located in the cemetery of St Nicholas: Delaville le Roulx, *Cartulaire*, III, 323–24, no. 4020.

[45] See Forey, 'The Military Order of St Thomas', pp. 490, 492–95.

[46] D. Jacoby, 'Conrad, Marquis of Montferrat, and the Kingdom of Jerusalem (1187–1192)', in *Atti del Congresso Internazionale 'Dai feudi monferrini e dal Piemonte ai nuovi mondi oltre gli Oceani'*, ed. by L. Balletto (Alessandria, 1993), pp. 210 and 234, n. 82 (reprinted in Jacoby, *Trade, Commodities and Shipping,* no. IV).

[47] See M. Barber, *The New Knighthood. A History of the Order of the Temple* (Cambridge, 1994), p. 199, also for additional relics kept at Acre before 1291.

[48] Text cited by R. Röhricht, 'Marino Sanudo sen. als Kartograph Palästinas', *Zeitschrift des Deutschen Palästina-Vereins,* 21 (1898), 109: 'Ad hanc civitatem [i.e. Acre] circa annos Domini

kept a precious silver gilt box said to contain the skull of a *beatus Gerardus*, considered the founder and first Master of their Order, in the Hospital's chapel at Manosque, France.[49] This box must have originally been in Jerusalem, was presumably transferred to Acre in 1191, and remained there until it was removed to Manosque.[50] The Hospitaller's relics still in Acre in 1291 were lost when the city fell to the Muslims.[51]

Before 1187 the church of the Nativity at Bethlehem owned precious relics. When Saladin expelled the Latins from the city in that year, the clergy moved first to Tyre and in 1191 to Acre, apparently taking along some of them. Although Saladin allowed two deacons to serve in the church of the Nativity, these relics remained at Acre and were preserved there around 1240, as we may gather from somewhat later evidence.[52] Between 1239 and 1245 Giovanni Romano, Bishop-elect of Bethlehem, together with some canons of that church in Acre, alienated various pieces of its property in that city and in the countryside.[53] In addition, presumably in the first half of 1245, they pawned for 1,500 besants various relics, including a nail and a hammer of the Crucifixion and a hand of St Thomas the Apostle, to the Templars at Acre, other clerics and laymen, among them Balian of Ibelin, lord of Beirut and later *bailli* of the Kingdom of

---

MCC nobiles principes in die de progenie Vaus perduxerunt aureum diadema pretiosissimis gemmis ornatum ipsius regis Arabie et Nubie Melchior, qui Christo tria numera obtulit [. . .], quod tamen postea a Templariis subtractum fuit'. The story originates in John of Hildesheim, 'Historia trium regum', ed. by E. Köpke, *Mitteilungen aus den Handschriften der Ritter-Akademie zu Brandenburg,* 1 (1878), 10–11. This author lived from 1310/20 to 1375. At Acre in 1272 the Master of the Templars, Thomas Bérard, transferred to the knight Alain de Lasalle various relics, which were authenticated by John, Bishop of Tyre, and Hubert, Bishop of Banyas: ed. by Abbé Batiffol in *Bulletin de la Société Nationale des Antiquaires de France* (1891), 237–38. In 1291 the Templars managed to rescue some of their relics from Acre; see previous note and 'Anonymi de excidio urbis Acconis Libri II', in *Veterum scriptorum et monumentorum amplissima collectio,* ed. by L. Martène and U. Durand (Paris, 1724–33), V, 782 (II, 12).

[49] See A. Luttrell, 'The Rhodian Background of the Order of Saint John on Malta', in *The Order's Early Legacy in Malta,* ed. by J. Azzopardi (Malta, 1989), p. 9 (reprinted in A. Luttrell, *The Hospitallers of Rhodes and their Mediterranean World* (Aldershot, 1992), no. XVIII).

[50] Some Hospitaller relics were transferred to France shortly before February 1282: Delaville le Roulx, *Cartulaire*, III, 433–34, no. 3797.

[51] Luttrell, 'The Rhodian Background', p. 10.

[52] Pringle, *The Churches*, I, 139, 155, reconstructs the history of the church and mentions the relics, yet does not refer to the latter's itinerary from Bethlehem to Acre.

[53] These dates can be deduced from papal letters. Pope Gregorius IX did not allude to relics when he annulled the election of Giovanni Romano to the Bishopric of Bethlehem on 20 December 1238: *Les registres de Grégoire IX,* ed. by L. Auvray (Paris, 1896–1955), III, cols 1201–02, no. 4699. Neither did his successor Innocent IV, when he first intervened with respect to the alienation of property on 7 February 1245: *Les registres d'Innocent IV,* ed. by E. Berger (Paris, 1884–1921), I, 155–56, no. 957. For the location of the houses in Acre, see next note.

Jerusalem.[54] Giovanni Romano was apparently prompted to act by the fall of Bethlehem to the Khwarizmian Turks in April 1244, which inflicted heavy damage upon the church of the Nativity and deprived it of the substantial revenues it had been enjoying from pilgrimage between 1229 and 1244.[55] Innocent IV intervened at the request of Gottifredo de' Prefetti, whom he recognized as Bishop-elect of Bethlehem, to ensure the return of the relics to his church and to raise funds for the latter's support.[56] It is unclear, however, whether the church of Bethlehem in Acre ever recovered its lost relics.[57] In any event, around a decade later it must have nevertheless owned a large collection of devotional objects, judging by its ranking in the *pardouns dAcre*.

Burchard of Mount Sion, who visited Acre around 1280, still considered that the city was not part of the Holy Land.[58] However, the progressive accumulation of relics

---

[54] The pawning of the relics is first mentioned in a papal letter of 20 August 1245: *Les registres d'Innocent IV,* I, p. 233, no. 1531. A later one, dated 25 June 1246, refers to 'domos in Acon [. . .] necnon pretiosas reliquias, which had not been recovered': ibid., p. 306, no. 2057. Laymen owning relics are attested in 1291. They took them along when they escaped from Acre: 'De excidio urbis Acconis', p. 770 (II, 3): 'thesauros omnes cum mercibus et sacrosanctis reliquiis'.

[55] Like the patriarchs in Jerusalem: see above, n. 7. On 17 June 1248 Innocent IV described the church of the Nativity as *destructam quasi totaliter*: Berger, *Les registres d'Innocent IV,* I, 612–13, no. 4044. However, it would seem that the collection of funds in the West sponsored by that pope on 3 February 1245 was initially intended for the impoverished church of Bethlehem relocated at Acre, in order to enable it to attend to paupers and pilgrims: ibid., I, 158, no. 980. Only later were the funds allocated to the restoration of the church of the Nativity itself.

[56] On the double election and the issue of the relics, see P.-V. Claverie, 'Un conflit entre deux évêques italiens de Terre Sainte: l'affaire "Giovanni Romano" (1245–48)', *Studi medievali,* 40 (1999), 291–304, yet with respect to the relics my reading of the documents differs from his; see also my reservations in the following note.

[57] Various liturgical objects, some from the twelfth and others from the thirteenth century, were excavated at Bethlehem; see T. S. R. Boase, 'Ecclesiastical Art in the Crusader States in Palestine and Syria', in *A History of the Crusades,* ed. by K. M. Setton (Madison, 1969–89), IV, 139; Pringle, *The Churches*, I, 155. It has been argued that these were the relics alluded to in the papal letters, which after being retrieved were sent back to Bethlehem: see Boase, as above, followed by Claverie, 'Un conflit', pp. 301–04. Such a scenario is totally excluded after the renewed loss of the city and the damage inflicted upon the church of the Nativity in 1244, which had not yet been repaired by 1248: see above, n. 55. It is likely, therefore, that the objects that were discovered, as well as a set of small thirteenth-century bells and some organ pipes, were buried by the canons in that year when the Khwarismian Turks were approaching Bethlehem.

[58] *Peregrinationes medii aevi quatuor: Burchardus de Monte Sion, Ricoldus de Monte Crucis, Odoricus de Foro Julii, Wilbrandus de Oldenborg,* ed. by J. C. M. Laurent (Leipzig, 1864), p. 23. On the dating of his pilgrimage and of the latter's report, see A. Graboïs, 'Christian Pilgrims in the Thirteenth Century and the Kingdom of Jerusalem: Burchard of Mount Sion', in

in Acre after 1191 had gradually turned the city into a sacred space. This development culminated after the final loss of Jerusalem in 1244 or, more likely, after the departure of King Louis IX for France in 1254, when a substitute expiatory pilgrimage was established in Acre. It should be stressed that this institutionalized urban pilgrimage was exclusively Latin in character and added yet another distinctive feature setting Latins apart from Oriental Christians. The *pardouns dAcre*, a guide compiled between 1258 and 1264 for the benefit of pilgrims and crusaders, provides the itinerary linking some forty among the sixty or so Latin churches, monasteries, hospices, and hospitals existing in the city around the mid-thirteenth century and states the indulgences gained at each site. It is noteworthy that by contrast to the centrality of the Holy Sepulchre in Jerusalem, there was no single focus of pilgrimage in Acre. The compiler of the *pardouns dAcre* was obviously a French speaker, yet his choice of that language does not necessarily imply that this was also the case of most pilgrims and crusaders. The urban pilgrimage in Acre could be performed by individuals on their own at any time of the year, yet it is likely that it was essentially carried out in large groups under the guidance of the local clergy during the spring and autumn pilgrimage seasons. As such it must have played an important role in the structuring of urban time and space in Acre.

Outremer, ed. by Kedar, Mayer and Smail, pp. 287–88. See also Graboïs, 'Les Pèlerins occidentaux', pp. 251–52, 260–61.

Sermons, Preachers, and the Law

PHYLLIS B. ROBERTS

Preaching and the development of sermon literature played an important role in the history of the medieval Church.[1] In a society where large numbers of people were unlettered, sermons were the primary means of instruction of the laity. The duties of a priest included preaching, which meant not only exhorting people to a better life but also instructing them in the tenets of the faith. On all levels of the clergy, from parish priest to university master, preaching was recognized as a vital aspect of Christian communal life.

By the last part of the twelfth century, sermons entered a distinctive stage influenced by the increasing importance given to popular preaching in the growing cities of western Europe. Preachers found that a sermon could be more effective if *exempla,* the anecdotes, the moral illustrations, the concrete examples—in short, the conceptual language mirrored a familiar kind of life experience. The stories told by preachers might not be original. They were, in fact, rarely so. But they had to have a meaningful context,

[1] See T. N. Hall's indispensable bibliography of medieval sermon studies in *Medieval Sermon Studies,* 36 (1995), 26–42, and the *International Medieval Bibliography*, which, since 1986, has identified a separate section on 'Sermons and Preaching'. On the study of medieval sermons, see L.-J. Bataillon, 'Approaches to the Study of Medieval Sermons', *Leeds Studies in English,* n.s. 11 (1980), 19–35; and B. M. Kienzle and D. L. D'Avray, 'Sermons', in *Medieval Latin: An Introduction and Bibliographical Guide*, ed. by F. A. C. Mantello and A. G. Rigg (Washington, D.C., 1996), pp. 659–69.

and their importance lies in their selection by preachers for audiences that would find them relevant and significant.

Exempla on kings and princes and on law and justice appear frequently in the sermons of medieval preachers. Connections with the theme God the King are obvious, and references to earthly kings and princes and to the exercise of law and justice carried a special moral message that was fundamental to popular preaching. Sermonizing about the royal nature of Christ could be made all the more effective if examples were drawn from the experience and image of earthly kingship. Weighty and difficult subjects such as divine law and justice could be more readily understood if translated into the conceptual language of the popular audience. This essay has as its purpose an examination of the intersection between sermons, preachers, and the law. As a remarkable source into the *mentalité* of the time, the medieval sermon, with its stories and *exempla* for audiences of laity and clergy, offers unique insights into how medieval people perceived law and justice.[2]

The growth of the preaching art in medieval Europe occurred in several stages. There was, of course, the very ancient tradition of preaching that primitive Christianity inherited from Judaism and was transmitted by the Church Fathers over the early medieval centuries. St Augustine (354–430) wrote one of the early guides to preaching in Book IV of his *De doctrina Christiana*[3] and Pope Gregory I (590–604) emphasized the close relationship of biblical interpretation, teaching, and preaching.[4] Already in the early Middle Ages, there was a distinction between preaching *ad cleros* and preaching *ad populum*. Legislation in the capitularies of Charlemagne (813) urged that sermons be preached to the people in the language they would understand.[5] The distinguishing mark of most early medieval preaching, however, was that it was essentially preaching by clerics for audiences of clerics, since the language was Latin. The monastic sermon of this period, which was typical of the style of preaching into the first part of the twelfth century, was rather simple in structure and style. Preachers expounded on a theme drawn from Scripture and concentrated on theological motifs such as grace, the sacraments, and redemption.[6]

---

[2] See also the *exempla* in the two sermons addressed to lawyers in the collection *Sermones ad status* by Jacques de Vitry. Paris, BNF, lat. 17509, fols 33–34v and fols 34v–36v. Cited by M. Sandor, *The Popular Preaching of Jacques de Vitry* (unpublished doctoral dissertation, University of Toronto, 1993), p. 319.

[3] Augustine, *De doctrina Christiana,* ed. by J. Martin, CCSL, 32 (Turnhout, 1962), pp. 116–67.

[4] See Gregory's *Liber regulae pastoralis*, PL, 77, cols 13–128.

[5] *Capitularia regum Francorum,* ed. by G. H. Pertz, MGH, Leges, 1 (Hannover, 1835), c. 14, p. 190: 'De officio praedicationis, ut iuxta quod bene vulgaris populus intelligere possit, assidue fiat'.

[6] M.-M. Lebreton, 'Recherches sur les principaux thèmes théologiques traités dans les

The later years of the twelfth century marked a turning point in the history of the medieval sermon. Popular preaching[7] became more important as the Church increasingly took the offensive against two principal enemies: Saracens abroad and Christian heretics at home. Sermons and preaching were valuable weapons in this effort to educate and to persuade. The importance attached to popular preaching was also reflected in Canon 10 of 4 Lateran (1215) which called for bishops to name men suited to fulfill the task of instructing the people by word and example.[8] Pope Innocent III (1198–1216), who was also a renowned preacher,[9] was an example to an age when the sermon was coming into its own not only as a weapon against the enemies of the Church but also in winning popular support for his plans of Church reform. Masters in the cathedral schools in Paris who were trained in theology, such as Stephen Langton, later Archbishop of Canterbury (d. 1228), Peter the Chanter (d. 1197), and Robert of Courson (d. 1219) responded to this call.[10] They were interested in the reinvigoration of Christian teaching and therefore attached great significance to popular preaching. Secular preaching masters were soon joined by Franciscans and Dominicans whose rapid spread throughout the cities of western Europe in the course of the thirteenth century should be seen as a part of this ongoing effort by the Church to educate and persuade the laity.

Exempla on kingship and the law, on the nature of equity and justice were a part of this popular preaching movement devoted to the spread of reform. Preachers found their sources and inspiration in the writings of theologians and canonists who had elaborated ideas and ideals of justice in the course of the twelfth century.[11] Note, for

---

sermons du XII siècle', *Recherches de théologie ancienne et médiévale,* 23 (1956), 6, 8.

[7] See P. B. Roberts, *Stephanus de Lingua-tonante: Studies in the Sermons of Stephen Langton* (Toronto, 1968), c. 3, for a summary of the growth of popular preaching and references. On the revival of popular preaching in the twelfth century, see B. Smalley, *Study of the Bible in the Middle Ages*, 3rd edn (Oxford, 1983), p. 244.

[8] *Conciliorum Oecumenicorum Decreta,* ed. by J. Alberigo et al. (Freiburg, Rome, and Vienna, 1962), p. 215: '[...] ut episcopi viros idoneos ad sanctae praedicationis officium salubriter exequendum assumant, potentes in opere et sermone, qui plebes sibi commissas [...] eas verbo aedificent et exemplo'.

[9] For the sermons of Innocent III, see PL, 217, cols 313–688. See J. C. Moore, 'The Sermons of Pope Innocent III', *Römische Historische Mitteilungen,* 36 (1994), 81–142. See also P. B. Roberts, 'The Pope and the Preachers: Perceptions of the Religious Role of the Papacy in the Preaching Tradition of the Thirteenth-Century English Church', in *The Religious Roles of the Papacy: Ideals and Realities*, ed. by C. Ryan (Toronto, 1989), pp. 277–97.

[10] See J. W. Baldwin, *Masters, Princes and Merchants: The Social Views of Peter the Chanter and his Circle*, 2 vols (Princeton, 1970); and J. Longère, *Oeuvres oratoires de maîtres parisiens au XIIe siècle: Étude historique et doctrinale,* 2 vols (Paris, 1975).

[11] F. Morenzoni, *Des Écoles aux Paroisses: Thomas de Chobham et la promotion de la*

example, the preaching of Stephen Langton, master of theology at Paris and Archbishop of Canterbury from 1206 to 1228. A major participant in events surrounding the Magna Carta, Langton was also a biblical scholar of some renown and a preacher whose reputation won him the contemporary sobriquet, *Stephanus De Lingua-tonante*. Langton's role as an important popular preacher in the evangelical movement in Paris in the last decades of the twelfth century attests to the participation of the Paris masters in a program directed toward the education of the laity, reform of the Church, and the reinvigoration of Christian teaching. What Langton (and others) observed about equity and justice, on the nature of kingship and law have, therefore, a special interest.

Langton's sermons include numerous references to these themes and reflect his thinking about the right order of society. Moreover, they are cast in language that was understandable to his audience. Absent from the sermons are the complex arguments that Langton reserved for his *Questiones* and his Paris lectures.[12] More typical in his preaching is the following comment which underscores the opposite nature of equity and iniquity:

> Equity and iniquity, as you know, are opposites. Equity means that a man should return that which he owes. For a man is bound in three ways: he owes a debt to God, to his neighbour, and to himself. Should he not honour this debt, this is iniquity. Notice that one does not use the singular *iniquity* but the plural *iniquities*, since he owes many debts [. . .] not one iniquity but many iniquities does he make. Consequently, he is obligated to return those things which he owes, and to whom he owes them.[13]

Langton's comments on the nature of justice are scattered in various sermons. They are brief and traditional aphorisms and well suited to his popular audiences. 'Justice', he said, 'is to render to each one that which is his'.[14] 'There are two parts to justice: one is to turn away from evil, and the other is to do good'.[15] 'Justice teaches obedience to

---

prédication au début du XIIIe siècle (Paris, 1995), p. 127.

[12] See R. Quinto, 'Doctor Nominatissimus: Stefano Langton (d. 1228) e la tradizione delle sue opere', *Beiträge zur Geschichte der Philosophie und Theologie des Mittelalters,* neue folge, 39 (1994), pp. 91–166.

[13] Paris, BNF, lat. 14859, fol. 272ra: 'Equitas et iniquitas ut scitis contraria sunt. Equitas est ut homo reddat quod debet. Quilibet enim homo tribus modis ligatur. Debitum enim debet Deo, proximo et sibi ipsi, quod si non reddit, iniquitas est. Non dicit iniquitatem sed iniquitates, quia plura debita debet [. . .] non inquitatem unam sed plures facit iniquitates. Tenetur ergo reddere ea que debet et quibus debet'.

[14] Arras, BM, 222 (334), fol. 78ra: '[. . .] iustitia reddere unicuique quod suum est'.

[15] Paris, BNF, lat. 14859, fol. 210rb: 'Due sunt partes iusticie, alteram partem habuisti que est declinare a malo; aliam non habuisti, quia bona non fecisti que est consummatio perfectionis. [. . .]'

one's superiors, counsel and aid to one's peers, and correction and protection of one's subjects'.[16] 'The good judge will not permit robbers to flourish in the land'.[17] Justice goes hand in hand with piety: 'For the just man returns to each man that which is his. [. . .] Piety consists in having compassion for the pauper and distributing one's goods to the poor. [. . .]'[18]

Langton's view of kings as practitioners of law and justice was traditionally defined: 'one is not a king unless he is a servant and minister of God'.[19] 'Kings are those who rule themselves well and do justice in their land'.[20] The lesson is repeated in more than one sermon: 'On the contrary, all will be kings who serve Him, i.e. all rule themselves who serve the Lord. For no one is a king unless he rules himself, and this, according to divine precepts'.[21] The good king acts justly: 'If a king orders peace to be preserved in a land that is not his own and that he has conquered while, in his own state, thieves rob and despoil, he cannot be said to maintain justice'.[22] 'The good king also punishes counterfeiters',[23] and 'one who disobeys his edicts may suffer a capital penalty'.[24]

Like other contemporary preachers, Langton also attacked the vices of kingship: their pursuit of vain glory, the favours they granted to usurers and Jews, their attachment to games and to the hunt to the exclusion of divine law, and the closer attention they gave to the advice of storytellers than to doctors and wise men. These

---

[16] Leipzig, Universitätsbibliothek, 443, fols 181vb–182ra: 'Iustitia vero maioribus obedientiam, paribus consilium et auxilium inpendi precepit. In subditis vero correctionem et custodiam. [. . .]'

[17] Ibid., fol. 41vb: 'Non diceretur bonus iudex qui terram aliorum pacificaret, et in propria latrones habitare permitteret. [. . .]'

[18] Brussels, Bibliothèque Royale, II. 953, fol. 137ra: '[. . .] enim iustus reddit unicuique quod suum est. [. . .] Est autem pietas pauperem misereri et distribuere pauperibus bona sua. [. . .]'

[19] Troyes, BM, 1100, fol. 289ra: 'Ipse enim rex non est nisi quidam servus et minister Dei'.

[20] Arras, BM, 222 (334), fol. 78rb: 'Reges sunt quicumque se bene regunt, et faciunt iustitiam in terra sua. [. . .]'

[21] Brussels, Bibliothèque Royale, II. 953, fol. 137rb: '[. . .] immo omnes erunt reges qui servient ei i.e. omnes regent se qui servient Domino. Nullus enim rex nisi regat se, et hoc secundum precepta Domini. [. . .]

[22] Ibid., fol. 142vb: 'Sequitur. Et iustitia. Si rex in terra sibi subdita et non propria pacem servari iubeat, in propria vero civitate eius fures spolient et furentur, non dicetur iustitiam observare [. . .]'

[23] Troyes, BM, 1100, fol. 246vb: 'Sed attendite quod principes terre generaliter puniunt fabricatores false monete. [. . .]'

[24] Leipzig, Universitätsbibliothek 443, fol. 97va: 'Certe siquis preceptum regis terreni transgreditur, pena capitali punietur. [. . .]'

were frequent complaints heard in the sermons of the age.[25] Langton also had a few things to say about tyrants who persecuted the Church. 'When such a tyrant attacks the Church, the Lord shall not forsake her'.[26] William Rufus was specifically singled out as an oppressor of the Church. The book of Maccabees, said Langton, offers us an instance of a people's refusal to yield to tyranny: 'It is better for us to die than to disobey ancestral laws'.[27] 'Thus does the threat of a tyrant and secular persecution try to shake just men rooted in their faith; but they are invincible against the blows of adversity, and against persecutions they are firm'.[28] This was the tyrant, oppressor of Holy Church and antithesis of the good king who rules himself and his subjects with wisdom and justice.

If Langton and many of his contemporaries spoke in general terms of the ideals of kingship, justice, and the law, there are other sermons that make these eulogies much more specific. David D'Avray's study of memorial preaching before 1350 cites several examples of kings and princes whose devotion to law and justice was noteworthy. King Edward I of England, for example, '[...] loved not just any justice, but legal justice, which is all virtue and all justice, and hated not just any iniquity, but hated that iniquity which is all vice and all injustice. [...]'[29] King Charles II of Anjou and Naples wins praise, 'for he made constitutions or statutes of the kingdom which contain both justice and judgement, so that he could be called not only an executor of the law, but also a legislator. [...]'[30]

Sermons also drew on experiences and images that were close at hand. The law and the law courts in England, for example, furnished the following comparison:

> The King of Heaven has in his kingdom two justiciars [*justiciarios*], even as the king of England has, and they are Mercy and Justice. Justice sits in the Common Bench, but Mercy sits in the King's Bench. If a man should find that the standard is too strict before the jurisdiction of the Common Bench, he can appeal to the higher judge and be saved within a time certain.[31]

---

[25] A. Lecoy de la Marche, *La Chaire française au moyen âge, spécialement au XIIIe siècle: d'après les manuscrits contemporains,* 2nd edn (Paris, 1886), p. 381.

[26] Troyes, BM, 1100, fol. 250vb: 'Cum tyrannus infestat ecclesiam, Dominus eam non relinquit desolatam'.

[27] Arras, BM, 222 (334), fol. 119rb: 'Melius est nobis mori quam patrias leges prevaricari. [...]'

[28] Ibid., fol. 60rb: 'Sic comminatio tirannica et persecutio secularis, iustos in fide radicatos concutere nititur, sed contra impulsus adversitatum sunt invincibiles, contra persecutiones rigidi. [...]'

[29] D. L. D'Avray, *Death and the Prince: Memorial Preaching before 1350* (Oxford, 1994), p. 71.

[30] Ibid., p. 103.

[31] Cambridge, University Library, Ii.iii.8, fol. 147 (Wimbledon?): 'Rex celorum habet in

The world of Florence as a merchant-banker republic is reflected in the sermons of the Dominican theologian and preacher Remigio de' Girolami. In his sermons of the 1290s and the early decades of the fourteenth century, Remigio based his ideas of 'practical, local law and justice upon the merchant-capitalist virtue of rational order'.[32] French preachers of the late Middle Ages also drew from their contemporary experience in sermons that idealized the monarchy and its exercise of justice as an earthly reflection of the divine.[33]

The other side of the story of justice idealized is the theme of justice for sale which our sources repeat again and again. 'For the preachers, an honest lawyer was a contradiction in terms'. Later medieval French preachers were also rather specific in their denunciations of the law and lawyers. Olivier Maillard (*c.* 1430–1502), for example, described the law 'as the single most dangerous profession from the point of view of personal salvation', and Michel Menot (*c.* 1473–1541) classified lawyers with 'horse sellers, liars, pimps, courtiers, and soldiers, saying that "there are few professions so damaging to the soul".'[34]

Later medieval preaching handbooks include collections of *exempla, similitudines* and *distinctiones* which provide a rather unflattering picture of what was said and what was heard about lawyers, the law, and contemporary justice. Modern 'lawyer jokes' have a long history. Medieval preachers could draw on an ample supply of anecdotes and *exempla* stories about the law and lawyers. Some examples follow: A lawyer accustomed to asking for delays asks for a delay when he sees demons before him at the point of death.[35] A man claimed that he would rather be defended by a dead lawyer than a living one because the former would be just and equitable in matters concerning worldly values.[36] A dishonest lawyer was carried up into the sky by demons. They

regno suo duos justiciarios, sicut habet rex Anglie, et sunt Misericordia et Justicia. Justicia sedet in bancho communi; sed Misericordia sedet in bancho regis. Et si homo inveniat nimium rigorem coram justiciario de bancho communi, adhuc potest appellare ad altiorem judicem et salvari infra certum tempus'. Quoted in G. R. Owst, *Literature and Pulpit in Medieval England: A Neglected Chapter in the History of English Letters and of the English People,* 2nd rev. edn (Oxford, 1961), p. 31, n. 2 (translation mine).

[32] See D. R. Lesnick, *Preaching in Medieval Florence: The Social World of Franciscan and Dominican Spirituality* (Athens, GA, 1989), pp. 108–09.

[33] H. Martin, *Le Métier de prédicateur en France septentrionale à la fin du moyen âge (1350–1520)* (Paris, 1988), p. 623.

[34] L. Taylor, *Soldiers of Christ: Preaching in Late Medieval and Reformation France* (Oxford, 1992), p. 148.

[35] F. C. Tubach, *Index Exemplorum: A Handbook of Medieval Religious Tales* (Helsinki, 1969), no. 2991.

[36] Ibid., no. 2995.

dropped him near an abbey, killing him.[37] A lawyer was given a bull by one litigant and his wife was given a cow by the other. He could not represent the donor of the bull because the owner of the cow would not permit it.[38] Two peasants threw a man into the mud when he told them he was a lawyer.[39] A peasant promises to give a lawyer some geese if he will teach him his trade. The lawyer says, 'Object freely, and prolong the suit until you win'. When he demands his geese, the peasant objects and prolongs the suit.[40]

Lawyers, and especially corrupt lawyers, were a favourite target of homilists. John Bromyard, the fourteenth-century Dominican and author of the *Summa predicantium,* a compendium of preaching materials, offers this satirical description of corrupt lawyers who fulfill the familiar prophecy of Isaiah: 'They shall beat their swords into ploughshares, and their spears into pruning-hooks (Isaiah 2. 4)'.

> First, because, instead of using the sword or spear of justice, which are 'straight' weapons—sparing neither friend nor foe, poor nor powerful, acting with strict impartiality, moved neither by love nor hate—they choose 'curved' instruments, designed for 'earthly' use and for temporal gain—ploughshares and hooks. So, too, as the curved reaping hook, though held in the right hand, is actually manipulated by the 'left' [*sinistra*], with this they seek to reap a 'lucrative' harvest, by 'crooked' methods. So again, like ordinary reapers, you can never move them to take action, until they see a 'harvest' ready waiting for them.[41]

Corrupt practitioners of the law are denounced, along with evil princes, usurers, wicked ecclesiastics, and other oppressors of the poor: 'Where, moreover, are the false wise men of the world, the judges, assessors, advocates, swearers and perjurers [...] who for bribes were wont to sell God and the kingdom of heaven, and purchase hell?'[42] The unfortunate person who turns to the law and the courts thus has many perils to face: 'he may have to steer clear of the Charybdis of a corrupt jury, as well as the Scylla of an unjust judge'.[43] Denunciation is piled upon denunciation. Advocates are like 'hawks', 'highway-robbers', 'false merchants', and 'demons'. There is no shortage of words to express the outrage of condemnation and censure.[44] The thirteenth-century French

[37] Ibid., no. 2996.

[38] Ibid., no. 2998.

[39] Ibid., no. 3003.

[40] Ibid., no. 2259.

[41] Quoted in Owst, *Literature and Pulpit*, p. 63.

[42] Ibid., p. 293.

[43] Ibid., p. 346.

[44] Ibid., p. 348.

preacher, Ranulphe de la Houblonnière, once compared the eloquence of advocates at court to a multitude of frogs that feed on eels and lampreys and destroy abbeys.[45]

Lawyers were not always thus. Seneschal, bailiff, or attorney were once amiable and charming enough in their student days but have become vicious and hateful to satisfy the greed of their own lords and masters and their own ambition.[46] Nor were all legal practitioners always worthy of complaint and denunciation. A preacher, after passing 'in brief review the crimes of the false plaintiff, the false defendant, witness, juror, advocate, pleader, procurator, attorney, notary, clerk, doomsmen civil and ecclesiastical', reminds us that 'of alle these degrees and astates, by the grace of God, there beth ful good men and trewe, and wel and truliche ruleth wel the lawe, bothe in spiritual lawe and temporal lawe. [. . .]'[47]

There may well have been a few good lawyers, but for the most part, they were, in the preacher's words a venal and corrupt lot. There was also criticism in the preaching literature of the attraction of law over theology. 'Why do men apply their sons more readily to Civil Law, to the king's court, to the work of secretaries and notaries rather than to philosophy or theology? Or, Why does the Law School have a hundred or two hundred pupils, where the School of Theology has not even five?'[48] The theme of 'too many lawyers' is echoed in a sermon by the thirteenth-century Franciscan Jean de la Rochelle who, in a section on *secularis scientia*, writes: 'The moon of secular knowledge is to disputation about earthly things as the sun of theology is to day, that is to contemplation of divine things. [. . .] This moon waxes extraordinarily in the consummation of the age, while [. . .] we now see that there are almost as many doctors of law as there are cities'.[49]

John Bromyard, cited earlier in this essay, could easily have added the modern phrase 'Money talks!' to his aphorisms and observations about law and justice: 'Money [. . .] is the only key that admits to the courts of false men of law. [. . .] Blessed is he that cometh in the name of Money!'.[50] 'Money conquers: money rules. Money bribes or gifts [. . .] will free the robber, the murderer, the deceiver in the law courts, and even in the prison [. . .] juries, judges, advocates, are all amenable to the same influence. Like weathercocks [. . .] they will turn automatically at every wind of silver. Laws will be stretched to meet the briber's case. Legal proceedings will be dragged out unnecessarily

---

45 See N. Bériou, *La Prédication de Ranulphe de la Houblonnière: Sermons aux clercs et aux simples gens à Paris au XIIIe siècle*, 2 vols (Paris, 1987), II, 126.

46 Owst, *Literature and Pulpit*, p. 323.

47 Ibid., p. 345.

48 G. R. Owst, *Preaching in Medieval England: An Introduction to Sermon Manuscripts of the Period c. 1350–1450* (Cambridge, 1926), p. 33.

49 D. L. D'Avray, *The Preaching of the Friars: Sermons Diffused from Paris before 1300* (Oxford, 1985), p. 117.

50 Owst, *Literature and Pulpit,* p. 345.

for the sake of greater fees. [...] And yet, I hear say of men that have proved both courts, that the court which is called more spiritually Christian is more cursed'.[51]

Church courts and their practitioners were thus not immune from the criticism of preachers. Bromyard elaborates on the venality and corruption of the ecclesiastical courts and how bishops and their ministers receive money or gifts: 'By means of a little money given to the sumners or the ecclesiastical judges, who ought to be punished along with them with an equal punishment, adulterers and fornicators are always able to persist'.[52] Church burials and dedications were also for sale: 'Through their [i.e. the bishops'] cupidity they have now become the Devil's Procurators and the promoters of vice'.[53]

Medieval sermons and preachers might denounce lawyers, the courts, and justice for sale. Their *exempla,* often caustic, sometimes amusing, may well reflect how medieval people viewed the exercise of justice and its practitioners. Justice realized, after all, was a far cry from justice idealized. When Thomas Brinton, the fourteenth-century Bishop of Rochester, preached on the subject of English justice, he complained of too many laws that were not obeyed. Nevertheless, Brinton also underscores a truth that bears repeating, that the law is essential to the very life of the state:

> And in the realm of England so many laws abound, and yet there is no utterance or observance of the laws. It seems likely that unless these injuries, injustices and wrongs are very quickly reformed by execution of the laws, it will be, in short, the destruction or at least the transference of this realm. [...][54]

[51] Ibid., p. 317.
[52] Ibid., p. 252.
[53] Ibid., p. 255.
[54] Ibid., p. 340.

Depriving Parents of the Consolation of Children: Two Legal *Consilia* on the Baptism of Jewish Children

AVIAD M. KLEINBERG

Forced baptism of children was a constant source of anxiety for Jewish communities throughout the ages. In ninth-century Lyon, Jewish children were seized and baptized against their parents' will.[1] In the eleventh century, the Jews of Worms (1074) and Speyer (1090) obtained from Emperor Henry IV privileges protecting them against forced baptism of their children. These privileges were renewed by Frederick I and Frederick II.[2] In times of persecution, when entire communities were forced to accept baptism, Jewish children shared the fate of their parents, but even in relatively calm times one finds the traces of incidents involving the baptism of Jewish children without parental permission.[3]

The following abbreviations occur frequently: DG = Decretum Gratiani; D = distinctio; C = causa; q = quaetio; c = capitulum; De cons. = *De consecratione*; Sext. = *Liber sextus* (1298); X = *Decretales Gregorii IX* (Liber extra); Digest = *Digesta* (in *Corpus Juris Civilis*); Codex = *Codex Justiniani* (in *Corpus Juris Civilis*).

[1] See, MGH, Epp., 5 ed. by E. Dümmle (Berlin, 1899), p. 239. The incident is described in a letter, attributed by Bernhard Blumenkranz to Agobard of Lyon. This attribution has been challenged by E. Boshof, *Erzbischof Agobard von Lyon: Leben und Werke* (Köln, 1969), pp. 135–38.

[2] W. Pakter, *Medieval Canon Law and the Jews* (Ebelsbach am Main, 1988), pp. 316–17.

[3] See C. Roth, 'Forced Baptism in Italy: A Contribution to the History of Jewish Persecution', in *Gleanings: Essays in Jewish History, Letters, and Art* (New York, 1967), pp. 240–63.

What complicated matters was the fact that according to Catholic dogma baptism imprinted an indelible character (*character indelebilis*) on the recipient. Theoretically, at least, it was—if properly administered—an irrevocable act. But what if the recipient was unwilling? Under what circumstances might the sacrament be considered invalid and the *character sacramenti* not impressed; and supposing it was impressed, should it always have the same legal implications?

The Church had traditionally denounced the use of force in the conversion of infidels, notably of Jews. Jews, it was held, should not be compelled to accept baptism. They should be drawn to the faith by kindness, not by force.[4] But a canon of the Fourth Council of Toledo (633) incorporated by Gratian into his *Decretum* set a precedent of a forcible conversion the effects of which were nonetheless binding:

> Concerning the Jews, the Holy Synod decrees that no one, from now on, bring force to bear on belief: Therefore He has mercy on whom He wills, and whom He wills He hardens (Romans, 9. 18). For such are not to be saved unwilling, but willing, so that the form of justice might be whole. So, just as man, by obeying the serpent, was lost by his own willing choice, so too is each one—the grace of God calling him—saved by believing through the conversion of his own mind. Therefore they must be persuaded, rather than compelled, to convert, not by force, but by their faculty of free choice. Those, however, who were forced in times past to become Christian, as was done in the days of the most religious prince, Sisebut [613], since it is clear that they have been associated in the divine sacraments, have received the grace of baptism, were anointed with the chrism, and took part in the body and the blood of the Lord, it is right that they be obliged to hold the faith which they received, albeit by force or by necessity, lest the name of the Lord be blasphemed and the faith which they have received considered worthless and contemptible.[5]

Medieval canonists saw in this canon an affirmation that a seemingly illicit act could have binding consequences and that, furthermore, the perpetrator of this transgression was not denounced, but given the honourary title most religious prince. In their effort to settle the contradiction between a denunciation of violence on the one hand, and an acceptance of its consequences on the other, the canonists formulated a concept of free will that enabled them to see forced conversion as voluntary and made it almost impossible for the victim of such coercion to escape punishment, if he or she wished to revert to Judaism. This, as we shall see, had a bearing upon the fate of children baptized against their parents' will.

In his influential summa on the *Decretum* (finished *c.* 1188) Huguccio of Pisa

---

[4] X 5.6.9: 'nullus invitos vel nolentes Judaeos ad baptismum venire compellat', DG, D. 45, c. 3: 'Qui sincera intentions extraneos a Christiana religions ad fidem cupiunt rectam perducere, blandimentis non asperitatibus debent studere'.

[5] DG, D. 45, c. 5.

argued that as long as the sacrament was properly conferred, and the minister had the intention of baptizing, the baptism was valid. Most canonists, as we shall see, eventually rejected this view. What was more important was Huguccio's distinction between the sacramental validity and the judicial efficacy of the sacrament. While the sacrament was always valid, it was sometimes without legal consequences.[6] Borrowing a concept from Rufinus,[7] Huguccio distinguishes between two types of coercion, absolute and conditional:

> If someone were baptized under absolute coercion, say, one person held him tied down and another poured water over him, unless he later consented, he must not be constrained to hold the Christian faith. (He is, however, baptized and receives the sacrament; for whether one is baptized willing or unwilling, awake or asleep [possibly comatose], as long as the proper ecclesiastical form has been observed, he receives the sacrament.) If, however, a person were baptized under conditional coercion, say [someone said to him]: I will beat you, or rob you, or kill you, or harm you, unless you are baptized, he is to be constrained to hold the faith, for such coercion turns one from unwilling to willing, and he is baptized willing. Coerced will is a will [nonetheless] and turns one into a willing [agent].[8]

Even those baptized under absolute coercion could be considered to have retroactively given their consent, if they participate in the sacramental life of the church after their conversion, especially if they partake of the Eucharist. In such a case their baptism becomes binding as if it were voluntary. Huguccio has few illusions about the effect of

---

[6] Huguccio was contesting the views of canonists, who taking an even more mechanistic approach than his, argued that not only was the sacrament, properly conferred, always valid, but that it should always have the same legal results. Thus Huguccio notes in his *Summa* (ad D. 45, c. 5, s.v. associates unctos corporis domini, Admont Stiftsbibl. MS 7, fol. 61v.): 'Magister tamen G[andulphus] et quidam alii dixerunt quod qualitercumque aliquis baptizetur, sive invitus, sive volens, sive postea consentit, sive non, cogendus est vivere secundum ritum Christianorum. Set sicut dictum est, male dixerunt'. See Mario Condorelli, *I fondamenti giuridici della tolleranza religiosa nell'elaborazione canonistica dei secoli XII–XIV: Contributo storico-dogmatico* (Milan, 1960), pp. 52–53. On legal definitions of voluntary acts, see S. Kuttner, *Kanonistische Schuldlehre von Gratian bis auf die Dekretalen Gregors IX*, Studi e testi, 64 (Vatican City, 1935), pp. 301–33; E. F. Vodola, 'Fides et culpa: The Use of Roman Law in Ecclesiastical Ideology', in *Authority and Power*, ed. by B. Tierney and P. Linehan (Cambridge, 1980), pp. 83–97.

[7] Rufinus, *Summa decretorum*, ad C. 22, q. 5, c. 1, ed. by H. Singer (Paderborn, 1902; repr. Aalen, 1963), pp. 399–402, s.v. qui compulsus.

[8] Huguccio, *Summa*, ad D. 45, c. 5. Although Huguccio does not mention Augustine, it is hard not to recognize the latter's influence. Augustine used a similar concept—that only the total absence of any will relieves from responsibility—to explain why fallen humanity, in a state of 'non posse non peccare', is nonetheless responsible for its sins.

forced conversion on the victims' inner convictions: 'How can one be forced to hold and maintain the faith [which he does not have]?'. One does not refer here to internal faith (*fides cordis*), but to external Christian faith, external Christian rites, and external Christian worship.[9] According to Huguccio, the reason—and here he seems to follow the spirit of Toledo IV—for compelling such people to maintain this exterior is that otherwise Christianity and its sacraments may seem worthless.

In 1201 Innocent III, a former student of Huguccio in Bologna, gave official sanction to his master's position, modifying it somewhat. In the decretal *Maiores,* Innocent dealt with the validity of the sacrament of baptism for infants, the insane, the comatose, and those baptized under duress. Innocent uses his master's legal distinction between conditional and absolute coercion, but rejects both the extreme view of Gandulphus and Huguccio's modification of it. There are cases when even though the sacrament is properly executed the character is not impressed. Only in such cases may a person continue to live as an infidel; otherwise he or she ought to be compelled to live as a Christian.

> Likewise, it was asked concerning the comatose and the insane whether they receive at least the character of the sacrament in baptism, so that when they are awakened from their coma or cured of their sickness they need not be re-baptized. There are some who say that the sacraments which produce their own effect, like baptism, holy orders and the like, confer the character, though not the grace (*rem*), not only to the comatose and the insane, but also to those unwilling and objecting (*contradicentibus*), since not only infants receive the sacrament, who do not consent, but also dissimulators, who though not by word, dissent at heart. In opposition to such [views], it can be said that those who were immersed unwilling and resisting (*reluctantes*), do come under ecclesiastical jurisdiction, at least by reason of the sacrament; hence they may reasonably be compelled to observe the standards of the Christian Faith. It is, however, contrary to the Christian religion that one totally unwilling and wholly opposed should be compelled to accept and observe Christianity. For this reason certain others have made a not unreasonable distinction between kinds of unwillingness and of coercion, so that he who is dragged violently by torture and fear and accepts the sacrament of baptism to avoid loss does receive the impressed character of Christianity, as does one who comes to baptism in dissimulation. Such a person is to be compelled to observe the Christian Faith as one conditionally willing (though in the absolute sense he is unwilling). It is as applying to such a case that the decree of the Fourth Council of Toledo should be understood. [. . .] He, however, who never gave his consent, but wholly objected, receives neither the character nor the grace of the sacrament, because to object expressly outweighs minimal consent; thus he does not incur any blame who, wholly objecting and protesting, was forced violently to burn incense for idols.[10]

---

[9] Ibid.

[10] X 3.42.3. Innocent lumped dissimulators together with those not fully conscious and those

The distinction between conditional and absolute coercion was adopted by almost all canonists. This was not merely an abstract concept. In a letter of 1277 Nicholas III ordered that Jews converted under threats of death be forbidden to revert to Judaism. Many of the said Jews, writes the pope, 'fearing death at the hands of the aforementioned Christians, though not absolutely and precisely coerced, accepted baptism. The pope ordered that those who persisted in their Judaizing be treated as heretics.[11] Some twenty years later, Boniface VIII in the decretal *Contra Christianos* echoes the same words, asserting that those baptized under threats of death, but not absolutely and precisely coerced fall under inquisitorial jurisdiction.[12]

The deliberations on the nature of consent in baptism affected the legal situation of the child baptized without parental consent by creating a frame of mind that saw baptism, however achieved, as an almost irreversible fact. The main problem that needed to be addressed was not the child's consent or lack thereof, but the infringement upon the rights of the (unwilling) parents, especially the father's *patria potestas*.

Gregory IX's decretal *Ex litteris* was written in 1229 in response to a query of Berthold of Tech (or Teck), Bishop of Strasbourg.[13] The case involved a man who converted to Christianity while his wife remained Jewish. The husband demanded that their four-year-old son be handed over to him to be baptized and raised as a Christian. The father based his claim on the fact that the child had not yet reached the age of discretion (and therefore cannot decide for himself) and on the advantage of the Catholic Faith. The mother argued that since the boy was still an infant, he was more in need of a mother than of a father. Marriage, she said, is called matrimony, not patrimony, because of the toil involved (for the mother) in giving birth and raising a child. The boy, then, ought to stay with her, or, at least, with neither parent (not follow any religion?). When he had reached legal age he would decide for himself.

The defence, then, was based on the child's age and an attempt to prevent any

---

converted under duress. But dissimulators really form a separate category. Unlike the insane and the comatose, they could not be assumed willing had some external obstacle not stood in the way, nor was their will changed by fear. Innocent IV notes this difficulty in his commentary on X 3.42.2. He states that while the coerced are compelled to want baptism, and are therefore truly baptized, dissimulators having no will to receive the sacrament are not truly baptized, but must be treated as such 'propter ignorantiam [ecclesiae]' (*In V lib. decretalium commentaria* (Franfurt, 1570), fol. 456v.). He does not say what should happen when a dissimulator later confesses his dissimulation.

[11] 'Plures ex dictis Judaeis metu mortis qui eis per prefatos Christianos inferebatur, non tamen absolute seu precise coacti, se baptisari fecerunt'. Cited in S. Grayzel, 'The Confession of a Medieval Jewish Convert', *Historia Judaica,* 17.2 (1955), 92–93, n. 11.

[12] Sext. 5.2.13: 'etiamsi hujusmodi redeuntes dum erant infantes aut mortis metu, non tamen absolute seu precise coacti, baptizati fuerint'.

[13] X. 3.33.2. There is a translation of this text in S. Grayzel, *The Church and the Jews in the Thirteenth Century* (Philadelphia, 1933; repr. New York, 1966), pp. 181–83.

change in the child's legal status until he had reached maturity. Gregory ruled in favour of the father for two main reasons: (1) a child is in the father's power, unless the father is of bad reputation; (2) in such a tender age he ought not to remain among people who might be suspected of endangering his salvation or his life: if he were to remain with the mother, she could easily lead him into the error of faithlessness. The possibility that the child continue to live with his mother or other (Jewish) relatives, at least temporarily, without the mother necessarily becoming his legal guardian (the solution, as we shall see, offered by Gaspar Calderini in his *consilium*) is flatly rejected.

In his influential commentary on *Ex litteris*, Hostiensis has taken Gregory's position a step further. What if the child were less than three years old? The child would still be given to the father, because all the mother had was milk, while the father had on his side all the reasons mentioned by the pope. But what, he asks, if the case were reversed, that is, the mother converted and the father remained Jewish? The child would then be given to the mother. Hostiensis gives five reasons why this should be so: (1) because the father in such a case is wicked; (2) because the father endangers the child's physical and spiritual life; (3) because in such a case the woman should be considered a man, since she acts in a manly fashion (*in hoc casu debet mulier reputari vir, quia viriliter agat*); if the father tried to claim his paternal right, the wife could respond: mine is the Father of fathers to whom all are subject and who ought to be obeyed more (than you); (4) because the father was the cause of the divorce; (5) because of the advantage of the faith.

Pope Gregory could have made things much simpler, he writes, had he stated in straightforward terms what Hostiensis had to toil proving: that whether younger or older than three, and as long as he had not reached the age of seven (when he may make up his own mind), the child always goes to the converted parent.[14] When the child was baptized against *both* parents' will, such a child, asserts Hostiensis, must be taken away from his parents.[15] What situation does the cardinal envisage? Hostiensis mentions 'those who kidnap Jewish children who are at the age of reason (*doli capaces*), and force them to accept baptism'. The cardinal considers such actions pious, though, illicit.[16] As for the children, since they now have a will of their own, they fall under the by now standard categories of conditional and absolute coercion.

The two legal *consilia* I shall now discuss should be studied against the backdrop of its period's common opinion. They both reflect it and deviate from it in some respect. Legal *consilia* are technical documents, intended for a very limited audience of legal professionals. Most did not survive beyond the specific incident they addressed; but some, usually those written by famous lawyers, did. They were collected in com-

---

[14] Hostiensis, *In V lib. decretalium*, ad X 3.33.2 fol. 124r., s.v. non suspectum, and s.v. Maxime Christianae fidei. See Innocent IV, *In V lib. decretalium*, fol. 429v, s.v. suspicio, and Thomas Aquinas, *In IV sent.* D. 39, q. 1, art. 4 ad 4.

[15] Hostiensis, *In V lib. decretalium,* ad X 3.33.2, fol. 124r, s.v. non suspectum: 'nam et si ambo parentes in Iudaismo permaneant, ilii tamen eorundem baptizati eis auferuntur'.

[16] Ibid., s.v. non suspectum.

pilations, organized in most cases according to the titles of Gregory IX's *Decretals*. Some collections of medieval *consilia* achieved considerable circulation and were later printed, sometimes in more than one edition. The two *consilia* appended at the end of this article appear in such collections.

Gaspar Calderini and Peter of Ancarano were roughly contemporaries.[17] Gaspar Calderini (born 1345) was the son of John Calderini (the adoptive son of Johannes Andreae). He studied and taught law in Bologna and died in 1390.[18] His *consilia* were published together with those of his father. Peter of Ancarano (near Orvieto) studied both canon and civil law under Baldus, Richard de Saliceto, and John and Gaspar Calderini. He served as judge and deputy of the *podestà* of Bologna. From 1384 to 1387 he was consultant to the Republic of Venice. He taught law at Siena from 1387 to 1390 and then, until his death (1416), in Bologna.[19] Calderini's *consilium* posed in general terms (rather than as a discussion of a specific case) was more influential than Peter of Ancarano's. He may have also benefited from his father's reputation (since his *consilia* were published among his father's).[20]

Calderini examines arguments for and against involuntary baptism. The most significant argument is the advantage of the faith (*favour fidei*): since there can be no higher goal than defending and promoting Christian faith, other considerations must give way to this basic policy. This, as we saw, can be traced back to *De Iudaeis*. If Jews were allowed to revert to Judaism after they had been baptized, albeit by force, the name of the Lord be blasphemed, states the canon, and the faith which they have received be considered worthless and contemptible.

Calderini rejects the validity of this approach, at least for the case in question. He cites the various texts that prohibit forced conversion and insists that the advantage of the faith must not come at the cost of causing injustice. He alludes to Aquinas's opinion that injury must be avoided and parents' natural rights respected, though he does not

---

[17] For the texts see Johannes and Gaspar de Calderini, *Consilia sive responsa*, *consilium*, 487.3 (third *consilium* under the heading of *De Judaeis*) (Venice, 1497), fols 72v–72r. I have also consulted Vatican City, Biblioteca Apostolica Vaticana, Vat. lat. 2651, fol. 221r. Peter of Ancarano, *Consilia* (Pavia, 1496), fol. 84v.

[18] See, *Dizionario biografico degli Italiani,* XVI, 605.

[19] See J. A. Clarence Smith, *Medieval Law Teachers and Writers: Civilian and Canonist* (Ottawa, 1975), p. 86.

[20] His position is cited approvingly by John of Anagni (d. 1457) *Super quintum decretalium,* ad X 5.6.9 (Lyon, 1553), fol. 75r; Felinus Sandaeus (1444–1503) in his commentary on the fifth book of the *Decretals* (cited in Pakter, *Medieval Canon Law and the Jews*, p. 330); and by Giacomo de Graffiis (1548–1620) in his *Decisiones aureae casuum conscientiae*, cited by Pope Benedict XIV in a letter of 28 February 1747 to the Archbishop of Tarso, see Benedict XIV (Prospero Lambertini), *Opera omnia,* 18 vols (Prato, 1839–47), XVII, 179. Benedict, who disagrees with Calderini, cites him as the main proponent of the view that baptized children are to be returned to their Jewish parents.

mention him by name (in the Middle Ages canonists rarely acknowledged their debts to theologians).

Calderini's most significant contribution to the debate is his discussion of the second question: that of custody. The *Ordinary Gloss* on *Iudaeorum* (*Decretum,* C. 28 q. 1, c. 11) states quite clearly that baptism annuls paternal authority (*per baptismum solvitur ius patriae potestatis*). Canonists have generally accepted this view. Together with the prohibition on cohabitation with Jews it meant that validly baptized children were to be removed from their parents' homes. Not so according to Calderini. In his *consilium* he simply ignores this widespread and authoritative position in favour of the Roman-law concept of the sacrosanctity of *patria potestas*. Jewish fathers maintain their paternal authority over their children. The only valid cause for removal is a father posing a threat to his child's well-being. To protect the baptized child—for Calderini does not question the validity of illegal baptism—the parents are required to provide a surety that they would not try to impose their infidelity on the child, nor prevent him or her from leaving when he had reached legal age (apparently twelve, according to Calderini). Calderini does not specify the nature of this bond. If parents fail to provide it, though, the child is to be taken away from them.

One of the reasons given by Pope Gregory IX in the decretal *Ex litteris* for not allowing the child of a converted parent to live among Jews was that such a child would inevitably be drawn to their perfidy. Calderini must have been aware of this, but chooses to ignore it. Of course the family could be subjected to constant harassment in the guise of inspections to make sure that the child is not being drawn to infidelity, and there would probably be considerable pressure on the child to reaffirm his or her sacramental state by leaving the Jewish community. We do not know enough about actual cases in the Middle Ages to decide what this solution meant in practice. If applied it was no doubt preferable to the loss of a child.

There is one earlier case where a similar arrangement seems to have been made. Grayzel has published a papal letter that he attributes to Pope Clement IV (1265–1268) in which a case of abduction and forced baptism of a child is referred to. The pope writes in response to the plea of a Jewish father, Eleazar, whose seven-year-old (*septennem*) daughter was abducted by a cleric. The child was kept in a monastery, and when the local lord intervened on behalf of the family, she was transferred to some distant place. Although this is not explicitly mentioned, Grayzel is probably right in assuming that the child was baptized. The pope orders the child's return, stating that the father would not object to his daughter's subsequently becoming Christian (*non curaturus si demum ad religionem transire voluerit fidei christiane*).[21] This seems to imply an arrangement not unlike the one suggested by Calderini: the child returns to the parents on condition that they would not try to prevent it from subsequently becoming Christian.

---

[21] S. Grayzel, 'Jewish References in a Thirteenth Century Formulary', *Jewish Quarterly Review,* 46 (1955), 63.

It is hard to know whether Calderini was aware of the precedents to his solution. He does not mention any, and all later commentators who accept it refer to him as its originator. We have later evidence that at least in one place an arrangement similar to that suggested by Calderini was applied. In Rome, children baptized against their parents' will were sometimes returned to their homes with the requirement that when they had reached the age of twelve or thirteen they be presented to the authorities for examination so that their religious identity could be finally determined.[22] I was unable to establish links between this practice in Rome and Calderini's text (rejected by papal authorities).

While Calderini offers a solution for all cases of baptism without parental permission, Peter of Ancarano's *consilium* hinges on a technicality peculiar to the case brought before him. It involved, it seems, one of those private baptisms that Jews always dreaded. We do not know the identity of the person who performed the baptism, nor the specific circumstances under which the baptism took place. Was it a domestic, a neighbour, some overzealous passer-by? Peter provides no answer. What matters for him is that whoever it was, he or she was not a priest. Unless there was a pressing necessity (fear of imminent death), only a priest, he says, may perform a baptism. He dwells on various defects of this improvised baptism (the absence of holy water, of a respondent, of catechetical instruction), and concludes that the baptism is invalid. It is particularly interesting that he considers of no consequence the active participation of the baptized child. Even were it to provide the baptismal responses itself, the baptism would remain invalid. Children under the age of discretion (seven according to most authorities) are incapable of rational behaviour and their commitments are devoid of any legal power.[23]

The problem with Peter of Ancarano's argument is that he jumps from proving that the baptism was illegal to arguing that it is therefore invalid. As we have seen earlier, this is not a permissible deduction. Calderini's solution was aimed at providing a solution to this incongruity. Most authorities agreed that illegal baptisms of this sort are nonetheless valid and have at least some of the consequences of a legal baptism. Peter decided that one could not subvert so many sacred canons and traditions and deprive parents of the consolation of children. He disregards the common legal opinion and rules in favour of the parents.

The legal *consilium* of Gaspar Calderini, then, rests on a solution that practically all authorities rejected—that validly baptized children may remain with their Jewish family; Peter of Ancarano's is based on the premise (again almost universally rejected)

---

[22] See A. Milano, 'Battesimi di Ebrei a Roma dal cinquecento all'ottocento', in *Scritti in memoria di Enzo Sereni: Saggi sull' Ebraismo Romano*, ed. by D. Carpi et al. (Jerusalem, 1970), p. 137. See also idem, *Il Ghetto di Roma: Illustrazioni storiche* (Rome, 1988), pp. 290–91; and S. Waagenaar, *The Pope's Jews* (London, 1974), p. 211.

[23] See A. M. Kleinberg, 'A Thirteenth-Century Struggle over Custody: The Case of Catherine of Parc-aux-Dames', *Bulletin of Medieval Canon Law*, 20 (1990), 53–70.

that an illegal baptism is invalid. What do these *consilia* tell us? If nothing else they prove that a legal expert could find ingenious solutions to specific problems and that such solutions were not necessarily mere extensions of theory. How common was this? For the time being we are faced with a puzzle that is still missing many pieces. Only when more evidence about practice will emerge will we be able to tell what a Jewish family faced when such a baptism actually occurred.

APPENDIX

TEXT I. Gaspar de Calderinis, *Consilia sive responsa, consilium,* 487.3.

An filii Iudeorum infra xii. annum constituti, invitis parentibus, baptizari possint? Et si de facto baptizentur, debeant ali penes iudeos vel christianos?

Ad primum videtur quod sic, propter fidei favorem, pro qua multa inducuntur contra regulas iuris communis (ii. q.vii. Si hereticus, De here[ticis], In fidei, Liber Sextus). Sed quod isti baptizentur est favor fidei, cum salvetur anima pueri (De consecra. dis. iiii. Quaeris), unde videtur[24] spiritualis elemosina ad quam quilibet tenetur (xlv. dis. Tria sunt, De spon[salibus] Inter opera). Item, quia dolus, si est bonus, commendatur (xxii. q.ii. Utilem, et ibi nota De conver[sionel coniu[gtoruml Dudum. Sic et violentia qua quis ad bonum inducitur, quia ista equiparamus (iii. q.i. Redintegranda, De pactis, Quamvis, Liber Sextus cum similibus). Et de his videtur casus xlv. dis. De Iudeis.

Sed contrarium videtur veritas, quia isti non sunt cogendi ad fidem (xlv. di. Qui sincera et c. De Iudeis). Nullus enim invitus fit bonus, quia voluntarium militem Christus elegit (xv. q.i. Non est). Ad hoc: De Iudeis, Iudei, et c. Sicut Iudei, ubi expresse dicitur quod Iudei inviti ad baptismum compellendi non sunt. Et licet illud loquatur in adultis, tamen idem est in parvulis, ut nota glossa xxviii. q.i. Iudeorum filiis. Et hoc tenuit Archidiaconus in dicto capitulo, Qui sincera. Hoc etiam suadet ratio naturalis, que dictat nulli debere fieri iniuria sive violentia, et specialiter ipsis Iudeis (De Iudeis Etsi Iudeos, et 1. Christianis C. De paganis). Unde concluditur: invitis parentibus non essent baptizandos. Nec obstat quod magnus favor debeatur fidei, tamen non debet preberi contra iustitiam (De fo[rol compe[tenti], Ex tenore, et De dona[tionibus] inter vi[ruml et uxo[rem], Nuper), et contra iustitia esset auferre[25] filios parentibus, ut supra dictum est. Nec obstat quod per hoc fieret magna elemosina, quia fateor, si hoc fieret, in adulto, inducendo eum verbis et predicatione.[26]

Ad secundum principale videtur casus quod non, ut in c. Iudeorum filios xxviii. q.i. et facit c. sequens. Et ratio est quia pupillus non debet educari penes illum qui insidietur saluti eius (ff. Ubi pu[pillus] educa[ri vel morari] debeat, l.i et penultimo, et De conver[sionel infi[deliuml c.ii. ubi videtur expressus). Immo ista est causa quare Christiani prohibentur cohabitare cum ipsis Iudeis vel Saracenis (xxviii. q.i. Iudei, et c. Sepe, et duobus c. sequentibus).

Sed ad questionem propositam, dico quod de iure parentes habent filium in potestate. Sive volens sive invitus filius detineatur, ipse filius potest peti a parentibus per interdictum De liberis exhibendis ff. De exhiben[dis] libe[ris], l.i., et quasi per totum, ff. De rei ven[dicationel, l.i., et nota in dicto capitulo finale De conver(sionel infi[deliuml. Ubi ergo non sit suspitio quod pater et mater filium baptizatum ad infidelitatem traha[n]t, est eis restituendus et maxime in casu isto quando eis invitis fuit baptizatus. Et si dicatur semper suspitio adest tamen, propter teneram

---

[24] 'Dicitur' in Vat. lat. 2651, fol. 22lr.

[25] 'Baptizare' in ibid.

[26] Ibid., fol. 221r reads: 'Nec obstat quod hoc potest fieri in adulto inducendo eum verbis et praedicatione'.

etatem, ut filii non subvertantur tamen propter cohabitationem, ut in dictis iuribus: Iudei, Sepe, et c. sequens, et in c. Ad hec, respondeo fateor quod de hoc praesumptio vel suspitio est [faciendum?]. Unde propter talem suspitionem vel praesumptionem dico quod ipsi parentes prestent ydoneam cautionem et sufficientem de ipso filio cum pervenerit ad etatem legitimam que videlicet fit doli capax, quod permittent libere abire et eundem tunc in sua cohabitatione nullatenus retinebunt. Item quod eundem interim non seducent per cautionem enim talem providetur contra suspectos (xxviii. di. De Siracusane, xxxii. q.i. de Benedicto, De rest[itutionel spo[liatorum], Literas, in fine). Si vero dictam cautionem ydoneam dicti parentes vel non possent vel nollent prestare, dico tunc eum nullatenus esse restituendum, ut in iuribus in contrarium allegantibus. Eo ergo casu quo prestatur dicta cautio, restituatur filius dictis parentibus. Nec obstant iura in contrarium allegantes, que loquntur in filiis puberibus, vel quando non sunt subtracti a parentibus, invitis vel si non caverent ut premittitur.

(Whether the children of Jews, under the age of twelve, may be baptized against their parents' will, and if in fact so baptized, whether they ought to be raised by Jews or by Christians.

It seems that the answer to the first question is yes, because of the advantage of the Faith, for which many things are done against the rules of common law.[27] That such children be baptized is to the advantage of the Faith, since the soul of the boy would be saved.[28] Hence it seems an act of spiritual charity to which all are obliged.[29] Likewise, if a wrong has good consequences, it is to be commended,[30] as is violence by which one is led to do good.[31] Concerning these things see D. 45 *De Iudaeis*.[32]

---

[27] DG, C. 2, q. 7, c. 26; Sext., 5.2.5. Both references state that heretics may accuse each other in court, although as excommunicates they cannot normally give testimony.

[28] DG, De cons. D. 4, c. 129 (the baptism of children pleases the entire Christian community).

[29] DG, D. 45, c. 12 (there are three types of charity: corporal, spiritual, and 'corrective' [correcting the errant]); X, 4.1.20 (to recall the erring from the path of error is an act of great charity).

[30] DG, C. 22, q. 2, c. 21 (dissimulation for a good purpose is allowed); X, 3.32.20 (a layman, led by false promises, made a vow of mutual abstinence with his wife; the contract is nevertheless binding).

[31] The references are confusing. Calderini cites DG, C. 3, q. 1, c. 3, which indicates that episcopal property forcibly taken is to be returned immediately to the bishop regardless of the reason that moved the confiscators to take such action. The second authority, Sext., 1.18.2, states that a daughter's promise to renounce, upon marriage, any claims to her father's property is not binding, unless it can be established that she took a free oath on the matter. This seems to be the opposite of what Calderini tries to argue in this section—that the end justifies the means. I cannot explain this discrepancy.

[32] DG, D. 45, c. 5 (Jews are not to be baptized forcibly; however, those who were so baptized must remain faithful Christians).

But the truth seems to be the opposite, because Jews are not to be forced to the Faith.[33] No one becomes good unwillingly. Christ chooses the willing soldier.[34] On this see the *Decretals*, title *De Iudaeis*, chapters Iudaei and *Sicut Iudaei,*[35] where it is said expressly that Jews are not to be compelled to accept baptism unwillingly. And although this is said regarding adults, it holds equally true for young children, as is said in the *Ordinary Gloss* to C. 28, q. 1, c. 11.[36] This is the view of the archdeacon (Guido de Baysio) in his commentary on *qui sincera*.[37] Natural reason also supports this, since it dictates that no one should suffer injury or violence,[38] and this is especially true with regard to Jews.[39] Hence it can be concluded: [Jewish children] are not to baptized against their parents' will. The advantage of the Faith must not be achieved contrary to justice,[40] and it would be contrary to justice to remove children from their parents, as was said above. Nor can it be said that through this a great act of charity is performed. I admit that this would have been so had we been dealing with an adult, persuading him through words and preaching.

To the second principal question, it seems that the answer is no.[41] The reason is that a ward should not be brought up by a person who would plot against his salvation.[42] Indeed this is why Christians are forbidden to live among Jews or Saracens.[43]

---

[33] DG, D. 45, c. 3 and c. 5.

[34] DG, C. 15, q. 1, c. 10 (citing Ambrose: 'voluntarium sibi militem elegit Christus').

[35] X 5.6.5 and X 5.6.9.

[36] The canon taken from Toledo IV orders that the children of Jews be taken away from their parents. The gloss clarifies that the children in question are children already baptized whose parents had a change of heart. If it were permissible to baptize the children of Jews without parental consent, Jews would soon disappear and the prophesies relating to the conversion of the remnant of Israel in the end of days be unfulfilled.

[37] Guido de Baysio ad D. 45, c. 3, s.v. non asperitatibus, *Rosarium* (*Lectura super decreto*) (Lyon, 1516), fol. 49v. While not allowing private individuals to baptize Jewish children, the archdeacon permits Christian princes the same action, since, in his opinion, as slaves of the prince, Jews have no parental rights vis-a-vis their master.

[38] See Thomas Aquinas, *Summa theologiae,* 2a2ae, q. 10, art. 12; 3a, q. 68, art. 10, *Quodlibet,* 2 q. 4, art. 2.

[39] X, 5.6.13 (Christian piety accepts the presence of Jews in the midst of Christian society) and Codex 1.11.6 (Christians are not to harass Jews and pagans who live their lives quietly).

[40] X, 2.2.11; X, 4.20.6 (both state that the charity due to widows must not come at the expense of injustice to others).

[41] DG, C. 28, q. 1, cc. 11, 12 (both say that the fellowship of Jews is to be avoided, especially by converts).

[42] Digest, 27.2.1, 27.2.5 (children are not to be in the custody of suspicious persons), X, 3.33.2 (the child of a baptized father ought not to be brought up among Jews who would risk his physical and spiritual well-being).

[43] DG, C. 28, q. 1, cc. 10, 12–14 (the first forbids socialization with Saracens and Jews; the others refer to Jews alone).

But to the proposed question I say that by right parents have their child in their power; whether he is held willingly or unwillingly [by some third party], this son can be requested by the parents through the interdict *De liberis exhibendis* and by an action through *De rei vindicatione*.[44] Where, therefore, there is no suspicion that the father and mother of a baptized child would draw him into infidelity, he is to be returned to them, especially if he was baptized against their will. And if it is said that, because of the children's tender age, the suspicion always remains that, living together, they would subvert their offspring, as in the following laws: *Iudaei, Saepe* and the following chapter, and *Ad haec*,[45] I say in response what ought to be done concerning such a suspicion. To solve this problem the parents are to offer a suitable and sufficient surety for the child that when he reaches legal age, that is when he becomes capable of doing wrong, they will let him go freely and will in no way hold him back with them. Likewise, it shall be provided by means of such a surety that the suspect [parents] will not lead the child astray in the meantime.[46]

If, however, the parents cannot or would not place this suitable surety, I say that then the child must in no way be returned to them ,as was stated in the laws that argue the contrary form of action [that is, laws that disallow baptized individuals to live among Jews]. When the said surety is placed by the parents, their child is to be returned to them. Laws that argue the contrary have no bearing on this case, since they deal with adolescents (not infants], or with cases where the children were not taken away from unwilling parents, or when they [the parents] did not take the precautions necessary to allow [cohabitation].)

TEXT II. Peter of Ancarano, *Consilia* (Pavia, 1496), 195.

In Christi nomine amen. Secundum ea que proposita sunt videtur quod dictus puer hebreus non debet nec dici possit baptizatus, et hoc rationibus et iuribus supradictis que possunt iuribus et rationibus corroborari. Deficit enim hic primo potestas ex parte baptizantis. Nam alius quam sacerdos baptizare non potest nisi in casu necessitates (De conse. di. iiii. c. Constat et c. In veritate [necessitate]). Deficit igitur hic baptismus propter defectum persone agentis et sic auctoritas traditionis (De conse. di. iiii. Sanctum est baptisma). Ideo de aliis solemnitatibus que requiruntur in baptismo non videtur necessario inquirendum ut l. Quidam referunt (De iure codi[cillorum]). Ex parte etiam suscipientis deficit hic impressio huius sacramenti. Parvulis enim quia non intelligunt quid agunt, non confertur nisi ab illo teneantur et offerantur qui interrogationibus sacerdotis respondeant (i. q.i. Spiritus sanctus). Et est speciale hoc casu ut fides parentum vel alterius offerentis obliget pueros ad fidem et possunt alienum [alieni?] suppleat [supplere?]

[44] Digest, 43.30 (an interdict which provides for the restitution of a child to the parents, except when the child stays willingly with the second party); Digest, 6.1 (an action allowing the father to demand the restitution of his child by an appeal to Quirital possession); X, 3.33.2 (Gregory IX gives paternal right as the main reason for giving custody of a child to the father).

[45] DG, C. 28, q. 1, cc. 10, 12, 13; X, 5.6.8.

[46] DG, D. 28, c. 13, C. 32, q. 1, c. 5; X, 2.13.13 (all cases where a bond is used to guarantee the proper behaviour of suspect persons).

defectum non alias intelli[gentis?] pupillaris etatis—que etas quod vide[alt ignorat—et eorum fides nihil operatur ut predicta probantur (De conse. di. iiii. per totum). In questions autem proposita defuit responsalis, quia nullus respondit pro parte parvuli hebrei, et per se responders ipse non potuit veluti furiosus et intellects carens et fide, ut nota in dicto capitulo Spiritus sanctus et l. i. ff. De acqui[renda vel amittendal po[ssessione]. Et si dicatur iste non-sacerdos qui infundit super caput huius pueri hebrei utrum eque potuit responders pro eo, respondeo hoc non est verum. Quia sicut in ista sacramentali generations alius debet esse qui spiritualiter generator, alius qui spiritualiter generate ita alius debet esse qui pro puero respondeat, alius qui baptizat, ut dicto capitulo Spiritus sanctus et c. Prima. Igitur sic non potest unus conferre beneficium et collationem recipere (c. finale De Insti[tutionibus]). Et est hic defectus ex parte aque, unde dicit beatus Ambrosius, non omnis aqua sonat, sed illa que habet gratiam Christi (De conse. di. iiii. Per aquam et c. finale [sequens?]). Frustra enim sacrificantes ad baptismum conferendum et aqua ibi posita deputata [deputati?] essent, si quis posset in qualibet aqua baptizari (facit capitulo dicto in principio et quod ibi nota[tur]). Deficit etiam hic solemnitas nathacismi [sic] que debet precedere baptismum in pueris et adultis (de qua solemnitate et in quibus consistat habetur De conse. di. iiii. Baptizandi (nomen] cum pluribus capitulis sequentibus). Quod ergo unus, non sacerdos, nulla necessitate cogente baptizando puerum hebreum possit subvertere tot sacrorum canonum traditiones et parentibus subtrahere solatium filiorum discretione carentium iniquissimum videretur. Et immo concludo dictum puerum non esse baptizatum per rationes et iura predicta que possunt multis aliis rationibus confirmari, gratia brevitatis omissis.

(In the name of Christ, amen. According to what was put forward, it seems that the said Hebrew boy is not, nor can he be said to be, baptized, and this for the reasons and laws mentioned above, which can be further corroborated by [the following] laws and reasons. First, missing here is the authority on the part of the baptizer. For no one but a priest may baptize, except in cases of emergency [literally necessity].[47] There is therefore no baptism, because of the defect in the person of the agent, and thus the authority of transmission.[48] It is not therefore necessary to inquire about other rites required in baptism.[49]

On the part of the receiver lacking here is the impression of the sacramental character.[50] Since young children do not know what they do, it is only conferred upon them, if they are held and offered by him who responds to the interrogations of the priest.[51] And it is special to baptism

---

[47] DG, De cons. D. 4, cc. 19, 21.

[48] DG, De cons. D. 4, c. 36 (the same as the two earlier references: baptism by laymen is allowed only in case of an emergency).

[49] Digest 29.7.14 (questions regarding the persons involved in a transfer of property precede any consideration regarding the procedural validity of the grant).

[50] Baptism, confirmation, and holy orders impress on the recipient an indelible character.

[51] DG, C. 1, q. 1, c. 58. The relevant part is actually in the dictum post (Peter may have had a text where there was no distinction between the body of the text and Gratian's addition). The case involved children baptized by friends as part of a game. The bishop inquired whether all the basic elements of the rite were present and whether all the responses were made and declared the

that the faith of the parents or of someone else offering the child commits children to the Faith, and others can supply what is missing in the child who has no understanding himself. [Children of] this age do not understand what they see,[52] and the faith of those of this age has no effect as has been proved above.[53] In this case a respondent was missing, because no one responded on behalf of the Hebrew child, and he could not make the responses himself, being similar to a madman, lacking both understanding and faith.[54]

And if it were asked whether that non-priest who poured the water over the Hebrew boy's head could not also respond on his behalf, I would answer that he could not. Because, just as in the sacramental bringing forth one is spiritually brought forth and another spiritually brings forth, in the same way there must be one person who responds on behalf of the boy, another who baptizes him.[55] Hence, one person cannot both confer a benefice and receive it.[56]

And there is also a defect on the part of the water, hence St Ambrose says: 'Not any water heals, but that which has the grace of Christ'.[57] It would be pointless to designate celebrants and special water for the celebration of baptism, if one could be baptized in any water.[58] Missing is also the solemnity of Catechism that ought to precede baptism in children and in adults.[59]

That someone, then, not a priest and with no pressing necessity could in baptizing the Hebrew boy subvert so many sacred canons and traditions and deprive the parents of the consolation of children lacking discretion seems most wicked. I conclude, therefore, that the said boy is not baptized for the reasons and laws discussed above which can be confirmed by many other reasons not mentioned for the sake of brevity.)

---

baptism valid (this contradicts Peter of Ancarano's earlier emphasis on the need to have a priest for a valid baptism; there was no question of emergency in the case described).

[52] See Codex, 9.24.1.6 ('quia aetas eorum quid videat ignorat').

[53] DG, De cons. D. 4 in its entirety. Though there is much in D. 4 about the importance of faith, the reference to the entire distinction is somewhat exaggerated.

[54] DG, dictum post C. 1, q. 1, c. 58 (this refers to the importance of a respondent), Digest, 41.2.3 (a minor and a madman cannot acquire possession without the authority of a guardian or a tutor). However, that the absence of a respondent obstructs the sacrament was not the prevailing view. See Felinus Sandaei's discussion in his *Commentaria V in decretalium,* 4 vols (Basel, 1568), III, 1084.

[55] DG, dictum post C. 1, q. 1, c. 58, De cons. D. 4, c. 73 (a sermon of Augustine on the baptismal responses).

[56] X, 3.7.7 ('cum inter dantem et accipientem debeat esse distinctio personalis').

[57] DG, De cons. D. 4, c. 9 and c. 10 (which has the same theme as c. 9).

[58] See previous note.

[59] DG, De cons. D. 4, c. 60.

Liturgy and the Foundation of Cults in the Thirteenth and Fourteenth Centuries

MICHAEL GOODICH

In the course of the 1202 translation of the relics of Gilbert of Sempringham (d. 1189), following his canonization by Innocent III, it is reported that 'some sick people came closer, and as they touched these holy objects, they were delivered from their illnesses, we know for certain, at that very same hour'.[1] Although Gilbert's biographer provides details about the ceremony itself and the accompanying activities, he does not discuss these particular cures or the reaction of the crowd. Other such cures, however, which took place just before or during the translation ceremony, often played a decisive role in the establishment of a cult, and are described in graphic detail in contemporary miracle collections. Hagiographical sources provide examples in which the performance of the liturgy served as the necessary context through which the power of the saint's relics was first publicly manifested, a private devotion was transformed into a public cult and certain basic themes of Catholic piety were reinforced. Such religious ritual performs two important roles: (1) certain central values and traditions are transmitted to both participants and spectators in symbolic form; and (2) the categories through which the structure of society, the natural and moral order, and the collective view of the world are perceived, re-enacted, or recreated.[2]

An earlier version of this paper was presented at the Hagiography Society workshop held at Ammerdown, 6–10 July 1998. I would like to thank the participants for their valuable comments.

[1] *The Book of Saint Gilbert,* ed. and trans. by R. Foreville and G. Ker (Oxford, 1987), p. 191.

[2] C. Helman, *Culture, Health and Illness*, 2nd edn (Oxford, 1990), p. 193.

Several well-documented cases illustrate how miracles have played a particularly decisive role in the establishment of a new cult. In all of these cases, an exorcism in which the perennial conflict between God and Satan, acted out in public, was the premier miracle. Anthropologists and others have noted that spirit possession, or 'the attribution of illness to the direct, hostile, arbitrary, or punitive action of some malevolent or affronted supernatural being', such as an incubus or succubus, is the most widespread type of supernatural cause of disease. In this respect, the following examples parallel paradigms of demonic possession observed in contemporary Pentecostal sects or in non-Christian tribal societies.[3] The exorcism provides a kind of social therapy for the entire group. If interpersonal stress had characterized this group, onlookers and participants are assured that such tensions will abate following a cure.

The first posthumous miracle attributed to Bishop Thomas of Hereford (d. 1282) reportedly occurred in 1284, about two years after his death.[4] But because it was not a public event, a more dramatic demonstration of the saint's power was required. In Thomas's canonization trial[5] it is reported that the focal miracle had taken place rather fortuitously on 28 March 1287, the Friday just preceding Palm Sunday. This was about a week before the scheduled translation of Thomas's relics, which were to be moved to the chapel of St Catherine on Maundy Thursday, 4 April 1287, in the course of an extensive renovation carried out at Hereford cathedral.[6] Because of flaws in the Bollandist transcription, the Vatican manuscript is more reliable in reconstructing this focal miracle.[7] A considerable number of persons, male and female, are named who

---

[3] G. P. Murdock, *Theories of Illness. A World Survey* (Pittsburgh, 1980), p. 20. Important works on this theme include I. M. Lewis, *Ecstatic Religion. An Anthropological Study of Spirit Possession and Shamanism* (Harmondsworth, 1971); E. Bourgignon, *Religion, Altered States of Consciousness and Social Change* (Columbus, OH, 1973). The classic account, in which medieval cases are also treated, remains T. K. Oesterreich, *Possession, Demoniacal and Other among Primitive Races in Antiquity, the Middle Ages, and Modern Times*, trans. by D. Ibberson (London, 1930). On demonic possession in a scriptural context, see J. D. Crossan, *The Historical Jesus. The Life of a Mediterranean Jewish Peasant* (New York, 1992), pp. 313–20.

[4] *Processus canonizationis Thomae de Cantilupo*, in AASS, 2 October, I, pp. 582–83, 694–95. For summary of miracles, see R. Finucane, *Miracles and Pilgrims. Popular Beliefs in Medieval England* (London, 1995), pp. 181–82. Thomas's servant William Jaudre and Robert Deynte (witnesses nos. 53, 60) told of the miracle-working power of the dead bishop's cloak. See AASS, 2 October, I, pp. 582, 696–97. A collection of articles on this hearing appears in *Saint Thomas Cantilupe, Bishop of Hereford: Essays in His Honour*, ed. by M. Jancey (Hereford, 1982).

[5] Recorded in early November 1307 at the chapel of St Catherine in Hereford.

[6] A sermon was preached at his funeral by Cardinal Girolamo Marei, Bishop of Palestrina, later elected Pope Nicholas IV. Thomas's heart had been sent to Ashridge in Buckinghamshire, while part of Thomas's relics had been interred at Orvieto where he had died on 25 August 1282.

[7] Vatican City, Biblioteca Apostolica Vaticana, lat. 4015, fol. 211r–219v. This miracle does

either witnessed the miracle, or immediately heard about it, including cathedral canons, artisans of various kinds, and dependents of both the king and bishop.

A demoniac named Edith, aged about twenty, the wife of Robert,[8] an iron merchant and citizen of Hereford (and the daughter of one Ralph Holdecrift) had been brought to Thomas's temporary tomb and was cured. Gilbert, the procurator of the church of Hereford, testified that she had been brought to the site of Thomas's bones in the Ladychapel because her behaviour would disturb the choir, which was some distance away.[9] Just after sunrise and right after prime, the chaplain John Godhyne was celebrating mass on the so-called altar of the Cross,[10] beside Thomas's temporary tomb. In the course of the celebration all the lamps and candles suddenly lit up around the altar, and then were immediately extinguished, although there had been no sign of a breeze. All those present were stunned.[11]

At the same time everyone heard an unusual sound of rushing water. The only light came from the candle which had been brought as an ex-voto offering and whose wick had been measured by friends to the length of Edith's body. Edith just then lay prostrate before the altar with hands and feet tied. The candle lit up miraculously with a 'celestial fire' in three places, at the top, bottom, and in the middle. When this candle suddenly began to burn, all the other lights in the church were rekindled. At the same time, Edith came free of her bonds and stood up, crying out repeatedly to the participants, 'It is Saint Thomas who returned my sanity to me'. Turning to a woman who was holding her, since her chains had fallen to her feet, she said, 'Let me go', approaching the altar and placing the lighted candle above it, while giving thanks to God and St Thomas for her recovery. When the mass was completed, Edith went unaided to Thomas's bones in the Ladychapel.

Those who viewed Edith's exorcism were already anticipating the festivities scheduled within a few days in Thomas's honour, and may well have been part of the constituency supporting his cult. Several of those who testified about Edith's cure appear to have come from the parish of Marden, which figures very prominently in Thomas's other posthumous miracles.[12] Anthropologists who have studied demonic

---

not appear among those cited in the bull of canonization.

[8] Ibid. fol., 216v.

[9] The Ladychapel was built by about 1240. N. Pevsner, *Hereford. History and Guide* (Harmondsworth, 1963). For a plan of the cathedral, see *An Inventory of the Historical Monuments in Herefordshire, I: South West*, 3 vols, Royal Commission on Historical Monuments (London, 1931–34).

[10] This was known as the Rood altar.

[11] This lasted about as long as one could recite ten times the Sunday prayer along with the Hail Mary ('decies orationem dominicam cum Ave Maria'); AASS, 2 October, I, pp. 622–23.

[12] This includes the revival of the drowned child Joan, daughter of the local sheriff. This particular miracle is more thoroughly discussed in Ronald C. Finucane, *The Rescue of the Innocents. Endangered Children in Medieval Miracles* (New York, 1997), along with a

possession have noted the presence of the extended family during exorcism and the need for a public ritual to restore unity to a fractured community.[13] After the participants prayed beside Thomas's temporary tomb, they returned to the altar of the Cross, where Gilbert celebrated mass. Edith participated fully in the offertory, kissed Gilbert's hand, and gave an offering of one penny, and remained until the mass had ended. After it was over, Gilbert gathered together all four cathedral canons who were to be found in the city. Edith remained in the church until nones, Edith and Gilbert recounted the miracle, the church bells were rung, the people and clergy joined in procession, and all heard of the miracle. Gilbert sang out loudly, as others followed in reciting the *Te Deum*.

The support of the canons for Thomas's cult rested on the saint's strong defence of their liberties during his episcopacy.[14] The canonization record reveals that Thomas's cult was not universally accepted, since Bishop Thomas had in fact died in the course of a jurisdictional dispute with the archbishop which had reached the curia.[15] Thomas had failed to appear at a hearing held in Lambeth palace, and was forced to withdraw to the abbey of Lyra in Normandy for a year and a half.[16] His canonization was therefore to be delayed until a special hearing was held proving that he had not in fact died excommunicate.[17] It was suggested by one of those who heard of Edith's liberation that the miracle was more likely to have occurred due to the merits of another former bishop of Hereford, Robert de Beton (d. 1147), also buried in the cathedral. Nevertheless, Edith herself rejected this suggestion, and insisted that Thomas had appeared to her in the course of her cure, looking as she had seen him when he was serving as bishop. Gilbert testified that when Thomas of St Omer, a canon of Hereford and member of Archbishop John of Canterbury's household, came to the city the day after Edith's cure in order to deal with problems connected to the recently vacant Welsh see of Llandaff,[18] Gilbert was severely reprimanded and suspended for seven days for publicizing the miracle without the archbishop's approval.

This suspension was, however, revoked by Master William de Montfort, dean of London and precentor of the church of Hereford, who admitted that this was the first posthumous public miracle which had been performed by Thomas of Hereford. Possibly on Maundy Thursday, 4 April 1287, Thomas's bones were removed from the

---

translation of the testimony, pp. 169–206.

[13] Helman, *Culture*, p. 204.

[14] A. T. Bannister, *The Cathedral Church of Hereford* (London, 1924), pp. 68–72.

[15] Two issues had been in dispute, one dealing with inheritance, another with matrimonial problems.

[16] Bannister, *The Cathedral Church*, pp. 87 ff.

[17] Vatican City, Biblioteca Apostolica Vaticana, lat. 4015, fol. 212r. The records of this investigation appear in Vatican, Biblioteca Apostolica, 4016.

[18] A ten-year vacancy occurred between the recent death of Bishop William de Breuse (1 May 1266–19 March 1287) and the consecration of John of Monmouth (10 February 1297–8 April 1323).

Ladychapel to the northwest transept.[19] The fact that Edith's cure had occurred so close to the translation of Thomas's relics suggests that the event may have been orchestrated in order to encourage participation in the cult and in the festivities surrounding the translation.[20]

Several witnesses provided the background to Edith's affliction, which conforms to the traditional symptoms of demonic possession and would require a ritual exorcism. Her husband Robert reported that they had been married for two years when, at the beginning of Lent (i.e. 23 February 1287) his wife began to suffer, namely for about a month prior to the miracle. She had eaten and drunk a bit, and while they were in bed at night she began gesticulating and speaking blasphemously against their neighbours.[21] The next day, since her condition had continued, he had her bound with cloth, while two neighbour women guarded her. She remained bound in that way until a week before Palm Sunday, highly weakened, often delirious, eating little and drinking only water or weak beer.

On his neighbour's advice Robert measured his wife and had two candles made out of a quarter of a pound of wax, one for the Holy Cross at Wistanton[22] and the other for the Holy Cross at Hereford. This devotional practice was noted by the commission investigating the miracles as a peculiarly English practice with historical precedents.[23] She was taken by her two neighbours to the church at Hereford in order to incubate there as a means of effecting a cure within five or six days. At vespers on the Thursday just before Palm Sunday she was moved at the advice of an unnamed cleric from the altar of the Cross to the Ladychapel, where Thomas's bones were interred, since the cleric said she could be cured through Thomas's merits. The next morning, Friday, Robert brought the other candle to the Holy Cross at Wistanton. On returning to Hereford he heard the bells of the cathedral pealing, and prayed to God that it would be because his wife had been cured. He met John Slaybond of the parish of Marden who told him that his wife had been cured due to Thomas's merits. When he got to the church he saw Edith taking part in the Eucharist service, and the candle which she had brought to the church was deposited in the treasury. Edith was accompanied home by the two neighbour women on the same litter in which she had come to church.

Edith recovered from her illness, but nevertheless died within two months, on the feast of Peter and Paul (i.e. 29 June 1287) and was buried in the cemetery of the church at Hereford. The victim herself therefore did not take part in Thomas's canonization

---

[19] He was buried in a tomb whose carvings included fifteen armed Templars treading on monsters, which stressed Thomas's role as a former grand master of the Templars in England.

[20] On the translation see AASS, 2 October, I, p. 584.

[21] She uttered blasphemies against God and the saints.

[22] Not otherwise identified.

[23] This is discussed in the report of Thomas's miracles, written between 1318 and 1320. For the text, see A. Vauchez, *Sainthood in the Later Middle Ages*, trans. by J. Birrell (Cambridge, 1997), pp. 540–58.

trial. Dyonisia, the wife of Robert the apothecary, testified that Edith may have been pregnant; at first she was saddened, then became mentally deranged.[24] A similar case of either false or unwanted pregnancy in a possessed woman appears in the unpublished 1265 summary of the miracles of Philip of Bourges.[25] It has been noted that ritual is often a way of reducing anxiety at a time of physiological change, and its cathartic effects help to relieve uncertainty and unpleasant emotions born of an unwanted pregnancy or other emotional stress in which family or other support is not forthcoming.[26]

The candle episode in this dossier parallels a similar miracle found in the canonization record of the hermit John Buoni (d. 1249), one of the forerunners of the Augustinian order.[27] The tale was corroborated by five witnesses who spoke at John's canonization hearing, and may likewise be regarded as the formative miracle initiating John's cult. At the time of the translation of John's relics, a group of youths from the St Nicholas quarter of Mantua had constructed a tall and elaborately decorated candle made of many smaller candles. On Whit Sunday, 4 June 1251, just after tierce, they came to the church of St Agnes with their unlit candle. The brethren processed from the church carrying holy water in order to bless the children and the accompanying throng, all of whom lamented that the candle was not burning. During the benediction, the candle had been lowered as the brethren sang, and all those present praised the name of Jesus. At the moment that the bearers raised the candle on high, it suddenly lit up and then went out. When this miracle took place, despite the rejoicing, a young woman impatiently demanded that the candle be rekindled due to John Buoni's merits.[28] Nevertheless, the brethren and throng of participants cried out, 'May the name of Our Lord Jesus Christ be blessed, who through the merits of brother John Buoni performed such a miracle for us sinners, and thus made clear that he is worthy'. At the time of John's translation, the region was harried by Frederick II's ally Ezzelino da Romano, who figures prominently as one of those enemies of the church who were strenuously

---

[24] Dyonisia also said that when the high mass was being celebrated spectators saw a small white object descend onto the candle (fols 216v–217r).

[25] *Processus super vita et miraculis domini Philippi archiepiscopi Biturcensis*, in Paris, BNF, lat. 5373A, fols 16v–17r.

[26] Helman, *Culture*, p. 207. See also C. Ward and M. Beaubrun, 'The Psychodynamics of Demon Possession', *Journal for the Scientific Study of Religion,* 19 (1980), 201–07, who note that demon possession is often a symptom of neurotic depression.

[27] *Processus apostolici de B. Joanne Bono*, in AASS, 22 October, IX, pp. 884–86. See G. J. C. Snoek, *Medieval Piety from Relics to the Eucharist* (Leiden, 1995), pp. 322–28, on miraculous light. See *Magna vita Sancti Hugonis*, ed. by D. Douie and H. Farmer, 2 vols (London, 1962), II, 220, on the great light which accompanied Hugh of Lincoln's coffin in 1200, since the lighted candles were not extinguished despite the rain and wind.

[28] She is described as a *muliercula*, which suggests perhaps a prostitute. See *Processus apostolici de B. Joanne Bono*.

opposed by John in his lifetime. Stress was particularly placed on his conversion of anticlerical Patarenes, and the doubting woman, who had died by the time of the canonization trial in 1253, may have been a member of this sect.[29]

A report of posthumous exorcism, similar to the case of Edith, also appears in the dossier of the Servite Joachim Piccolomini, and again it is the miracle that initiated the cult.[30] Christopher of Parma (writing in about 1335) reported that in May, 1310, five years after Joachim's death, pilgrims had gathered at the monastery of San Galgano at Chiusdino, about twenty-two miles from Siena. They had come because of the indulgences granted to Galgano, the early Augustinian whose shrine was one of the most important in Tuscany. Gathered around a fire because of the cold, they recalled the life and miracles of some local saints, including the Dominican Ambrose of Siena (d. 1287), the Franciscan Tertiary Peter Pettinaio (d. 1289), and others. One of them sought to praise Joachim, but wondered why, although he had performed many miracles in his lifetime, no miracles had been performed through him since his death. This suggests that a dramatic cure was needed in order to initiate a cult in his honour. A *conversus* of the Servite order, who was present around the fire, had been told that day by a physician that a growth would have to be removed. After hearing about Joachim, he fearfully beseeched the saint, saying, 'Oh most holy father Joachim, if what I have heard about you is true, ask almighty God to begin to show your miracles through me; I promise to proclaim it publicly, and to personally bring to you a waxen offering replicating me'. The next morning, when he went to the physician for the operation, he found the growth was gone, and fulfilled his promise.

But since this Servite was an interested party and this cure had been a private event, a more dramatic public cure was required in order to encourage Joachim's cult. This occurred shortly thereafter. During Pentecost, on 7 June 1310, as friar Nicholas of Siena was preaching at the Servite cloister after nones (i.e. about 3.00 PM), a demoniac woman named Christianella was brought in. After the preacher had told of the preceding miracle, the incubus possessing the woman cried out, 'The time has come for me to exit, and for Christianella's liberation'. This attracted a large number of spectators. When the spirit was asked why the other saints had not expelled him, the demoniac moved to Joachim's tomb, and said, 'Because God has reserved this miracle for this saint, and it is pleasing to the divine wisdom to do so'. After being conjured up again, the demon said, 'When I leave her, I will break a lamp and leave Christianella as if she were dead'. The demon then broke the lamp and darparted. In addition, even though she was a simple and unlettered woman, she spoke perfectly. The demon added, 'Remove the clothes from her back, cut the hair on her head, and hang it on his tomb as proof of this miracle, lest I have the power to return'. It is clear that prior to this miracle, Joachim's merits had not been universally recognized. The mere recitation of the first miracle

---

[29] *Processus apostolici de B. Joanne Bono,* pp. 813, 834, 828.

[30] 'Vita et miracula beati Ioachimi Senensis ordinis servorum sanctae Mariae virginis', ed. by P. M. Soulier, *Analecta Bollandiana*, 13 (1894), 391–92.

would not suffice. A dramatic demonstration of the saint's merits through the exorcism of a well-known incubus in the presence of a large gathering on an important feast day was necessary in order to encourage the establishment of his cult.

A further example of a public miracle as the dramatic event which initiated a cult comes from the miracles of the shepherdess and hermit Giovanna da Signa (d. 1307?).[31] Giovanna was reportedly a local miracle-worker in her lifetime who specialized in the problems of the rural peasantry, but her cult apparently began to flourish during the plague in 1348, and was active again during the secondary plague years of 1363–66 and 1383; she was the patroness of one of the few confraternities devoted to a recent, uncanonized saint, attested to at Signa in 1385, and the subject of a cycle of frescoes at the parish church.[32] The founding episode of her *devotio* probably occurred in 1348, with the miraculous cure of Nuta da Signa, who had known Giovanna in her lifetime. Suffering from the plague and despairing of human help, Giovanna appeared to her at night and she was cured.[33] The second miracle also occurred privately, when Francesco Nerozzi in his sleep envisioned his wife beseeching Giovanna's aid against the plague.[34]

But, here again, a more public event occurred afterward. According to the author of her dossier, in order to deal with the shortage of food, medicine, and religious services which accompanied the plague, in 1348 twenty-four men had joined together to establish the Compagnia dello Spirito Santo, a group of *Bianchi*, or penitential flagellants.[35] In the course of their activities, they came to the Carmelite house near Signa in order to take counsel, confess, and receive communion from the provincial prior of Tuscany, Pietro di Lapo. One of their number, Morozzo Tendi Mori da Signa, said that he was going to confess, although he did not do so.

Dressed in white, the members of the confraternity took an oath of mutual loyalty and provided assistance to the needy in Signa and in the regions of Gangalandi and Montelupo. Several days later, probably after the plague had reached Signa in March, 1348, a general penitential procession came to the church of Signa, where Giovanna's relics were housed.[36] During a solemn mass, the penitents called upon God to put an end to the plague. The priest who was celebrating the mass offered the relics of Giovanna's

---

[31] 'Vita e miracoli della Beata Giovanna da Signa', ed. by S. Mencherini, *Archivum fratrum historicum,* 10 (1917), 367–86; *Vita*, in AASS, 9 November, IV, pp. 280–88. J. Delarun, 'Jeanne de Signa, ermite toscane du XIVe siècle ou la sainteté ordinaire', *Mélanges de l'École française de Rome. Môyen Âge*, 98, pt. 1 (1986), 187, reasonably places Giovanna's death closer to 1348.

[32] G. Kaftal, *Iconography of the Saints in Tuscan Painting* (Florence, 1952), pp. 539–50; D. Russo, 'Jeanne da Signa ou l'iconographie au féminin. Études sur les fresques de l'église paroissale de Signa (milieu du XVe siècle)', *Mélanges de l'École française de Rome. Môyen Âge*, 98 (1986), 201–18.

[33] Mencherini, 'Vita e miracoli', p. 379, n. 5.

[34] Ibid., p., 382, n. 16.

[35] Ibid., p. 385, n. 27.

[36] Delarun, 'Jeanne de Signa', p. 183.

arms to the congregants in order to kiss them. During the plague years, such processions and masses were a focal point of penitential requests to God to mitigate his anger, which was regarded as the cause of the great catastrophe that had befallen Europe. Morozzo, who had yet not confessed and had not done so for twenty years, attempted to kiss the relics. Nevertheless, he was driven back three times, as though pushed aside by force. The third time, he fell to the ground accompanied by a loud crash which sounded like a falling pillar. The author of Giovanna's dossier suggested that it appeared as though he was being held down by a demon. After being lifted up by the startled onlookers, he publicly confessed his sins and admitted that he had not confessed for twenty years and expired three days later.

Although the author does not say this, Morozzo may well have died of the plague, since three days generally elapsed between the first appearance of its symptoms and the victim's death. The author regarded this as both the just punishment of one who had acted without faith, failing to confess, and as proof of the value of Giovanna's relics. Morozzo's origins in Signa would suggest a previous acquaintance with Giovanna, and his punishment implies an insufficient display of the kind of local patriotism so closely associated with cults such as Giovanna's. His experience was immortalized in a fresco cycle executed at Signa in 1441 and 1462 by the Bicci atelier.[37]

Catalogues of miracles that took place during the procession and display of holy relics contain further accounts of exorcising doubt during the liturgy. Such miracles encompass the saint's constituency and symbolize the patron/client relationship which governed the economy of the sacred. The failure to mobilize the community in order to show its respect for its patron could have baleful results. For example, several days after Whit Sunday, on Wednesday, 2 June 1322, all of the clergy, nobility, and people of Temse near Ghent took part in a traditional barefoot circumvolution of the town to the accompaniment of mimes, clowns, and various kinds of musicians in which the relics of St Amalberga and others were held on high.[38] Because fewer than usual had taken part in the ceremony that year, the sacred carriage was borne with difficulty to the altar, and a great storm arose in which the village was nearly destroyed by hailstones. Afterward, apples were found which allegedly bore devilish faces. This was taken as the just judgement of God and as a warning that Amalberga's cult should be honoured, since the storm did not extend beyond the borders of Temse. On the other hand, the following year, the entire community took part in the festivities and an increase in miracles was recorded.

Another kind of miracle in which religious liturgy and the expression of doubt were linked appears in the *topos* of vengeance against those who acted sacrilegiously in the course of witnessing a translation ceremony. Hagiographical accounts of the first translation of a saint's relics often contain a catalogue of those miraculous cures which

---

[37] Russo, 'Jeanne de Signa', p. 208, n. 7.

[38] *Miracula S. Amalbergae virginis*, in AASS, 10 July, III, pp. 100–107.

occur during the solemn procession preceding the interment of sacred relics.[39] Such expressions of doubt may be caused by: (1) personal animus against the saint; (2) resentment of clerical greed in the establishment of the cult; (3) sympathy for such heresies as Waldensianism, which rejected the cult of the saints; (4) rivalry between religious orders, each of which preferred its own saints; and (5) local patriotism, which denigrated the saints belonging to other regions.[40] But despite the prevalence of this theme in hagiographical sources, the only case which passed the curial standards for judging the validity of a miracle and was, as a consequence, noted in a bull of canonization, is found in the bull canonizing Louis of Toulouse (d. 1297) issued by John XXII on 7 April 1317. The pope's bull reports that 'When a certain man had made detracting remarks concerning the miracles of the saint, his eyesight was blurred, and his face was twisted. He remained in this condition for six days, until he made a vow out of devotion to the saint. Coming to the tomb, offering a head fashioned of wax, before leaving the church, he was completely cured'.[41]

This episode refers to Guillaume de Moissac, a stonemason and citizen of Marseilles, who was about fifty at the time of the miracle, two months after Louis's burial. His affliction and cure were reported by the victim himself, along with two other witnesses. It was reported that he had come one Sunday morning to the Franciscan church at Marseilles. After mass had been sung, a large crowd had gathered in the church. 'Some were carrying candles, others full images, some effigies, some various kinds of candles and waxen figures in honour of the saint'. Guillaume reported at the hearing that he had mockingly said, 'From now on the other saints in Paradise have little to do, since Saint Louis is doing everything'. One of his fellow stonemasons reported that he had contemptuously said, 'Would that Louis could perform virtues and miracles, just as an ass does'. Guillaume's face was immediately disfigured; out of shame and grief he covered his face with a cape.[42] Physicians were unable to cure his condition,

---

[39] See, for example, the circuit of the relics of Atto of Pistoia, in AASS 22 May, V, pp. 199–204.

[40] M. Goodich, 'Miracles and Disbelief in the Late Middle Ages', *Mediaevistik,* 1 (1990), 23–38.

[41] Patres Collegii S. Bonaventurae, 'Processus canonizationis et Legendae variae Sancti Ludovici', in *Analecta franciscana,* VII (Quaracchi, 1951), p. 399: 'Cum homo quidam, qui miraculis huius sancti detrahere nitebatur, reversionem faciei et oculorum turpiter incurrisset sicque manens per dies sex huic sancto se cum devotione qua poterat devovisset, ad sepulchrum eius veniens et offerens caput cerae, antequam exiret ecclesiam perfect reperit se curatum'. This canonization inquiry is discussed more thoroughly in M. R. Toynbee, *S. Louis of Toulouse and the Process of Canonisation in the Fourteenth Century* (Manchester, 1929).

[42] Patres Collegii S. Bonaventurae, 'Processus canonizationis', pp. 233–36. The hearing was held at Marseilles in 1308, and the event took place in 1297. Guillaume was sixty at the time of the trial. The testimonies of three witnesses are found in the protocol, although seven names appear. The only person who appears to have been present when he cursed the saint, became

and after remaining at home for three days, he returned to work, although his affliction continued.[43] He only recovered completely after he expressed full contrition and beseeched the aid of Louis of Toulouse. A week later he came to the church as a penitent carrying a waxen offering in the form of a head and a candle, reporting the miracle to the custodian. Although others were equally punished for mocking the saint,[44] Guillaume's affliction allegedly dated from the mass celebrated in Louis's honour and, because of its citation in the canonization bull, may be regarded as one of Louis most important miracles.

In all of the previous exorcisms, the victims were quite adamant as to which saint had been responsible for their liberation, despite the voices of doubt and opposition which had been raised. It was in fact not unusual for demoniacs to specify which saint was to be their preferred liberator. In one of the very earliest public miracles attributed to the Franciscan Gerard Cagnoli (d. 1342) a woman from the village of Santa Maria a Monte near Pisa, after suffering for a year and eight months, told her husband, who had himself never heard of the saint, that 'There is no remedy or medicine except what is provided by friar Bartholomeo Albizi'.[45] Having composed a special prayer in Gerard's honour, Bartholomeo performed a mass in her presence with the saint's relics. Two days later, he prepared a kind of ritual plaque with which she was signed and which was fastened to her, leading to her cure. Sixteen members of the victim's family appeared at Pisa with a wax ex-voto offering of four pounds, confirming her recovery.

In all of the cases cited above, the interaction between a wider audience of believers and the victim-performer may be seen as a kind of sacred theatre in which the recurring drama of the cosmic conflict between God and Satan is re-enacted. The presence of spectators, including relatives, friends, local parishioners, clergy, and curious onlookers, is a sine qua non of the demoniac's successful therapy. The victim becomes a willing performer in what appears to be an orchestrated effort to encourage the creation of a cult with the cooperation of the audience.[46] Some observers have argued with respect to

---

disfigured, and recovered was one Gerald de Albana, who was dead at the time of the trial (ibid., p. 234).

[43] The witnesses reported that Guillaume worked as a stonemason 'in opere Philippi Corderii', and that at the time was employed 'in carreria de Cordis' (ibid., pp. 235–36). Since the Franciscans, who were the chief proponents of Louis cult, were called 'Cordeliers', this may imply some economic dependence on the Franciscans which would encourage Guillaume and his compatriots to testify. Although the largest number of miracles reported at Louis's trial refer to persons from Marseilles, we do not know if a confraternity existed at this date in that city, although one is documented in Aix.

[44] Patres Collegii S. Bonaventurae, 'Processus canonizationis', pp. 236–39.

[45] 'La Leggenda del B. Gerardo Cagnoli, O.Min. (1267–1342) di Frà Bartolomeo Albizi, O.Min. (+ 1351)', ed. by F. Rotolo, *Miscellanea franciscana,* 57 (1951), 402.

[46] C. Garrett, *Spirit Possession and Popular Religion from Camisards to Shakers* (Baltimore, 1987), pp. 1–10.

contemporary cases of possession, that 'situations of social tensions such as the following are often indicated as the causal context of possession: class antagonisms rooted in economic exploitation, conflicts between traditions where revered traditions are eroded, colonial domination and revolution'.[47] This premise cannot be fully proven based on our knowledge of the cults here noted. All of these cults appear to have enjoyed the support of a wide constituency of both urban and rural devotees. None of the demoniacs, however, come from the clerical or noble classes.

Possession was apparently more common among women, who may have faced both straitened economic circumstances and emotional pressure. For example, Edith's husband Robert himself testified that he was a poor man who lived by charity and alms. This rather contradicts a description of him as an iron merchant; perhaps he had once been employed, but had fallen on hard times, or perhaps he lived by the charity now provided through the thriving cult of Thomas of Hereford. The possibility that Edith's behaviour was a symptom of an undiagnosed and fatal illness (she died two months later), perhaps brought on by pregnancy, should be considered. In the case drawn from the protocol of Louis of Toulouse, the victim, Guillaume de Moissac, was a stonemason, although we cannot ascertain whether he was wealthy or not. The social background of Christianella, the victim exorcised via Joachim of Siena, is not stated; although Joachim's socially identifiable *miraculés* include a soldier, wine merchant, rural man, and several members of the Servite confraternity of *Laudesi*.[48] The victim in Giovanna of Signa's case, Morozzo, was clearly from the governing classes, appearing as the parent of persons who occupied the highest magistracies in Tuscany.[49] Unlike the other victims, however, he does not recover at all.

None of the cited cases directly refers to the traditionally prescribed rituals of exorcism in which a priest officiates; the participants thus did not choose to follow the normally prescribed method for exorcising a demon.[50] The clergy appear rather as preachers, administering communion, conducting the mass, perhaps serving as stage managers of the drama in which both the victim and the larger community play active roles. The demoniac is transformed into the focus of this theatrical event, and the saint and his relics function as a *deus ex machina* which brings about dramatic resolution. Liturgy, recitation of the mass, prayers, proper timing (namely on or near an important feast day), sacred objects, flashing light, heavenly music, a possessed individual whose evil alter ego announces his intentions, and a receptive audience, including the extended family and others, are all mobilized as a means of renewing the faith of the

---

[47] P. Hollenbach, 'Jesus, Demoniacs and Public Authorities: A Socio-Historical Study', *Journal of the American Academy of Religion,* 99 (1981), 567–88.

[48] Soulier, 'Vita et miracula', p. 394 ('soldatus'), p. 393 ('quidam habebat unam vegetem vini meri et optimi, quam pro suis necessitatibus vendere intendebat), pp. 393–94 ('rusticus quidam qui per silvam laci transiret').

[49] Delarun, 'Jeanne de Sigua', p. 180.

[50] E. Martène, *De antiquis ecclesiae ritibus libri*, 2 vols (Antwerp, 1736), II, 970–94.

community.[51] As Barbara Newman has suggested, 'Thus the beliefs and actions of the mentally ill, beyond any personal idiosyncrasies they reveal, can represent collective desires and anxieties through the performance of cultural scripts, whose authority is in turn reinforced with each repetition'.[52] The presence, real or implied, of those who would cast doubt on the saint or his relics adds to the tension, which is resolved by the successful exorcism; or, as in the case of Guillaume de Moissac, it is a cure of a condition brought on as revenge against sceptical remarks. It is suitable that the utterance of blasphemies by the demoniac would call for the balm of miracle. William of Auvergne, for example, noted that blasphemy represents a form of diminished belief in God; while miracles, which cannot be performed by the idolatrous, Moslems, or heretics, bring spectators to the faith.[53] Such a dramatic, ritualized public miracle often initiated the enthusiasm which enabled a large number of thaumaturgical miracles at the site of the tomb. In Thomas of Hereford's case, several days after Edith's miracle, on April 2, four blind persons recovered their sight at his tomb, and scores of others were cured.[54]

---

[51] R. N. Swanson, 'Medieval Liturgy as Theatre: The Props', *Studies in Church History,* 28 (1992), 239–53, regarding the use of copes, crosses, images, etc. in creating a theatrical setting. See *The Age of Chivalry: Plantagenet England, 1200–1400,* ed. by J. J. G. Alexander and P. Binski (London, 1987), pp. 83–97, on the architectural setting.

[52] B. Newman, 'Possessed by the Spirit: Devout Women, Demoniacs, and the Apostolic Life in the Thirteenth Century', *Speculum*, 73 (1998), 758. This is a highly textured and provocative study of possession among early thirteenth-century female saints and mystics.

[53] William of Auvergne, *De fide*, c. 3, in *Opera omnia*, 2 vols (Paris, 1674), I, 16–17.

[54] *Processus canonizationis Thomae de Cantilupo,* in AASS, 2 October, I, p. 655.

Text and Context: On the Rise of Physiognomic Thought in the Later Middle Ages

JOSEPH ZIEGLER

In spite of years of discredit (in particular after the fusion of physiognomy with racial theory in the nineteenth and early twentieth centuries) physiognomic thinking is still prevalent today at various crossroads of our society. Ask any policeman responsible for investigation whether he or she can detect a liar by his external appearance and behaviour, and you will be likely to receive a positive answer. The belief that liars fidget, stutter, and avoid eye contact is widespread among the police forces. This stereotyped view of how people behave when they lie may be holding back criminal investigation because research in applied social psychology has shown that practised liars often behave in the opposite way and appear unnaturally calm, making fewer gestures, maintaining eye contact, and giving a rehearsed, ordered, and rigid impression to onlookers. Physiognomy, the art of deciphering one's character by the external appearance of his or her bodily organs and an analysis their size, proportion, shape, colour, hairiness, and motion, is today more controversial than ever. In the scientific community few if any would think that a physiognomic analysis can provide valid data concerning a person's character or that physiognomy can be regarded as a science. This view is reflected in the writings of contemporary historians of medieval science when they come to treat physiognomy in their narratives.

It is not surprising, therefore, that a recently published annotated bibliography of medieval science and technology contains no independent entry for physiognomy, not even among the 'quasi-sciences'.[1] This, however, creates an anachronistic image of

---

[1] *Medieval Science and Technology: A Selected Annotated Bibliography*, ed. by C. Kren (New York and London, 1985).

medieval science since there is no justification for historians of science to exclude certain subjects and to label them as occult or pseudoscientific simply because they have been rejected from the canon of modern science.[2] From the last third of the thirteenth century physiognomy (*scientia physionomie*) was recognized as a science (i.e. a body of knowledge which derives its roots from a system of knowable causes which can be deciphered through rational reasoning and logic) by medieval academics. In this essay, I shall therefore speak of the science of physiognomy in this medieval sense. Furnished by a set of canonical texts attributed to Arab and Greek authorities (Rhazes, Hippocrates, and from the 1260s Aristotle himself) medieval natural philosophers, physicians and laymen alike possessed a sound basis for a scientific discourse which was focussed in physiognomy and its use. To this sound basis they added commentaries and occasionally compiled original treatises.

How can one explain the rise of physiognomy in the twelfth and thirteenth centuries after years of neglect and oblivion?[3] The renewed exposure of the Latin West to lost classical texts (through translations from the Arabic or Greek) provides only a partial answer. In this respect Jole Agrimi's seminal studies have added much substance to our knowledge of the process by which physiognomy came to be accepted by the medieval academic culture in the thirteenth and fourteenth centuries.[4] But scientific texts are transmitted from one culture to another because there is a need for them, not only because their author is much revered. Intention not coincidence guides the process of assimilation of new knowledge. It is this need or intention that I would like to decipher here through looking at the codicological context of some physiognomic texts and at the actual use of physiognomic thought.

With respect to physiognomy the question of its reception is all the more intriguing because of its potentially dangerous consequences for Christian ethics. 'Mental character is not independent of and unaffected by bodily processes, but is conditioned

[2] D. C. Lindberg, 'Medieval Science and Its Religious Context', *Osiris*, 10 (1995), 61–79 at p. 65.

[3] From the early medieval period there are only traces of physiognomic thought and no physiognomic texts. See P. Squatriti, 'Personal Appearance and Physiognomics in Early Medieval Italy', *Journal of Medieval History*, 14 (1988), 191–202.

[4] J. Agrimi, 'La ricezione della *fisiognomica* pseudoaristotelica nella facultà delle arti', *Archives d'histoire doctrinale et littéraire du Moyen Age*, 64 (1997), 127–88; idem, 'Fisiognomica e "Scolastica"', *Micrologus*, 1 (1993), 235–71; idem, 'Fisiognomica tra tradizione naturalistica e sapere medico nei secoli xii–xiii, con particolare riguardo alla Scuola di Salerno', in *Atti del Congresso Internazionale su Medicina Medievale e Scuola Medica Salernitana (Salerno, 8–9 Maggio 1993)* (Salerno, 1994), pp. 44–57; and idem, 'Fisiognomica: Nature allo specchio ovvero luce e ombre', *Micrologus*, 4 (1996), 129–78. For a concise and useful overview of the main medieval physiognomic texts, see A. G. Clarke, 'Metocoscopy: An Art to Find the Mind's Construction in the Forehead', in *Astrology, Science and Society*, ed. by P. Curry (Woodbridge, 1987), pp. 171–95, at pp. 173–77.

by the state of the body', is the opening sentence in Pseudo-Aristotle's *Physiognomonics,* which was available in Latin from the mid-1260s through the translation of Bartholomew of Messina who was active in the court of Manfred, King of Sicily.[5] If the external traits of the body teach us all we need to know about one's character and since all these external traits inhere in one from birth, then one's behaviour is determined in birth, there is little place for free will or voluntary choice and the consequences for Christian pastoral theology are dire.

How could the Church accept the physiognomic theory which predisposes one's behaviour to one's physical appearance and thus potentially undermines free will? The thirteenth-century person was sometimes ambivalent about physiognomy, which came to be regarded as a dubious science. It was associated with the necromantic sciences but did not become part of them and hence escaped the condemnation which they suffered. For those who accepted astronomical principles as indicators for the validity of a body of certain knowledge, there was a simple way to eliminate the doubt. Physiognomy was nothing but a reflection of the overwhelming powers of the stars over nature and hence could not be regarded as a superstitious divinatory art. For example, chapter 17 of the *Speculum astronomie* attributed to Albertus Magnus identified the necromantic texts which should be put aside (not destroyed). When he came to chiromancy, the author explained his ambivalence towards making a precipitous determination about it 'perhaps because it is a part of physiognomy, which seems to be collected from the significations of the control (*magisterium*) of the stars over the body and over the soul, while it makes conjectures about the character of the mind from the exterior figure of the body; not because the one might be the cause of the other, but because both are found to be caused by the same thing'.[6]

The ecclesiastical ambivalence towards physiognomy may be reflected in article 167 among those condemned in 1277 by Etienne Tempier, the Bishop of Paris. The rejected opinion which does not specifically name physiognomy reads as follows:

> That by some signs human intentions and changes in intentions can be known, and whether these intentions will be carried out and that by such shapes the fate of pilgrims is known, [as well as] captivity, release of captives and whether they will be sages or criminals.[7]

---

[5] *The Complete Works of Aristotle: The Revised Oxford Translation*, ed. by J. Barnes, (Princeton, 1984), I, 1236. 'Quoniam et animae sequuntur corpora et ipsae secundum se ipsas non sunt impassibiles a motibus corporis', in the thirteenth-century translation of Bartholomew of Messina, in *Scriptores physiognomonici graeci et latini*, ed. by R. Förster, 2 vols (1893; repr. Stuttgart and Leipzig, 1994), I, 5 (henceforth *SPGL*).

[6] P. Zambelli, *The 'Speculum Astronomiae' and its Enigma: Astrology, Theology and Science in Albertus Magnus and his Contemporaries,* Boston Studies in the Philosophy of Science, 17 (Dordrecht, Boston, and London, 1992), pp. 272–73.

[7] R. Hissette, *Enquête sur les 219 articles condamnés à Paris le 7 Mars 1277* (Leuven,

The source of this article is unknown, but it is tempting to link it to the rise of physiognomy whose canonical texts had newly reappeared in the Latin West. In addition to the general physiognomic rationale of deciphering one's intentions through bodily signs, particularly evocative here are for example chapters 25 ('De comparatione vel emptione captivorum') and 51 ('Signa hominis philosophi') in book II of Rhazes' *Liber ad regem Almansorem* (or *Liber almansoris*), translated by Gerard of Cremona (d. 1187). Yet even if this is so, physiognomy as such was not condemned, but only its divinatory dimension which is generally absent from the physiognomic texts.

That the learned people of the medieval West occasionally sensed the tension between physiognomic judgment, which relied on analyzing innate, unchangeable, and uncontrollable bodily signs and Christian morality, is apparent from many proemia to physiognomic texts. Beyond the attempt to structure the science so that erroneous judgment would be reduced to a bearable minimum, many medieval writers made specific attempts to limit the scope of physiognomy thereby eliminating its potential danger for Christian morality.

Albertus Magnus devoted the second paragraph in his introductory chapter to physiognomy to an apologetic debate which justified the preoccupation with the topic.[8] Physiognomy merely shows inclinations which reflect the quality of the blood and physical spirits (*ostendit inclinationes ex sanguine et spiritibus physicis*). But these inclinations can be, if necessary, curbed by reason (*retineri possunt freno rationis*). The legend about Hippocrates' disciples who clashed with the physiognomer Phylemon over his judgment that their master was lascivious, devious, and sexually compulsive was Albertus's exemplary proof that one can control all negative inclinations, that philosophy is nothing but abstinence and the subjugation of lust, and that nothing is predetermined by nature. In the case of Phylemon, it was by the love of philosophy and decency (*amor philosophie et honestatis*) that he subdued his lust. What has been denied him by nature he received through intellectual effort (*studium*). The legend, which Albertus drew from the physiognomy included in the *Secretum secretorum,* appeared with some variations in other medieval sources,[9] and was introduced into sermons as will be shown below.

1977), no. 178, p. 273. See also Jole Agrimi in 'La ricezione', p. 129, n. 5, for another article (Hissette, no. 105, p. 174) which may echo some critique of physiognomy since it cites a phrase from the first sentence in Pseudo-Aristotle's physiognomy: 'Quod in hora generationis hominis in corpore suo et per consequens *in anima, quae sequitur corpus*, ex ordine causarum superiorum et inferiorum inest homini dispositio inclinans ad tales actiones vel eventus' (my emphasis).

[8] Albertus Magnus, *De animalibus libri XXVI*, I.2.2, ed. by H. Stadler, 2 vols, Beiträge zur Geschichte der Philosophie des Mittelalters, 15 (Münster, 1916), I, p. 46, par. 127; *Quaestiones de animalibus*, I, q. 21, in *Alberti magni . . . Opera omnia*, xii, ed. by E. Filthaut (Münster, 1955) pp. 94–95: 'Utrum physiognomia sit possibilis haberi per partes corporis'.

[9] *Physiognomoniae secreti secretorum*, in *SPGL,* II, 187–91. In another version of the story Socrates substitutes Hippocrates, and Zopyros is the physiognomer instead of Phylemon.

Before 1257 Roger Bacon in his gloss on the *Secretum secretorum* praised the value and usefulness of physiognomy but specifically warned his readers not to pronounce on the basis of physiognomic analysis any judgment concerning Christians. Physiognomy teaches natural aptitude to behavioural characteristics which if bad can be defeated by divine grace.[10]

In *c.* 1257, Aldobrandino da Siena introduced the physiognomy which constituted the fourth part of his *Regimen sanitatis* (written for Beatrice of Savoy, Duchess of Provence) as a tool to know the nature of the person according to his external organs.[11] But he too stressed that this nature imposed no necessity and that for both mankind and beasts *nutritiva* (nourishment in the broadest sense, both spiritual and intellectual) can be stronger than nature and hence effectively change it.[12]

It is rash, we are told about a century later by a mid-fourteenth-century theologian who produced a commented summary of Aristotle's metaphysics and natural philosophy, to reach a judgment concerning a person (*de homine iudicare*) because physiognomy proves the existence of an inclination and not of a necessity. It is dangerous to reach such a judgment based on external signs because this endangers the concept of human freedom (*humana libertas*). Furthermore, many of those created imperfect by nature prove to be of superior character. The fact that some signs are introduced by custom which can be freely suppressed shows that what seems to be a natural inclination can be freely suppressed. Moreover, the fact that one person evinces contradictory signs renders invalid any judgment which does not rely on a thorough knowledge of the person involved. All this, however, does not lead the writer to reject physiognomy whose principles he then summarizes. If one is aware of its limits, if one

---

[10] *Opera hactenus inedita Rogeri Baconi,* V: *Secretum secretorum cum glossis et notulis*, ed. by R. Steele (Oxford, 1920), pp. 164–71 at p. 166: 'nec de Christianis debet aliquis judicare nisi aptitudinem naturalem ad mores, non quod talis erit, quia gracia Dei gratum faciens potest vincere malam disposicionem animi ad quam excitatur ex complexione et composicione corporis et ceteris proprietatibus'.

[11] *Le Régime du corps du maître Aldebrandin de Sienne*, ed. by L. Ladouzy and R. Pépin (Paris, 1911), pp. 193–202. F. Féry-Hue, 'Le Régime du corps d'Aldebrandin de Sienne: Tradition manuscrite et diffusion', in *Santé, médecine et assistance au moyen âge, Actes du 110e Congrès national des Sociétés savantes. Histoire médiévale, 7.1, Montpellier, 1985* (Paris, 1987), pp. 113–34. Aldobrandino derived much of his physiognomic details from Rhazes' physiognomy in *Liber almansoris,* II, cc. 26 ff. By including physiognomy in his *Regimen*, this physician from Troyes turned it into an integral part of preventive medicine.

[12] Oxford, Bodleian Library, Can. misc. 388, fol. 36ra (a Latin translation of the original French version): 'In ista quarta particula intendimus docere qualiter poteritis cognoscere naturam hominis per membra exteriora et quamuis naturaliter et racionabiliter debent esse ut dicemus preterea non est ibi necessitas et bene possit aliter esse et hoc propter bonas doctrinas et bonum rationem hominis. Et multociens accidit quod nutritiua preualet nature et sepe in hominibus et bestiis apparet. [. . .]'

accepts the fact that it reveals an inclination or an aptitude, not an inevitable destiny, its principles can be discussed.[13]

That around 1300 physiognomic thought was incorporated into the clerical imagery is clear from the appearance of explicit references to physiognomic theory in biblical commentaries, sermons, and other sorts of preachers' literature.[14] In his commentary on Ecclesiasticus 13. 31 (13. 25 in the Revised English Bible: 'It is the heart that changes the look on the face either for better or for worse'), Nicholas of Lyra supplied a concise definition of physiognomy, explicitly referred to Aristotle's physiognomy, and recognized the ability of experts to decipher from an inspection of the face the disposition of the heart as well as a person's thoughts.[15]

In his sermons, Giovanni da San Gimignano OP (d. *c.* 1333) extensively used the human body and its organs as a source of similes and analogies for spiritual interpretations of Scripture.[16] Occasionally, he needed to explain to his audience his method of interpretation of Scripture. In one case he presented Holy Scripture as a storehouse of physiognomic knowledge which the physiognomer (i.e. the exegete or the preacher) uses when he reads the signs of the body (biblical verses which discuss the human body,

---

[13] Paris, BNF, lat. 6752, fol. 166v: 'Secundum phisonomiam de homine iudicare temerarium est quia signa solum arguunt non necessitatem sed inclinationem. Et quia omni inclinationi superest humana libertas, ideo per signa exteriora de homine iudicare periculum est quia plures ex natura imperfecti fuerunt et tamen laboribus et moribus melioribus famosi fuerunt. [. . .] His ergo attentis, nouerit lector quod ea communia que subscribuntur sic intelligenda sunt quod non arguunt necessitatem nec ineuitabilitatem sed solum inclinationem seu aptitudinem dummodo impedimentum non interueniat ut puta alterius signi oppositi vel consuetudinis seu libertatis aliud disponentis'.

[14] In a collection of model sermons from the late thirteenth century (in L.-J. Bataillon, 'La Prédication populaire d'un dominicain italien à la fin du XIIIe siècle', *Archivum fratrum praedicatorum,* 65 (1995), 171–83 at p. 177) one finds the following: 'Dicit Albumasar: cuius facies carnosa est piger est et stultus'. This is an exact reference to Rhazes' physiognomy in *SPGL,* II, p. 153, c. 3, ll. 20–21.

[15] Nicholas of Lyra in *Biblia sacra, cum glossa ordinaria [. . .] et postilla Nicolai Lyrani,* (Lyons, 1589), III, 2038: 'Hic consequenter docet distinguere bonos a malis, dicens: 'Cor homini im'. Dispositio enim cordis apparet in facie, plus quam in aliis partibus corporis: quia vigent ibi omnes sensus: et potissime apparet in oculis, eo quod visus plures differentias ostendit .j. Metaph. propter quod cogitatio cordis in bonum siue in malum a peritis hominibus frequenter percipitur in facie. Et quia pauci sunt boni et virtuosi respectu malorum, secundum quod dicitur Eccl. j.d. 'Stultorum infinitus et numerus' [Ecclesiasticus 1. 15]. ideo subditur'. *Physiognomia metaphorica* or *metaphoricae* are conventional names for Pseudo-Aristotle's physiognomy.

[16] J. Ziegler, 'Medical Similes in Religious Discourse: The Case of Giovanni da San Gimignano OP (ca. 1260–ca. 1333)', *Science in Context,* 8.1 (1995), 103–31, and idem, *Medicine and Religion c. 1300: The Case of Arnau de Vilanova* (Oxford, 1998), pp. 65–68, 79–82, 108–11, 187–90, 196–99, 200–02, 277–93.

its functions, senses, and pathologies) in order to divulge the hidden parts of the person's soul and mind (i.e. the spiritual message of the Bible). This he did in a sermon on the theme of John 5. 3: 'In them lay a great number of sick people, blind, lame and paralysed'. In order to explain to his clerical audience that the corporeal diseases of the people in the verse are nothing but signs of internal spiritual diseases, Giovanni devotes the introductory part of the sermon to physiognomy. The ancients, he tells, found a certain knowledge (*scientia*) which is called physiognomy and which teaches us how to pass a judgment concerning the accident of the soul according to the accidents of the body. To elucidate this he brings two examples.

The first, which he attributes to Aristotle's *De animalibus,* is that of a large forehead which signifies mental heaviness tending to stupidity.[17] Giovanni is not content with the simple citation of this general rule; he supplies his audience with the reason (*ratio*) for its validity. Large foreheads are always linked to large heads. In large heads the specific effects (*species*) disintegrate and hence are weakened. Consequently they are insufficient for the regimen of the senses and of the body and cause the person to act slowly and indiscreetly. This condition is caused by superfluous matter in the head and the consequent weakness of its power. It can be detected only in the context of the proportions of the whole body. That is, if the neck and the shoulders do not correspond in size with the head.

The second example, which Giovanni attributes to the physiognomers, is that of an oblong head which resembles a hammer. This signifies mental subtlety, studiousness, and wisdom because the oblong shape of the head allows the optimal separation and distinction between those forces and cerebral operations that serve the intellect.[18] Giovanni continues with an exposition of the forces of the brain according to their location in the brain (common sense followed by the imaginative force at the front, reason in the middle, and memory at the back of the brain). In an oblong head they can be perfectly separated, something which cannot happen in a round head. Like physiognomy which reads the body in order to reach the depth of the mind and soul, so Holy Scripture uses bodily signs in order to express spiritual messages. The daily reading of the Gospel talks of some ill persons whom Christ found lying, and teaches us to identify the vices of the soul through the diseases of the body ('per languores corporum cognoscere vitia animarum').[19]

---

[17] Albertus Magnus, *De animalibus,* I.2.2. par. 136, p. 49; Psuedo Aristotle, *Bartholomaei de Messana interpretatio Latina*, in *SPGL,* I, c. 64, p. 71; Palemon, *De physiognomonia liber*, in *SPGL,* I, c. 27, p. 230; Rhazes, *Liber almansoris,* ii.31, in *SPGL,* II, p. 168.

[18] Albertus Magnus, *De animalibus,* I. 2. 2. par. 135, p. 49; according to *Anonymus latinus,* c. 16: 'caput malleo simile ante ac retro impudentem monstrat', in *SPGL,* p. 27, and Anonyme Latin, *Traité de physiognomonie*, ed. and trans. by J. André (Paris, 1981), p. 64.

[19] Giovanni da San Gimignano (Gorus), *Convivium quadragesimale hoc est conciones et sermones* . . . (Köln, 1612), pp. 138–39: 'Antiqui inuenerunt quandam scientiam que vocatur physiognomaia [*sic*], que scilicet per accidentia corporis docet nos iudicare de accidentibus

A sermon on the treachery of the Jews (on the theme of Luke 22. 2: 'And the chief priests and the scribes were trying to devise some means of doing away with him') allows Giovanni a small digression to elaborate on the theme of what makes people unfaithful and traitors. Jewish treachery was triggered by their envy (*ex invidie impulsione*); it was caused by a flaw in their soul and was not a result of their physical complexion. This makes their character evil beyond limits since they freely chose to kill Christ without being forced by physical traits, which anyhow create a disposition and an inclination that can always be avoided. As for those who become traitors by reason of their complexion, Giovanni elaborates on the common belief that those who are red (ruddy complexion or red hair) are unfaithful. But there are two kinds of red: there are ruddy people who are more bright in their red colour and whose redness inclines to white. These red people are not thought to be particularly unfaithful because the heat in them is calm; humid though it is, it is also of an earthen character. All this makes them fairly stable and constant. But those who are deep red are another story altogether. Their redness is caused by hot, burning choler which causes them to be inconstant, unstable, and unfaithful, and consequently they are not to be trusted. But all this should not be understood as an inevitable outcome of the colour deep red, says Giovanni. This is a disposition, and while it reflects a real complexion, it creates only an inclination which can be avoided by the aid of reason.[20]

---

anime. Verbi gratia dicit Philosophus in lib. *De animalibus* quod quando frons hominis fuerit magna significat ponderosum declinantem ad stultitiam. Et ratio huius quia magnitudo frontis sequitur magnitudinem capitis. In capite autem magno disgregantur species et ita debilitantur quod sunt insufficientes ad regimen sensus et corporis: propter hoc tales tarde et indiscrete faciunt opera sua. Hoc autem est verum, quia magnitudo frontis et capitis procedit non ex fortitudine virtutis in ipso operante sed potius ex superabundantia materie et virtutis debilitate; quod perpenditur quando alie propinque, puta collum vel spatule non correspondent magnitudini capitis, puta quod sint graciles et parue. Item dicunt physiognomones quod caput oblongum et malleo simile est signum subtilitatis et studiositatis et sapientie et ratio est quia figura capitis existente oblonga optime possunt distingui operationes et virtutes diuerse cerebri que scilicet deseruiunt intellectui. Tunc enim in prima parte cerebri situabitur sensus communis, deinde imaginatiua, deinde in medio ratiocinatiua et in posteriori parte memoratiua. Non sic autem possent distingui si esset caput rotundum. [. . .]'

[20] Giovanni da San Gimignano, *Convivium Quadragesimale,* pp. 612–13: 'Nota hic, quod aliqui efficiuntur proditores siue traditores quandoque quidem corporis complexione. Communiter dicitur quod rubei sunt infideles. Et distinguunt aliqui quod est duplex rubedo. Quedam scilicet magis tendens ad claritatem et albedinem. Et tales ruffi, ut dicunt, non sunt multum infideles, quia hi sunt habentes calidum quiescens, humidum tamen terrestre, et tales sunt aliquando bene stabiles. Alia est rubedo magis vergens ad obscuritatem. Et talis rubedo causatur ex calida adurente cholera. Et tales ruffi cholera adusta sunt mobiles propter subtilitatem cholere et non habent stabilitatem, nec per consequens fidelitatem et quicquid eis apparet, videtur eis

Another example for the infiltration of physiognomic thought into sermon literature comes from Giovanni's discussion of the adjective 'human' (*humanum*) in a sermon which deals with the moral and spiritual fragility of humans. The theme of the sermon is Romans 6. 19 ('I speak after the manner of men (*Humanum dico*) because of the infirmity of your flesh'). When he discusses the capacity and propensity of the human heart towards evil, Giovanni attributes to Aristotle's *Ethics,* book VII, the notion that sometimes this propensity to evil emerges from complexion. This is the case with the bestial people who cut up the bellies of pregnant women and devour their embryos, wild men (*silvestres homines*) who live a solitary life beside the Pontic Sea and eat human flesh including their children.[21] Another cause for human propensity for evil is a specific celestial constellation by which he who is born under Saturn is prone to sloth, he who is born under Mars is prone to anger and so forth. But neither complexion nor celestial constellation impose necessity since the rule of reason (*dominium racionis*) can resist and hinder this evil. Two exemplary sources buttress this argument. The first is a commentary on [Pseudo] Ptolemy's *Centiloquium* attributed to Albertus Magnus. Albertus apparently spoke of a king whose astrological indicators (*significationes*) were the worst possible ones, yet he lived a life of glory and glitter with the best company. Though attracted by filthy desire, he chose honourable company and remained master of his own acts. The other example is attributed to the physiognomy of Polus (a corruption of Phylemon or Polemon) and deals with Hippocrates. According to all signs, physiognomic and astral, he appeared to be a sorcerer (*sortator*) and indecent. Yet he was amongst the best of all intellectuals and nobody surpassed him in integrity and decency. This could only have happened by the choice to be decent (*honestatis electio*).[22]

These physiognomic examples would have been inconceivable had physiognomy been a religiously rejected discipline at that period. Giovanni's sermons teach us that preachers' literature was another important channel through which physiognomy was communicated to the larger public. Physiognomy was a legitimate source of antique knowledge which the congregation should know and it was employed not merely as a rhetorical device. The congregation thus would not be outraged to hear their preacher explaining an idea *ut dicunt physionomici*. The third example is banal and rudimentary, and reflects a vulgarization of the Hippocartes legend in the *Secretum secretorum* physiognomy; the first two suggest a deeper familiarity with physiognomic knowledge.

---

bonum et mouentur ab uno in aliud, primum bonum dimittendo; et hoc est propter mobilitatem et ideo non in eis confidendum. [. . .]'

[21] Aristotle, *Nicomachean Ethics,* VII.5, p. 1814.

[22] Paris, BNF, lat. 14941, fols 107v–108r: 'Consimile exemplum ponitur in phynosomia [*sic*] poli de ypocrate. Ypocras enim in omnibus signis corporis, que stellas secundas uocat tholomeus, sortator et turpis apparebat, et tamen optimorum erat studiorum et honestatem conuersacionis in tantum ut optimus omnium hominum [diceretur] quidam fieri non potuit nisi per honestatis electionem. Unde patet quod constellacio aut complexio necessitatem non imponit. [. . .]'

But all suggest that Giovanni did not feel ill at ease when touching the theme of physiognomy.

What was the source of Giovanni's information? Some of the physiognomic utterances are derived from common knowledge that demanded no direct contact with any literary source. It is also possible that some preachers had access to the popular physiognomic sources, such as the treatises attributed to Aristotle, the *Secretum secretorum* physiognomy, Albertus's commentary on Aristotle's *De animalibus,* or even the earlier *Anonymus latinus* text (a fourth-century text with specific reference to Aristotle, Loxus, and Phylomen as its authorities; it reappeared in a Latin version in the beginning of the twelfth century but manuscripts containing its first eighty chapters started circulating as a popular compendium of physiognomic knowledge only a hundred years later). But preachers could also have drawn their information from encyclopaedias which often devoted long chapters to discussion of the human body and its organs. Though physiognomic thought could hardly be systematically drawn from the great thirteenth-century encyclopaedias which were compiled before the assimilation of the pseudo-Aristotelian physiognomy,[23] the picture dramatically changes throughout the fourteenth century. I shall cite here only two examples which represent a much more intensive infiltration of physiognomic thought into fourteenth-century encyclopedias. The *Responsorium curiosorum* (a preachers' manual prepared to provide answers to the curious natural philosophical questions which the faithful presented the preachers) attributed to the Dominican Konrad of Halberstadt the Older (fl. 1330) included eleven chapters that supplied his reader with an abridged version of physiognomic theory principally drawn from Albertus Magnus's commentary and questions on *De animalibus.*[24] There are several questions around which Konrad supplies his reader with basic physiognomy of the face: Is physiognomy concerning the character possible through [examination] of other bodily organs? According to which organ can physiognomy be best executed? Why does a large and broad forehead signify a

---

[23] Thomas Cantimpratensis, *Liber de natura rerum*, ed. by H. Boese (Berlin and New York, 1973), pt. 1, I.ii (*De capite*), pp. 13–14, introduced the *signa virtutis* which appear on the face (in particular the forehead, the brows and the eyes) according to Aristotle's *De animalibus.* Vincent of Beauvais, *Speculum naturale* (Douai, 1624), xxviii.95, cols 2058–59, devoted a chapter to physiognomy. Vincent's authorities for this chapter were: (1) Pliny's *Natural History* xi.114, 273–76, where the author refers with wonder and amazement to Aristotle's active interest in bodily signs. Acknowledging his doubt vis-à-vis the practice and openly judging it fatuous, *vana,* Pliny nevertheless writes on the topic. (2) Trogus (via Pliny) who is Vincent's source for the relationship between bodily signs and individual morality. (3) Rhazes' physiognomy. From Rhazes Vincent borrows the instruction to refrain from judgment on the basis of one sign, and how to cope with contradictory signs. See also cc. 50, *De physiognomia oculorum*; 94, *De pedibus*; 96, *De medicinis ex humano corpore*.

[24] Konrad of Halberstadt, *Responsorium curiosorum compilatum per fratrem Conradum de halberstad ordinis predicatorum* (Lübek, 1476), II, cc. ccclxix–ccclxxix.

[mentally] heavy person tending to stupidity whilst a small forehead signifies a good [mental] disposition? Why do eyebrows curved toward the nose signify good intellect whilst those curved toward the temples signify softness and weak intellect? Why do bushy eyebrows which bend downwards signify envy and lust? Why do bulging eyes signify a mental and visual disturbance but deep-set eyes signify the opposite? Why does wide opening of the eyes or their stillness signify immodesty, whilst their [excess] mobility signifies fickleness?[25]

The *Reductorium morale* of the Benedictine Pierre Bersuire (d. 1362) adds to the chapter on eyes the physiognomic observation that eyes which are wide open and which rarely shut signify shamelessness, according to Aristotle, whilst eyes which open slowly mark out a defect in the mental power, and those which remain shut for too long denote imbecility.[26] In the chapter on eyebrows he again refers to Aristotle who allegedly claimed that eyebrows have some hidden power to decode the passions of the soul. Straight eyebrows signify soft and effeminate character; low eyebrows indicate envy; thick and elevated eyebrows denote courage; long and thin eyebrows represent timidity; eyebrows so bushy as to obstruct vision signify anger and a hot complexion; fleshy eyebrows denote lack of perception; and the absence of eyebrows signifies a pathological condition such as the corruption of the blood in the case of lepers, the consumption of the humour in the case of those suffering from hectic fever, and the obstruction of the pores of the human body as in the case of the *castrati*.[27] Then follows the moral interpretation according to which every deviation from the ideal form of an eyebrow (characterized by moderateness, *mediocritas*) signifies a sin. The chapter on the nose opens with a paraphrase of the opening sentence in Aristotle's *Physiognomy* (according to Bersuire, Pseudo-Aristotle as we know today) that justifies drawing lessons from the nose about the character. Bersuire brings one example only: widely flaring nostrils suggest aggressiveness and an easily indignant mind.[28]

---

[25] Other questions with a physiognomic aspect include the following: 'Quare sternuatio est diuinatoria cum exitus aliarum ventositatum de pectore et ventre non sint tales? Quare linee communes manus longe et aperte sunt signum longe vite et breues econuerso? [. . .] Quare magnitudo manus in viris significat bonum, in mulieribus malum?'.

[26] *Reductorii moralis petri berchorii pictaviensis* (Venice, 1583), II.4 (De oculo), p. 31, col. 2: 'Oculi quandoque valde aperti et raro clausi inverecundiam significant secundum Arist. Tarde vero apertionis oculi defectum virtutis designant. Inverecundi enim oculos valde apertos tenent. Imbecilles vero ipsos ultra debitum habent clausos'. See *Bartholomaei de Messana interpretatio latina*, in *SPGL,* I, c. 17, p. 31.

[27] *Reductorii moralis petri berchorii,* II.7 (De superciliis), p. 33, col. 2: 'Dicit igitur Aristoteles quod supercilia habent quandam vim occultam passiones anime indicantem. Unde etiam, ut communiter videmus, in superciliis apparet signum superbie, iracundie, audacie et timoris. [. . .]'

[28] *Reductorii moralis petri berchorii,* II.11 (De naso), p. 36, col. 1: 'Cum conditiones anime secundum dispositiones corporis varientur, sicut dicit Aristoteles in princicpio physionomie (sicut

The manuscripts which include physiognomic texts occasionally reveal a strong sense of religiously motivated ambivalence towards physiognomy. Sometimes it was sufficient to draw the reader's attention to the danger of rash physiognomic judgment and to the possibility and desirability of defeating the natural inclinations, by adding pointing fingers and other *nota bene* signs at the margins of the story of Hippocrates' disciples or the last paragraph of the *Secretum secretorum* version which warns against rash judgments based on one sign only. The scribe could add at the closing title his own remark which would underline the fact that physiognomy is about probability and not about necessity.[29] Another ingenious way to divert attention from the danger of physiognomy was to entitle it in a manner which turned it into a pious piece of Christian morality. Thus, in thirteenth-century Cerne Abbey (Dorset) a version of the *Secretum secretorum* Physiognomy (with a few omissions and a few additions and some reordering of the items) was entitled in red: *Ypocras de contemptu mundi.*[30] By turning the story of Hippocrates' disciples and its moral lesson to the centre of the science of physiognomy, the scribe could both diffuse the danger inherent in this science and fully expose his readers to all its principles. For if the message of the text is so perfectly congruent with the monastic ideal of *contemptus mundi*, surely it can be read by all. It would be tempting to speculate that this strange title was cunningly adopted by the scribe, who facing critique of the science and its practitioners devised a way to salvage the knowledge and supply it to the brethren.

But MS Egerton 843 is of particular interest also because of the codicological context in which the physiognomic text is situated and which sheds some more light on the actual use of physiognomic thought and its relevance to religious contemplation. Tacked on to the physiognomy in the same hand are three treatises: (1) a short treatise which links complexion with elemental theory and the size (weight and height) of people;[31] (2) a short treatise which commences: 'Legitur in annalibus hebreorum'; (3)

---

vinum album in vitro rubeo rubeum videtur), hinc est quod secundum dispositionem nasi et aliorum membrorum de conditionibus anime iudicatur. Et sic dicit quod nares nimis aperte et multi aeris attractive ferocitatem animi pretendunt et mentem faciliter indignantem.' See *Bartholomaei de Messana interpretatio latina*, in *SPGL,* I. c. 1, p. 5.

[29] See for example Paris, BNF, lat. 6298, fols 155rb–156rb, a fourteenth-century compendium of Aristotle's natural philosophy, that includes a physiognomy based on the *Secretum secretorum.* At fols 155rb–155va there are *nota bene* signs, and at fol. 156rb the scribe ends the treatise thus: 'Explicit physonomia aristotelis de signis corporis hominis que non sunt necessaria sed probabilia'.

[30] London, British Library, Egerton 843, fol. 35v. The manuscript was once united with Cambridge, Trinity College 1149, where it followed astrological tables and was followed by a calendar. *The Western Manuscripts in the Library of Trinity College, Cambridge*, ed. by M. R. James (Cambridge, 1902), III, 150–60, at p. 152 are the contents of Egerton 843.

[31] London, British Library, Egerton 843, fol. 37v. Cf. Oxford, Bodleian Library, Digby 95, fol. 6v.

a therapeutic *lapidarium* against demons, incantations, snakebites, abortive women, sterility, poisons, and captivity.

It is the second treatise which is unique, since it brings forth a physiognomic description of Christ, as someone who was 'fairer than the children of men', having a perfect physiognomic complexion.[32] The text does not directly derive from the *Secretum sercretorum* physiognomy which precedes it. The anonymous author depicted Christ as a sanguine, Jovian type (the opposite of the melancholic Saturnine type)[33] and did not try systematically to apply the physiognomic signs to the imagined body of Christ. However the close vicinity of this text to the physiognomic treatise may suggest a conscious attempt on behalf of the scribe to legitimize the science of physiognomy. This science is designed to teach who the human beings around us really are; but it also can get us nearer to knowing what Christ looked like.

Whether this textual tradition left any iconographic impact, and how it is connected to the known iconographic presentations of Christ, demand an independent study. But a close comparison between Christ's physical traits and the description of the more balanced type (*aequior et temperatior creatura*) in the *Secretum secretorum* physiognomy shows some close affinities which support the hypothesis concerning the meaning of the co-appearance of the two texts. What were Christ's physical characteristics which explicitly reflected physiognomic categories? The ideal type of a perfectly balanced

---

[32] London, British Library, Egerton 843, fol. 37v–38r; Psalms 45. 3: 'Legitur in annalibus hebreorum apud romanos existentibus quod dominus Christus qui dictus fuit propheta veritatis stature fuit procere mediocris et multum spectabilis. Vultum habens hylarem quem possent intuentes diligere et formidare. Capillos habuit coloris nucis auellane pre mature et planos fere usque ad aures. Ab auribus [. . .] crispos aliquantulum ceruliores et fulgentiores ab auribus ventilantes. Discrimen habens in medio capitis iuxta morem nazareorum. Frontem planam et serenissimam cum facie sine ruga et macula quam rubor moderatus venustuerat. Narium et oris nulla prorsus reprehensio. Barbam habens copiosam, [. . .] sed in mento parum bifurcatam. Aspectum simplicem et maturum oculis glaucis et variis et claris existentibus. In increpatione terribilem et in admonitione blandum et amabilem se exhibebat. Hylaris fuit seruata grauitate, aliquando fleuit sed numquam risit. In statura corporis propagatus et rectus. Manus et brachia visu delectabilis erant. Alloquio grauis rarus et modestus fuit et merito secundum Psalmista dicentem: Speciosus forma pre filiis hominum dicitur, et verum est'. See London, British Library, Add. 33969, fol. 97r–97v. For a mid sixth-century description of Christ which stresses his beauty and which does not use physiognomic categories, see in the description of an image (icon) that the anonymous pilgrim to the Holy Land reports to have seen on the spot where Christ was judged by Pilate. *Antonini placentini itinerarium*, c. 23, in *Itineraria et alia geographica*, ed. by P. Geyer, CCSL, 175 (Turnhout, 1965), p. 141: 'Pedem pulchrum, modicum, subtilem, nam et staturam communem, faciem pulchram, capillos subanellatos, manum formosam, digita longa'.

[33] Pietro d'Abano, *Liber compilationis phisonomie* (Padua, 1474), III.3.2, p. 40v; *Bartholomei Coclitis Chiromantie ac physionomie anastasis cum approbatione magistri Alexandri de Achillinis* (Bologna, 1504), III, 2.

creature in the *Secretum secretorum* physiognomy version is characterized by medium and erect stature (*mediocritas stature, rectitudo stature*).[34] Christ had a medium-sized (*mediocritas*), erect (*rectus*) stature. The ideal type according to the *Secretum secretorum* version does not laugh too much (*modici risus*), and his whole face radiates joy and cheerfulness (*cuius aspectus quasi commixtus est laetitie et iocunditate*).[35] Christ had a cheerful face (*vultus hylaris*) but no signs of laughter. Christ had straight hair (*capili plani*) almost down to his ears and the colour was the colour of an unripe hazelnut (*avellana*). From the ears it fell in shining waves of curls. *Capili plani mediocres* are one of the signs of the person who is naturally well formed (*bene compositus in natura*) in the *Secretum secretorum* version.[36] Christ had a straight, fair forehead of moderate redness (*rubor moderatus*) and a face without wrinkles or warts. Moderate redness is an essential part of the ideal physical complexion in Rhazes' physiognomy and the Jovian type.[37] Christ wore a dense beard which was slightly split at the chin, a typical characteristic of the Jovian type. His eyes were blue, variegated and bright (*glauci, varii, clari*). An ideal physiognomic complexion should include eyes which are *'inter varios et nigros medii'*.[38] His voice was deep (*gravitas*), and he was sparing in words (*rarus, modestus*). The ideal type in the *Secretum secretorum* version has a voice which is moderate in sound (*mediocritas in sonoritate vocis*) and he is generally not very talkative (*raritas verborum*).[39]

Sometimes a more explicit textual alteration seemed to be necessary in order to minimize the potential dangers of physiognomy. The scribe of a pastoral codex which includes a version of the *Secretum secretorum* physiognomy altered the last chapter of the text and turned it into a moral excursus about the possibility to resist and defeat the apparently innate character which nature had forced upon man.[40] For him the

---

[34] *SPGL,* II, 195–96.

[35] Ibid., II, 220; an earlier version of the text actually uses the noun *hilaritas*.

[36] Ibid., II, 218.

[37] Ibid., II, 174. A Flawless forehead is a negative physiognomic sign which signifies a litigious, disputative, harmful, ill-tempered, and not very clever nature. *SPGL,* II, 167, 205.

[38] Ibid., II, 166, 175.

[39] Ibid., II, 196.

[40] Paris, BNF, nouv. acq. lat. 711, fol. 29r–29v: 'Verumtamen non oportet te precipitare tuam propter unum istorum signorum. Sed collige testimonia diuersorum signorum vel omnis. Item antequam feras tuum iudicium, pro aliquo istorum signorum respicias modum viuendi seu conuersacionem hominis de quo vis proferre tuum iudicium pro aliquo istorum signorum. Quamuis enim omnia signa predicte magnam inclinationem et promptitudinem naturalem inducant ad illa vicia vel turpitudines morales, et peccata que signant tibi, difficile est obuiare et resistere et multis hominibus sicut secutoribus passionum et concupiscentiarum videatur quasi impossibile esse. Et tamen satis possibile resistere omnibus viciis et peccatis ad que videntur inclinare aliquem sua anathomia vel disposicio corporalis. Si talis homo nitatur facere opera virtutum contra viciis seu turpitudinibus et peccatis ad quem videtur ipsum declinare sua natura

physiognomic discourse fuses smoothly with the discourse about vices and virtues. Physiognomy reveals only potential sins, so for an accurate judgment it is essential to compare the signs and their meanings with the actual deeds and behaviour of the person. Though it is difficult to obviate lust and other desires to which we are naturally inclined by virtue of our anatomy and corporeal disposition, it is still possible to do so. In this struggle, good deeds which counter the vices and a soul governed by a well-functioning rational appetite (*racionalis appetitus*) are the main means. The story of Hippocrates is the example of this possibility to fight the natural inclinations.

Some physiognomic texts are in manuscripts which are essentially compilations of pastoral treatises. This suggests yet another religious context for the use of physiognomy: priests needed it and used it for fulfilling their pastoral duties perhaps as a lay mirror of vices and virtues.[41]

A monastic provenance of a significant number of manuscripts is one of the findings which emerge from the survey I have made of manuscripts containing physiognomic treatises in French and British libraries. By monastic provenance I do not mean that the manuscript was simply in a monastic library at a certain stage of its history (such manuscripts are abundant, but they teach us little about the reception of physiognomic knowledge in monasteries), but that the physiognomic text is found in

---

et hoc fit quando anima intellectiva vel racionalis appetitum bene et sane iudicans et contra vicia et peccata dominantur remunerans in omnibus appetitui sensitiuo sicut rex dominatur in suo regno vel specialiter in aliqua sua ciuitate ita quod homo semper in omnibus secundum rectum iudicium appetitus racionalis operatur appetitu sensitiuo per omnia ad suum imperium vel secundum bene placitum obediente sicut ypocras faciebat ut dictum fuit de ipso superius'.

[41] Agrimi, 'Fisiognomica: Nature allo specchio', p. 178. For example, Paris, BNF, nouv. acq. lat. 711, fols 25v–29v (fifteenth century) is a pocket-size (142 x 100 mm) pastoral book which starts with a version of the *Secretum secretorum* followed by the section on physiognomy, a *Tractatus de septem viciis capitalibus siue mortalibus* and other miscellaneous pastoral works. Strasbourg, BM, 98, fols 138v–140r (fifteenth century: German provenance) is a moralistic, pastoral handbook which includes miscellaneous treatises that should help the priest in his daily work of teaching, hearing confession, and assigning penitential duties. It includes Thomas Aquinas's *Summa de articulis fidei et ecclesie sacramentis*, prayers and sermons, Seneca's *Tractatus de virtutibus cardinalibus* with a gloss, a treatise entitled *De confessione*, John Nider's *Manuale confessorum,* and Hermanus de Saldis (de Schildig), *Speculum manuale sacerdotum*. Then on fols 137v–138v appears a short medical treatise entitled *De Ypocrate philosopho et dieta hominis et sanitate*. It is followed by the physiognomy (which is a shortened version of the *Secretum secretorum* version). London, British Library, Royal 8 F VI, fols 53ra–53va (fifteenth century), is a priest's manual with simple, short moralistic treatises and practical advice (sometimes in English) for the confessor or priest (*De custodia cordis, De tentatione, De viciis, De penitentia, De confessione, De horis canonicis, Remedia contra omnia peccata*). The physiognomy is a revised version of the *Secretum secretorum* physiognomy and is preceded by a gynaecological treatise entitled *Secreta nature*.

a manuscript which is clearly a manual (spiritual or practical) for a monastic community. This suggests a possible use of physiognomy for recruiting new members to the monastery or the will to furnish the monks with basic principles of physiognomic theory for the administrative tasks of running the monastic community, tasks which involved frequent negotiations with people who were not part of the monastic community. The disappearance of oblates, brought up within the monasteries from childhood, in favour of the recruitment of older novices, is an intensifying process after 1200 and may account for the monastic interest in practical physiognomy. Bearing in mind Bernard of Clairvaux's view that the beauty of the soul (*decor anime*) is outwardly expressed in the appearance of the body, in its motions, gestures, and way of walking and laughing,[42] all this is not surprising. Furthermore, it is as if thinking 'physiognomically' became part of the intensive monastic soul-searching process. You need it to know yourself in order to be able to protect yourself. Like the practical medical treatises which preceded the physiognomy in Cambridge, Corpus Christi College, MS 481 and which were supposed to save the reader who practised the desirable regimen from the need to seek medical aid, the physiognomy was meant to protect the soul.[43]

---

[42] C. Stephen Jaeger, *The Envy of Angels: Cathedral Schools and Social Ideals in Medieval Europe, 950–1200* (Philadelphia, 1994), pp. 110–11; J.-C. Schmitt, 'The Ethics of Gestures', in *Fragments for a History of the Human Body*, ed. by M. Feher with R. Naddaff and N. Tazi, 3 vols (New York, 1990), II, 129–47.

[43] For example: Paris, BNF, nouv. acq. lat. 401, fols 138r–146r (second half of fifteenth century: Monastery of Saint Benedict of Polirone). This pocket-book (85 x 58 mm) is a monastic northern Italian compilation of chants, prayers, and general monastic liturgy for daily use. Between a list of readings for Sundays and holidays around the year and a letter in verse attributed to Urban V followed by more devotional poems (in Italian) relating to the cult of Mary, the book includes what is entitled as 'Notabilia artis physionomie secundum diuersos auctores'. This is a unique text. It is in the shape of aphorisms drawn from two physiognomic sources. It starts with a portion from the physiognomy contained in Hugo Riplin's *Compendium theologie veritatis* (from the beginning until the end of the paragraph dealing with the head) in *Alberti magni opera omnia*, 34, ed. by A. Borgnet (Paris, 1895), p. 79, col. b. Then it continues with physiognomy which heavily relies on the *Secretum secretorum* version (starting from the face of the temperate person: vultus, cf. *SPGL* II, p. 195). Later on he reverts to Riplin (fol. 141r for example) but essentially the text is the *Secretum secretorum* version, slightly edited and restructured. It ends with the same moral excursus as found in Paris, BNF, nouv. acq. lat. 711, fols 29r–29v.

Cambridge, Corpus Christi College, MS 481, pp. 385–404 (thirteenth century). A small book which includes miscellaneous moralistic, pastoral, and psychological treatises, many of which suggest a monastic provenance. (Hugues de Fouilloy's (Folieto) various treatises on the soul, Alcuinus Levita, *De utilitate anime*, excerpts from Ecclesiasticus, *meditationes* (attributed to St Bernard), various guides to monastic life including the rule of St Augustine, and Augustine's *De spiritu et anima*). The physiognomy (a version of the text known as *Auctoris incerti de*

As for the actual presence of physiognomic texts in monastic or religious libraries in the middle ages, it will be necessary to survey systematically all their catalogues. What follows is just a partial list of libraries which held at a certain stage a physiognomic text. The list suggests that at least in the fifteenth century it was not unconventional for an ecclesiastical institution to possess a physiognomic text. The 1480 catalogue of Cîteaux includes as item no. 294 the following description: 'Liber phisicorum et phisonomia aristotelis. Et liber metaphysice. Et de causis in medio uolumine'.[44] This is probably a conventional compendium of Aristotle's natural philosophy and metaphysics. But it is significant that of all the Aristotelian treatises the compiler of the catalogue chose to mention the physiognomy by name. For him the physiognomy was important enough to be mentioned together with *Physics*, *Metaphysics,* and *Liber de causis* as the essential pillars of Aristotelian natural philosophy. Specific physiognomic entries appear in the fourteenth-century catalogue of the Abbey of Saint Denis[45] and the 1521 inventory of Claîrvaux.[46] As for the British scene, there are no physiognomic entries in the catalogues of the libraries of the English Cistercians, Gilbertines, and Premonstratensians;[47] a single entry (from Glastonbury) appears in the

---

physiognomonia libellus in R. A. Pack, 'Auctoris incerti de physiognomonia libellus', *Archives d'histoire doctrinales et littéraire du Moyen Âge,* 41 (1974), 113–38, at pp. 126–38), which is attributed here to Aristotle, is preceded by *Epistola Aristotelis ad Alexandrum regem de sanitate corporis conservandam,* which is composed of various short treatises that stress the tight relationship between body and soul (*De quatuor temporibus, De quatuor humoribus, Alteratio cordis et oculi, Alteratio carnis et spiritu*). It is followed by *De interpretatione sompniorum.*

London, British Library, Sloan 513, fol. 77v–83r (fifteenth century: Buckfastleigh, Devon). This monastic book (copied by 'Ricardus Dove monachus de Bukfestre') of miscellaneous treatises of astrology, arithmetic, practical astrology, divination, chiromancy, alchemy, and monastic statutes contains the *Auctoris incerti de physiognomonia libellus.* The physiognomy comes in the divinatory part of the manuscript and is preceded by *Tractatus astrologicus de dispositione hominis* (discusses the effects of astrological constellation during birth) and is followed by a short chiromantic treatise.

[44] Dijon, BM 610, fol. 25r. The catalogue includes at least four medical books: Constantinus Africanus's *Viaticum* (no. 299); Galen's *Aphorisms* (no. 301); *Compendium medicine* (no. 302); Avicenna's *Canon* (no. 303).

[45] D. Nebbiani-Dalla Guarda, *La Bibliothèque de l'abbaye de Saint-Denis en France du IXe au XVIIIe siècle* (Paris, 1985), p. 201, no. 61, identified now as Paris, BNF, Fr. 1201 (which includes the pseudo-Aristotelian physiognomy in French).

[46] *La Bibliothèque de l'abbaye de Claîrvaux du XIIe au XVIIIe siècle*, ed. by A. Vernet (Paris, 1979), p. 503, no. 1041a; p. 523, no. 1267; and p. 524, no. 1271. Two of the entries are part of a compendium of Aristotle's natural philosophy, one is an independent version of Pseudo-Aristotle's physiognomy.

[47] *The Libraries of the Cistercians, Gilbertines and Premonstratensians*, ed. by D. N. Bell (London, 1992).

shorter catalogues of the English Benedictine libraries and two entries appear in the catalogue of Dover Priory from 1389.[48] Of all the fragmentary lists from the Friars' libraries in the British Isles only the 1372 catalogue of the library of the Austin Friars of York provides some evidence of a physiognomic text. Item 271 among books classified as *'Logica et philosophia cum scriptis et commentis'* includes Aristotle's physiognomy preceded by *De motu cordis* attributed to Magister Ricardus and followed by *De disciplina scolarium* attributed to Boethius.[49] Item 371, classified among the books of Master John Erghome, includes the *Anonymus Latinus* version of physiognomy, preceded by a treatise on astrological divination and followed by a chiromancy.[50] Item 458 among the books classified as *'Auctores et philosophi extranei'* concludes with a versified physiognomy which is preceded by a lapidary.[51] As for the papal library, there is no record of a physiognomy in Boniface VIII's library or in the 1353 *recensio*. Concrete evidence for the existence of a book of physiognomy in the library of the popes first appears in the *recensio* of 1369. This commentary on the physiognomy (*exposicio phisonomie*) in a single volume bound in red vellum reappears as item no. 452 in the *recensio* of Gregory XI in 1375 and number 612 in the catalogue of 1411. It has been identified by Anneliese Meier as the commentary in Rome, Biblioteca Alessandrina, MS 81, fols 1–93.[52]

So, despite some reservations, clerical writers vindicated physiognomy. The manuscript evidence suggests some interest of monastic communities in physiognomic texts. The sermon evidence suggests the incorporation of monastic thought into clerical discourse. Let me introduce one last contextual factor, this time based on a single manuscript and on a close reading of the text itself. It will link the instrumental ecclesiastical approach to physiognomy depicted above to the broader social values in thirteenth-century Europe and will fuse the general need for physiognomic analysis with the ecclesiastical acceptance of a science which had some religiously dubious meaning.

---

[48] *English Benedictine Libraries: The Shorter Catalogues,* ed. by R. Sharpe et al. (London, 1996), p. 164, no. 26. The entry ('a. Fisonomiam b. Lapidarium. c. Librum Petri Alfunsi') is from a list of books copied for Abbot Henry of Blois (1126–71) in the earliest portion of the *Libellus* attributed to the Glastonbury monk Adam of Damerham and written in the mid-thirteenth century. *Dover Priory*, ed. by W. P. Stoneman (London, 1999), p. 134, no. 323a; p. 161, no. 409d.

[49] *The Friars' Libraries*, ed. by K. W. Humphreys (London, 1990), p. 66, no. 271; cf. Dublin, Trinity College, 359, fol. 21v.

[50] Ibid., no. 371, pp. 91–92.

[51] Ibid, no. 458, p. 112.

[52] 'Item quedam exposicio phisonomie, cooperta corio rubeo que incipit in secundo folio: bonum, et finit in penultimo folio: qualitatum'. *Historia bibliothecae romanorum pontificum tum bonifatianae tum avenionensis*, ed. by F. Ehrle (Rome, 1890), no. 618, p. 335 and no. 452, p. 489 ('Item in volumine signato per XLIII exposicio phisonomie'); A. Meier, 'Der Katalogue der Päpstlichen Bibliothek in Avignon vom Jahr 1411', in *Archivum historiae pontificae* (Rome, 1963), I, 168, no. 612.

Starting from Michael Scotus's physiognomic treatise all the original medieval contributions to the science of physiognomy were dedicated to noble men. Michael Scotus wrote his *Liber phisionomie* for Frederick II;[53] an anonymous author may have compiled a short treatise on physiognomy for King Václav (Wenceslas) II of Bohemia (r. 1283–1305);[54] Peter of Abano dedicated his *Liber compilationis phisionomie* of 1295 to Bardellone de Bonacossi the lord (*capitaneus generalis*) of Mantua (1292–99); Roland l'Ecrivain proffered his physiognomy to the Duke of Bedford;[55] Michele Savonarola dedicated his *Speculum phisionomie* to Leonello d'Este, the Marquis of Ferrara (1441–50), whose personal physician he had been since 1444; the Bolognese physician Bartolommeo della Rocca Cocles dedicated in 1504 the last medieval physiognomy to Alessandro Bentivoglio, the son of Giovanni Bentivoglio, the dictator of Bologna.[56] All this suggests a useful working hypothesis: physiognomy served somehow the interest of the nobility in the Occident. But how exactly? Here comes William of Aragon or of Spain[57] who composed a commentary on the Pseudo-Aristotelian physiognomy and shed fascinating light on the cultural and social context into which physiognomy fitted so perfectly.

His commentary opens with a detailed, scholastic discussion of what nobility really is. The opinion of the author is clear from the beginning: by linking nobility to notability the author declares that nobility cannot be caused just like that, as it is nothing but the distinction of good action. He then proceeds to the scholastic examination of the topic and asks: is he nobler who is only noble by virtue of his noble parents, or is he noble [only] by the goodness of his own actions?[58] It is a common notion that he who has noble parents is generated and consequently nurtured as a nobler person. On the other hand, he who is noble *in se* and by virtue of intrinsic principles is nobler than a person who is noble merely by virtue of external principles. William determines unequivocally that since nobility is the distinction of good deeds, he who is made noble by virtue of his own goodness is nobler.[59] Quotations are given from Sallust's *The War*

---

[53] Agrimi, 'Fisiognomica e "Scolastica"', pp. 253–63; D. Jacuqart, 'La Physionomonie à l'époque de Frédéric II: Le Traité de Michel Scot', *Micrologus,* 2 (1994), 19–37.

[54] *Lapidarius. Quomodo virtutes pretiosorum lapidum augmentantur. Physiognomia* (Merseburg, 1473), fols 1–2, 29vb–38vb. Incipit: 'Attendite a falsis prophetis. [. . .]'

[55] Lisbon, Bibl. Ajuda, 52. XIII. 18; Oxford, St John's College, 18; London, British Library, Royal 12 G. XII.

[56] See n. 33 above.

[57] On William of Spain and his commentary see Agrimi, 'La ricezione', pp. 152–65.

[58] Paris, BNF, lat. 16089, fol. 244va: 'Primum est utrum nobilior sit qui sola nobilitate parentum est nobilis, aut qui bonitate operationum propriarum sit nobilis? Et arguitur quod noblior sit qui sola nobilitate parentum est nobilis. [. . .]'

[59] Ibid., fol. 244vb: 'Ad questionem istam dicendum est breuiter quod cum nobilitas nichil aliud sit quam bone operacionis notabilitas, nobilior est qui bonitate propria fit nobilis, quam qui nobilis dicitur sola bonitate parentum. [. . .]'

with Jugurtha (85, 25, 36–43) in which Marius hails nobility *in se* of a consul who was rejected by the nobility because of his lower birth, and from Aristotle's *Rhetoric* (I, 5: 1360b, 31–33) where Aristotle displays the political setting for nobility which in ancient times was determined by good deeds performed in the political context (i.e. protecting the ancient laws), and by judgment based on common sense, for no sane person would dare to allege that he, who has a white father and is himself black, is white. Nobility is determined not by blood but by character and virtue. Hence the need for a tool which will enable people to determine nobility that can no longer be determined automatically. The science of physiognomy was invented by philosophers, according to William, to serve as this useful tool, which enables the person to know how to choose his companions and associates so that by knowing their natural inclinations, he will avoid detrimental company and properly select his friends.[60] All this fits well with Alexander Murray's description of the growing literary campaign against carnal nobility from the mid-thirteenth century onwards.[61] The link between nobility and virtue and the rejection of the hereditary ideal became in the thirteenth century a widespread trend particularly among clerics. Later on, in Guelph Florence it received special impetus and could be fostered by the nobility itself to counter the *nouveaux riches* who lacked aristocratic virtues.

William supplies here a scholastic treatment of the topic. Consequently, he must cope with the inevitable question of whether, on the basis of the suppositions that *nobiles operationes* determine nobility and that there are two kinds of such *operationes* —active and speculative, the speculative is nobler than the active ('utrum speculatiuus nobilior sit actiuo').[62] In his answer, William refers to Algazel's *Logic* and Cicero's *Ad Tusculanos* and determines that speculative activity is nobler than active operation since he who is not active will not be speculative ('quia non erit speculatiuus quin sit actiuus').

He does the same thing in more detail in the treatise *De nobilitate animi* which precedes the commentary in Paris, BNF lat. 16089.[63] By stressing that speculative activity was superior to active life as a vehicle towards nobility, William expressed the

---

[60] Ibid., fol. 244ra–b: 'philosophi [. . .] viderunt esse necessariam scienciam per quam possent de facili iudicare de quolibet utrum sic esset naturaliter dispositus quod suas haberet operaciones nobiles siue uiles, que phisonomia dicitur.' Ibid., fol. 244rb: 'Multum enim necessarium et utile est homini quod aliquam artem habeat per quam uilium et pravorum sciat uitare consortium et sciat societates eligere studiosas. [. . .]' Ibid., fol. 244va: 'ualde enim utile est hominis scire eligere cum quibus poterit ducere bonam uitam'. See also Agrimi, 'La ricezione', pp. 154–56.

[61] A. Murray, *Reason and Society in the Middle Ages* (Oxford, 1978), pp. 270–81.

[62] Paris, BNF, lat. 16089, fol. 245r.

[63] M. Thomas, 'Guillaume d'Aragon, Auteur du *Liber de nobilitate animi*', *Bibliothèque de l'école des Chartes,* 106 (1945–46), 70–79; Marvin L. Colker, '"De Nobilitate Animi"', *Medieval Studies,* 23 (1961), 47–79 at pp. 53–78.

notion that it was the clerk's occupation (i.e. learning and education) which was thought to be the best road to true nobility. Are all men naturally noble? ('Utrum omnes homines sint nobiles per naturam?') asks William in *De nobilitate animi*.[64] It seems they are, since all those things in nature which are of the same species are of the same action and form. However, William holds the opposite opinion. For him there is a variety of people whose nobility depends on the quality of their deeds (*forma nobilitatis*) and is not necessarily natural. Aristotle's physiognomy is the foundation of his argument: soft flesh signifies apt mind (*molles carne aptos mente*),[65] and if someone should insist that rational soul does not depend on the body, I say it is wrong, determines William. For even though the soul does not depend on the body as its subject, it does depend on it as its object. William feels the need to qualify the nature of the dependence between soul and body and possibly reflects here some doubt that the physiognomic theory undermines Christian teaching about the soul. What exactly infuses the individual with that dimension which creates different properties and character among humans? Some say astral influences at the time of birth, but William distances himself from this 'meta-natural solution' and prefers to stick to natural causation. Aristotle's opening words in his physiognomy concerning the interdependence between body and soul should be understood in one way only: the soul has a natural inclination towards the body which it uses as its organ and essential object. This inclination the astronomers show by the stars and the 'naturals' or physiognomers by the shape of the organs.[66]

The preoccupation of the late thirteenth-century academic milieu with questions concerning the definition and origin of nobility is evident from two questions in a *quodlibet* of Jean Vate (*c*. 1290, master of philosophy in Paris) reported as a *reportatio* in the same Paris, BNF lat. 16089. Does a good person generate good persons? Jean distinguishes between Good according to complexion and Good according to morals. The first is transmitted biologically, the second is not; it is not innate but must be sought after and acquired through immersion in good deeds.[67] The penultimate question reverts to a similar problem: Are those noble by virtue of their parent's nobility nobler than those noble by virtue of their morals and character? After distinguishing different kinds

---

[64] Colker, '"De Nobilitate Animi"', p. 65.

[65] Ibid., p. 66. See Pseudo-Aristotle, *Physiognomonica*, 15, in *SPGL*, I, p.29 (sign of the 'bene nati'); *Secretum secretorum*, 23, in *SPGL*, II, p. 218.

[66] Colker, '"De Nobilitate Animi"', p. 67: 'Et istam talem inclinationem significant astronomi per stellas et naturales vel phisionomi per menbrorum figuras. [. . .]'

[67] Paris, BNF, lat. 16089, fol. 75ra: 'Consequenter queritur utrum bonus generat bonum? Dicendum quod aliquem bonum esse hoc est dupliciter, uel secundum complexionem vel secundum mores et scienciam. Primo modo dico quod bonus debet generare bonum quia agens intendit generare sibi similem. Secundo tamen modo bonus non generat bonum quia bonitas secundum mores non est innata sed inest magis per assuefactionem in bonis operibus et per inquisitionem et aquisitionem'. P. Glorieux, *La faculté des arts et ses maîtres au XIIIe siècle* (Paris, 1971), p. 240.

of nobility (for example, by descent, or character), Jean determines the absolute priority of nobility according to morals. But he does not entirely reject descent as a source of nobility and adds at the end that the ideal or the most perfect state is a combination of the two (nobility by descent and morals).[68]

It is thus not a coincidence that medieval literature from the twelfth century onwards dealing with aristocratic representation evinces a clear physiognomic link.[69] It is possible to identify a nobleman by seeing and hearing him; it is possible to explain his behaviour by understanding his physiognomic complexion. But the fact that Lancelot, the noble hero, is described as a choleric type, or that Chaucer's Wife of Bath had physical marks which were imprinted by Mars and Venus, is mere traces of popular physiognomy and has little to do with learned physiognomy. The physiognomic traces in medieval literature were usually folklorist in character, and relied on the principle of the eternal struggle between beauty which was automatically connected with goodness versus ugliness which was connected with evil. They thus reflected no scientific pretensions of having found an ultimate tool by which one could judge and know all fellow humans.[70] But sometimes, more elaborate and explicit types of physiognomy penetrated literature and introduced the humoral physiognomy to the wider readership. Thus Section 2.4.2 in the commentary of Évrart de Conty (*c.* 1330–1405) of *c.* 1440 on the *Livre des éschez amoureux* is entitled 'The face reveals the person' (*Le visage révèle la personne*).[71] According to this master of medicine of the faculty of medicine in Paris, the face is the key to decoding the disposition of the body as well as the character and the natural inclinations of the soul. Amongst all the organs of the body it is the most efficient in this respect, as it appears in physiognomy which uses it more than any other

[68] Paris, BNF, lat. 16089, fol. 75va: 'Consequenter queritur utrum nobiles nobilitate parentum sint nobiliores nobilibus nobilitate morum? [. . .] Dico ergo quod nobiles nobilitate morum sunt nobiliores quia perfectiores sunt in nobilitate. [. . .]'

[69] I. Hahn, 'Zur Theorie der Personenerkenntnis in der deutschen Literatur des 12, bis 14. Jahrhunderts', *Beiträge zur Geschichte der deutschen Sprache und Litteratur,* 99 (1977), 395–444; H. Wenzel, 'Hören und Sehen. Zur Lesbarkeit von Körperzeichen in der höfischen Literatur', in *Personenbeziehungen in der mittelalterlichen Literatur,* ed. by H. Brall, B. Haupt, and U. Küsters (Düsseldorf, 1994), pp. 191–218 and esp. pp. 215–18; idem, 'Zur Repräsentation von Herrschaft im mittelalterlichen Texte. Plädoyer für eine Literaturgeschichte der Herrschaftsbereiche und ihrer Institutionen', in *Adelsherrschaft und Literatur,* ed. by H. Wenzel (Bern and Frankfurt am Main, 1980), pp. 339–75; C. Connochie-Bourgne, 'Lancelot et le tempérament colérique', in *De la science en littérature à la science-fiction,* ed. by D. Jacquart (Paris, 1996), pp. 11–22.

[70] F. Neubert, 'Die volkstümlichen Anschauungen über Physiognomik in Frankreich bis zum Ausgang des Mittelalters', *Romanische Forschungen,* 29 (1911), 557–679, at 672–73.

[71] Évrart de Conty, *Le livre des 'éschez amoureux' moralisés*, ed. by F. Guichard-Tesson and B. Roy (Montreal, 1993), p. 32.

organ ('come il appert par la phisonomie, qui use des signes de la face que de quelques autres). Besides the face, celestial constellation unravels many secrets. It is thus not surprising that Évrart calls the sky and its planets 'the face of nature'.

The link between the changing concept of nobility and the rise of physiognomy, may enhance our understanding of the acceptance of physiognomic thought by ecclesiastical writers. For if *mores* and not birth determine nobility, one can easily add to the noun *'mores'* the adjective 'Christian' and thus recruit physiognomy to the ecclesiastical programme which sought to enforce Christian ethics everywhere and on all levels of society. After all, the strong noble element among the clergy created common interests and shared values which enabled both groups to adopt and propagate physiognomic thought. Church and society were thus inseparable.

The growing interest in physiognomy may have been related to this new ideal of nobility, fostered by the clerical, literate milieu. But it also served the practical needs of the nobility as a ruling class. For the political leader, lay or clerical, physiognomy was an auxiliary tool which supplied him with basic information regarding the character and the adaptability of a candidate for a political or public job. According to Roger Bacon in his gloss on the *Secretum secretorum,* which was written before 1257, it was particularly important for kings and other magnates to be well versed in physiognomy for choosing their friends and servants. For position, wealth, honours, and gifts corrupt even those who appeared to be good at the time of their election for joining the ruling court.[72] This, of course, was not particularly a new thirteenth-century phenomenon. The *Secretum secretorum* was composed as a *speculum regis* perhaps as early as the eighth century, and the physiognomy contained in it was designed to help the leader to choose his associates. Rhazes' *Liber ad regem Almansorem* (whose second book is a physiognomy which from the beginning of the thirteenth century circulated independently in the Latin West in the translation by Gerard of Cremona) did the same thing in the tenth century. In the sixteenth century, the Ottoman court chose its élite and promoted its high officers with reference to physiognomy and with the aid of a court-physiognomist whose office had been created specially for that purpose.[73] Though I found no specific reference to physiognomic check-ups in the *Specula principiorum* literature, physiognomy could easily detect the *sapiens, fidelis, non velox et impetuosus* —the most sought-after characteristics of civil servants in medieval government.[74]

---

[72] *Opera hactenus inedita rogeri baconi,* p. 166: 'Super omnes autem valet regibus et magis viris ut essent periti in hac sciencia in eleccione amicorum et ministrorum, quia etsi boni primo eligantur ad curias regum et prelatorum cito depravantur per divicias et delicias et honores et munera. Propter quod Aristotiles voluit instruere Alexandrum in hac sciencia utilissima pro omnibus, et maxime pro magnatibus, ut possit cavere a malis et eligere bonos'.

[73] G. A. Russell, 'Physicians at the Ottoman Court', *Medical History,* 34 (1990), 243–67 at 251–52.

[74] *Vincenti beluacensis de morali principis institutione,* ed. by R. J. Schneider (Turnhout, 1995), c. 12, pp. 64–68.

While physiognomy was an integral part of 'guides to the ruler' literature in the Arab world, the Latin *Speculum principis* literature I have checked shows that only that attributed to Engelbert of Admont (*c.* 1250–1331) contains a physiognomy.[75] Physiognomy was also used in the thirteenth century as a tool for recruiting personnel in other professional preoccupations such as selecting students and directing them to the study of the discipline they were suited to, or determining the professional adeptness of the astrologers.[76]

The rise and dissemination of physiognomy from the twelfth century onwards can only be understood in their medieval context. I have discussed here only one social need which can help us better to understand the rise of a new science. Surely there are other factors and variables which should be taken into consideration. In a world which had no data bases that recorded essential information about people, where the ways of communicating immediate information concerning individuals were long, inefficient, and often unreliable, there was a specific need for classifying tools that would enable people to pass an immediate judgment concerning people they met for the first time in social, commercial, or political circumstances. This need became particularly urgent from the second half of the twelfth century onwards when the vibrant Latin West opened up to economic and cultural exchanges that involved high, fast, and wide-ranging mobility. This in turn increased one's exposure to foreigners, reinforcing the need to devise reliable and user-friendly mechanisms by which these people may be at least superficially known.[77] Physiognomy was one of these mechanisms and its full history in the Middle Ages still needs to be told. For this purpose, a systematic study of the context in which the physiognomic texts (both Latin and vernacular) appear is at least as important as the study of the texts themselves.

---

[75] G. B. Fowler, 'Manuscript Admont 608 and Engelbert of Admont (*c.* 1250–1331)', *Archives d'histoire doctrinale et littèrraire du Moyen Âge,* 44 (1977), 149–242, at 206–42 and esp. pp. 235–39. I Have checked the *Specula* according to W. Berger, *Die Fürstenspiegel des hohen und späten Mittelalters* (Leipzig, 1938).

[76] Agrimi, 'La ricezione', p. 135, n. 3. According to Roger Bacon in his *De laudibus mathematicae* the astrologer should have 'an open and well-disposed face, a free and lofty brow, as a sign of good imagination, because the instrument of the imagination is the anterior part of the brain; and he should have clear, strong, and healthy eyes because of the multiple viewing of rays by instruments in delicate contemplation and many other things that signify wise dispositions, as is taught in books of physiognomy (*ut in libris phisionomie docetur*)'; see G. Molland, 'Roger Bacon's *De laudibus mathematicae*: A Preliminary Study', in *Texts and Contexts in Ancient and Medieval Science: Studies on the Occasion of John E. Murdoch's Seventieth Birthday*, ed. by E. Sylla and M. R. McVaugh (Leiden, 1997), pp. 68–83, at pp. 77–78.

[77] On the pre-modern lack of means for establishing a person's identity see M. Eliav-Feldon, 'Invented Identities: Credulity in the Age of Prophecy and Exploration', *Journal of Early Modern History*, 3 (1999), 203–32.

The Peasant Community and its Laws: Medieval Bavaria

MICHAEL TOCH

Medieval Bavaria, a sizeable and quite distinctive part of Germany then as it still is today, was probably the most rural and least urbanized of the many territorial units making up the German *Reich*. Its social history has traditionally been seen as dominated by lordship—*Herrschaft*—in its two chief manifestations, the territorial and the manorial one. On one hand there was the quickly developing ducal state of the Wittelsbacher dynasty (*Landesherrschaft*), basing itself on comparatively modern political resources as well as on extensive manorial possessions.[1] On the other hand there was manorial lordship—*Grundherrschaft*—which too has been subjected to intensive research for now over forty years.[2] Most of the latter work has been directed towards the landed holdings of ecclesiastical establishments. The lay ones were held to be politically less important because of the early taming of their lords by the Bavarian

[1] The magisterial account of Bavaria's way to statehood is still *Handbuch der bayerischen Geschichte*, ed. by M. Spindler, 2nd edn (Munich, 1977), II. It is supplemented by *Bayerischer Geschichtsatlas,* ed. by M. Spindler and G. Diepolder (Munich, 1968). For the manorial aspects of ducal rule, see I. Heeg-Engelhardt, *Das älteste bayerische Herzogsurbar. Analyse und Edition* (Munich, 1990).

[2] The fruits of which can be found in the many volumes of the *Historischer Atlas Bayerns*. On this enterprise see Erwin Riedenauer, 'Der Historische Atlas von Bayern. Zur Geschichte und Methode eines landeskundlichen Unternehmens mit besonderer Berücksichtigung Frankens', *Jahrbuch für fränkische Landesforschung,* 43 (1983), 21–58.

dukes.[3] In both cases the main emphasis has been on the territorial and political aspect of landlordship as a constitutive element of incipient Bavarian statehood. The social history of rural society has barely been touched upon.[4]

With such overwhelming dominance of lordship as the historical backdrop and early modern statehood as the horizon, the village community has been either of no interest at all, or was seen as little and only lately developed. This line of thought can be found as early as the sixteenth century:

> the common man of the countryside is solely dedicated to the working of the land and the tending of the cattle; he is forbidden to deal in matters of the authorities; he is not taken into councils and estates; besides that he is free [that is in matters concerning his holding]. [. . .][5]

This general image of the feebleness of Bavarian peasant organization runs until the last and even into the present generation of research, a conservative view befitting the dominant political culture of the country. Witness one of the leading historians of Bavarian agriculture and rural society, writing on the insignificance of the early sixteenth-century peasant uprisings in Bavaria: 'such partial insurrections could not damage the strengthened territorial state'.[6] On the contrary, as befitting the ancestors of later-day loyal subjects, these peasants were even credited with possessing 'an early form of state outlook'.[7] Still, maybe one is seeing a collusion of conservative opinion where the plain facts of history really left only little or no room for communal development.[8] None less than Peter Blickle, a 'progressive' historian if there ever was

---

[3] See the close to forty volumes of manorial records, belonging almost exclusively to ecclesiastical establishments, edited under the auspices of the Kommission für bayerische Landesgeschichte of the Bayerische Akademie der Wissenschaften in the series *Quellen und Erörterungen zur bayerischen Geschichte*, Munich.

[4] The exception is the work of French scholar P. Dollinger, *L'Èvolution des classes rurales en Bavière depuis la fin de l'époque carolingienne jusqu'au milieu du XIIIe siècle* (Paris, 1949), used in the updated German translation *Der bayerische Bauernstand vom 9. bis zum 13. Jahrhundert,* ed. by F. Irsigler (Munich, 1982). As implied by the title, this most important work reaches however only to the thirteenth century. A further work, despite its title, deals only with the legal history of rural lordship: Friedrich Lütge, *Die bayerische Grundherrschaft. Untersuchungen über die Agrarverfassung Altbayerns im 16.–18. Jahrhundert* (Stuttgart, 1949).

[5] Aventin, *Chronik*, cited by A. Sandberger, 'Die Landwirtschaft', in *Handbuch*, ed. by Spindler, II, 660.

[6] A. Sandberger, 'Die 21 Artikel', in idem, *Altbayerische Studien zur Geschichte von Siedlung, Recht und Landwirtschaft* (Munich, 1985), p. 250, my translation.

[7] 'eine frühe Form der Staatsgesinnung': Sandberger, 'Die Landwirtschaft', II, 663.

[8] For a comparative approach to the problem, which brings out the manifold varieties, see *Les Communautés rurales. Quatrième partie,* I: *Europe occidentale,* Recueils de la Société Jean

one, has characterized peasant self-administration in Bavaria as *peu devéloppée*.[9] Even a recent addition to the literature, the highly competent and interdisciplinarily inclined catalogue of the 1992 state exhibition on 'Peasants in Bavaria', has very little to say on communal organization.[10] Still, this does not mean that historians have been totally oblivious of the possibility of peasant self-rule. Following the search led after World War II by such eminent historians as Karl Bosl for early, yet peculiarly German forms of incipient democracy and social mobility,[11] some beginnings of 'popular participation in public life' were also confirmed in the Bavarian countryside. They were located in the local militia, the communal administration of parish property and funds, and the local courts.[12] The empirical proof for such general considerations has been partly provided by Pankraz Fried. While reconstructing for a restricted area the puzzle of local landlordship, Fried discovered sizeable areas of peasant-owned land, up to almost 15% of all holdings.[13] This would imply considerable spaces void of lordship and filled by forms of peasant organization yet to be discovered. Another of Fried's findings was the early development of holdings so small that they had to be supplemented by regular wage labour and rural crafts.[14] This has important implications for social structure and conflicts within the village. Chronologically, these features appear a long time before the onset of the processes of social stratification in the village that have usually been dated to the early modern centuries.[15] Fried's work on legal sources has led him to stress

---

Bodin, 43 (Paris, 1984); L. Genicot, *Rural Communities in the Medieval West* (Baltimore and London, 1990); G. Sivéry, *Terroirs et communautés rurales dans l'Europe occidentale au moyen age* (Lille, 1990).

[9] P. Blickle, 'Formes de l'administration paysanne autonome en Europe Central', in *Histoire compareé de l'administration (IVe–XVIIIe siécles),* ed. by W. Paravicini and K. F. Werner (Zürich and Munich, 1980), 392–404, here p. 397.

[10] *Bauern in Bayern von der Römerzeit bis zur Gegenwart,* ed. by Haus der Bayerischen Geschichte (Munich, 1992).

[11] K. Bosl, 'Freiheit und Unfreiheit. Zur Entwicklungsgeschichte der Unterschichten in Deutschland und Frankreich während des Mittelalters', *Vierteljahrschrift für Sozial- und Wirtschaftsgeschichte,* 44 (1957), 193–219; idem, 'Über soziale Mobilität in der mittelalterlichen Gesellschaft', ibid., 47 (1960), 306–32.

[12] Sandberger, 'Die Landwirtschaft', II, 662f.; idem, 'Altbayerns Bauernschaft', in *Altbayerische Studien*, pp. 368, 378; and 'Studien an Chiemgauer Maierhöfen', ibid., p. 65f.

[13] P. Fried, *Herrschaftsgeschichte der altbayerischen Landgerichte Dachau und Kranzberg im Hoch- und Spätmittelalter sowie in der frühen Neuzeit* (Munich, 1962), pp. 7–8, 66.

[14] P. Fried, 'Zur Geschichte der bayerischen Landgemeinde', in *Die Anfänge der Landgemeinde und ihr Wesen,* ed. by T. Mayer (Lindau and Konstanz, 1964), I, 79–106, here p. 86f.; in full P. Fried, 'Historisch-statistische Beiträge zur Geschichte des Kleinbauerntums (Söldnertums) im westlichen Oberbayern', *Mitteilungen der Geographischen Gesellschaft München,* 51 (1966), 5–39.

[15] H. Haushofer, 'Bäuerliche Führungsschichten in Altbayern', in *Bauernschaft und*

the community of court, the co-operation of the peasants in the workings of lordship and political rule.[16]

When these revisions and the detailed results of local research were incorporated within a comparative approach, the supposed embryonic state of the Bavarian peasant community appeared in a rather different light. Heide Wunder has differentiated between two forms of peasant organization, of which an earlier one grew out of the manorial lordship (*Hofmarksgemeinde*) of ecclesiastical and lay lords.[17] A later one initiated by the dukes bound the peasants of a given geographical area, regardless of their manorial attachment, within the framework of the 'community of the regional court' (*landgerichtische Gemeinde*).

The latest development in the field has gone far beyond re-examination and adjustment. In a number of important studies, Renate Blickle has dismantled the peacefulness with which Bavarian peasants were supposed to have suffered their lords and rulers. Integrating Bavaria into pre-modern Europe, she has shown confrontation and resistance as a central part of late medieval and especially early modern peasant behaviour patterns.[18] There were basic rules for such conduct, rules that made possible long struggle, retreat, and entrenchment. In all this the village community with its well-defined ways of interaction played a central part, much more than was to be expected of an institution supposedly ill developed. Renate Blickle has also demolished the easy identification between economic elite and community leadership, thus giving the community a much deeper-seated social dimension.[19] However, most of her very convincing findings come from Alpine regions of the early modern centuries. It still has to be demonstrated that the picture of a much more complex Bavarian peasantry is also valid for the late medieval centuries and for areas outside the mountain region.

One very much wishes to be able to provide such proof. Renate Blickle's work illustrates the difficulties better than anything else. Only by the patient reconstruction of quite dramatic and well-documented local events of peasant revolts—petitions, confrontations, legal action, troops called in, peasant marches into the capital city—was she able to uncover a deep-rooted structure of village life rightfully termed 'communal-

---

Bauernstand 1500–1970, ed. by G. Franz (Limburg, 1975), pp. 103–35.

[16] Fried, 'Zur Geschichte', p. 96.

[17] H. Wunder, *Die bäuerliche Gemeinde in Deutschland* (Göttingen, 1986), pp. 72–74.

[18] R. Blickle, 'Spenn und Irrung im Eigen Rottenbuch', in *Aufruhr und Empörung? Studien zum bäuerlichen Widerstand im alten Reich,* ed. by P. Blickle (Munich, 1980), pp. 69–145; idem, 'Die Haager Bauernversammlung des Jahres 1596. Bäuerliches Protesthandeln in Bayern', in *Festschrift für Günther Franz,* ed. by P. Blickle (Stuttgart, 1982), pp. 43–73; idem, 'Agrarische Konflikte und Eigentumsordnung in Altbayern 1400–1800', in *Aufstände, Revolten, Prozesse,* ed. by W. Schulze (Stuttgart, 1983), pp. 166–87; idem, 'Die Tradition des Widerstandes im Ammergau', *Zeitschrift für Agrargeschichte und Agrarsoziologie,* 35 (1987), 138–59.

[19] R. Blickle, 'Besitz und Amt', *Zeitschrift für bayerische Landesgeschichte,* 40 (1977), 277–90; see also idem, 'Spenn und Irrung', p. 129, n. 6.

ism'.[20] How much more frustrated must one be when dealing in earlier, less well documented periods, or in regions lacking such dramatic occurrences? Building on the work of Fried and Renate Blickle, this study shall suggest two possible steps to take us from the event into the structure. First, going through the typical terms coming up in the sources to designate the peasant community, we shall look for linguistic indicators that might hint at communal institutions during the Middle Ages proper. Having established their existence, we shall then attempt to flesh out their approximate nature by focusing on one particular feature accessible even through a case study. This is the complex of peasant solidarity as evidenced by the institution of pledging. We shall then take up a recent suggestion to ask whether the village is indeed the right place to look for the props that supported peasant life.[21] We shall enquire on the geographical horizons of peasant solidarity, asking whether they were of the family, of the village neighbourhood, or possibly of a regional nature. For both ventures we begin with the earliest sources extant and, taking the Peasants' War of 1525 as a cue, make a full stop in the early sixteenth century.

How are peasants designated as a collectivity? There seem to be three groups of phrases that come up in the sources. Chronologically the first ones, from the mid-thirteenth century onwards but also to be found much later, are some terms that indicate the village and peasant communality by relating them in a hierarchical manner to the manor and the lordship. Obviously tinged by the seigneurial origin of the evidence, these sources indicate 'the people of [. . .]' (*plebs, homines nostri de [. . .], homines de villa, ville homines*);[22] 'those of [. . .]'; 'the peasants of [. . .]';[23] and in general the *villa.*[24]

A second semantic group designates the 'common', in German *Gemain* and its derivatives. The earliest mention of *Gemain* occurs in the mid-thirteenth-century records of the monastery of Diessen: *locus communis quod in vulgari dicitur gmainde.*[25] A little

---

[20] For the concept of 'communalism' see P. Blickle, 'Der Kommunalismus als Gestaltungsprinzip zwischen Mittelalter und Moderne', in *Studien zur geschichtlichen Bedeutung des deutschen Bauernstandes* (Stuttgart and New York, 1989), pp. 69–84 (originally published in 1982). For an ongoing discussion of the concept see *Landgemeinde und Stadtgemeinde in Mitteleuropa,* ed. by P. Blickle, Historische Zeitschrift Beiheft, 13 (Munich, 1991).

[21] Anne DeWindt, 'Redefining the Peasant Community in Medieval England: The Regional Perspective', *Journal of British Studies,* 26 (1987), 163–207.

[22] J. Chmel, 'Die Besitzungen des Benediktinerklosters Niederaltaich in der Passauer Diöcese', *Notizenblatt der kaiserlichen Akademie der Wissenschaften* (Vienna): V, p. 282 (1257); p. 116; VI, p. 575 (1261); IV, p. 570 (1268); VI, p. 355 (1254); VI, p. 355 (1280).

[23] Friedrich Hector Graf Hundt, *Die Urkunden des Klosters Indersdorf* (Munich, 1863–64) (henceforth cited as *UB Indersdorf*), II, no. 1284 (1482); no. 1214 (1480); I, no. 721 (1446): 'die von [. . .], die pawrn von [. . .], die pawläut zu [. . .]'.

[24] Chmel, *Notizenblatt,* VI, p. 355 (1280).

[25] *Urkundenbuch Diessen,* ed. by W. Schlögl (Munich, 1970), no. 25, p. 148 (1248).

bit further on in the same document this is explained as *locus pascualis*, or grazing ground. A hundred years later, the same monastery refers to the same matter as *articulum de communitate*,[26] distinguishing in yet another document between meadows that are *proprium ecclesie nostre* and others *hoc est commune*. The identification of common property with the commune is still found at the end of the fifteenth century and again in the midst of the Peasants' War of 1525.[27] Common property is rightfully enclosed by the village, as in a document of 1414 where the two concepts are carefully distinguished.[28] Other terms for the same thing are *ad communem culturam*,[29] *ad pratum publicum*.[30] All this clearly does not mean a community but rather land held at common use, the commons. The monastery of Osterhofen used the terms *communitas, communio,* and *in der Gemain* interchangeably to signify rights to land in common use.[31]

Yet *communitas* and *Gemein* are of course fore and foremost terms for the village and peasant community. The Latin phrase appears in the thirteenth-century records of the monastery of Niederaltaich[32] and in the mid-fourteenth-century accounts of the monastery of Scheyern.[33] The aforementioned monastery of Diessen used the term *gemeinde* also to signify the burgher community of its nearby market town of the same name.[34] According to Renate Blickle, the term *Paurschafft gemeiniglich* was not just aimed at the collectivity of peasants, but indeed established the communal institutions of the whole of the Ammergau peasantry, that is their regional commonalty.[35] On a much smaller scale this was the case in a triple agreement between a priest, the lord, and the community of the parish.[36] The institutional meaning is obvious when the phrase

---

[26] Schlögl, *Urkundenbuch Diessen,* no. 180, p. 361.

[27] J. Grimm, *Weisthümer* (Göttingen, 1876), VI, 198 (abbey of Thierhaupten 1475–1502): 'Item es sol auch die vichwaid oder die gemeind verboten sein [. . .]'; *Der deutsche Bauernkrieg. Aktenband,* ed. by G. Franz (Darmstadt, 1980), p. 164: 'Das Aichholz zu Wiedergeltingen gelegen, sagen die pawrn, es sey vor alter ain gemaindt gewesen [. . .]'.

[28] *UB Indersdorf,* I, no. 446: '[. . .] die von Aspach von ir gemain wegen, wie si die eingeuangen hieten, wann die gemain allain zu dem Dorff gehört'.

[29] Niederaltaich mid-thirteenth century: Chmel, *Notizenblatt,* V (1855), p. 115.

[30] Chmel, *Notizenblatt,* V (1855), p. 116.

[31] *Die Urkunden und das älteste Urbar des Stiftes Osterhofen,* ed. by J. Gruber (Munich, 1985), nos 245, 256, 752, 1160, 1195, 1234, 1630, 3555, 3558, 3561, 3568, 3569.

[32] Niederaltaich 1254: Chmel, *Notizenblatt,* VI, p. 355.

[33] *Die ältesten Rechnungsbücher des Klosters Scheyern 1339–1363,* ed. by M. Toch (Munich, 2000), entry 1324.

[34] Schlögl, *Urkundenbuch Diessen,* no. 140, p. 300.

[35] R. Blickle, 'Tradition des Widerstandes', p. 143; the text of the imperial chancery of 1330 is in *Monumenta Boica,* 7, no. 4, p. 232; similar in 1405: *Monumenta Boica,* 7, no. 106, p. 97.

[36] A. Sandberger, 'Zur mittelalterlichen Kirchengeschichte von Prien am Chiemsee', in *Altbayerische Studien*, p. 217 f. (1385): 'daz ich mich veraint han mit meinem genädigen herrn [. . .] und gemeinleich mit meinen pfarrläuten'.

comes up in a struggle over access to common grazing ground and is used by a village community itself: 'We the peasantry commonly poor and rich'.[37] Such moments of communal action can cause the whole 'communality' (that is the village) to appear 'communally' on the scene.[38] Even more intense conflicts lie behind the wording of the documents drawn up in 1409 and 1425 by the ducal chancery to arbitrate between landlords and their peasants. In both instances the peasants are called *Gepaurschaft gemainiklich*.[39] There can be no doubt at all to the spirit of communalism when peasants themselves draw up their petition and again use the same phrases.[40] Here we are already in the vicinity of the structured rules of revolt behaviour discovered by Renate Blickle.[41] To mention but a few of her instances, in a petition of 1466 the Rottenbuch peasants complain of their lord's disregard for their community of court, which is again called *gemain*.[42] In a later moment of rare concord both sides petitioned the duke on an economic matter. Again the peasants' organization is termed *gemaine Paurschaft*.[43] To close the circle, when the rebellious men of Wiedergeltingen complained about their commons (the *gemaindt*) being alienated, they wanted it restored to them, namely to their *gemaindt*.[44] So the commons are the community or commonalty and vice versa, not surprisingly if one remembers the importance of dairy-farming and cattle-raising and thus of grazing grounds for many parts of Bavaria. As suggested by the geographical scope of our sources, this organized and relatively homogenous peasant community constituted one of the constant features not only in the early modern Rottenbuch researched by Renate Blickle, but in later medieval Bavaria as a whole.

The third and chronologically latest group of phrases are the ones used internally. Obviously the community must have a name for its members. Often they are called 'fellow inhabitants' (*hawsgenossen*), a phrase sometimes coupled with 'peasantry' (*pauernschaft*), and there are also the 'settled men of worth' (*angesessen piderman*) and the 'men of the land' (*landleut*).[45] All this conveys not only the feeling of commonality,

---

[37] *UB Indersdorf*, I, no. 267 (1376), no. 742 (1447): 'Wir die pawrschafft gemainchleich arm und reich; Wir dy von Aspach und Uettenhoffen all gemainklich, Rich und arm als wir dann yeczo da gesessen sen'.

[38] *UB Indersdorf*, I, no. 1636 (1494): 'es sind gekommen die gantz gemaind gemainlich zu Kümetzhouen'.

[39] *Monumenta Boica*, 8, no. 64, p. 86; G. Franz, *Quellen zur Geschichte des Bauernkrieges* (Darmstadt, 1963), p. 9.

[40] Sandberger, 'Die 21 Artikel', p. 252 (1514): '[. . .] in der Sach zwischen ainer herrschaft zu Wildenwart und unser gemain daselbs [. . .]'.

[41] Blickle, 'Agrarische Konflikte', n. 29 (1352); idem, 'Spenn und Irrung', pp. 77, 82.

[42] Blickle, 'Spenn und Irrung', p. 86, n. 9.

[43] Ibid., p. 95, n. 71 (before 1515).

[44] Franz, *Aktenband*, p. 164: '[. . .] wollen das hinfuero wiederumb ainer gemaindt zugestellt werde'.

[45] *Urkunden zur deutschen Agrar-Geschichte*, ed. by H. Wopfner (Stuttgart, 1925–28), no.

but also one of the major constituent elements of inclusion, namely the exclusion of less privileged and less propertied others. The most frequent term in the earlier Latin documents, however, reaching back to the early medieval *Lex Baiwariorum*, is *vicini* and in the later German sources 'neighbours' *(nachbarn, nachtpern, nachpawren)*.[46] Neighbours are by definition good ones, friendly and pious, and not supposed to behave otherwise.[47] This is not just a devout call for godliness, but a necessary condition for social life, as witnessed by a tenancy contract between a peasant and his lord of 1491. The tenant commits himself 'to be a dutiful tenant, man of the court and of the lordship, to keep himself in a neighbourly way, to hire together with the neighbours a herdsman (for the cattle), to fence in his fields and to be mindful of his horses and cows'.[48] So important was good neighbourhood that the original German verb *verfriden* (here translated as 'to fence in') still conveys the public function of making or maintaining the peace (*Frieden*). A bad neighbour was the exactly the opposite, he was a disturber of the peace: 'as I proved myself in an unneighbourly way, cut their wood [. . .] and also caused some trouble with my cattle in their sown fields'.[49] These two sources, appearing one after the other in the court-minutes of the monastery of Indersdorf, are a humble counterpart to the feudal vassal's duty of not hurting as well as actively aiding his lord. However, not to encroach on someone else's property was all right, but not quite enough. There is a distinct feeling of intimacy about neighbours. Many times the 'neighbour' is part of a connected group of terms signifying close relationships: 'friends (that is kin) and neighbours'; 'good friends (kin) and neighbours'; 'fathers and

---

254, p. 339 (Kloster Frauenchiemsee, Hofmark Seebruck, 1392–98); *Monumenta Boica*, 8, no. 61, p. 83 (Rottenbuch, 1393); Sandberger, '21 Artikel', p. 253 (Wildenwart, 1514); Sandberger, 'Die Entstehung der Herrschaft Aschau-Wildenwart', in *Altbayerische Studien*, p. 163 (1477).

[46] *Lex Baiwariorum*, XII, 3; for later (mid-fourteenth-century) occurrences of *vicini*, see Toch, *Rechnungsbücher*, entries 7272, 7273; for the German terms see G. Franz, *Quellen zur Geschichte des deutschen Bauernstandes im Mittelalter* (Berlin, 1967), no. 188, p. 482 (Berchtesgaden, 1377); *Österreichische Weistümer*, V, no. 3, p. 17 (Weihenstephan, 1381); Grimm, *Weisthümer*, VI, p. 128 (Kloster Aspach, 1481); L. Hanser, *Rechtsgeschichtliche Forschungen über das Kloster Scheyern* (Munich, 1921), p. 120 (1493); Sandberger, 'Das Landrecht der Herrschaft Aschau-Wildenwart', in *Altbayerische Studien*, pp. 168, 174, 177–80 (Wildenwart, end of fifteenth century); R. Blickle, 'Spenn und Irrung', pp. 60, 73, 74, 81, 87 (Rottenbuch, 1393, 1470 ff.); Franz, *Aktenband*, p. 163 (village of Türkheim, 1525); and most frequently in the late fifteenth-century court book of the monastery of Indersdorf, cited above and below as *UB Indersdorf*.

[47] *UB Indersorf*, II, nos 1581, 1241, 1584: 'früntlich und güt, früm nachpauren'.

[48] *UB Indersdorf*, no. 1528: 'Ein gehorsamer hindersaß, gerichtsmann und ehafftman sein, sich nachperlich halten, mit den nachpern einen hutter bestellen, seine velder sol er verfriden und seine roß und kue in acht haben'.

[49] *UB Indersdorf*, no. 1527: 'Als ich mich unnachperlich bewiß, in ir holtz abhawet, [. . .] auch ettlich schaden mit meinem vich in irn besaten veldern gethon'. For *unnachperlich* see also no. 1323.

respectable neighbourhood'; 'kinship, fathers and good neighbours'.[50] This coupling of positive traits was a moral norm and sometimes even a social reality. Neighbours are found interceding in favour of one of their number, petitioning the lord or the court to let mercy rather than justice prevail.[51] They also arbitrate, urging the parties to drop their disruptive quarrel.[52] The neighbourhood was obviously only one part of the social fabric of the village, catering for a segment of needs, but it was a very important one. For it appears that in Bavaria at least *nachperschafft* served also another word for *gmainde*. There are many cases of village communities being involved in this or other issue concerning one of their number. This took place 'in the presence of the neighbourhood'; 'with full authority of the whole neighbourhood and commonality'.[53] Thus we get a coupling of community and neighbourhood.[54] So it is full circle again, with the neighbourhood as a distinctive and very important element of village life, up to the point where it too becomes synonymous with the peasant community.[55]

What were the prevailing frames of reference in the day-to-day lives of Bavarian peasants of the late Middle Ages? Where did these people seek help and assistance when in a difficult situation? Was it with the family group (however defined), the neighbourhood, the village, or maybe some larger entity? Following the lead provided by English scholarship, we propose to use the institution of pledging as an gauge for such preferences.[56]

---

[50] *UB Indersdorf*, nos 1400, 1416, 1454; 1432, 1527; 1472: 'freunt und nachpern; gut freunt und nachpern; vatern und ain erber nachperschafft; frewntschaft, väter und gut nachpern'.

[51] On peasants negotiating with the lord, see M. Toch, 'Ethics, Emotions and Self-Interest: Rural Bavaria in the Later Middle Ages', *Journal of Medieval History,* 17 (1991), 135–47.

[52] *UB Indersdorf,* no. 1584 (1492): 'Darauff legten sich die frumen nachpern oben benent darein und erbaten [. . .]'.

[53] *UB Indersdorf,* II, no. 1474 (1488): 'in peywesen der nachperschafft'; *UB Indersdorf,* I, no. 771 (1449): 'mit vollem gewalt der ganntzen nachpaurschaft und gemain'.

[54] *UB Indersdorf,* I, nos 667, 931; II, 1011, 1174, 1260: 'gemain nachtperschaft, nachpawrschafft gemainklich, gantz gemain nachpawrschaft'.

[55] For the vicinity as a synonym for the peasant community in other parts of Europe, see Genicot, *Rural Communities*, p. 16.

[56] E. B. DeWindt, *Land and People in Holywell-cum-Needingworth* (Toronto 1971), pp. 242 ff.; M. Pimsler, 'Solidarity in the Medieval Village? The Evidence of Personal Pledging at Elton, Huntingdonshire,' *Journal of British Studies,* 17 (1977), 1–11; Z. Razi, 'Family, Land and the Village Community in Later Medieval England' (reprinted in *Landlords, Peasants and Politics in Medieval England,* ed. by T. H. Aston (Cambridge, 1987), pp. 360–93, here pp. 368–69). The most inclusive study is R. M. Smith, 'Kin and Neighbours in a Thirteenth-Century Suffolk Community', *Journal of Family History,* 4 (1979), 219–55. For doubts on the validity of pledging as a gauge to 'village emotional ties and loyalties' see B. A. Hanawalt, *The Ties That Bound. Peasant Families in Medieval England* (New York and Oxford, 1986), p. 260.

The need to have someone else stand surety for one's behaviour or ability to fulfil an obligation was a constant one for the medieval peasants of Germany as it was for their English counterparts. It was demanded by landlords and courts, and therefore has the great advantage of being written down in the minutes of the manor court. Unlike medieval England with its outstanding manorial records,[57] very little of this (or of manor-court books in general) has been preserved on the continent at large and almost nothing at all in Germany.[58] There is however some extant material from Scheyern and Indersdorf, two monasteries and adjoining landlords in Upper Bavaria. Both monasteries and the bulk of their landed property were situated in the hilly lowlands edged in between the River Danube to the north and the Munich plain to the south, the River Lech to the west and the River Isar to the east.[59] Geographically, this area was quite far removed from the Alpine valleys, whose free spirit of communalism has recently been reaffirmed in Renate Blickle's work.[60] We are using the mid-fourteenth century account-books of Scheyern and the late fifteenth-century *Tädingbuch* of Indersdorf ('Book of Settlements'), that is the monastery's manor-court book.[61]

People were obliged by the manorial court to provide personal pledges, people of solid standing and material means, for a multitude of reasons but most commonly for arrears of taxes, dues and other tenurial charges. Indebtedness to the lord appears to have been a widespread occurrence in that period. However, only the most blatant cases led to legal or disciplinary action by the lord.[62] The findings from mid-fourteenth

---

[57] On the English record, see the magisterial volume edited by Z. Razi and R. Smith, *Medieval Society and the Manor Court* (Oxford, 1996).

[58] For an overview on manorial records, see R. Fossier, *Polyptiques et censiers,* Typologie des sources du moyen âge occidental, 28 (Tournhout, 1978). On those of Germany, see the introduction to my forthcoming edition of *Die ältesten Rechnungsbücher des Klosters Scheyern 1339–1363*. For the Bavarian records see J. Wetzel, *Die Urbare der bayerischen Klöster und Hochstifte vom Anfang des 11. Jahrhunderts bis 1350* (unpublished doctoral thesis, Ludwig-Maximilian-Universität, Munich, 1976). See the introduction to my edition, *Rechnungsbücher.*

[59] For the historical landscape of the area, see the following volumes of the *Historischer Atlas Bayerns*: G. Diepolder, *Das Landgericht Aichach* (Munich, 1950); P. Fried, *Die Landgerichte Dachau und Kranzberg* (Munich, 1958); M. J. Hufnagel and S. Hiereth, *Das Landgericht Rain* (Munich, 1966); V. Volckamer von Kirchensittenbach, *Das Landgericht Pfaffenhofen und das Pfleggericht Wolznach* (Munich, 1963).

[60] This is not to say, however, that there were no contacts between lowlands and highlands. On the contrary, see M. Toch, 'Peasants of the Mountains, Peasants of the Valleys and Medieval State Building: The Case of the Alps', in *Montagnes, fleuves, forets dans l'histoire,* ed. by J.-F. Bergier (St Katharinen, 1989), pp. 65–70.

[61] Toch, *Rechnungsbücher*, passim; *UB Indersdorf*, nos 1078–1605 (1478–93). For the nature of the first source, see the introduction to my edition, for the latter, see my 'Ethics, Emotions and Self-Interest', pp. 136–37.

[62] M. Toch, 'Local Credit in an Agrarian Economy: The Case of Bavaria (14th and 15th

century Scheyern (nine documented years between 1339 and 1363) are quite straightforward. Out of a 156 cases of pledging only 20 (13%) were carried out by clearly recognizable relatives. Of these relatives the greater numbers were brothers. They are followed in order of decreasing frequency by relatives designated in general terms, then by sons, fathers, and in-laws. Clearly this is a sample much too small, but it does tell the anticipated story of a hierarchy of family ties and the obligations going with them. The main fact emerging is that the vast majority of pledges were sought and found not within the family circle but rather outside it. Since people of every socio-economic standing were in need of pledges, this is not a case of poor people seeking help from richer ones outside their family circle. Even the few relatives did not usually stand surety on their own, but rather together with other people not of the family. In 87% of the cases, that is 135 instances, no family member was involved at all. Even if we weigh for undetected relatives, a real possibility given the nature of the source and the present state of family reconstruction in this case-study, the percentage is not likely to change in a decisive way.[63]

Amongst the non-relatives of Scheyern peasants acting as pledges there are a number of people of local and even regional standing: a knight, priests, burghers, two ducal judges, the keeper of a ducal granary, millers, a forest-keeper, and most significantly, five of the landlord's regional officers (*Probst, prepositus*) and eighteen village headmen or substantial peasants, depending how one translates the Latin *villicus*. Altogether there were forty instances of pledges in positions higher than the average peasant. Although our Bavarian sources allow at this point nothing of the complex analysis undertaken in English case-studies,[64] we do get an inkling that here too might have been significant differences between the various layers of peasant society. However, these people of higher standing too usually did not act on their own but rather together with other pledges taken from the peasantry itself. So the typical pledge would be non-family, non-noble, not educated, not a holder of town citizenship or of manorial office, in other words a peasant like the person seeking his assistance. Indeed, there are numerous examples of reciprocal pledging, up to the one case where four peasants from the same neighbourhood take the stand one after the other, each stating his willingness to secure the others' obligations to the lord.[65] Was the typical pledge a neighbour then, defined as someone who lives in the same village? Out of the 156, we find the following distribution of origin: in 24% both sides are from the same village; in 15% part of the pledges come from the same village, while others are from different places; in 12%

Centuries)', in *Fra spazio e tempo. Studi in onore di Luigi de Rosa,* ed. by I. Zilli (Napoli, 1995), I, 793–803. The findings there should be supplemented by Toch, 'Ethics, Emotions and Self-Interest', p. 143.

[63] I hope to present more exact findings in a book on the later medieval Bavarian peasantry presently in preparation.

[64] Smith, 'Kin and Neighbours', pp. 242–46.

[65] Toch, *Rechnungsbücher*, entries 7272–74.

origin could not be established. But in close to half of the cases (49%) the pledges came solely from places other than the home of the man helped by them.

Now for the evidence from Indersdorf, another monastery situated a mere twenty kilometres to the south-west. It is much more explicit and sometimes long-winded manor-court book (*Tädingbuch*) lists 80 cases of pledging for the years 1478 to 1493, giving many more details than the previous source on the persons called to perform this duty. Let us ask again for the distribution of relatives, neighbours, and co-villagers acting as pledges. More relatives do stand surety, a total of 36% as compared to the 13% in Scheyern a hundred and fifty years earlier. We have already stated the suspicion that the Scheyern relatives have not all been identified. In Indersdorf too the relatives were mainly ones whose exact status could not be established, followed in order of decreasing frequency by brothers, fathers, in-laws, and sons. Here too then the greater majority of pledges were non-relatives, 64% as compared to the 87% in Scheyern. Again, was the typical pledge a neighbour living in the same village? 20% were indeed co-villagers, a figure similar to the 24% of Scheyern. In 30% of the cases pledges come both from the same village and from other places as well. Finally, exactly the same percentage as in Scheyern, close to 50%, lived in places other then the one of the man or woman helped by them. Despite the differences of the two databases, the picture is essentially the same and appears to have remained so over one and a half century. It is also similar to the findings from England, where in all case-studies only a minority of personal pledging involved members of the same family.[66]

So what is this, yet another atomized society of people with little family and village ties, a re-issue of Alan MacFarlane's 'Origins of Individualism' in Bavaria?[67] Of course not. The solution lies in the geography, settlement patterns, and prevalent forms of landholding in the region. Such features also explain how Bavarian peasants, lords, and scribes could consistently equate the neighbourhood with the village. First, both lordships lay in the same undulating lowland country that is structured into tiny and secluded settlement areas by a number of smaller rivers, low hills, and the prevalence of woodland.[68] Second, unlike other areas of Bavaria, most prominent amongst them the broad and fertile *Gäuboden* of the Danube valley, this thinly populated region had few consolidated villages. Thus the prevailing form of settlement was (and still is) the hamlet (*Weiler*), usually not more than a handful of homesteads. Yet communications between these nuclei themselves and the manorial and trade centres located in small

---

[66] Smith, 'Kin and Neighbours', pp. 224–25.

[67] Alan MacFarlane, *Origins of English Individualism*(1978; repr. Oxford, 1985).

[68] E. Meynen and J. Schmithüsen, *Handbuch der naturräumlichen Gliederung Deutschlands* (Bad Godesberg, 1953–62), pp. 72–73, 92–93, 97–99, 107–08, 112–13, 124–27, 131–33. The nature of the region has been painfully demonstrated to me during a cycling tour undertaken with my friends Alexander and Gregor Patschovsky of Munich. I thank both for their patience while waiting for me to get my breath back.

market towns involved no great distances. Third, this was an area of short-term leases called *Freistift*.[69] Thereby the landlord could move his tenants from one holding to another, or remove one tenant and take on another. Research has tended to focus on the more stable leases, including hereditary ones, granted during the fifteenth century by the Bavarian dukes to their men and tenants. This was supposed to have sparked off an *Erbrechtsschub*, a wave of more permanent leases granted by other landlords too.[70] However, we have found that ecclesiastical landlords remained very reluctant to follow the generous lead provided by the prince and father of the country. Instead, they tended to cling tenaciously to short-term leases, having little other means to prevent the alienation of their land. A last point, manorial structures were not consolidated but rather dispersed. The mean number of tenancies belonging to the monastery of Scheyern for instance was 1.8 per village.[71] As all other Bavarian landlords, the duke, lay aristocrats, and ecclesiastical establishments, in all the places where Scheyern had possessions it shared lordship with others.

All these factors must have led to a great extent of peasant mobility, the exact amount and dynamics of which are still under study. Yet such movements of peasant families, many of them still legally serfs,[72] tended to take place within a confined geographical range encompassing the lordship and its immediate manorial neighbours. Thus peasants had to rely to a considerable extent on networks of support outside their immediate vicinity and beyond kinship. These however were placed in accessible distances. Pledges would be called up from other villages and hamlets located at distances of not more than two to ten kilometres, including the few towns or market-places of the area. Given the geography and settlement structure mentioned before, extra-village and extra-kin solidarity were thus both a need and a working proposition.

---

[69] H. Lieberich, 'Die Rechtsformen des bäuerlichen Besitzes in Altbaiern', *Mitteilungen für die Archivpflege in Oberbayern*, 6 (1941), 159–76; L. Holzfurtner, 'Die Grundleihepraxis oberbayerischer Grundherren im späten Mittelalter', *Zeitschrift für bayerische Landesgeschichte*, 48 (1985), 647–75. For the actual praxis, see M. Toch, 'Lords and Peasants: A Reappraisal of Medieval Economic Relationships', *Journal of European Economic History*, 15 (1986), 163–82; Toch, 'Local Credit'; idem, 'Hauling Away in Late Medieval Bavaria: The Economics of Inland Transport in an Agrarian Market', *Agricultural History Review*, 41 (1993), 111–23.

[70] G. Kirchner, 'Probleme der spätmittelalterlichen Klostergrundherrschaft in Bayern', in *Zeitschrift für bayerische Landesgeschichte*, 19 (1956), 1–94. Such lordly benevolence was supposed, amongst other things, to have prevented the Bavarian peasants from joining their revolting Swabian and Tyrolian brethren at the time of the German Peasants' War.

[71] Toch, 'Introduction' to *Rechnungsbücher*, c. 1.3.1.

[72] On serfdom in Bavaria, see H. Lieberich, 'Die Leibeigenschaft im Herzogtum Baiern', *Mitteilungen für die Archivpflege in Oberbayern*, 28 (1948), 741–61; A. Sandberger, 'Entwicklungsstufen der Leibeigenschaft in Altbayern seit dem 13. Jahrhundert', in idem, *Altbayerische Studien*, pp. 224–43.

So there were distinctive features to the community life of peasants in Upper Bavaria. Their immediate physical vicinity was much more limited than that of the village, the unit upon which most of our thinking about peasant life has until now been focussed. Yet at the same time, their social contacts extended in arches larger than the ones prescribed by the nucleated village. Thus we need to shift our perspective as to the focal points of peasant life. We shall be better off thinking in terms of spatial layers and geographical circuits of social ties, units which were more complex than the ones usually associated with the village or lordship proper.[73]

Having pre-dated peasant communalism in Bavaria to the thirteenth century at the latest, we should inquire again into the specific background and reasons for its establishment. These must have been different from the ones adduced for the early modern centuries or even for the period following the Black Death of the mid-fourteenth century. Thus the much used, one might say overused, idea of a 'Crisis of the Later Middle Ages' is not applicable for the problem at hand.[74] Neither will general concepts such as manorial lordship and territorial (ducal) rule be helpful to explain the complexity of social development. With both the neighbourhood and the region as yet other frameworks of peasant life, at a much earlier date than previously envisioned, the structure and functioning of this society will have to be re-thought again.

[73] A recent addition to the literature is looking at lordship too from a spatial perspective: E. Riedenauer, K. Kauczor, I. Niedermaier, K. Schaelow, C. Schedler, W. Seufert, A. O. Weber, 'Gestaltung der Landschaft durch die Herrschaft. Beiträge zu einem Thema der historischen Landeskunde', *Zeitschrift für Bayerische Landesgeschichte,* 57 (1994), 567–718.

[74] One might add that our researches into the mid-fourteenth-century demographic history of the region have not come up with any proof that the Bavarian countryside has indeed suffered from the ravages of the Black Death of 1348–50. See the introduction to my edition of the *Scheyern Rechnungsbücher,* c. 1.3.3.

Who Desecrated the Host?

ESTHER COHEN

On the Friday following the feast of Corpus Christi, 1493 (7 June), a thirty-six-year-old priest named Jehan Lenglois walked into the Cathedral of Notre-Dame in Paris. Inside, he went to the chapel of Saints Crispin and Crispinian, near the choir, where high mass, with deacon and subdeacon, was being celebrated. There, he did an extraordinary thing. When the chanting priest reached the *Agnus Dei,* Lenglois burst out: 'you are lying, it is not as you say' (*tu mens, il n'est point comme tu dis*); he grabbed the host, broke it in his fingers, and scattered the pieces on the ground, adding insult to injury by seizing the chalice and spilling the wine. He then attempted to trample the spilled sacrament, but the deacon prevented him.

As might be expected, the uproar was immediate. One of the communicants, a nobleman, tried to attack the desecrator with his dagger, but others present prevented him, claiming the man was undoubtedly mad. Eventually, he was taken to the prison of the Parlement, the Conciergerie, for interrogation. Apparently, the first assumption of the interrogators, whom we cannot identify, was that the man had indeed been suffering from some temporary mental disorder or devilish possession. Lenglois, however, insisted that he was in his right mind and had planned his deed carefully. In fact, he had meant to commit the outrage in front of a much bigger audience, on the very day of Corpus Christi at the main altar, but had failed to fulfill his intent.

Though sane, Lenglois, it appears, had still been under undue influences. According to the main source of his story, Jean Molinet,[1] Lenglois had at one time lived in

---

[1] *Chroniques de Jean Molinet*, ed. by G. Doutrepont and O. Jordogne, 3 vols (Brussels, 1935–37), II, 373–76.

Avignon. There he had met Jews and been influenced by them. He believed in one God, creator of heaven and earth, but not in Christ or the Virgin. Like the Jews, he still expected the Messiah to come in the future. Naturally, he considered the Eucharist meaningless. All the same, to perform such an overtly provocative act meant far more than mere disbelief. The Jews had seduced Lenglois into performing such a spectacular gesture at the very heart of Christendom, where the greatest faculty of theology flourished, precisely in order to prove the superiority of Jewish belief over Christianity. Their hope was that a manifest proof of the Eucharist's inefficacy would promptly convert the greatest authorities in Christianity to Judaism, and the rest would inevitably follow their lead.

Who was Jehan Lenglois? The most detailed story of his case comes from the pen of Jean Molinet, canon of Valenciennes and *indiciaire* to the dukes of Burgundy.[2] As the biographer of Charles the Bold, his work is indispensable. But other than a short trip to Paris in his youth, decades before the scandal, he had never visited the French capital. Had he been the only source, one could easily have discounted the story as one of the numerous accusations of host desecration attached to Jews at the time. After all, Molinet's information was all hearsay. Unfortunately, whether Jewish influence did or did not stand behind his act, Jehan Lenglois's existence and deed are amply documented. He graduated from the faculty of theology in Paris on 21 March 1491, and another hand added next to his graduation record the following text: 'Johannis [*sic*] de Villeria, preacher. I heard that he had snatched a consecrated host from a priest's hand'.[3] The story is also told in the *Liber de origine reformationis canonicorum regularium in Francia,*[4] a contemporary account of the Collège de Montaigu and its influence upon French cathedral chapters and monasteries. Written by William Gregory, a monk of Château-Landon, *c.* 1520, it contains a highly laudatory biography of Jan Standonck, director of Montaigu, who was involved in the Lenglois case.[5] Like the entire text, the account is obviously based upon first-hand recollections; Château-Landon was one of

---

[2] N. Dupire, *Jean Molinet. La vie—les œuvres* (Paris, 1932), pp. 7–60; J. Devaux, *Jean Molinet, Indiciaire bourguignon* (Paris, 1996).

[3] Paris, BNF, lat. 15446 (pièces diverses), p. 351: 'Johannis de Villeria, praedicator. Audivi eum arripuisse hostiam consecratam in manu sacerdotis'. The manuscript continues with a summary of Lenglois's execution: 'Nota quod 21.6.1493 Johannes Anglici [*sic*] de Surcaeo comburitur post degradationem et truncationem brachii propter haeresim in foro porcorum. Et Ma. Standon eum astitit et bene moritur'.

[4] Paris, BNF, lat. 15049, fols 24r–v: 'quisdam familiaris collegii [. . .] a judeis in eorum heretica pravitatis dictus est et reali corpori Christi in sacramento altaris [. . .] negavit'. Augustin Renaudet, 'Jean Standonck, un réformateur catholique avant la réforme,' *Bulletin de l'histoire du protestantisme français,* 57 (1908), 1–81 (reprinted in *Humanisme et Renaissance, Travaux,* 30 (1958), 114–15, n. 2); all further references to this article are to the reprinted edition.

[5] Bk. 3, entitled 'De vita ac sancta conversatione venerabili magistri Standoncki'.

the first abbeys reformed by Standonck, and Gregory must have known Standonck personally.

Though established, Lenglois's identity is full of contradictions. On the one hand, Molinet describes him as a 'notable confessor [. . .] a respectable and impressive cleric', and the local *curé* of Ivry, near Paris.[6] On the other hand, the *Liber de origine reformationis* portrays him as the brother of a servant at the Collège de Montaigu in Paris.[7] Though not mentioned by name, he is referred to as 'someone attached to the college' who had denied the sacrament of the altar. Another northern chronicler, Christian Massaeus from Cambrai, simply describes him as 'a certain Master Jehan Lenglois.[8] Ten years after Massaeus (who had published his work in 1540), Gilles Corrozet, writing in Paris, repeated the story in different words, merely calling the culprit a heretical priest.[9] Seemingly, with the passage of time the connection both with Montaigu and with Judaism became more and more vague to the point of vanishing; conversely, his priestly identity was consistently affirmed.

Molinet alone presents a picture of Lenglois's convictions. When questioned how, given his beliefs, he could have celebrated the mass, he said that in order to satisfy people he had pretended to do as other priests did. Only instead of pronouncing the correct words of the ritual he had said, *'Hic est verus panis'*, rather than *'verus corpus'*. In any case, he had only performed the ritual twice in his life: once, to show the man

---

[6] Molinet, *Chroniques*, p. 374: 'notable confesseur [. . .] assez clerc et beau personage [. . .]'.

[7] This could mean a closer connection with the college than one might expect. Standonck had founded a special house for poor students in the college. By 1493, there were over eighty such students, living under monastic discipline. Many of them eventually joined monastic orders, especially Dominicans and Franciscans. During their studies, they often earned some money as servants to richer students. M. Godet, *La Congrégation de Montaigu (1490–1580)*, Bibliothèque de l'école des hautes études, 198 (Paris, 1912), pp. 9–11, 25–28, 39–40.

[8] C. Massaeus, *Chronicorum multipliciis historiae utriusque testamenti* (Antwerpen, 1540), p. 268: 'Anno 1491, postridie sacramenti, tertia iunii, quidam magister Ioannes Lenglois Parisii in facello sancti Crispini presbyterum celebrantem deiecit in terram, hostiam et calicem iam consecratum essudit et conculcavit. Captus ilico, negavit ibi corpus esse Christi. Post multa conanima, cum respicere nollet, combustus interiit'. Like William Gregory, Massaeus had met Standonck personally while the latter was in Cambrai; see Renaudet, 'Jean Standonck', 150; Godet, *La Congrégation de Montaigu*, p. 114 and n. 3.

[9] G. Corrozet, *Les Antiquitez, histoires et singularitez de Paris, ville capitale du Royaume de France* (Paris, 1550), pp. 147–48: 'L'an mil cccc iiiixx.x Jehan l'englois prestre heretique, osta l'hostie & le calice de dessus l'autel ou on chantoit messe en la chapelle saint Crespin & saint Crespinian dans la grande eglise de Paris, & la getta par terre. L'iniure reparee envers dieu [. . .] degrade & brule au marche aux pourceaux. Iehan Standon docteur en theologie se mit en devoir de le povoir convertir [. . .]'. The only later source to repeat the story, copying Massaeus verbatim, is Charles du Plessis d'Argentré, *Collectio judiciorum de novis erroribus* . . . , 3 vols (Paris, 1725–36), I, pt. 2, pp. 323–24.

who had taught him, and the second time, for the benefit of the Jews, who wanted 'to perform a certain superstition from the body of Our Lord'.[10] While the first statement is possible, and that people had failed to notice the difference in his Latin, the second one is incredible. It would have meant that the local priest of Ivry, who pretended to have been privately tutored rather than possessing a proper ordination, had never once celebrated mass for his parishioners. Finally, he claimed that, after returning from Avignon, it had taken him three years to find the proper opportunity to desecrate the host. Since two years before the outrage he had graduated from the faculty of theology, it would mean the sojourn in Avignon had preceded his studies, and that Lenglois had enrolled as a student of theology after being fully convinced that Christianity was no more than a sham.

One thing, however, is certain: Jehan Lenglois was attached in some way to the Collège de Montaigu. This much is proven by the involvement of its director, Jan Standonck, from 1483 till his death in 1504. Like Erasmus and Calvin later on, Lenglois may well have studied theology there. Since Standonck had become its director in 1483 and reformed it, the college had become famous for its academic level, as well as its ascetic and monastic lifestyle.[11] Standonck was equally noted for his piety, his reforming zeal, and his concern for poor students. Whether Lenglois was a preacher or not, Standonck was certainly better known as a preacher than as a theologian. In fact, all that remains of his written work (unfortunately, his sermons were never taken down) are a series of proposed reform articles for the clergy, propounded in November 1493 at the council of Tours,[12] and legislation for Montaigu and other monastic foundations and colleges he had either founded or reformed. His influence, however, was far-reaching. He had preached to and reformed religious communities also outside Paris, in northern France and in the Low Countries, where his fame was considerable. Jean Molinet was Standonck's admirer, mourning his death in one of his poems: 'the good Standonck, purer than fine gold'.[13] There is no evidence that the two knew each other,

---

[10] Molinet, *Chroniques,* p. 375.

[11] For Jan Standonck and the Collège de Montaigu in the late fifteenth century, see A. Renaudet, *Préréforme et humanisme. Paris pendant les premières guerres d'Italie (1494–1517)*, 2nd edn (Paris, 1953; repr. Geneva, 1981), pp. 178–83; The Lenglois affair is mentioned in ibid., pp. 110–11, wrongly dated 1491; idem, 'Jean Standonck', pp. 114–61; Godet, *La congrégation de Montaigu,* pp. 1–42 (the Lenglois affair is mentioned on p. 8); J. K. Farge, *Orthodoxy and Reform in Early Reformation France: The Faculty of Theology of Paris, 1500–1543* (Leiden, 1985), pp. 9, 72; P. G. Bietenholz and T. B. Deutscher, *Contemporaries of Erasmus*, 3 vols (Toronto, 1985–87), III, 281–82.

[12] Paris, BNF, lat. 13116, fols. 44r–50r, 'Articles de Standon docteur en theologie sur la reformation de gens d'eglise'. For details of Standonck's proposal, see Renaudet, *Préréforme*, pp. 178–80.

[13] *Le Debat du poisson et de la chair,* vv. 179–82: 'Le bon Standon, plus pur que n'est or fin'. Quoted in Renaudet, 'Jean Standonck', p. 159; Dupire, *Jean Molinet,* pp. 21, 36.

but it is very likely that Molinet had received his information concerning the Lenglois case either directly from the director of Montaigu or from Thomas Warnet, Standonck's student and emissary in Valenciennes.[14]

From the judicial point of view, the case is equally strange. Though a priest, Lenglois was promptly incarcerated in a secular jail, and no account tells of his transfer to ecclesiastical authorities, or of any trial before the Bishop of Paris.[15] Again according to Molinet, the transgressor spent eight days in jail, being visited constantly by four theologians, the most expert in the faculty, who tried to reconvert Lenglois into the Catholic faith. Neither their exhortations, nor those of his mother, served to change his mind. When faced with arguments he could not answer, Lenglois claimed that the rabbi who had taught him in Avignon would have been able to do so. When threatened with death, he maintained that he would willingly endure martyrdom for Almighty God's law, 'while hurling also several insults concerning our saviour Jesus Christ'.[16] Eventually he was ritually excommunicated and defrocked in a ceremony that reversed, step by step, his ordination,[17] and handed over to lay authorities. But at no point, seemingly, had the bishop claimed jurisdiction over Lenglois, an odd attitude on the part of an ecclesiastical authority jealous from times immemorial of its jurisdiction over the clergy.[18]

Furthermore, though placed in the jail of the Parlement, Lenglois was not tried there. The criminal records of the Parlement, extant for the period in a continuous series, make no reference to him. The indecent haste, in which the whole business was conducted from crime to execution in two weeks, does tend to disqualify the Parlement from being the 'lay court' in question. Parlement trials took a long time, sometimes years. Very likely, he was tried at the Châtelet, since he is mentioned in one of its collections of proclamations and special cases, the *Livre bleu du Châtelet*.[19] That same record, though, simply states that he was tried 'in lay court', without specifying which

---

[14] Godet, *La Congrégation de Montaigu,* pp. 109–31; Renaudet, 'Jean Standonck', pp. 150, 154; Bietenholz and Deutscher, *Contemporaries,* III, 281–82. Standonck had visited Valenciennes and preached there, in Latin and Flemish, at least twice during Molinet's life.

[15] Ecclesiastical prisoners were normally held at For-l'évêque prison. Even if arrested by the civil authorities, they were promptly transferred there as a rule.

[16] Molinet, *Chroniques,* p. 375.

[17] For identical ceremonies of defrocking, including the shaving of the head (to erase the tonsure), and the scraping of the chrism from the fingers a century earlier, see *Chronique du réligieux de Saint-Denys, contenant le règne de Charles VI,* ed. by M. L. Bellaguet, 6 vols (Paris, 1839–52), II, 662–69; and E. Cohen, *The Crossroads of Justice: Law and Culture in Late Medieval France* (Leiden, 1993), pp. 184–85.

[18] R. Génestal, *Le Privilegium fori en France du décret de Gratien à la fin du XIVe siècle,* 2 vols (Paris, 1921–24).

[19] The Châtelet criminal records, unfortunately, were destroyed during the French Revolution. The proclamation is in Paris, Archives Nationales, $Y6^2$, fols. 38r–39r.

one. In short, a clergyman was arrested by lay authorities for blasphemy and heresy, imprisoned in a secular jail, first interrogated by an unknown layman, subsequently harangued by four famous, though mysteriously anonymous, theologians to no avail, then excommunicated and defrocked by the same authorities that had never had him placed under their jurisdiction, and finally tried and condemned by a lay court which remains unidentified. While the irregularities of Parisian jurisdictions were notorious at the time, the case—if taken at face value—exceeds the boundaries of probability.

The final chapter of the drama is equally sensational and equally mysterious. Here, the judicial account supports the narrative sources. According to both the Châtelet record and Molinet, the execution was long and painful. On 21 June 1493 he was first dragged from the Conciergerie on a hurdle at the tail of a tumbril or garbage-cart to the cathedral doors. There, at the site of his crime, he had his right arm cut off. Thence he was carried in the same tumbril out of town, to the pig-market (where executions by burning usually took place), and there, tied to a stake, had his blasphemous tongue cut out. Finally, at the same spot, he was burned to death.[20]

But this was only one half of the drama. Did Lenglois die recusant or repentant? Each version of the case tells another story, but each follows the rhythm of recantation and denial. The *Liber de origine reformationis canonicorum* and one manuscript of Molinet's chronicle claim that while still imprisoned, Lenglois had offered to recant in exchange for a life sentence, but once it had been made clear to him that his fate would undoubtedly be death, he decided to remain steadfast in his heresy.[21] Nevertheless, Molinet's main version is more dubious. Apparently, towards the very end of the very long and painful execution Lenglois made some sign that he had repented. Standonck, at all events, was convinced of this, though others insisted that he had died a heretic.[22] The *Liber*, though highly laudatory towards the preacher who had accompanied the heretic all the way to the pyre, hazarded the guess that the final conversion was due not only to Standonck's exhortations, but also to the pain of torture.[23] The final remaining impression, apparently, is that Lenglois died converted, a good Catholic. *'Et bene moritur'*, says the note next to his graduation registration.[24] Surprisingly, the source that most outdid itself in describing the heartfelt contrition of the tortured heretic was the judicial note in the Châtelet archives:

> And on the afternoon of the same day, after the pronunciation of the sentence, the said Jehan Lenglois, by the grace of God, reconciled himself to God, confessed and

---

[20] *Livre bleu*, fol. 39r; Molinet, *Chroniques*, pp. 375–76.

[21] Molinet, *Chroniques*, p. 375, n.a.

[22] Renaudet, 'Jean Standonck', pp. 25–26; *Liber de origine reformationis canonicorum*, fol. 23r; Molinet, *Chroniques*, p. 375.

[23] *Liber de origine reformationis canonicorum*, fol. 24r.

[24] Paris, BNF, lat. 15446, p. 351.

> repented his crime, and like a good Christian [. . .] suffered the execution of the said sentence sweetly and patiently. Of this the people later praised God and rejoiced.[25]

The case of Jehan Lenglois is extraordinary on several counts. Even discounting the inconsistencies among the various versions, the tale as such merits closer examination. There is no question of establishing the facts, for those are beyond our knowledge. All we can safely assume is that Jehan Lenglois existed, that he was accused of desecrating the host in a spectacular act of ideological blasphemy, and that he was executed for his deed. Far more important than the facts are the context of the story and reasons for the telling.

If we accept the evidence of the narrative and judicial sources, and assume that Lenglois indeed committed the crime, there can be two interpretations for his motivations. One is that Molinet was telling the truth, and indeed the priest had been influenced by Jewish attitudes that the host was simply a piece of bread, unchangeable in its substance by any human ritual.[26] The other possibility is that he had adsorbed the ideas of various pre-reformation movements which—though usually accepting the symbolic value of the ceremony—denied that transubstantiation actually took place. We shall begin by examining the intra-Christian criticism of orthodox eucharistic doctrine.

Of the various possible doubts as to the efficacy of the sacrament, one concerned the validity of the rite administered by corrupt or simoniacal priests. This problem, however, does not concern the Lenglois case; the central problem is that of transubstantiation. As Rubin notes, doubts about this point go back to the tenth century, long before the Reformation.[27] But during the fifteenth century, these took on stronger forms. The remaining Cathars in southern France still considered that spirit could not reside in a material object, and the host was no different from any other piece of bread; John Wyclif himself considered the host more of a token of spiritual presence than the true body of Christ. He eventually developed the doctrine of remanence or consubstantiation, which postulated that the host was both bread and Christ. Wyclif's Lollard followers in the fifteenth century did not maintain his subtle distinction, considering the host no more than a piece of unaltered bread. 'By the fifteenth century, most formulations [. . .] had become far simpler, such as that attributed to William Mundy of Wokingham that the body of Christ consecrated by the priest at the altar was blessed bread and

---

[25] Paris, Archives Nationales, Y6^2, fol. 39v.

[26] On Jewish attitudes towards transubstantiation, see M. Rubin, *Gentile Tales: The Narrative Assault on Late Medieval Jews* (New Haven, 1999), pp. 93–103.

[27] Eadem, *Corpus Christi: The Eucharist in Late Medieval Culture* (Cambridge, 1991), pp. 319–34; see also S. Beckwith, *Christ's Body: Identity, Culture, and Society in Late Medieval Writings* (London and New York, 1993), pp. 33–37. Israel J. Yuval's book, *'Two Nations in Your Womb': Perceptions of Jews and Christians* (Tel Aviv, 2000) [in Hebrew], came out too late to be discussed in this article.

nothing more'.[28] Blessed it might be, but its substance remained that of bread, not the body of Christ.

All these heresies were far from Paris, the locus of our drama. The faculty of theology in Paris was the cornerstone of orthodoxy. The only other case of heterodoxy known at the Collège de Montaigu came somewhat later, in 1506, when Noël Beda's youthful ideas concerning benefices were adjudged to be perilously close to Wyclif's.[29] There was no other whiff of heresy emanating from the highly orthodox and ascetic college, and benefices had nothing to do with the nature of the Eucharist. To the contrary: in so far as Standonck and Montaigu maintained close connections with Low Countries religiosity, exporting its reforming spirit to Windesheim and back to France,[30] it was far more likely to sin in the opposite direction: namely, the stubborn attempts of northern mystics, especially women, to gain direct access to the host on a daily basis.[31] But even this divergence was unlikely: the students at Montaigu were all clerics, regular or secular, many of them ordained priests. None of them, Lenglois included, could have had any trouble getting hold of a consecrated host, had they wanted to. None of Standonck's remaining writings refers to any such problem, and whatever Standonck's connections with the *Devotio Moderna* movement, unlike his Flemish friends he does not seem to have devoted any attention to eucharistic meditations.[32]

All the same, some of the formulations put in Lenglois's mouth by Molinet echo Lollard and Cathar words. The words *'Hic est verus panis'*, which he was supposed to have uttered while performing the mass instead of the liturgical formula, and his statement *'le sacrement estoit nul'* both sound remarkably like the heretical formulations of eucharistic doubts which both Standonck the theologian and Molinet the canon regular and chronicler would have recognized—and perhaps put into the desecrator's mouth.

But while Standonck was a model of orthodoxy, the university of Paris in its entirety was not free from eucharistic speculations. Almost exactly ten years after the Lenglois scandal, on 25 August 1503, another outrage took place. It happened on the day of the feast of St Louis, while high mass was celebrated at the Sainte-Chapelle in the presence of the president and councillors of the Parlement. Hémon de la Fosse, a student at the Collège de Bourgogne, originally from Abbeville, grabbed the host from the priest and tried to run away with it. He was immediately mobbed, and the host fell

---

[28] Rubin, *Corpus Christi*, p. 327.

[29] Farge, *Orthodoxy and Reform,* pp. 163–64.

[30] R. R. Post, *The Modern Devotion: Confrontation with Reformation and Humanism,* Studies in Medieval and Reformation Thought, 3 (Leiden, 1968), pp. 632–36; idem, 'The Windesheimers after c. 1485: Confrontation with the Reformation and Humanism', in *The Reformation in Medieval Perspective*, ed. by S. Ozment (Chicago, 1971), pp. 157–84.

[31] C. W. Bynum, *Holy Feast and Holy Fast: The Religious Significance of Food to Medieval Women* (Berkeley, 1987), pp. 115–29 and passim.

[32] Farge, *Orthodoxy and Reform,* pp. 248–49.

on the ground and broke. One councillor prevented the mob from tearing him apart, so as to save him for judicial punishment. Arrested, he was first taken to the Conciergerie like Lenglois, but subsequently tried by an inquisitorial court. Like Lenglois, he was condemned to have the hand that had desecrated the host cut off, and to be burned at the pig-market.

Had host desecration become fashionable? Two contemporary chroniclers describe the events. Jean d'Autun, official chronicler of Louis XII, tells the story in a florid and intricate way. The student had approached the celebrant, pretended to be a believer and to help, but as soon as the host was consecrated he grabbed it, crying out, 'will this madness still persist?' While in jail, he declared that he believed only in Jupiter and Hercules as gods, denying all principles but the natural ones. Furthermore, there was no paradise beyond the Elysian Fields.[33] D'Autun's contemporary Jean Bouchet, however, tells a much less dramatic tale. The man had made no declaration; he was undoubtedly insane, for the judges had sent for physicians who pronounced him *maniaque* and lacking half his senses. Bouchet terms him pityingly *'ce pauvre foul'*.[34] Both, however, agree that he was condemned, degraded, excommunicated, and handed over to the secular arm for execution; and that he died unrepentant.

Is there any similarity between the cases? The one clear connection is the fact that Standonck, practically on his deathbed, was called in once more to argue with the desecrator.[35] Moreover, both desecrations were performed by university people, and on a Friday. The day of the week, more than the calendar date, does indicate the importance of the Eucharist and the Crucifixion to the desecrators. But there the similarity ends. There is no proof that Hémon de la Fosse was actually trying to desecrate the host. Whether he was mad or not, all he initially did was grab it and attempt to run. His act was interpreted as heresy by one, as madness by another. It might also have been a form of perverted eucharistic piety. In any case, nobody levelled the accusation of judaizing against him. But this second case, a mere decade after Lenglois, does indicate that eucharistic preoccupations were rife in late fifteenth-century Paris.

While the heretical, proto-Protestant interpretation of Lenglois's act comes from the historians' pen, contemporaries attributed the scandalous act to Jewish influences. But though the former interpretation carries some air of verisimilitude, the second is bizarre in the extreme. Three sources bring up the accusation of 'judaizing', though never of an actual conversion to Judaism: Molinet extensively, adding the Avignon episode; the *Liber de origine reformationis* simply, stating that he had acted at the instigation of the Jews; finally, the Châtelet record, naming him *'prestre judaizant'*.

Two centuries earlier, in 1290, Paris was the locus of the first full-fledged host desecration accusation, which was destined to serve as a basis for all the later ones. The

---

[33] 'Et durera tousjours ceste folye!'; Jean d'Autun, *Chroniques de Louis XII*, ed. by R. Maulde de la Clavière, 4 vols (Paris, 1889–95), III, 270–72.

[34] Jean Bouchet, *Annales d'Aquitaine* (Poitiers, 1524), fol. 66r.

[35] Renaudet, 'Jean Standonck', p. 158; idem, *Préréforme,* pp. 357–58.

story took place (as most of the later accusations were wont to) at Eastertide. A Jew persuaded a Christian woman (either his servant or his debtor) to give him the host she had received during Easter communion. He proceeded first to stab it with a knife, whereupon it bled, then tried to burn it, eventually throwing it into a cauldron of boiling water; at this point, it was transformed into the image of the crucified Christ.[36] The outrage was promptly reported by the Jew's son to a devout Christian woman, and the Jew came by his due punishment: he was burned at the stake while his family, having evidenced the miracle, converted. The miraculous host was kept in the church of St-Jean-en-Grève, and was carried in processions throughout the city as late as the fifteenth century.[37]

The story of Jewish host desecration was thus undoubtedly familiar to all Parisians. A recurring motif in this accusation is Jewish empiricism. Time and again the accusations stated that Jews tortured and abused the host in order to find out whether it was indeed the true body of Christ. Only in one case, however, was the Jew convinced by the evident miracle and went on to convert.[38] As a rule, the story tells that the Jews were so frightened by the evidence of their error that they tried to get rid of the host, usually with the aid of a Christian or a convert, and were thus denounced and discovered.[39]

How does the case of Jehan Lenglois fare in light of this fairly homogenous tale? Very badly indeed. True, Molinet claims that Lenglois had indeed cooperated with the Jews of Avignon in some sort of secret host abuse, but the trial and the scandal had nothing to do with that episode. Here we have a born Christian, not even a converted Jew, and a priest to boot, committing the sacrilege. Furthermore, the entire desecration is different. Unlike the Jewish crimes, which took place either at home or in a synagogue, secretly and privately, this desecration takes place in full view, in the middle of the mass, on the weekly day of the Crucifixion. Indeed, had Lenglois had his way, it would have been an even more public desecration. It includes not only the host, but the wine as well, the flesh and the blood of Christ. And to top it all, there is no miracle: the host, when thrown on the floor, does break into pieces, but does not bleed, nor was there any other miraculous manifestation commonly associated with host desecrations. But the most striking difference lies in the motivation attributed to the desecrator. Jews were assumed by Christians to torture the host precisely because they suspected it might indeed be God—otherwise why would anybody bother to stab or boil a piece of bread? Like true empiricists, they were subjecting their object to a laboratory experiment, approaching it with an open mind. 'If you are indeed God, prove it to me', they say. Lenglois's motivation is opposite. He proceeds not from a question, but from the

---

[36] Rubin, *Gentile Tales,* p. 41.

[37] Ibid., pp. 159–61.

[38] Ibid., p. 84.

[39] Ibid., pp. 181–89 and passim.

certitude that the host is meaningless. His act is meant merely to prove this fact to others. Ironically, he succeeded in one sense: no miracle was produced whcre expected. Why was the story constructed this way, so divergent from the standard? To begin with, by 1493 there had been no Jews in France for a century, the last ones having been expelled in 1394.[40] True, there were Jews in papal Avignon,[41] but their existence must have been of little interest to the mystics and theologians of northern France. If one had to produce a Jewish 'education' for Lenglois, Avignon was a possible source, far enough to defeat any casual attempt at verification.[42] Secondly, the story of a Jewish plot to convert Christians in Paris by Lenglois's example is not part of the standard tale. Usually, the accusations attributed a far more malevolent motivation to the Jews: not proof by example, but vindictiveness and evil. The only hint in Molinet's version of the traditional accusation is that the Jews in Avignon had requested that Lenglois perform a mass for some malefic reason of their own, directed against Christ.

If the perpetrator was a Christian priest out to prove the inefficacy of the sacrament, it is also clear why the blasphemy had to be committed in public. Traditional host desecration tales speak of furtive stealing and clandestine stabbing, boiling, and burning of wafers. No Jew performed such a sacrilege in public, since the efficacy of the act lay in the attack, not in its visible results. But the only way to strip the host of its charisma was to desecrate it publicly.

The only way of explaining the case of Jehan Lenglois as told by its various sources is to place it within the context of the telling. The sources are all either Parisian or Netherlandish, and the connection between the two, as we have seen, lies in the person and life of Jan Standonck. Given the abundance of sources, it is unlikely that Standonck could have invented the flesh-and-blood Lenglois; he had indeed existed, and suffered execution. It is possible, however, that Standonck re-invented him posthumously.

The evidence in the case belongs to two different categories: those which Standonck could not have affected, namely, the Châtelet record bearing the judicial evidence of crime, trial, and punishment, and those he could have formed, which include the graduation record with its 'marginal gloss', the *Liber de origine reformationis canonicorum,* and chronicles of Jean Molinet and Christian Massaeus. The second

---

[40] I. Loeb, 'Les expulsions des Juifs de France au XIVe siècle', *Jubelschrift H. Graetz* (Breslau, 1887), pp. 39–56.

[41] For the Jews of Avignon in the late fifteenth century, see Armand Mossé, *Histoire des juifs d'Avignon et du Comtat-Venaissin* (Paris, 1934); D. Iancu, *Les juifs en Provence (1475–1501). De l'insertion à l'expulsion* (Marseilles, 1981); B. Delpal, *Juifs et chrètiens à Avignon et dans le Comtat-Venaissin* (unpublished master's thesis, Université de Nanterre, 1968); R. Moulinas, *Les Juifs du pape en France: Les communautés d'Avignon et du Comtat Venaissin aux 17e et 18e siècles* (Paris, 1981), pp. 24–29.

[42] I have found no mention of Jehan Lenglois either in the municipal archives of Avignon or in the Archives dèpartamentales of Vaucluse. While the absence of archival justification proves nothing, it does strengthen my hypothesis somewhat.

category bears the clear mark of his hand. Though the note next to the graduation record was written at a later date, and is obviously second-hand, they were all obviously written by people very much under Standonck's influence. Given both Molinet's connections with Standonck and William Gregory's adulation of the same, it is clearly the context of pre-reformation Paris that we must examine.

The most notable watchword of Standonck and his college was reform. He reformed the college, he founded a special house for poor students, and brought all, rich and poor, 'ad [. . .] confugii religionis reformatam'.[43] Not content with the college, he tried to impose reform upon the entire French clergy, and preached on the same theme throughout his career.[44] But the word meant different things in different contexts. Within the college, it meant asceticism, monastic discipline, and high academic standards. For the clergy, especially canons regular, it meant imposing monastic discipline and enclosure.[45] For the laity, it meant an internalization of a moral and religious code.

It is here that the Lenglois case came in so opportunely. Here was a way to tie Montaigu reform standards with the world at large, or at least with Paris. The ones to crucify Christ again and again are not the Jews, but—as another contemporary countryman of Standonck's, Jan of Ruysbroeck, had noted—Christian sinners: '[. . .] and so it is even now in the world: the sinners crucify our Lord by their sins, as did the Jews and the heathens with their hands'.[46] And for one dedicated to the reform of the clergy, what better sinner to crucify Christ than a sinful priest?

In addition, there is the nature of Lenglois's motivation. In the texts that Standonck touched, Lenglois is neither avaricious nor evil. His motivation is ideological. Sin no longer lay in the physical desecration, but in the denial of faith. That is why no physical miracle of a bleeding host was forthcoming. It would not have been fitting within the new context. It is not likely that either Standonck or Molinet were so utterly and woefully ignorant of the original traits of the host desecration accusation. They must have known it, but were not interested in the external devil anymore, when the internal one was far more threatening and dangerous. Therefore, the miracle of the host was of a new order as well. The miracle consisted in Lenglois's near-death reconversion to the

---

[43] *Liber de origine reformationis canonicorum,* fols 23r–v.

[44] Renaudet, 'Jean Standonck', passim.

[45] Post, *Modern Devotion*, p. 633; idem, 'Windesheimers', pp. 157–60; Standonck attempted to reform the Windesheim community in 1495, founding there a school for poor pupils, as he had done at his college; then brought its people back to reform the canons of St-Victor in Paris.

[46] Jan of Ruysbroeck, *De vera contemplatione [Vanden XII beghinen],* ed. by M. M. Kors, English trans. by H. Rolfson, Latin trans. by L. Sirius (1552), CCCM, 107–107A (Turnhout, 2000), pp. 316–17:'Sic hodie in mundo agitur: Homines peccatis dediti, suis sceleribus crucifigunt Dominum, sicut olim Iudaei et Pagani manibus' ('[. . .] ende alsoe eest noch in de werelt: die zondaren crucem onsen heere met haren sonden, ghelijckerwijs dat die jueden ende heiden daden met haren handen').

Christian faith. How miraculous this was is highlighted by Molinet's statement that four eminent theologians had wrought unsuccessfully with Lenglois for a whole week. It was only Standonck who managed to bring him back into the fold, and only at the foot of the scaffold. Obviously, the preacher did not consider the conversion his handiwork, but a manifest grace of God. So powerful was the impact of this conversion, that in gratitude the rector of Montaigu observed 'perpetual Lent' thereafter, forswearing meat for the rest of his life.[47]

The perpetual Lent of Standonck, in the wake of the conversion and execution of Lenglois, also closes the calendar cycle. Host desecration accusations began by taking place around Easter, but the date was not invariable. They occurred also at other times, and with the growth of the feast of Corpus Christi, it is natural that this case should have taken place in relation to the popular late medieval feast.[48] With Lent, one returns to the Easter setting of eucharistic devotion and desecration. Standonck had indeed brought a double coup: first the desecration drama, then the conversion and execution drama. The first was short but intense, the second long and drawn out but equally intense. Almost to the very last, people were probably watching the procession, hearing Standonck's constant exhortations and Lenglois's cries of pain, and guessing, will he or will he not recant? Until finally at the climax—or so Molinet tells it—the chief actor consented to play his role, and the miracle of conversion took place. In truth, admits Molinet, the end was ambiguous. Some said he had died a stubborn recusant, but not only Standonck was convinced that he had cried out of his tongueless mouth something resembling 'Jesus'. The hangman also thought so, and begged the judge to have the man strangled prior to burning so that he would not fall into the sin of despair, seeing that he was repenting already.

Does this mean that the whole story is spun from the same cloth as other host desecration accusations? We cannot tell, or even make a fair guess. The trial irregularities do raise some serious questions. Why did the Bishop of Paris never intervene until the defrocking if Lenglois was indeed a local priest? If he was an impostor, how had he graduated from the faculty of theology and why did he have to be properly defrocked? The protocol is missing, the 'lay court' is unspecified, the whole business took an exceedingly short time. Did a proper trial ever take place? Did Lenglois admit his guilt before a court? Or, more embarrassingly, had he denied it and threatened to ruin the whole show?

If one eliminates the impossible, says Sherlock Holmes, the improbable, however unlikely, must be true. Jehan Lenglois must have existed and been executed. Whether he did or did not commit the crime he stood accused of is immaterial. What remains is the story of outrage and penitence, heresy and conversion. At a time when preachers

---

[47] *Liber de origine reformationis canonicorum,* fol. 24r. This custom was probably adopted from the example of Saint François de Paule and his order of the Minimes.

[48] For other cases of accusations connected with the feast of Corpus Christi, see Rubin, *Gentile Tales*, pp. 48, 55, 79.

were repeatedly exhorting their audiences to repent and reform, Standonck being at the forefront of the movement, the story had no value unless it carried this moral. Whether he did recant or not, the story had to be told as such. What remains is the story, as crafted by Jan Standonck, director of Montaigu college.

The final question that remains is the tale's short life. It is repeated twice during the sixteenth century, and once in the eighteenth. Despite the presumed uproar the case ought to have caused, it vanished nearly without a trace. Possibly, it was engulfed in the bigger eucharistic storms of the Reformation shortly thereafter. By the sixteenth century, the faculty of theology in Paris had far graver problems than keeping alive the memory of a dubious heretic. What looked in 1493 as the promising beginnings of a new type of host desecration tale, this time by Christians, became completely outdated within little more than a generation. The one attempt to repeat the coup (if it was such an attempt at all in the case of Hémon de la Fosse) brought no reminiscences from contemporary chroniclers. Today, Jan Standonck is remembered mainly because of the humanists and reformers who had come out of his college. Jehan Lenglois, who might have done nothing to deserve his short notoriety and violent death, lies totally forgotten.

List of the Published Writings of Amnon Linder

1967

Recherches sur l'idée de la tyrannie au Moyen Age (doctoral thesis, Université de Dijon, 1967).

1974

'The Roman Government and the Jews under Constantine', *Tarbiz,* 44 (1974), 95–143 [in Hebrew].

1975

'The Myth of Constantine the Great in the West: Sources and Hagiographic Commemoration', *Studi medievali,* 16 (1975), 43–95.

1976

'Ecclesia and Synagoga in the Medieval Myth of Constantine the Great', *Revue belge de philologie et d'histoire,* 54 (1976), 1019–60.

1977

'John of Salisbury's *Policraticus* in Thirteenth-Century England: The Evidence of MS Cambridge Corpus Christi College 469', *Journal of the Warburg and Courtauld Institutes,* 49 (1977), 276–82.

'The Knowledge of John of Salisbury in the Later Middle Ages', *Studi medievali,* 18 (1977), 315–66.

1978

'Christlich-Jüdische Konfrontation im kirchlichen Frühmittelalter', in *Die Kirche des früheren Mittelalters*, ed. by K. Schäferdiek (Munich, 1978), pp. 397–441.

'L'expédition italienne de Charles VIII et les espérances messianiques des Juifs: temoignage du manuscrit BN lat. 5971A', *Revue des études juives,* 137 (1978), 179–86.

'*Ex mala parentela bona sequi seu oriri non potest*: The Troyan Ancestry of the Kings of France and the *Opus Davidicum* of Johannes Angelus de Legonissa', *Bibliothèque d'humanisme et renaissance,* 40 (1978), 497–512.

1979

'Jerusalem as a Focus of Confrontation between Judaism and Christianity: Anti-Jewish Aspects in the Jerusalem Church since the Fourth Century', in *Jerusalem in the Middle Ages: Selected Papers,* ed. by B. Z. Kedar (Jerusalem, 1979), pp. 5–26 [in Hebrew].

'Jerusalem between Judaism and Christianity in the Byzantine Period', *Cathedra,* 11 (1979), 110–19 and 136–40 [in Hebrew].

1981

Review: R. J. Richards, *Consul of God: The Life and Times of Gregory the Great* (London, 1980), in *Numen,* 28 (1981), 262–6.

1982

'An Unpublished Charter of Geoffrey, Abbot of the Temple in Jerusalem', in *Outremer: Studies in the History of the Crusading Kingdom of Jerusalem Presented to J. Prawer*, ed. by B. Z. Kedar, H. E. Mayer, and R. C. Smail (Jerusalem, 1982), pp. 119–29.

'Roman Law as a Source in the Study of Jewish History: A Reappraisal', in *Proceedings of the 8th World Congress of Jewish Studies* (Jerusalem, 1982), pp. 29–32 [in Hebrew].

Review: P. Riché, *Les Écoles et l'enseignement dans le occident de la fin du Ve siècle au milieu du XIe siècle* (Paris, 1979), in *Kiryat Sepher,* 56 (1982), 148–52 [in Hebrew].

1983

Jews and Judaism in Roman Imperial Legislation (Leges Imperatorum Romanorum ad Res Iudaicas pertinentes) (Jerusalem, 1983) [in Hebrew].

'Charles VIII and the Ideal King According to the *Opus Davidicum*', *Zmanim,* 11 (1983), 30–38 [in Hebrew].

'The Roman Law in the Study of Jewish history', *Proceedings of the Israel Academy of Sciences and Humanities*, 6 (1983), 243–57 [in Hebrew].

1984

'An Unpublished 'pronosticatio' on the Return of Charles VIII to Italy', *Journal of the Warburg and Courtauld Institutes,* 47 (1984), 200–03.

1985

'La Loi romaine et les juifs d'Afrique du Nord', in *Actes du colloque 'Juifs et judaisme en Afrique du Nord jusqu'au XIIIe siècle, Montpellier 1983* (Montpellier, 1985), pp. 57–61.

'Jerusalem as a Focus of Confrontation between Judaism and Christianity', in *Vision and Conflict in the Holy Land*, ed. by R. I. Cohen (Jerusalem and New York, 1985), pp. 1–22.

1986

'The Christian Medieval Tradition of the Destruction of Jerusalem and the Temple: Two New Sources', in *Proceedings of the 9th World Congress of Jewish Studies* (Jerusalem, 1986), pp. 87–91.

'Law, Jewry', in *Dictionary of the Middle Ages*, ed. by J. R. Strayer (New York, 1986), VII, 499–502.

1987

The Jews in Roman Imperial Legislation, Edited with Introductions, Translations and Commentary (Detroit and Jerusalem, 1987).

'The Christian Communities in Jerusalem', in *The History of Jerusalem: The Early Islamic Period (638–1099)*, ed. by J. Prawer (Jerusalem, 1987), pp. 97–132 [in Hebrew].

1988

'Constantine's Ten-Laws Series', *Fälschungen im Mittelalter*, Schriften der Monumenta Germaniae Historica, 33, 6 vols (Hannover, 1988), II, 491–507.

'The Destruction of Jerusalem Sunday', *Sacris erudiri,* 30 (1987–88), 253–92.

1989

'An Easter Homily on the Destruction of Jerusalem and the Temple', in *Culture and Society in Medieval Jewry. Studies Dedicated to the Memory of Haim Hillel Ben-Sasson* (Jerusalem, 1989), pp. 19–26 [in Hebrew].

1990

'The Liturgy of the Liberation of Jerusalem', *Mediaeval Studies,* 55 (1990), 110–31.

1992

'Ps. Ambrose's *Anacephaleosis*: A Carolingian Treatise on the Destruction of Jerusalem', *Revue d'histoire des textes,* 22 (1992), 145–58.

1993

'Aspects du retour aux ecritures au Moyen Age: le cas de Jerusalem', in *Les retours aux écritures: fondamentalismes présents et passés*, ed. by E. Patlagean and A. Le Boulleuc, Bibliothèque de l'École des Hautes Études, sect. des sciences religieuses 99 (Leuven and Paris, 1993), pp. 343–55.

1995

'The Status of the Jews in the Early Middle Ages: Sources of Civil and Ecclesiastical Law', in *Frontier, Town and the Transition from Antiquity to the Middle Ages*, ed.

by M. Toch and D. Mendels (Jerusalem, 1995), pp. 101–12 [in Hebrew].

'"Deus venerunt gentes": Psalm 78 (79) in the Liturgical Commemoration of the Destruction of Jerusalem', in *Medieval Studies in Honour of Avrom Saltman*, ed. by B.-S. Albert, Y. Friedman, and S. Schwarzfuchs (Ramat Gan, 1995), pp. 145–71.

1996

'Christian Communities in Jerusalem', in *The History of Jerusalem: The Early Muslim Period (638–1099)*, ed. by J. Prawer and H. Ben-Shammai (Jerusalem, 1996), pp. 121–62.

Review: S. Simonsohn, *The Apostolic See and the Jews* (Tel Aviv, 1994), in *Zion,* 61 (1996), 481–7 [in Hebrew].

1997

The Jews in the Legal Sources of the Early Middle Ages (Detroit and Jerusalem, 1997).

1998

'Individual and Community in the Liturgy of the Liberation of Jerusalem', in *Information, kommunikation und Selbsdarstellung in mittelalterlichen Gemeinden*, ed. by A. Haverkamp, Schriften des historischen Kollegs, Kolloquien, 40 (Munich, 1998), pp. 25–40.

1999

'The Loss of Christian Jerusalem in Late Medieval Liturgy', in *The Real and Ideal Jerusalem in Jewish, Christian and Islamic Art*, ed. by B. Kühnel (Jerusalem, 1999), pp. 165–78.

'The Loss of Christian Jerusalem in Late Medieval Liturgy', in *Jerusalem: Its Sanctity and Centrality to Judaism, Christianity and Islam*, ed. by L. I. Levine (New York, 1999), pp. 393–407.

'The Liturgy of the Liberation of Jerusalem', in *Verso Gerusalemme. II Convegno Internazionale nel IX Centenario della I Crociata, Bari 1999*, ed. by F. Cardini (Lecce, 1999), pp. 57–66.

'The Liturgy of the Latin Kingdom of Jerusalem', in *Knights of the Holy Land: The Crusader Kingdom of Jerusalem*, ed. by S. Rozenberg (Jerusalem, 1999), pp. 95–99.

Forthcoming

Speculum subversionis Hierusalem, CCCM (Turnhout).

Raising Arms: Liturgy in the Struggle to Liberate Jerusalem in the Late Middle Ages, Cultural Encounters in Late Antiquity and the Middle Ages, 2 (Turnhout).